Reforming Ideas in Britain

Between 1789 and 1815 Britain faced a surge of challenges brought about by the French Revolution. Growing tensions with France, then the outbreak of war, exacerbated domestic political controversy, giving rise to new forms of political protest, to which the government responded with ever-increasing severity. *Reforming Ideas in Britain* brings together a series of essays to provide a vibrant historiography of Britain's political thought and movements during the 1790s and beyond. Challenging traditional perceptions of the period, Mark Philp prompts us to reconsider the weight of various ideas, interpretations and explanations of British politics and language, showing us instead that this dynamic world of popular politics was at once more chaotic, innovative and open-minded than historians have typically perceived it to be. This is an essential interdisciplinary text for scholars of history, political theory and romanticism that offers a fresh perspective on radicalism, loyalism and republicanism in Britain during the French Revolution.

MARK PHILP is Professor of History and Politics in the Department of History, University of Warwick.

Reforming Ideas in Britain

*Politics and Language in the Shadow of the
French Revolution, 1789–1815*

Mark Philp

CAMBRIDGE
UNIVERSITY PRESS

CAMBRIDGE
UNIVERSITY PRESS

University Printing House, Cambridge CB2 8BS, United Kingdom

One Liberty Plaza, 20th Floor, New York, NY 10006, USA

477 Williamstown Road, Port Melbourne, VIC 3207, Australia

4843/24, 2nd Floor, Ansari Road, Daryaganj, Delhi - 110002, India

79 Anson Road, #06-04/06, Singapore 079906

Cambridge University Press is part of the University of Cambridge.

It furthers the University's mission by disseminating knowledge in the pursuit of
education, learning and research at the highest international levels of excellence.

www.cambridge.org
Information on this title: www.cambridge.org/9781316648490

© Mark Philp 2014

First published 2014
First paperback edition 2017

A catalogue record for this publication is available from the British Library

ISBN 978-1-107-02728-2 Hardback
ISBN 978-1-316-64849-0 Paperback

G. A. C. 1941–2009
Pauca tecum velim

Contents

Figures

Tables

Acknowledgements

My thanks are registered in many of these essays to those who were helpful at the time of writing, and I wish to reiterate those thanks while also singling out several people with whom I have worked and argued over the time it took to write these essays. Richard Fisher at Cambridge University Press was involved in the first of these essays and has been a stalwart supporter subsequently, enabling this collection to appear. My 1790s 'colleagues' – especially John Barrell, Martin Fitzpatrick, Kevin Gilmartin, Harriet Guest, Iain McCalman, Jon Mee, David O'Shaughnessy and Gillian Russell – have been a long-standing and endlessly stimulating group to work with, and have introduced me to new generations of scholars from whose work I have also learnt much. I also learnt a great deal from the reading group set up initially by Bonnie Honig from Northwestern and involving my politics colleagues, Lois McNay, Liz Frazer, Michael Freeden, and Mark Stears. My family, especially my children, Joe, Ruth and Hannah, who used to distract me from work, have graduated into some of my sharpest critics, for which I am doubly grateful. I especially want to thank Jo Innes, who has been an Oxford 'half-colleague' (given our different disciplinary locations) but who has consistently prodded me to think more carefully about a range of topics over the last twenty years, and has been unfailingly 'up' for talking through new ideas and projects. Some of the fruits of our joint project 'Re-imagining democracy 1750–1850' are evident in the later essays in this volume. I have also benefited from support from the Department of Politics and International Relations in the final months of the completion of this book, and would like to thank Dustin Kramer and Robert Cane for help preparing some of the text. Thanks are also due to Cambridge University Press's Mike Richardson for his scrupulous attention to the text and Gaia Poggiogalli for her tolerance.

Several of these essays were first published elsewhere. They remain essentially unchanged, save for the correction of mistakes and adjustments to create a uniform style in the footnotes. Chapters 5, 10 and 11 have not previously been published. My thanks are due to the publishers and the editors for allowing me to reprint them. The details of how the essays appeared previously are as follows.

Chapter 1: 'The fragmented ideology of reform', in Mark Philp, ed., *The French Revolution and British Popular Politics* (Cambridge University Press, 1991), 50–77.

Chapter 2: 'Vulgar conservatism, 1792–3', *English Historical Review* 110 (1995), 42–69 (© Oxford University Press).

Chapter 3: 'Disconcerting ideas: explaining popular radicalism and popular loyalism in the 1790s', in Glenn Burgess and Matthew Festenstein, eds., *English Radicalism, 1550–1850* (Cambridge University Press, 2007), 157–89.

Chapter 4: 'English republicanism in the 1790s', *Journal of Political Philosophy* 6 (1998), 235–62 (© Wiley-Blackwell).

Chapter 6: 'Paine and science', *Enlightenment and Dissent* 17 (1998), 210–49 (© University of British Columbia).

Chapter 7: 'Revolutionaries in Paris: Paine, Jefferson and democracy', in Simon P. Newman and Peter S. Onuf, eds., *Paine and Jefferson in the Age of Revolutions* (Charlottesville: University of Virginia Press, 2013).

Chapter 8: 'Godwin, Thelwall, and the means of progress', in Robert M. Maniquis and Victoria Myers, eds., *Godwinian Moments: From the Enlightenment to Romanticism* (University of Toronto Press, 2011), 59–82.

Chapter 9: 'Politics and memory: Nelson and Trafalgar in popular song', in David Cannadine, ed., *Trafalgar in History: A Battle and Its Afterlife* (Basingstoke: Palgrave Macmillan, 2006), 93–120.

Introduction

This is a collection of essays in the traditional sense. They are a series of 'assays' – attempts qualitatively to weigh certain ideas, interpretations and explanations, using a mixture of evidence and reasoned judgement. Their focus is on the politics, writing and language in Britain in the 1790s and beyond; in particular, on the rise of movements for reform, on the associated statements made and principles appealed to, and on the ways in which these were responded to. Individually, the essays raise a series of questions about how best to think about some of the key figures, practices and puzzles in the interpretation of the period. Collectively, they attempt to understand what was going on in one of the most vibrant periods of British intellectual and political life.

Britain in the 1790s might be thought to stand somewhat in the shadow of the French Revolution. It was certainly profoundly affected by events in France, but its experience had a character and logic that was very much its own. As events in France first unfolded there was widespread support for France, a certain degree of condescension and a profound sense that the events might lead to more peaceful relations between Britain and France. As the revolution took a more radical turn, hostility towards it began to crystallise, with Edmund Burke's 'Speech on the army estimates' in February 1790, and his subsequent *Reflections on the Revolution in France* (November 1790), providing the first powerful statement of resistance both to France and to what were seen as collateral attempts at reform in Britain (as the proposals for the repeal of the Test and Corporations Acts, and for extensions of the franchise came to be depicted, despite their origins in the 1780s). The 'revolution controversy' demonstrated the breadth and (albeit less often) the depth of political opinion in Britain, and fuelled both demands for reform and resistance to it. Several of the essays here deal with processes of politicisation, with understanding the relationships between these processes and their associated forms of expression and with a set of underlying and recurrent questions about the real character of radical thinking and of the organisations that sprang up to further or oppose it. How should we understand the radical artisan

1

societies? Were they a potentially revolutionary movement? Was their failure a function of internal conflicts or external repression? Should we see the loyalist associations that emerged in response as diametrically opposed in both principle and practice, or as sharing a number of common features with those they denounced?

The period has attracted a number of eminent historians, and has increasingly received attention from specialists in literature and Romanticism. E. P. Thompson's *Making of the English Working Class* (1968) helped revitalise the study of the decade and challenged scholars to think more systematically about the social foundations of its political movements. Albert Goodwin's *Friends of Liberty* (1979) gave further impetus for scholars by his detailed work on the organisation of the movements, in particular on the provincial corresponding societies. And J Ann Hone's *For the Cause of Truth* (1982) extended Goodwin's London narrative into the 1820s, while James Epstein's and Gareth Stedman Jones' work produced some major rethinking of the connections between the movements of the 1790s and those of the 1830s and 1840s.[1] Goodwin's, Hone's and Epstein's research was, like Thompson's, focused on reformers; subsequently, work by Robert Dozier, Harry Dickinson, Linda Colley, David Eastwood and Stuart Semmel broadened the scope by charting and explaining the rise of loyalism, linking it with that of a popular nationalism.[2] There has also been a renewed attention to a range of aspects and figures of the 1790s that have contributed more broadly to our thinking on the period – such as Olivia Smith's analysis of the politics of language;[3] Gregory Claeys' accounts of John Thelwall and Robert Owen and of the pamphlet literature of the debate;[4] Marianne

[1] James Epstein, *Radical Expression: Political Language, Ritual, and Symbol in England, 1790–1850* (Oxford University Press, 1994); Gareth Stedman Jones, *Languages of Class: Studies in English Working Class History 1832–1982* (Cambridge University Press, 1983). See also Jenny Graham's *The Nation, the Law and the King: Reform Politics in England, 1789–1799*, 2 vols. (Lanham, MD: University Press of America, 2000).
[2] Robert R. Dozier, *For King, Constitution, and Country: English Loyalists and the French Revolution* (Lexington: University Press of Kentucky, 1983); Harry T. Dickinson, 'Popular conservatism and militant loyalism, 1789–1815', in Dickinson, ed., *Britain and the French Revolution, 1789–1815* (Basingstoke: Macmillan, 1989), 103–26, and 'Popular loyalism in Britain in the 1790s', in Eckhart Hellmuth, ed., *The Transformation of Political Culture: England and Germany in the Late Eighteenth Century* (Oxford University Press, 1990), 503–33; Linda Colley, *Britons: Forging the Nation 1707–1837* (New Haven, CT: Yale University Press, 1992); David Eastwood, 'Patriotism and the English state in the 1790s', in Mark Philp, ed., *The French Revolution and British Popular Politics* (Cambridge University Press, 1991), 146–68; Stuart Semmel, *Napoleon and the British* (New Haven, CT: Yale University Press, 2004).
[3] Olivia Smith, *The Politics of Language, 1791–1819* (Oxford: Clarendon Press, 1984).
[4] See *The Politics of English Jacobinism: Writings of John Thelwall*, ed. Gregory Claeys (Philadelphia: University of Pennsylvania Press, 1995), *Citizens and Saints: Politics and*

Elliott's studies of Ireland;[5] Frank O'Gorman's studies of elections and Paine riots;[6] John Cookson's detailed work on the armed forces and the 'Friends of Peace';[7] Nick Rogers' studies of riots;[8] Gillian Russell and the late Jane Moody's work on theatre;[9] Michael Durey's work on transatlantic radicals;[10] Austin Gee and Katrina Navickas's books on volunteering and later provincial radicalism and loyalism;[11] Vic Gatrell's study of caricature;[12] and so on. At the same time, literary scholars with interests in the intellectual movements of the period also turned to ask questions about how their work connected with this broader historiography; Marilyn Butler was a major influence in this process.[13] This has produced a generation of literary/historical writing that embraced the linguistic turn but that also sought to give the analysis a firmer grounding in a detailed historical understanding of the period. I am thinking here of Iain McCalman's detailed investigations of the radical underworld;[14] Jon Mee's work on radical literary London;[15] Kevin Gilmartin's studies of

Anti-Politics in Early British Socialism (Cambridge University Press, 2002) and *The French Revolution Debate in Britain: The Origins of Modern Politics* (Basingstoke: Palgrave Macmillan, 2007).

[5] Marianne Elliott, *Partners in Revolution: The United Irishmen and France* (New Haven, CT: Yale University Press, 1982) and *Wolfe Tone: Prophet of Irish Independence* (New Haven, CT: Yale University Press, 1989).

[6] Frank O'Gorman, *Voters, Patrons and Parties: The Unreformed Electorate of Hanoverian England, 1734–1832* (Oxford: Clarendon Press, 1989) and 'The Paine burnings of 1792–1793', *Past and Present* 193 (2006), 111–55.

[7] John Cookson, *The British Armed Nation 1793–1815* (Oxford University Press, 1997) and *Friends of Peace: Anti-War Liberalism in England, 1793–1815* (Cambridge University Press, 1982).

[8] Nicholas Rogers, *Crowds, Culture and Politics in Georgian England* (Oxford: Clarendon Press, 1998) and forthcoming work on the Royal Navy and impressment.

[9] Gillian Russell, *The Theatres of War: Performance, Politics, and Society 1793–1815* (Oxford: Clarendon Press, 1995); Jane Moody, *Illegitimate Theatre in London, 1770–1840* (Cambridge University Press, 2000).

[10] Michael Durey, *Transatlantic Radicals and the Early American Republic* (Lawrence: University Press of Kansas, 1997).

[11] Austin Gee, *The British Volunteer Movement 1794–1814* (Oxford University Press, 2003); Katrina Navickas, *Loyalism and Radicalism in Lancashire 1798–1815* (Oxford University Press, 2009).

[12] Vic Gatrell, *City of Laughter: Sex and Satire in Eighteenth-Century London* (London: Atlantic Books, 2006).

[13] Perhaps most through those she taught and talked to (including me), but encapsulated in the volume she has edited, *Burke, Paine, Godwin, and the Revolution Controversy* (Cambridge University Press, 1984), and her *Romantics, Revolutionaries and Reactionaries: English Literature and its Background 1760–1830* (Oxford University Press, 1981).

[14] Iain McCalman, *Radical Underworld: Prophets, Revolutionaries, and Pornographers in London, 1795–1840* (Cambridge University Press, 1988).

[15] Jon Mee, *Romanticism, Enthusiasm and Regulation: Poetics and the Policing of Culture in the Romantic Period* (Oxford University Press, 2003) and *Conversable Worlds: Literature, Contention, and Community 1762–1830* (Oxford University Press, 2011).

print culture;[16] and John Barrell's seminal work on the Treason Trials and the 1790s more widely.[17] The scholars of this latter groups, it seems to me, have combined an impressive attention to historical detail with a critical intelligence that has redrawn our understanding of the decade and of the first twenty to thirty years of the nineteenth century.

The essays in this collection have been written over a twenty-year period. In that time I have been fortunate enough to know and work with, in different ways, many of those I have mentioned above. The intellectual community of scholars of the 1790s has some similarities to the free and easy debating clubs of the period: an egalitarian culture of discussion and debate, informed by different interests and experiences, and always critically probing the work of others. As a result, my thinking on issues has developed over time in interaction with their work. It has also, in part, responded to other literatures I have worked with in other contexts that remain largely off-stage in these essays. These 'outside' influences are most evident in the first three essays in the collection, which chart my attempts to analyse the popular movements of the period by drawing on some of the insights of theorists of social movements as well as that of other historians, and responding to analyses that I felt were dismissive of the reformers – for example, seeing in their disagreements and controversies an explanation of their failure.[18] Having read widely in the then emerging literature on social movements in political sociology, and following the discussions about the place of class in understanding the rise of Chartism, I found unpersuasive the implied standard for political movements that some of the literature worked with, and I sought to explain why. I did not then fully appreciate the dangers of treating 'the reformers' as a unity, when their identity was in large part a function of a polarising struggle, arising out of the responses to events in France. This sense that the lines between reform and loyalism were products of the decade led me to turn my attention to John Reeves' Association for the Protection of Liberty and Property against Republicans and Levellers and to the dynamics of that movement. 'Vulgar conservatism' is an attempt to read popular loyalism using the same attention to performance and to the tentative character of meaning that I used in 'The fragmented ideology

[16] Kevin Gilmartin, *Print Politics: The Press and Radical Opposition in Early Nineteenth-Century England* (Cambridge University Press, 1996) and *Writing against Revolution: Literary Conservatism in Britain, 1790–1832* (Cambridge University Press, 2007).
[17] John Barrell, *Imagining the King's Death: Figurative Treason, Fantasies of Regicide 1793–1796* (Oxford University Press, 2000) and *The Spirit of Despotism: Invasions of Privacy in the 1790s* (Oxford University Press, 2006).
[18] Ian R. Christie, *Stress and Stability in Late Eighteenth-Century Britain: Reflections on the British Avoidance of Revolution* (Oxford: Clarendon Press, 1984).

of reform'. But what came out of the two pieces was the recognition that I was suggesting an asymmetry between the two movements (and a unity to each of them), in which radical 'insincerity' was a function of tactical responses to repression while loyalist insincerity was simply opportunistic. I do think that there is something right about that suggestion, and 'Disconcerting ideas' tries to defend that view. But it does so with a sharper sense of the dangers of making assumptions about the stability and dimensions of the political spectrum, suggesting instead that there are things that themselves need to be explained. Through these pieces I think I now have a better sense of the complexities of interaction in the 1790s, and of the way in which commitments were forged, worked through and issued in action; and I hope I have made the case for not sequestering accounts of loyalism and radicalism off from each other.

If the histories of the 1790s and work on social movements were the dominant sources in the first three pieces, the second pair of essays draws on wider debates in political theory on republicanism and on methodology in the history of ideas. J. G. A. Pocock's work on civic humanism has had a deservedly major impact on our understanding of British and American political culture in the eighteenth century.[19] Moreover, following work by Philip Pettit and Quentin Skinner, it has resulted in a more nuanced 'neo-Roman' model of liberty, which Pettit has done much to ensure has relevance in politics today.[20] Thanks to Iain McCalman and Jon Mee I was fortunate to be visiting the Australian National University when Pettit was developing his ideas, and we were able to talk about them at length. His thinking dovetailed in many respects with the work I was then engaged in on political corruption. Nonetheless, while I believed that there was much to be learnt from this work, I had a nagging concern that there were substantial objections to thinking that republicanism, as a language and set of intellectual commitments, was something that could be said to be at work in any very determinate way in the 1790s. These two essays follow through these objections in rather different ways, the first by looking at the detail of what people were saying and doing in the 1790s and beyond, the second by pressing the question of what it might mean to commit oneself to republican manners, and to ask how far these sort of commitments were able to sit comfortably alongside a range of developments in society and culture at the end of the eighteenth century. While I

[19] See below, Chapter 4, and see esp. his *The Machiavellian Moment: Florentine Political Thought and the Atlantic Republican Tradition* (Princeton University Press, 1975) and *Virtue, Commerce, and History* (Cambridge University Press, 1985).
[20] Philip Pettit, *Republicanism: A Theory of Freedom and Government* (Oxford University Press, 1997); Quentin Skinner, *Liberty before Liberalism* (Cambridge University Press, 1998).

do not claim that republican commitment is impossible, I do suggest that it is something that depends on a range of very special circumstances, and that in turn casts doubt on exactly what meaning we should ascribe to republican language in the period.

In the course of the last thirty years I have worked extensively on the lives and writing of William Godwin and Thomas Paine – especially Godwin. In the essay on Godwin here I examine an issue that has troubled me for some time. E. P. Thompson was hostile to Godwin (and once described me as an overcommitted Godwinian), but he was hostile in the way that the left sometimes have of being harder on those who are close to them than those they oppose.[21] The heroes of the decade, for Thompson and many others, are the orator John Thelwall and the London Corresponding Society (LCS) secretary Thomas Hardy, rather than the more aloof and rigidly intellectual Godwin. For Thompson, Godwin's greatest apostasy was when he apparently turned against Thelwall in his *Considerations on Lord Grenville's and Mr Pitt's Bills* in 1795, criticising the pyrotechnics of Thelwall's oratory, which he saw as potentially inflaming an ill-informed and uneducated class. That action casts Godwin beyond the pale for Thompson. This account seems to me to be based on a misreading of Godwin's position, and of the events of the period more widely. Godwin's actions revealed the distance he had always maintained from political radicalism, but they also demonstrate his commitment to the steady progress of ideas and their gradual diffusion through society. Thompson reads Godwin as an enlightenment rationalist, whereas, in fact, Godwin had a nuanced understanding of the power of Burke's thought, which framed his attempt to think through how it might be possible to influence men and women and to help them take ever greater responsibility for their destinies. For all the utopianism of Godwin's *Enquiry concerning Political Justice* (1793), it was as much rooted in a historical sociology of some power as it was in what we tend to think of as enlightenment rationalism.

The first essay here on Paine was also prompted by a problem in knowing how to approach the diverse writings and activities of the writer and polemicist. Must we think of someone's oeuvre as a consistent and coherent, interrelated whole? Or does that impose a coherence on our reading that cannot be justified? This kind of issue is prominent in this period, in part because of the tendency to sweep together people's activities into a universal bin labelled 'enlightenment', or, subsequently, to do so into another called 'romanticism'. Against that temptation, and the

[21] See E. P. Thompson, *The Romantics: Wordsworth, Coleridge, Thelwall* (Woodbridge: Merlin Press, 1997), 96–106; see also 87–95.

corresponding sense that people need a single framework within which to arrange their ideas, I use the work of the anthropologist Dan Sperber to think about the different kind of propositional claims Paine might be making in different areas of his life.[22]

If coherence across domains is too often anticipated, so too is coherence across time. The image we have of Paine is that of a blunt and forceful character (and writer) whose revolutionary credentials were nailed to the mast in 1776, and remained there through his experience of the French Revolution and the British agitation for reform. For most commentators he seems to have been hardly affected by the specificity of the contexts in which he wrote. In the second essay on Paine, my concern is to argue that aspects of Paine's thought that people tend to brush over – for example his lack of interest in universal manhood suffrage until after the second part of the *Rights of Man* (1792) had been published – need to be taken seriously as evidence that the way in which he saw the world was far from as simple as it is usually portrayed and that it had an evolving character. In the essay, I am particularly concerned with the way that Paine's thinking evolved, not in response to Burke but prior to his clash with Burke, and arising from his membership of a group in Paris in the late 1780s that was responding to both the opening events of the French Revolution and the debates arising out of the Federal Convention in the United States.

All these essays are also concerned with the nature of evidence. As a graduate student in political theory I found the most persuasive work on method was that which argued for a contextualist history of political thought, as exemplified in the work of Quentin Skinner, John Dunn and J. G. A. Pocock.[23] Within this emerging body of work there was a strong tendency to treat context linguistically, however, and to treat linguistic context as comprised of substantive works of political thought. That predilection was in part a function of their resistance to a legacy of reductionism within Marxist historical and literary interpretation, but it tended to assume that the answer to the methodological question 'Which context?' was rather easily given. What I tried to do in my first book was to use a wider reading of context by identifying Godwin's conversational circles as a crucial forum for the development of his ideas, and I have subsequently sought to take a wider account of the way in which writing

---

[22] Dan Sperber, *On Anthropological Knowledge* (Cambridge University Press, 1985).

[23] Quentin Skinner, *Visions of Politics*, vol. I, *Regarding Method* (Cambridge University Press, 2002); John Dunn, 'The identity of the history of ideas', *Philosophy* 43 (1968), 85–104; J. G. A. Pocock, *Politics, Language and Time: Essays on Political Thought and History* (New York: Atheneum Books, 1973). I have discussed this movement from the perspective of political theory in 'Political theory and history', in David Leopold and Marc Stears, eds., *Political Theory: Methods and Approaches* (Oxford University Press, 2008), 128–49 (ch. 7).

and reading are partly framed by practices and institutions as well as by other texts.[24]

Even if one does not treat the character of 'the archive' in quite such labyrinthine complexity as Michel Foucault, many of his questions remain pertinent: why not accord the same status to laundry bills as to literary texts?[25] Not that we should; but we need to know how we are answering that question in dealing with the various forms of evidence available. My concern with these issues runs through all these essays. What counts as evidence for the existence of particular beliefs or commitments? What are the boundaries for what has been best described as 'the revolution controversy'[26] (does it include canonical works of literature at one end, and handbills and chalked slogans on walls at the other?)? Why does material appear in one genre but not another? What lines of demarcation seem to exist that break the connection between performances in one domain and those in another (as in Paine's scientific experiments and his political commitments)? One area I became increasingly fascinated by was that of popular song – as an expressive medium for ideas and sentiments; as a vehicle for news and information; as a highly flexible performance that could respond to its audience's demands; and as an expression of a partly local and partly national culture. Over the course of many years of identifying songs, in manuscript collections, chapbooks, songsters, broadsides and newspapers, it became clear to me that this was a major field of study, and one that does not simply add a further dimension to our understanding of the decade but might actually lead us to change how we read other elements in the period. I have not yet done this material the justice it demands, and, despite excellent work by Vic Gammon, Terry Moylan and others,[27] there is clearly room for more. Nonetheless, the piece in this collection on Nelson is partly an attempt to see what can be made of this type of evidence. When I was originally asked for the piece I thought I had found about ten major Nelson songs. By the end of my research I had identified between eighty and ninety. I do not claim to have identified everything that existed, but I do not think there were others in wide circulation in the period (and that is the crucial point for the argument

[24] See my *Godwin's Political Justice* (London: Duckworth, 1986).
[25] Michel Foucault, *The Archaeology of Knowledge* (London: Tavistock Publications, 1972).
[26] By Marilyn Butler in *Burke, Paine, Godwin, and the Revolution Controversy*, and in contrast to Alfred Cobban's *The Debate on the French Revolution, 1789–1800* (London: A. & C. Black, 1950).
[27] Vic Gammon, 'The grand conversation: images of Napoleon in British popular balladry', *Journal of the Royal Society of Arts* 137 (1989), 665–74; Terry Moylan, *The Age of Revolution in the Irish Song Tradition: 1776 to 1815* (Dublin: Lilliput Press, 2000).

I make). If the argument is right, the piece points to a degree of control by loyalist forces over something as mercurial as popular song, which gives us a much more forbidding picture of the loyalist upsurge in the early 1800s than is usually acknowledged.

This has also been a fertile period for those working on the French Revolution, and interpretations of France have had a considerable impact both on more theoretical approaches to the study of intellectual history and on the way in which people think about Britain in the period. But one result of a turn against social history and the development of a more intellectual and cultural approach to the French Revolution is the development of a certain element of discursive determinism: a tendency to see events as unfolding from the way in which people conceptualise and talk about the world. This reintroduction of political language and discourse as a primary driver of human actions does, indeed, add an important dimension to our understanding, but it has its limits. One problem is that the intellectual coherence of a position is in many respects an artefact of the reader and the historian. It is we who attribute intellectual and conceptual coherence as a way of accounting for roads taken or not taken – and, while there are clearly moments when political languages do take a determining role, we tend to overstate their monolithic character, to underplay their fragility and to obscure the power and violence that are required to turn propositional coherence into social and political reality. In the two final chapters I turn to a broader example of the way in which political ideas are seen as connected with social reality. In the 1790s and early 1800s, in France, Britain and elsewhere, the language of popular sovereignty, the nation and liberty becomes more widely used, giving rise to a sense that it is in this period that something like a principle of national self-determination is first articulated. Yet, although intellectual historians notch the progress of such ideas up in the emergence of a new modernity, my concern is to show that, while the idea may be there, it is deeply flawed, and in a major sense indeterminate. It is made real in various forms, as in the 1792 French declaration of aid to oppressed peoples, in the *levée en masse* and in the development of various national rhetorics. But we need to see this not as an idea come to fruition but as a set of claims from which social forces and political power forge practical instantiations of commitments that are not in themselves very intellectually coherent. On this kind of history of political thought and conceptual change, the word is made concrete through power, and it is through power that its insistencies and indeterminacies are ironed out – not once and for all, but in this context, on this occasion, in this instance. I do not try to defend the view that this is always the right way to understand ideas, but, if this kind of interpretation can be defended, it suggests that the history of political thought and conceptual change may need to be much more historically located than it often is, not just in other texts or textual contexts but in patterns of discourse and in the practices, institutions and behaviours that are integral in turning principles into action, and through which power is exercised and order imposed.

This more sceptical account of ideas and their place is also a key theme in the final essay, 'Time to talk', in which I turn back to the LCS and its papers to suggest that, rather than there being an underlying coherence to the positions of the society, we can understand what they say and what they do better by recognising that their commitments were barely, if at all, doctrinal, being for the most part tactical, exploratory and provisional. They shared a broad programme, and they could see that some convictions might damage their capacity to see that programme through, but they did not look for uniformity, and they remained, in many respects, genuinely open-ended about what might happen next. This, and the earlier essays, are both, in this sense, an attempt to recognise in the period the possibilities for other voices, other outcomes, other ways of drawing lines and identifying dangers and possibilities. It was an age in which ideas were re-forming – but that process was one that contained possibilities and potentials for individual and collective agency that became fought over, negotiated and realised to greater and lesser degrees. It was a period in which much changed, even when it did not change in ways that the ideas that people shared and fought over feared or predicted. What I have tried to do in these various essays is to understand better how people negotiated this set of shifting sands, not just in their discourse and publications but also in other aspects of their lives, and in doing so to see the way that their lived experience and their language changed together, not unidirectionally, and often unpredictably. My hope is that we get a better sense of how that world appeared to those who lived in it, a better sense of the extent to which, in different ways, things might have been other than they were, and a better sense of the complex interaction between ideas, practices and commitments in Britain in the revolutionary period.

1   The fragmented ideology of reform

Historians have invoked a wide range of factors to explain why reformers in the 1790s failed to obtain their objectives. Government repression, the strength of the popular loyalist movement, the pervasive influence of a sophisticated conservative ideology, the resilience of the institutions of monarchy, aristocracy and the Church of England, and the pluralism of British culture and the responsiveness of its institutions to the needs of the poor have all been cited as key factors in this failure.[1] So too have the ideological disagreements amongst reformers and the factionalism in the organisations for reform:

The reform movement was hopelessly divided on what changes ought to be made and none of the competing elements could rally adequate support in or out of

---

[1] Part of this formulation is owed to Dickinson's opening section to his 'Popular loyalism in Britain'. Dickinson is referring to J. C. D. Clark's *English Society 1688–1832* (Cambridge University Press, 1985) (for the 'resilience thesis') and to Christie's *Stress and Stability in Late Eighteenth-Century Britain* (for the 'pluralism and responsiveness thesis'; see also his 'Conservatism and stability in British society', in Philp, *The French Revolution and British Popular Politics*, 169–87). Clark also contributes a 'radical extremism thesis', which neatly complements Dickinson's account of popular loyalism. Compare, for example, Clark, *English Society*, 346 – 'Yet if the facts of suffering, poverty and (what radical intellectuals never saw) the horrors of war failed to be widely translated into popular politics directed against the establishment, a major reason must be the activities of those theorists who, even before 1789, had defined their position in terms so extreme (in relation to society's ruling orthodoxy) that radicalism itself could easily be equated with the destruction of civilisation' – with Dickinson, 'Popular loyalism in Britain', 503: '[H]istorians have often been so captivated by the noble and heroic efforts of reformers that they have exaggerated their strength and unity. They have usually failed to recognize that the reformers agreed on very little except the need for a more equal representation of the people, that they never developed the organizations, strategies, or tactics capable of bringing irresistible pressure to bear on the governing élite, and that they failed to rally the majority of either the middling or the lower orders behind their political demands.' The 'repression' thesis is given short shrift, on the basis that Clive Emsley's work has shown how much the repression has been exaggerated: see 'An aspect of Pitt's "terror": prosecutions for sedition during the 1790s', *Social History* 6 (1981), 155–84, and 'Repression, "terror" and the rule of law in England during the decade of the French Revolution', *English Historical Review* 100 (1985), 801–25. The thesis does have a long pedigree, however, starting with many of the participants of the decade, as discussed in my *Godwin's Political Justice*, 224–8.

Parliament... The evidence ... shows how the radicals were divided among themselves, how most of them failed to take their ideas to their logical conclusions and how all of them failed to devise any effective means of implementing their policies.[2]

It is primarily with this last claim that this chapter takes issue. I do not deny that there were substantial disagreements among reformers over both means and ends, but I do challenge the view that these contributed significantly to their failure to achieve parliamentary reform. In doing so, I also seek to cast doubt upon the adequacy of explanations of the failure of reform that do not recognise that the radical agenda was as much the outcome of the political struggles of the 1790s as it was their cause.

I

There is no doubt that, despite the apparently widespread favourable response to the French Revolution and the formidable initial critical reaction to Burke's *Reflections on the Revolution in France*, by the end of 1792 and throughout the rest of the decade there were deep and obvious divisions in the ranks of those sympathetic to reform.[3] Most obviously, there was the split in the Whigs between the Duke of Portland and the Foxites, but equally important were the tensions between Charles Grey's Friends of the People and the extra-parliamentary organisations for reform.[4] Although there were brief moments of temporary and uneasy alliance between parliamentary élites and these extra-parliamentary organisations, the general tenor of their association was one of mutual distrust and antagonism.[5] It is not difficult to identify other divisions, such

---

[2] Harry T. Dickinson, *Liberty and Property: Political Ideology in Eighteenth Century Britain* (London: Taylor & Francis, 1977), 271. See also his 'Popular loyalism in Britain'.

[3] On the initial response, see Cobban, *The Debate on the French Revolution*; P. A. Brown, *The French Revolution in English History* (London: Allen & Unwin, 1918), ch. 2; and Albert Goodwin,*The Friends of Liberty: The English Democratic Movement in the Age of the French Revolution* (London: Hutchinson, 1979), ch. 4. A slightly more nuanced picture can be gained from Derek Jarrett, *Three Faces of Revolution: Paris, London and New York in 1789* (London: G. Philip, 1989); and Leslie Mitchell, 'Introduction', in *The Writings and Speeches of Edmund Burke*, vol. VIII, *The French Revolution 1790–1794* (Oxford: Clarendon Press, 1990), 1–51.

[4] Compare Mitchell, 'Introduction', and John Derry, 'The opposition Whigs and the French Revolution 1789–1815', in Dickinson, *Britain and the French Revolution*, 39–59.

[5] The three key periods for cooperation between the parliamentary and extra-parliamentary forces are at the very end of the 1780s, when there was considerable agitation to remove the Test and Corporation Acts, and a good deal of support for the move in parliament; in 1792, after the formation of the Whig-led Association of the Friends of the People; and again around 1795/6, over the campaign to repeal the Gagging Acts. In the interim period Fox at first spent much energy attempting to hold the increasingly divided party together, and was forced to do so in ways that muted his endorsement of the reform movement. There was

as between 'Painites' and those operating with a less universalist, more home-grown set of assumptions about the appropriate structure for the British polity; Thelwall, for example, was not a Painite, nor a democratic republican.[6] This division was reflected within the reform movement between those with strong 'independent' or Whig leanings and those whose commitment to France pulled them away from their traditional protestations of the sanctity of the Englishman's liberty towards more internationalist aspirations (which were rarely integrated adequately into a consistent ideological position). Similarly, there were divisions within the corresponding societies – over the discussion of religion, between those with a republican bent and those with more moderate leanings, between local divisions and the central committee over the treatment of certain delegates, and, as the decade wore on, between those who favoured radical action and those who lacked the stomach for it or felt it served no point.[7]

The reform movement was also marked, as are most movements, by personal and ideological differences between leading reformers – such as Godwin's disagreement with Thelwall over the 'Gagging Acts', Thomas Spence's rather riotous relationship with Thomas Bewick, or Joseph Ritson's summary dismissal of most of the leading intellectuals associated with the reform movement, bar Thelwall:

To confess the truth, the more I see of these modern patriots and philosophers the less I like them... Their constant cant is, the force and energy of mind, to which all opposition is to be ineffectual; but none of them, I say, has ever chosen to rely upon that irresistible force in his own case. I really think that Thelwall is the best of them, and yet I find myself pretty singular in my good opinion of him.[8]

also tension between prominent Whigs and reformers when the former presumed the right to direct the latter's activities. See Goodwin, *The Friends of Liberty*, ch 2, 203–15, ch 10; John Ehrman, *The Younger Pitt*, vol. II, *The Reluctant Transition* (London: Constable, 1983), 108–10, 172–4; and J. Ann Hone, *For the Cause of Truth: Radicalism in London 1796–1821* (Oxford: Clarendon Press, 1982), ch. 1.

[6] Gregory Claeys, *Thomas Paine: Social and Political Thought* (London, Unwin Hyman, 1989), chs. 3, 4; Iain Hampsher-Monk, 'Civic humanism and parliamentary reform: the case of the Society of the Friends of the People', *Journal of British Studies* 18 (1979), 70–89. See also Dickinson, *Liberty and Property*, 237–69.

[7] See *Selections from the Papers of the London Corresponding Society 1792–1799*, ed. Mary Thale (Cambridge University Press, 1983), passim, but, on secession from the society, see esp. 241–52. Some of these divisions were felt still more acutely in the Irish reform movements, particularly on the question of religion. See Elliott, *Partners in Revolution* and *Wolfe Tone*.

[8] *The Letters of Joseph Ritson*, ed. Joseph Frank, 2 vols (London, 1833), II, 69. See also II, 117. On Godwin and Thelwall, see my *Godwin's Political Justice*, 117–19, 196–7; and Thelwall's *The Tribune* (a periodical published in London in 1795 and 1796), vol. II of the collected issues, vii; vol. III, 101–3. On Bewick and Spence, see Thomas Bewick, *A Memoir*, ed. Iain Bain (Oxford University Press, 1975), 53; and Marcus Wood, 'Thomas Spence and modes of subversion', *Enlightenment and Dissent* 10 (1991), 51–77.

Moreover, the presence of numbers of people whose opinions changed during the period added to the sense of division and incoherence amongst reformers – whether it be those who reneged on their earlier radical enthusiasms, those who were radicalised permanently or those who moved from early but essentially moderate enthusiasm for France ultimately to countenance domestic rebellion and revolution.[9]

Two further, related elements add to the impression of diversity, division and incoherence among reformers. The first concerns the extent to which the principles and ideology of reform were subject to ongoing innovation throughout the period. The second concerns the complex relationship that developed between radicals' aspirations, their commitments and their rhetoric.

There is a growing body of writing detailing the way in which reformers (and loyalists) changed and developed their theoretical positions in response to the arguments and events of the decade. Certainly, it seems that, without the impetus of Burke's *Reflections*, Paine would have had little cause to formulate a full natural-rights-based account of popular sovereignty and the limits of government legitimacy. Moreover, it was in responding to Burke that Paine turned to issues of welfare and distributional justice, the fruits of which appeared first in part two of his *Rights of Man* and subsequently, under the impetus of a rather different set of events in France, in *Agrarian Justice* – in which the intellectual justification for a distributive rather than an entitlement conception of justice is expounded.[10] Similarly, for others 'radicalism' was not a standard that they either stood beside or deserted; it was a developing political practice whose principles and ideological commitments were as much forged in the struggle as they were fetched from the arsenal and brought to it. Thelwall's account of his endorsement of a rights-based perspective on government should certainly caution us against thinking that the relationship between political practice and principle was a one-way process:

---

[9]   We should also recognise that at least some of those who might be claimed to have reneged on their earlier enthusiasms remained profoundly influenced by their earlier sympathies; see David Eastwood, 'Robert Southey and the intellectual origins of romantic conservatism', *English Historical Review* 104 (1989), 308–31. There is also the vexed question of how committed and realistic many of the more literary radicals were, on which compare E. P. Thompson, *The Poverty of Theory* (London: Merlin Press, 1978), 372, and *The Making of the English Working Class*, 2nd edn (Harmondsworth: Penguin Books, 1968), 193, with Nicholas Roe, *Wordsworth and Coleridge: The Radical Years* (Oxford: Clarendon Press, 1988), and my *Godwin's Political Justice*, ch. 10.

[10]   See my *Paine* (Oxford University Press, 1989), ch. 3; and Claeys, *Thomas Paine: Social and Political Thought*, chs. 4, 8 (although, in many respects, Claeys overemphasises the continuities in Paine's thought, and underplays the impact of Paine's immediate context on his writing).

It was only in the solitude of the Tower (awaiting his trial for High Treason), where the mind had leisure for the investigation of abstract and difficult propositions, that every objection was removed, and I became convinced, that the only practicable means of ameliorating the condition of mankind, is to restore them to the full possession of their just and inalienable rights.[11]

What we get from Thelwall, and from many others on both sides, is a sense of the period as transforming or traumatising people so as to produce highly individual personal and intellectual responses, rather than a pattern of simple conformity to a creed.

The sense of diversity in the radicalism of the decade is enhanced by those analysts of the 'debate on France' who see the decade as marking a break from eighteenth-century traditions of thought and argument.[12] There have, however, been recent attempts, by J. G. A. Pocock and Gregory Claeys, to illuminate the decade by recognising in the assumptions and arguments deployed by reformers the continuing influence of the discourses of country party opposition, civic and civil humanism, and Scottish political economy.[13] At base,

British radicalism . . . continued to be expressed in terms of a sustained attack on the Whig oligarchy, variously known as 'Old Corruption' and 'The Thing'. [. . .] We know that the language in which Old Corruption was defined was by this time a century old, and as much Tory as Whig in its origins and transmission; the time has now come to claim that it remained paradigmatic.[14]

Yet this is a rearguard action, and one that risks conflating different levels of abstraction. A language is not a paradigm, and we should not confuse the weaponry of reformers and radicals with the battle that they were fighting. While many clearly did use the language and imagery of 'old corruption', there should be little doubt that new paradigms of political thought and participation were being tabled. It is one thing to recognise the continued force of the language of 'independence', but quite another to think that this necessarily dominated the new universalist and national forms of political language that were an increasing presence in British political life from the 1760s onward and that had a major impact on

[11] Cecil Thelwall, *Life of John Thelwall, by His Widow* (London: J. Macrone, 1837), 115.
[12] For some commentators, it is precisely in Burke's attempt to purify Whiggism and in Paine's attempt to repudiate Burke that the principles of the two wings of modern liberal thought were forged. See, for example, Philippe Raynaud, ed., *Reflexions sur la Revolution de France* (Paris: Hachett, 1989), lxxxvii–lxxxviii.
[13] Pocock, *Virtue, Commerce, and History*, 279–94; Gregory Claeys, *Thomas Paine: Social and Political Thought* and 'The French Revolution debate and British political thought', *History of Political Thought* 11 (1990), 59–80; see also Iain Hampsher-Monk, 'John Thelwall and the eighteenth-century radical response to political economy', *Historical Journal* 34 (1991), 1–20.
[14] Pocock, *Virtue, Commerce, and History*, 289.

political debate and practice in the 1790s, even if they were subsequently
(if temporarily) eclipsed by older concerns.[15]

The further issue that both adds to and complicates this sense of disorder
and that is insistently present as the reader pores over the documents and
literature of the period is the question of how far, or in what ways, people
can be taken as meaning what they said. This is not straightforward. For
example, as D. O. Thomas has recently noted, when the good Dr Richard
Price raised his glass at the commemorative dinner held by the London
Revolution Society on 4 November 1790 and proposed a toast to '[t]he
Parliament of Britain – may it become a NATIONAL Assembly', he
certainly did not mean what he said.[16] Nor was Price alone in this. Quite
where John Horne Tooke stood on a number of rather crucial issues, from
monarchy to the use of extra-legal force to encourage Parliament to see the
wisdom of reform, remains unclear. And Thelwall's activities did much to
leave questionable the extent of his radicalism: '[I]n nothing was he more
representative of his generation than in the unrestrained violence of his
rhetoric and in the temporising moderation evident in his own conduct and
the political advice he gave to his popular audiences.'[17]

Given the range and nature of the divisions that it is possible to
identify among reformers in the 1790s, we have good reason to doubt
the adequacy of the various explanations offered for the failure of the
reform movement. Such explanations implicitly assume that there was a
sufficiently discrete entity, 'the reform movement', with objectives of
which success or failure can be predicated. Not only is this assumption
questionable, so too is the idea that there is agreement about the nature
of the movement. Different explanations of the failure of reform are inti-
mately related to divergent accounts of the nature of that movement and to
conflicting counterfactual claims about the kind of movement it ought to
have been for it to have succeeded; the accounts of what did not happen in
the 1790s, of why it did not happen and of how close it came to happening
are far from uncontentious.[18] Nor can differences between accounts of the
nature of radicalism be settled by appealing to the intentions and activities

---

[15] See O'Gorman, *Voters, Patrons and Parties*, 300–16, for an account that carefully avoids
equating 'independence' with radicalism. The shift towards a national political agenda
and more universal forms of political discourse is reflected in the very language in which
political debate was conducted in this period; see Smith, *The Politics of Language*; and
Butler, *Burke, Paine, Godwin, and the Revolution Controversy*.

[16] David Oswald Thomas, *Response to Revolution* (Cardiff: University of Wales Press,
1989), 41.

[17] Goodwin, *The Friends of Liberty*, 321.

[18] Compare Christie's *Stress and Stability in Late Eighteenth-Century Britain* and Roger Wells'
Insurrection: The British Experience, 1795–1803 (Gloucester: Alan Sutton, 1983) and
Wretched Faces: Famine in Wartime England, 1793–1803 (Gloucester: Alan Sutton,

of the reformers, since, as we have seen, different groups (and single groups at different points in time) could have different views of their objectives and of the steps required to achieve them.

Reformism or radicalism in the 1790s is protean stuff. It resists a simple definitive classification of its nature and objectives and it demands a more complex understanding of its ideology and political objectives than is often offered. To treat reformism or radicalism (or, indeed, loyalism) as a single, consistent, continuous programme throughout the decade is to ignore, at the very least, the extent to which reformist and loyalist movements shaped and conditioned each other's objectives and tactics, the way that government and judicial action against reformers helped focus and narrow the range of strategies open to them and the manner in which events in France fed into each group's understanding of the dangers of and potential for reform in Britain. The reform associations of the 1790s did not spring fully formed onto the stage of British politics with a clear sight of their historical destiny.[19] Over a ten- to fifteen-year period the complex of attitudes towards social and political reform that first responded to the opening events of the French Revolution underwent great changes, few of which can be ascribed to the immanent logic of radical principles. On the contrary, many of those principles were themselves the outcome of responses to events, or of reactions to others' responses to events. To analyse the reformism of the 1790s in these terms involves pre-empting questions about why there was no revolution in the period, or about why the reform movement failed, by asking instead how the agenda of radicalism, loyalism and government response was set, and how revolution came to be on it – if indeed it did.

II

That there is a good deal of evidence to show that the reform movement was not united should not surprise us; it is difficult to think of a reform movement or revolution, successful or unsuccessful, without significant divisions. What is at issue is how far these divisions were positive or containable, and how far they brought about the collapse of the reform movement from within. To establish this we need to consider not only how serious these divisions were but also from where they originated. In

---

1988) and their respective contributions to Philp, *The French Revolution and British Popular Politics*: 'Conservatism and stability in British society' and 'English society and revolutionary politics in the 1790s: the case for insurrection', 188–226.

[19] Jonathan Clark's caution on the latter point (historical destiny) in *English Society*, 347, needs supplementing by the former (springing fully formed).

the analysis of the reform movement, insufficient attention has been paid to the role played by the broader political context in generating some of the deeper and more debilitating divisions in the radicalism of the 1790s.

A central element of this broader context is the developing conflict between reformism and loyalism, which occurs not just in the theoretically sophisticated and principled tracts of the 'debate on France' conducted in the opening years of the decade but also, and equally importantly, in the tide of propaganda that, by 1793, was increasingly displacing the intellectual confrontation from the centre of political activity.[20] To grasp the process of contestation between the loyalist and reformist presses through the decade, we must recognise that three elements came into play at the beginning of the 1790s in a way that broke apart the existing lines of popular and élite political division: the French Revolution, Burke's *Reflections* and Paine's *Rights of Man*.[21] The precise impact of the French Revolution is difficult to assess. J. G. A. Pocock has said some very complex things about the problems of translating the French example into English terms and about the use of French rhetoric and symbols in a British context, but these risk missing the simple point that the French Revolution was seen immediately as speaking to an English experience (the Glorious Revolution of 1688), and that, having made this connection, events in France provided a running and, it was assumed, relevant commentary on British politics.[22] The outbreak of war between the new republic and the Duke of Brunswick's coalition, the internationalising of the revolution, the eventual declaration of war between Britain and France, and the ongoing problems of financing and manning the conflict inserted into British popular politics an insistent pressure to link experience at home with French affairs. This pressure was not intrinsically more

---

[20] Works that have extended our understanding of the principles in play in the 'debate' include Clark, *English Society*; Claeys, 'The French Revolution debate' and *Thomas Paine: Social and Political Thought*; Pocock, *Virtue, Commerce, and History*; Dickinson, *Liberty and Property*; T. P. Schofield, 'Conservative political thought in Britain in response to the French Revolution', *Historical Journal* 29 (1986), 601–20; and Robert Hole, *Pulpits, Politics and Public Order in England 1760–1832* (Cambridge University Press, 1989). But all these tend to place greatest weight on the first three years of the decade and underplay the less principled aspect of the confrontations that followed.

[21] This is not to deny the influence on the 1790s of the American Revolution, the Wilkes affair, Christopher Wyvill's reformist Yorkshire Association or the experiences of the Dissenters in their campaign to remove their disabilities in 1787, 1789 and 1790, but these are not in themselves enough to account for the events of the decade. See Goodwin, *The Friends of Liberty*, ch. 2; Eugene C. Black, *The Association: British Extraparliamentary Political Organization 1769–1793* (Cambridge, MA: Harvard University Press, 1963); and G. M. Ditchfield, 'The parliamentary struggle on the repeal of the Test and Corporation Acts, 1787–1790', *English Historical Review* 89 (1974), 551–77.

[22] Pocock, *Virtue, Commerce, and History*, 283–4.

favourable to reformers or loyalists, but its existence gave British domestic political confrontation a momentum it would otherwise have lacked. The other two elements – Burke's *Reflections* and Paine's *Rights of Man* – encouraged this connection and helped frame the interpretation and course of that momentum.

Gregory Claeys has suggested that much of the 'debate on the French revolution' was 'waged in terms not immediately given in the two combatants' main texts'.[23] While this is true, it remains the case that Burke and Paine did much to set the parameters within which the ideological confrontation between loyalism and reform was fought. Burke's *Reflections* sketch a conspiracy theory that his later works paint in, in ever more gruesome colours. The works of the Abbé Augustin Barruel and his translator merely complete and systematise a project that is implicit in Burke's revolution writings from 1790 onward, and while not all loyalists necessarily saw things in these terms the very existence of this perspective served to condition loyalist response and to shape its strategies.[24] This is particularly so after the outbreak of war with France, when radicalism could be tainted with disloyalty and identified as an enemy within. Moreover, although Burke's opening salvos against the French were treated by many with a mixture of disbelief, scorn and amusement (with the caricaturists depicting him as a befuddled Quixote, Don Dismallo, tilting at imagined horrors), as events progressed he came to be seen as increasingly prescient. Loyalists could find in Burke ample justification for a strenuous defence of their patrimony, and, even if they did not necessarily use the same principles or rhetoric in that defence, his work increasingly set the tone for those attacking radicalism. Indeed, one feature of its success was the fact that its complex and cultivated rhetorical style found (or perhaps called into being) an audience who could recognise in it a clarion call to fulfil their responsibilities.[25]

---

[23] Claeys, 'The French Revolution debate', 59.

[24] See Augustin Barruel, *Memoirs Illustrating the History of Jacobinism*, 4 vols., trans. Robert Clifford (London: T. Burton, 1797–8); and Robert Clifford, *Application of Barruel's Memoirs of Jacobinism, to the Secret Societies of Ireland and Great Britain: By the Translator of That Work* (London: T. Burton, 1798). See Seamus Deane, *The French Revolution and Enlightenment in England 1789–1832* (Cambridge, MA: Harvard University Press, 1988), 5–20; and Mitchell, 'Introduction', on Burke and conspiracy.

[25] The tendency to disaggregate the various elements of Burke's and Paine's works – their rhetoric, their audiences and supporters, and their ideas (between, roughly speaking, literary theorists, historians and political theorists) – although often unintended, has had the effect of underplaying the extent to which these elements were indissolubly connected; consequently, the extent to which what was being mapped out in the opening salvos of Burke and Paine was as much a plan of battle in a practical struggle for political ascendency as the intellectual contours of a new debate on the Whig legacy.

Paine's *Rights of Man* had a similar impact on the decade, even when his democratic republicanism was not embraced. Paine, more than any other pamphleteer in the initial wave of responses to Burke, endorsed the French Revolution by appealing to principles of natural rights and popular sovereignty – principles that questioned the legitimacy of the British state. And, by his open and inclusive rhetorical style, which constituted its readers as citizens not subjects, and through his own and others' efforts to arrange the wide circulation of his work, he ensured that these principles and the example of the French would be firmly lodged at the centre of radical politics throughout the decade. It is possible to imagine French affairs playing a relatively slight role in the British reform movement of the 1790s, but, in the wake of Burke's conspiratorial linking and Paine's willingness to endorse the conflation of the French example and the principles of British reformers, events in France assumed a direct significance for the British movements for reform. This, in part, accounts for the continuing recourse to imagery and rhetoric borrowed from France alongside vernacular idioms in the confrontation between loyalism and reformism. Loyalists had to deny the force of 'French principles', and did so by attempting to link them directly to the bloodshed of the decade; radicals might seek to deny the practical example of France, but they remained committed to defending, in some form, the principles it proclaimed. Hence, much of the argument and rhetoric of the decade revolved around the presence or absence of a link between principles and practice in France, with conspiracy theories being espoused by loyalists and being countered by reformers and radicals arguing that the bloodshed there was the result of a conspiracy of European states against France – with Burke's *Reflections* being partly responsible.[26]

In this confrontation, prose, poetry, print, caricature, pottery, painting and even coinage were mobilised, and what began as the 'debate on France' quickly degenerated into a propaganda war.[27] Certain motifs, often drawn from France or incorporating a French reference point, recurred in loyalist writings, such as the claim that reformers put into jeopardy that most natural and fundamental unit of sentimental

---

26   And didst thou hope, by the infuriate quill
        To rouse mankind the blood of realms to spill?
        Then to restore, on death devoted plains
        Their scourge to tyrants, and to man his chains?
        To swell their souls with thy own bigot rage
        And blot the glories of so bright an age?

Joel Barlow, *The Conspiracy of Kings* (London: J. Johnson, 1792), 12.
27 See David Bindman, ed., *The Shadow of the Guillotine: Britain and the French Revolution* (London: British Museum Publications, 1989), passim.

relationships, the family, beginning with the depiction of the treatment meted out to the French royal family by the French mob and culminating in the heart-rending scenes of Louis being taken from his family to be executed.[28]

Loyalism also used the straight Anglo-French contrast as a way of summarising the respective virtues of loyalism and reform. This is exemplified in the print *The Contrast* (1792) by Thomas Rowlandson, after a design by Lord George Murray, which offers two cameos: one of Britannia, beneath an oak, with lion and liberty cap;[29] the other, a French Medusa, with snakes for hair, one foot on a corpse whose head is impaled on her trident, with the 'lantern' and its traditional sacrifice in the background. England offers 'Religion, Morality, Loyalty, Obedience to the Laws, Independence, Personal Security, Justice, Inheritance, Protection, Property, Industry, National Prosperity, Happiness'; France 'Atheism, Perjury, Rebellion, Treason, Anarchy, Murder, Equality, Madness, Cruelty, Injustice, Treachery, Ingratitude, Idleness, Famine, National and Private Ruin, Misery'. A more culinary orientated version of the opposition is deftly put by James Gillray in *French Liberty, English Slavery*.[30]

The Contrast was just one amongst hundreds of prints that poured into the print shops between the summers of 1792 and 1793. There was also a simultaneous outpouring of loyalist songs and broadsides. The objective was to combat the successes of the radical associations and the dominance of radical literature in the arena of popular political debate.[31] Whether or not the insurrectionary plot of 1792 was an invention, the government certainly seems to have believed that extraordinary measures were required to counter the success of the reform associations and to rally

---

[28] See John Brewer, '"This monstrous tragi-comic scene": British reactions to the French Revolution', in Bindman, *The Shadow of the Guillotine*, 1–24, 22–4. The motif was continued subsequently in caricatures of sexual excess and libertinage amongst the 'Jacobins' and extended through to the pillorying of Godwin and his memoirs of Mary Wollstonecraft.

[29] On the ambiguous nature of the liberty cap, see James Epstein, 'Understanding the cap of liberty: symbolic practice and social conflict in early nineteenth century England', *Past and Present* 122 (1989), 75–118, esp. 86–91.

[30] Although the use of the contrast as a style of print was not restricted to the loyalist camp; see Rowlandson's *A General Fast in Consequence of the War* (c.1795).

[31] Both Claeys, in his 'The French Revolution debate', and Gayle Pendleton, in her 'Towards a bibliography of the Reflections *and the* Rights of Man controversy', *Bulletin of Research in the Humanities* 85 (1982), 65–103, show that there were more loyalist than reformist pamphlets. Nonetheless, given circulation figures and the evidence of the reform associations, it is legitimate to claim that in the field of *popular* political debate the radicals were ascendant, both in 1791/2 and again, though not continuously, after 1795.

public support as it faced the prospect of war with France.[32] It had become increasingly alarmed at the spread of reform principles after the spring of 1792, when Paine's works were being distributed on an unprecedented scale and the Whig association of the Friends of the People was formed, and when neither the royal proclamation against seditious writing of May 1792 nor the instigation of the prosecution of Paine had had much impact. The alarm had grown with the London Corresponding Society's inauguration of correspondence with the French Republic, with the transformation in French military fortunes and with the recognition that British reformers were increasingly coming to see the French as champions of universal liberty – and as their best defence against growing domestic repression.[33]

It is in this context that the loyalist movement emerged, and it is against this background that we can recognise that the 'debate' on France had metamorphosed into something rather different.[34] There is a strong sense in which we can see Paine as engaging Burke in a debate of principles,[35] but by the middle of 1792 the term 'debate' was a misnomer – except perhaps in certain élite circles relatively immune from popular politics. The pamphlet had become a weapon, the debate a struggle over popular mobilisation and political ascendancy. In the loyalist propaganda at the end of the year, the cause of reform was being cast as levelling, egalitarian and anarchical. For their part, the radicals focused on their new areas of strength, the circulation of pamphlets through the constitutional and corresponding societies in the metropolis and the provinces. Moreover, by their exclusion from the parliamentary arena and the challenge posed to their very legitimacy by the royal proclamation of May 1792 – an exclusion that the war with France and the increasingly violent direction taken by the revolution considerably accelerated – the radicals were forced to explore new ways of challenging the political status quo and making the government responsive to their interests. And, in being forced to countenance new methods, they also had to recognise the extent to which the stakes were being raised.[36]

---

[32] Clive Emsley, 'The London "insurrection" of December 1792: fact, fiction, or fantasy?', *Journal of British Studies* 17 (1978), 66–86.

[33] Goodwin, *The Friends of Liberty*, 239–67.

[34] See Donald E. Ginter, 'The loyalist association movement of 1792–3 and British public opinion', *Historical Journal* 9 (1966), 179–90; Austin Mitchell, 'The association movement of 1792–3', *Historical Journal* 4 (1961), 56–77; Dozier, *For King, Constitution, and Country*; and Dickinson, 'Popular conservatism and militant loyalism' and 'Popular loyalism in Britain'.

[35] See my *Paine*, ch. 3.

[36] See, for example, Goodwin, *The Friends of Liberty*, 280–2, on the failure of Grey's motion for reform in May 1793, and the message taken from this by the democratic societies.

There is insufficient space here to detail the highways and byways of this increasing polarisation, and the gradual elimination of the distinction between a reformer and a Jacobin revolutionary. It is a complex map, shaped by the judicious use of prosecutions, propaganda and the creation of states of emergency, with the suspension of habeas corpus, the deployment of the militia, and so on. Some areas of activity were more affected than others; Daniel Eaton, for example, spent some time going to court to answer charges of sedition (with great success), but 'higher' areas of literary activity remained relatively untouched – as with the Godwin circle prior to 1798. But only relatively so: Godwin did not face prosecution, but he did play an important part in the treason trials of 1794, and a perhaps less creditable one in the campaign against the 'Two Acts' in 1795; and throughout the period he was conscious of the government's willingness to transgress people's liberty in the name of resisting reform, and it is unlikely that he felt completely secure from prosecution.[37] In contrast, by 1796 Thelwall had no doubts as to the speed with which his public platform was being eroded by a combination of loyalist statutes and loyalist staves. The activities of the reform societies in the last four years of the century became more covert, increasingly linked with the United Irishmen and more wholeheartedly subversive.[38] By the turn of the century political reform was a cause canvassed largely in private, and, in at least some areas, it was broached in increasingly insurrectionary terms. The suggestion, then, is that the 'debate' became a practical struggle between loyalists and radicals over reform, with the loyalists seeking to discredit their opponents among the political and social élite and to counter the spread of radical principles and sympathies amongst the lower orders, who, as the war became more unpopular and as food shortages fuelled popular discontent, offered an attentive audience for radical propaganda. The radicals in turn attempted to extend popular support and agitation for reform to the point that the government would be forced to concede, but they did so against this background of increasing public unrest. Given that, from May 1793, the radicals were effectively cut off from established and respectable methods of reform, they were forced to consider alternatives. Hence the development of conventionist demands,

---

[37] On Godwin's view that the government's declaration of war with France was motivated almost wholly by a desire to challenge the spread of French principles, see Abinger manuscripts, Bodleian Library, Dep b. 227/1g. One indication of Godwin's sense of his vulnerability was the withdrawal of the preface to the first edition of *Things As They Are; or, The Adventures of Caleb Williams* (London: S. Crosby, 1794).

[38] This is territory best commanded by Roger Wells, in his *Insurrection* and *Wretched Faces* and in his 'English society and revolutionary politics'. But see also Marianne Elliott's *Partners in Revolution*, on the Irish dimension.

which led first to the Scottish trials and subsequently, and in part motivated by a fear that the government in England was aiming at a similarly
draconian repression, to the call for a British Convention and to the
English treason trials of 1794.[39] Hence their later alliance with the popular
discontent arising from the war and food shortages in 1795/6 and again in
1800/1801, and their more obscure connections with the mutinies of
1797. But hence, also, the reluctance on the part of some reformers to
become involved with these developments, and their unwillingness to
follow the path to insurrectionary activity or to risk prosecution and prison
or transportation. Government prosecutions for the 1790s are hardly
credible as a 'terror' of the same order as that experienced under both
'red' and 'white' on the other side of the channel, but the prosecutions
were sufficiently numerous, and many were sufficiently notorious (particularly the Scottish trials, which may have done much to pre-empt more
extensive government action in England), that it is impossible to believe
that they had no impact either on reformers' interpretation of what was
now politically possible or, more critically, on the price that might have to
be paid to achieve one's ends. Moreover, in the light of foreign war,
domestic repression and a government committed willy-nilly to sticking
it out, seemingly regardless of the cost in terms of popular support or the
suspension of the shibboleths of the Englishman's liberties, some reformers found themselves forced to revise their estimate of the ends they
should pursue; agendas change with circumstances. Of course, to find
one's cause forced along a path that must rely on foreign invasion, insurrection and revolutionary excess to achieve its ends is not to be forced to
take that path. There were other, more quietist, options. Some took these
early: the emigrations of Joseph Priestley, Eaton and others; the retire-
ments of Thomas Hardy[40] and ultimately of Thelwall himself. The corresponding societies found new leaders, who had gained their political
education when the stakes had already been raised, and who in consequence might well have found the road to insurrection a less alarming
prospect, or a more urgent necessity.

---

[39] See T. M. Parsinnen, 'Association, convention and anti-parliament in British radical
politics, 1771–1848', *English Historical Review* 88 (1973), 504–33, esp. 513.

[40] Nonetheless, Hardy remained an acute interpreter of the political scene. In 1801 he wrote
to Major Cartwright that the government had become 'terrified at the word *reform* least
[sic] it should tend to a *revolution* and terminate in a republic – they have effected [sic]
such a *revolution* in the country which the most violent reformer never had the most
remote idea of. The word reform may *now* be blotted out of the vocabulary – repeatedly
and honestly have the rulers of this country been told within these forty years of the
necessity of a reform in the democratic part of the constitution in order to save the Crown
but the die is cast!!!' Cited by John Dinwiddy, 'Conceptions of revolution in the English
radicalism of the 1790s', in Hellmuth, *The Transformation of Political Culture*, 535–60, 559.

This might be put another way. What forced the debate into the realm of practical political struggle was the government's refusal to contemplate reform. The radicals had no strategy against the government's refusal to negotiate or make concessions except to try forcing it to pay attention, and as they tried to do this they found themselves overstepping the bounds of legality. If it is fair to talk of the radicals losing the debate, it is so only if we also recognise that it is difficult to win a contest when the other side will not play.

We should not, however, overemphasise the radical side of the story as simply a reaction to government intransigence and repression and loyalist intimidation. The loyalist and government reading of radicalism might be a caricatured one – and the smear tactics used against both radical writers and their principles might also consciously exaggerate their evil intent and levelling aspirations – but it seems equally caricatural to think of loyalists or William Pitt's ministry as engaged in a wilful conspiracy against the liberties of Englishmen. It may be the case that Pitt could have conceded moderate political reform and found himself at the head of a more united and loyal people, but there seems to have been no way that he could have been certain of this outcome, and there were grounds in the activities of the radicals for wishing to temporise on reform. Once the war with France had begun, and given the direction that events in France had taken, reform seemed pregnant with even greater dangers.[41] While loyalism seemed to offer confirmation of the backing of the bulk of 'the people', it is also clear that the movement had lost a good deal of its impetus by the middle of the decade.[42] Moreover, although the volunteers were partly an

---

[41] Consider, for example, the remarks made by Lord Grenville in his letters to his brother the Marquis of Buckingham. '[I]t is perfect blindness not to see that in the establishment of the French Republic is included the overthrow of all the other Governments of Europe' (17 September 1794). 'I do verily believe that we must prepare to meet the storm here... It seems too probable that it is decreed by Providence that a stop shall be put (for reasons probably inscrutable to us) to the progress of arts and civilisation among us... Do not think me dispirited by what has happened. I see the extent of our danger, and think that danger much greater than is commonly apprehended; but the effect of that opinion on my mind is no other than that of increasing the conviction with which before I was impressed, of the necessity of perseverance and exertion. France and Spain and the Netherlands, and Geneva, most of all (small as it is), show us that this danger is not to be lessened by giving way to it, but that courage and resolution are in this instance, as in most others, the surest roads to self-preservation' (27 September 1794). Duke of Buckingham and Chandos, *Memoirs of the Court and Cabinets of George the Third*, 4 vols. (London, 1853), vol. II, 303, 305, 306–7.

[42] There was little in the petitions to the House of Commons over the 'Two Acts' (the 'Gagging Acts') to give Pitt confidence that he had the backing of the nation. The number of signatories against the bills substantially outweighed those in support: ninety-four petitions, with some 130,000 signatures, as against sixty-five, with around 30,000. See *The History of Two Acts...* (London: G. G. & J. Robinson, 1796).

outgrowth of the loyalist movement, and were a major adjunct to domestic policing, they were not without their dangers.[43] There were, then, times when the government felt that the reform movement was a threat to internal stability and the continuation of the war. Perhaps this is not surprising, since it did much to ensure that the cause of reform was a lost one unless reformers could gain substantial extra-parliamentary leverage against the government, but this should not obscure the fact that this was precisely what reformers were increasingly trying to do. The logic of confrontation between the reform movement and government and loyalist forces was such that each provided ample confirmation to the other of their threat.

To see why radicals might have taken positions that might further stimulate government measures against them, we need to look not simply at the way in which paths to alternative forms of reform activity were successively closed but also at the radical rhetoric that did much to alarm government and that increasingly seemed to lead towards insurrection.

III

There are two aspects of the relationship between rhetoric, ideology and action that demand careful attention. The first tackles the issue of how far reformers and radicals in the 1790s were operating within the established conventions of an attack on 'old corruption', and how far we can find in the decade evidence of a displacement of older frameworks of radical thought and their replacement with newer, more universalistic, democratic and populist ideological commitments. The second, albeit related, issue returns to the questions raised earlier about the connection between radical rhetoric and radical intent.

One consequence of the preceding analysis of the changing logic of confrontation between reformers and loyalist and governmental forces is that we should be prepared to forgo the prospect of identifying a new paradigm for those demanding parliamentary reform. Because radicalism evolved to a significant extent in the process of confrontation, and because, early in the decade, this confrontation became one of practical political struggle and propaganda, it becomes extremely difficult to read

---

[43] See Eastwood, 'Patriotism and the English state'; J. R. Western, 'The volunteer movement as an anti-revolutionary force', *English Historical Review* 71 (1956), 603–14; John Bohstedt, *Riots and Community Politics in England and Wales 1790–1810* (Cambridge, MA: Harvard University Press, 1983), esp. 49–51, 114–16; and John Cookson, 'The English volunteer movement of the French wars, 1793–1815: some contexts', *Historical Journal* 32 (1989), 867–91.

off ideology from rhetoric. It is true that there is extensive use, across the board, of the rhetoric of 'old corruption', and that the older tradition played a predominant role in the formal statements of the reform societies,[44] but there was also a great deal of rhetoric influenced by France and tied to the radicals' defence of the right of the French to their revolution. We have already seen why this should be so: France had been pushed firmly into the limelight by Burke, and its centrality to issues of reform in Britain had been confirmed by Paine. But events in Britain and France alike did much both to continue and to transform the role of French affairs. One reason for the corresponding societies sending addresses to the French Republic in the autumn of 1792 was a growing sense that France now stood as liberty's best ally, while Britain seemed to be sinking towards oppression. Some of the analysis of this development was doubtless indebted to 'independent' ideology; but it should also be recognised that one reason for using such language was the purchase it had within British political culture. Even while flirting with 'French principles', reformers could make pointed use of traditional forms of opposition rhetoric. How are we to tell whether or how it was meant?

One way of answering this question, which follows up the argument presented thus far, is to suggest that reformers in the 1790s were faced with at least four reference points when taking their ideological bearings. First, there was the theoretical and principled defence of reform, not just in the works of Paine, Thelwall and other contemporaries but also in those classical works of republicanism and radicalism that appeared in extracts in journals such as *Pig's Meat* and *Hog's Wash/Politics for the People*, and that were also reprinted and circulated by the constitutional societies. Second, the developing events in Britain and France acted as an ongoing commentary, capable of diverse interpretation, on the principles and prospects of reform. Third, the outpourings of the loyalist presses provided a constantly moving field of rhetorical contest for reformers while also acting as an alternative commentary on France. Finally, there were the existing traditions of political participation, with their rhetoric, expectations and codes.[45] Clearly, each point could be affected by other points; moreover, this is not offered as a definitive account of all potential influences. Nonetheless, we come closer to the realities of the 1790s if we think of people as responding to events, debating issues and affirming or

---

[44] See Dinwiddy, 'Conceptions of revolution', esp. 537–42.
[45] On which see O'Gorman, *Voters, Patrons and Parties*, esp. ch. 5; see also John Brewer, *Party Ideology and Popular Politics at the Accession of George III* (Cambridge University Press, 1976); and J. A. Phillips, *Electoral Behavior in Unreformed England, 1761–1802* (Princeton University Press, 1982).

changing commitments within this frame, rather than as subscribing to a particular set of radical principles or a particular ideology. Furthermore, if we recognise that the pressure of events in France and from the war with France fed into a polarising conflict between the cause of reform and loyalism, we can also see that as the decade progressed the paradigm of opposition thought was increasingly displaced and its language put to instrumental use. No new framework emerged to replace the old, although there were innovations.[46] Indeed, by the end of the 1800s we can recognise a revival of this ideology. But for a time, during the 1790s, popular political discourse broke with its traditions, and is best understood as increasingly tactical and innovative. Two areas symptomatic of this movement were the use of French references and motifs amongst radicals and the development of a distinctive language of protest.

One surprising feature of reform throughout the decade is the persistent use of French reference points. A whole panoply of symbols, images, styles and rhetoric continued in use amongst radicals throughout the decade[47] – much to the horror of the Committee of Secrecy:

Subsequent to the Declaration of War, which interrupted this System of direct Correspondence and Concert with France, and down to the present Time, the Society has continued, on various Occasions, to manifest their Attachment to the Cause of the French Revolution, and have affected to follow, in their Proceeding, and in their Language, the Forms and even the Phrases which are adopted in that Country.[48]

Reformers' attachment to French principles was signalled in the way they addressed each other, their dress and their hair. Moreover, as the Committee of Secrecy's report suggests, these practices continued after the outbreak of war; as far as the use of the term 'citizen' is concerned, the LCS used it from early in its history, as did some of the more respectable sympathisers, such as Ritson. At times the use of French symbolism could take a more complex form. When Joseph Gerrald was sentenced in Scotland he appeared before his judges with his neck bared, French style, his unpowdered hair hanging loose, and his shirt had a large collar

---

[46] See, for example, Claeys, *Thomas Paine: Social and Political Thought*, ch. 4; and Hampsher-Monk, 'John Thelwall'.
[47] Dinwiddy, 'Conceptions of revolution', 537–8.
[48] Committee of Secrecy, *First Report of the Committee of Secrecy: Ordered to be Printed 17th May 1794* (London: J. Debrett, 1794). See also the accusation of systematic French design to overthrow the British constitution and all its works, for which the dissemination of French principles was the instrument, in *House of Commons Sessional Papers of the Eighteenth Century: Reports and Papers 1798–9*, vol. CXXI, 'Report of the Committee of Secrecy', 317–18.

doubled over in the French fashion of the day.[49] While the contrast with his judges was stark, the intent and effect might have been more subtle than merely establishing his heterodoxy. His judges might have been reminded of other occasions on which French necks were bared. If so, the instance is instructive. To stand before his accusers representing the martyred king was to cast them as revolutionists. The tension between this rhetorical strategy and Gerrald's own ideological commitments is immaterial: the point and force of the act was not to take a stand on principle but to discomfit his judges. It is true that the strategy seems to have paid few dividends, save ensuring an equal martyrdom, but it is instructive of the way that symbolism and rhetoric might be used with serious practical intent but without direct ideological import.

A further feature of the identification with the French was the occasional willingness of some reformers to embrace the terms 'sans-culotte' and 'Jacobin' as self-descriptions, and the much more common use of 'citizen' amongst themselves.

I am a *sans-culotte*! one of those who think the happiness of millions of more consequence than the aggrandizement of any party junto! or, in other words, an advocate for the rights and happiness of those who are languishing in *want* and *nakedness*; the thing in reality which the *whigs* pretend to be.[50]

Cases of publicly subscribing to 'Jacobin' were rarer; even Richard Dinmore, in his *An Exposition of the Principles of the English Jacobins*, provided only a third-person account of the beliefs of the English Jacobins, and Eaton's *Politics for the People* seemed keener to reveal the English Jacobins as creatures of the imagination than to endorse the ascription.[51] Nonetheless, Dinmore did suggest that some radicals were prepared to be counted as Jacobins:

I call them jacobins because their enemies chose so to call them, with a view to confusing the public mind; to render it incapable of distinguishing their merit from the brutal cruelty of the second order of French jacobins. This nickname these

---

[49] Thompson, *The Making of the English Working Class*, 139.
[50] C. Thelwall, *The Life of Thelwall, by His Widow*, 128.
[51] See Daniel Eaton, *Politics for the People; or, Hog's Wash*, vol. 1, pt 2, no. 5 (1794), 15. But the description of them as non-entities is on the same page as the rhyme *Marat's Descent to the Shades* [emphasis in original]:

> The infernal realms, in wild afright, receive his spotted shade,
> Aristocratic imps and fiends were horribly dismay'd;
> They fear'd his democratic rage might all distinction level,
> Make Hell with loud Ca Ira's ring, and *Guillotine the Devil*.

persons readily adopted. They cared not by what names they were called, which rendered the malice of their enemies pointless.[52]

But there is no doubt as to the widespread use of 'citizen'. Ritson used it extensively in correspondence, and it became the standard form of address within the corresponding societies.[53]

The preparedness to use such terminology in self-description had obscure roots. The pejorative use of 'Jacobin' may well originate from the time of the reformers' correspondence with the French societies, but it came to have a much greater significance as events progressed.[54] Loyalists increasingly used the term interchangeably, to all intents and purposes, with 'French', it being used to describe all those implicated in the bloodshed in France from, at the very latest, September 1792. It was also increasingly used in association with the term 'leveller', thereby fusing French and English idioms in the attempt to discredit the movement for reform. When reformers embraced the terms 'Jacobin' or 'leveller', or used other terms valorised by French events (such as 'convention'), they could have had a number of purposes: to assert the legitimacy of the French Revolution; as part of a strategy to counter loyalist assertions as to their fiendish nature; or as a symbol to elicit affirmations of commitment from fellow radicals and a gesture of defiance and resistance to their opponents.[55]

Again, the rhetorical intent and effect was of greater significance than the principles that might be deduced from such a self-ascription. 'English

---

[52] Richard Dinmore, *An Exposition of the Principles of the English Jacobins* (Norwich: John March, 1796), 6.

[53] See Dinmore, *An Exposition of the Principles of the English Jacobins*, 37–8. It is difficult to know quite when 'citizen' came into common usage amongst the radicals. Judging from *Selections from the Papers of the London Corresponding Society*, it seemed to become frequent in 1793 and normal from 1794 on, but its presence in records might be a misleading indication of its actual use.

[54] Again, judging when 'Jacobin' became an epithet is also difficult. It appeared in loyalist songs from very early in 1793 – as in *King, Liberty, Laws*, which also appeared in the *Anti-Gallican Songster I*, as *Song* (first line, 'Ye Britons, so brave, so bold and so free'):

> No religion or laws the vile Jacobins own;
> Their God they deny, and their King they dethrone.

That they only dethrone their king suggests it was written prior to the king's trial (December 1792). Prior to the end of 1792 there would have been no cause to associate the Jacobins in particular with revolutionary extremism, although thereafter the left sections of the club did play a leading role in the inauguration of 'terroristic' policies. The loyalist linking of British reformers and the French Jacobins might well have been grounded on the apparent similarities in organisation and educational objectives between the provincial Jacobin clubs and the British societies, however.

[55] Not unlike the process of the inversion of terms derogatory of minority groups brought about by their positive affirmation by members of those groups – a common enough strategy in black, homosexual and feminist groups in the last thirty years.

Jacobins' is a wildly misleading description of British radicals in the 1790s, even if we think it possible to translate the category from the French experience to the English. What it does do, however, is indicate an implicitly international dimension to the radical cause, reinforced by the earlier exchanges of messages and the sending of delegates, which pushes radicalism beyond the boundaries of the more local and confined language of opposition thought. There was no wholesale conversion to French principles or terminology, but either might be invoked as a way of enriching, by universalising, the language of reform. This might be said of the use of 'citizen', which can be used as an equivalent to 'freeman' (possessing civic rights and privileges) but which, in virtue of its place in the French revolutionary lexicon, brings into play more universalist connotations.

The innovative character of radical writing in the period has been the subject of renewed critical study.[56] We should not underestimate the prior existence of a popular print culture, but the period was distinctive in the development of a popular style of political discourse. Paine is an exemplar of this style, but we can also see in the works of Spence, Eaton and others a process of working out ways of communicating effectively with an audience, many of whom were called into political debate on broader, national issues for the first time by the efforts of the corresponding and constitutional societies. This 'democratical' writing is important for the way it constructs its reader, making accessible to all political issues that were customarily shrouded in a refined language that confined them to an educated élite. Frank O'Gorman has made a convincing case for recognising widespread popular participation in elections in the hundred years before the 1832 Reform Act, but he has also stressed the localised character of the political issues.[57] The case for claiming innovation in politicisation in the 1790s and 1800s on the part of radicals rests with their introduction of a more abstract and principled form of political literature to a plebeian audience. But these writings are also significant in their development of ways of demythologising élite political discourse, and in undercutting the rituals, symbols and conventions of political, social and religious authority.[58] Although the role of loyalist counter-propaganda in

---

[56] Most prominently, Smith, *The Politics of Language*; and Butler's collection *Burke, Paine, Godwin, and the Revolution Controversy*. For a detailed analysis of Spence's methods, see Marcus Wood, 'Thomas Spence and modes of subversion', *Enlightenment and Dissent* 10 (1991), 51–77.
[57] O'Gorman, *Voters, Patrons and Parties*, ch. 5 ('Ideological aspects of electoral behaviour').
[58] See, for example, Eaton's 'Gulielmo Pittachio', in *Politics for the People*, vol. II of the collected issues, (issue 25) 388–9, (issue 26) 406–7; it is probable that the piece was by

defusing elements of this radical challenge should be recognised, it should not be exaggerated; it is more likely that the *Cheap Repository Tracts* were taken as entertainment than as gospel.[59] But it may well be that the net effect of all this activity was to increase the reader's scepticism toward print culture, and this doubtless worked in favour of the status quo.

These examples confirm the importance of moving the analysis of the debate from the level of contrasting political principles and theories to that of the conflicting rhetorical strategies and devices, the developing polarisation of loyalist and reformist claims with its associated denial by the authorities of the existence of a moderate middle ground, and the tactical extension of the boundaries of debate through to sections of the population with little previous involvement in politics. One consequence of doing this is that we have to develop a more nuanced understanding of the relationship between the practical, tactical struggle for reform and the terms that they used to justify, elaborate and reflect upon their activities and objectives. We also need a better understanding of the place of rhetoric and language within the reform movements. Even while recognising the existence of rhetorical flourishes, we need seriously to reflect upon their meaning and function.

For example, how was Thelwall's story 'King Chaunticlere', for the publication of which Eaton was charged with sedition, meant to be understood? The anecdote follows a story of a slave who had revolted for freedom and was being brutally tortured, but who instinctively defended himself against a blow intended by a companion to put him out of his misery. Thelwall purported to be exploring the distinction between mental and muscular action (or intentional and reflex), to demonstrate that we cannot conclude that the love of life is stronger than the love of liberty:

I had a very fine majestic kind of animal, a game cock: a haughty, sanguinary tyrant, nursed in blood and slaughter from his infancy – fond of foreign wars and *domestic rebellions*, into which he would sometimes drive his subjects, by his oppressive obstinacy, in hopes that he might increase his power and glory by their suppression...

This cock would not give the farmyard a moment's peace, and, despite certain prejudices predisposing him to reverence, Thelwall also felt a

Spence, and it is discussed as such by Wood in his 'Thomas Spence and modes of subversion'. There was also the use of offensive parody in *The Pernicious Principles of Tom Paine, Exposed in an Address to Labourers and Mechanics by a Gentleman*, in which the force of 'gentleman' suggests a class connotation absent from much reform literature. *The Pernicious Principles* was published both as a short pamphlet and in full in *Politics for the People*, vol. 2, issue 1 (1794), 4–9. See also Bindman, *The Shadow of the Guillotine*, esp. ch. 8; and Brewer's introductory essay, '"This monstrous tragi-comic scene"'.
[59] Susan Pedersen, 'Hannah More meets Simple Simon: tracts, chapbooks, and popular culture in late eighteenth-century England', *Journal of British Studies* 25 (1986), 84–113.

degree of aversion to barefaced despotism, which suggested to him 'that the best thing to do for cocks and hens, or men and women, was to rid the world of tyrants'.

> So I believe, if guillotines had been in fashion, I should have certainly guillotined him: being desirous to be merciful, even in the stroke of death, and knowing, that the instant the brain is separated from the heart, (which, with this instrument, is done in a moment,) pain and consciousness are at an end.

Instead, Thelwall was forced to use a knife and block, which he did to good effect. Beneath the bird's finery he found it to be no better than 'a common tame scratch-dunghill pullet'. But the point of his story is that, after the head had been cut off, the bird continued to bounce around, so that had someone tried to knock it down he or she would have concluded that the bird was trying to save itself, and that this 'proceeded from the conviction that life was worth preserving even after he had lost his head: which, in my opinion, would be just about as rational as supposing that it can be worth preserving to (the) man who is writhing about in *the frying pan of despotism*'.[60]

The story is a brilliantly constructed satire on loyalist dogma and monarchical pretensions – one that works even better as a performance than in the written word. But it is far from clear quite what Thelwall (if indeed it was Thelwall) was recommending. How, in particular, is the quite detailed reference to the virtues of the guillotine to be read?! It is worth asking whether Thelwall was just colossally imprudent, or whether it is evidence of a form of collective impudence. It is notable that the meeting broke up in disorder when a minority tried to prevent Thelwall from speaking when he went on to praise the exertions of France in favour of liberty. How much was it the frisson of danger, the thinking of the unthinkable, that generated the disorder? Perhaps what comes out most clearly from this and similar examples is a clear sense that writers were playing with ideas and principles, and with their audiences' intellectual and emotional reflexes. In a great deal of the material of the 1790s we are dealing less with a clear-cut ideological division with well-worked-out opposing principles and more with experimentation, both in the use of particular media and in the position being advanced. Such rhetorical experimentation often leads people to innovate in their commitments and break new ideological ground. Instead of reading these texts,

---

[60] Eaton, *Politics for the People*, vol. 1, issue 8 (1793), 102–7 [emphasis in original]. This is reprinted, omitting a report of the subsequent evening's debate, in Butler's *Burke, Paine, Godwin, and the Revolution Controversy*. Thelwall later denied that the story was given in these terms, and claimed that Eaton had dressed it up in much stronger terms: C. Thelwall, *The Life of Thelwall, by His Widow*, 108–9.

utterances and symbolic statements for the deeper, principled, meaning behind them, we should recognise that it is often in their superficial diversity, idiosyncrasy and imprudence that their force lies – a force that affects not just the audience but, in many cases, the writer or speaker as well. There is a temptation when looking at controversies to see writing and speaking as expressing already existing ideas, but there is much to be said for recognising a more complex relationship. It is frequently in the act of writing and speaking that we form ideas and make them choate. This is not invariably the case, but it is more likely to be so when writing and speech become invested with an immediate practical political significance.

There is a final area of concern in the analysis of reformism in the 1790s that requires our attention before we return to the questions raised in my opening statements about the impact of the fragmentation of radical ideology on the prospects of the reform movement. I have argued that we should understand the 1790s in terms of the development of a logic of confrontation and an associated shift from ideology to rhetoric and propaganda. I have also suggested that, in this process, some people were persuaded that they required new tactics to attain their ends and that, at each step, the stakes in the struggle were raised – both in the sense of increasing the costs of agitating for reform and in the sense of making moderate reform less likely and less possible. That is, as the decade progressed there was less chance of securing reform, and there was less chance, were such reform to be attained, that it would remain moderate. To complement this account we need some sense of the way that reformers reacted to these changing parameters of reforming activity. Clearly, there were, in fact, many different individual responses, some moving to a withdrawal from political activity, others being willing to countenance armed insurrection, but it is still possible to make some general comments about the processes involved in people's developing commitments.

The least plausible account of radical motivation is an instrumental one in which reformers saw reform as a way of improving their lot, but abandoned it as a strategy either when they ceased to need it[61] or when they saw the probable short-term costs outweighing the increasingly improbable long-term gains. This kind of calculation, particularly the latter, probably played some role in people's willingness to remain active

---

[61] A cynical account of Hardy would suggest that once he thought he could rely on the financial support of his rich friends he lost interest in the reform movement (he would certainly have been imprudent to do so, given that his friends seemed more willing to give out promises than cash). See Thomas Hardy's *Memoir of Thomas Hardy* (London: James Ridgway, 1832).

in political associations, but to see this as all is to rely on a very emaciated picture of human motivation and to be satisfied with a very inadequate account of the 1790s. We need to combine a more complex account of motivation and ideological commitment with a recognition of the changing nature of the options and costs faced by reformers, and with an appreciation of the factors that shaped their perceptions of these options. Ideology plays some part in this, but so too does the complex process of identifying interests and making commitments, and interpreting and reinterpreting these in a context that increasingly seeks to classify them and their concerns as subversive.

We should begin by recognising that becoming involved in agitation for reform was not a uniform experience. For someone such as Charles James Fox, his flirtation with the reform movement was not radically discontinuous from his previous activities; for someone such as Godwin, identification with it offered the prospect of fame and fortune within a literary culture in which he already played a minor role, or even, perhaps, a more glorious role as one of the intellectual leaders of the new society. But, for men such as Place and Hardy, reform offered a more practical kind of emancipation or empowerment, together with a degree of social mobility. Hardy's comments that in the first five nights he and his first associates in the LCS spent the time discussing whether they, as 'Treadesmen [sic] – Shopkeepers and mechanicks', had any right to seek parliamentary reform should alert us to the dramatic impact that democratic politics and the spread of Painite and other literature had on the common man. Thomas Preston recorded the awakening he experienced in the 1790s, which subsequently led him to trial for high treason for his part in the 1816 Spa Fields riot:

The increase in reading had dissipated the delusion, and people now knew the meaning of words, whether spoken in the Senate, written in a lawyer's bill of costs, or printed on an impress warrant. The charm of *ignorance* which had so long lulled my mind into comparative indifference at people's wrongs, was now beginning to disappear. The moral and political sun of TRUTH had now arisen. The arguments, the irresistible arguments, laid down by the 'Corresponding Society' had rivetted my heart to the cause of liberty.[62]

In other words, for some the experience was transformative – and this sense of personal enlightenment, indeed empowerment, was very much associated with the development of artisan-based organisations that made their own rules and ordered their own proceedings.[63] But it also suggests

---

[62] Thomas Preston, *The Life and Opinions of Thomas Preston* (London: A. Seale, 1817), 13.
[63] As Günther Lottes argues, in part in his 'Radicalism, revolution and political culture: an Anglo-French comparison', in Philp, *The French Revolution and British Popular Politics*,

that the experience could also be welded together with older and often deeply potent popular traditions of thought and practice – not just 'independent' or opposition traditions, but also millenarian and apocalyptic visions. The diverse languages, imageries and ideas available to those who now had a sense of a unique destiny in clearing the shrouds of superstition and imposture from the body politic could be combined and utilised in many ways – but not as creeds to conform to so much as a tool kit with which to innovate.[64]

There is, then, a recurrent sense in the 1790s of people's commitments being transformed, particularly amongst the artisans and the middling orders. This is one factor that distinguishes the popular participation of the 1790s from that which existed in the arena of electoral struggles and which has been brought sharply into focus by O'Gorman. But a further distinguishing feature is that, where electoral participation was rooted in local issues and reciprocal relations, reformers could interpret their activity in more universal terms, as a matter of moral truth and political integrity. Similarly, this feature also served to sanctify personal preferences by representing them as demanded by a higher morality, and this in turn might lead people to ignore instrumental calculation; prudence might speak against demanding reform, but truth would have the higher claim. And, when the force of law was brought to bear against this morality, it lost its impartial character and became seen as progressively more corrupt, both forcing and making legitimate active measures to challenge its authority. This progressive movement towards greater radicalism – this commitment to a radical 'career' – was made additionally attractive to many in the 1790s by the gradual erosion of legitimated alternative forms of political activity. Having made the initial commitment, people rarely fell at the first obstacle.[65] While events at home and in France – the royal proclamation, the September Massacres, the rise of loyalism and the Reevite societies, and so on – served increasingly to

---

78–98, but also in his *Politische Aufklärung und plebejisches Publikum: Zur Theorie und Praxis des englischen Radikalismus im spätem 10. Jahrhundert* (Munich: Oldenbourg, 1979).

[64] The metaphor of 'bricolage' is helpful here; see Claude Levi-Strauss, *The Savage Mind* (London: Weidenfeld & Nicolson, 1972), ch. 1; and Jon Mee, *Dangerous Enthusiasm: William Blake and the Culture of Radicalism in the 1790s* (Oxford: Clarendon Press, 1992), ch. 1.

[65] Although Godwin's experience did not extend across the whole social spectrum, it is worth recalling this suggestion of his: 'Down to the spring of 1797, when petitions were being sent up from many parts of England for the removal of the King's ministers, scarcely one of those persons who had declared themselves ardently and affectionately interested for the success of the French, deserted their cause.' William Godwin, *Thoughts Occasioned by the Perusal of Dr Parr's Spital Sermon* (London: Taylor & Wilks, 1801), 4.

stigmatise and increase the costs of radical activity, there were also gains to radicals from this process, in terms of collective solidarity and, through this and the higher public profile attained, an implicit affirmation of one's new political identity. It might well be, however, that these gains were greater for the newly politicised, those who rose with events, than they were for the older élite, whose role in the political and social order might itself be under threat. Further polarisation made escape routes more attractive – emigration, quiescence, volte-face – but, again, there were class and status differentials. Who could gain by reneging (James Mackintosh, but not Francis Place or Thomas Hardy)? Who could afford emigration? Quiescence was not necessarily a more attractive prospect than continued involvement, especially if there were side benefits, such as participation and status gains, a sense of empowerment, and so on, or when there were innovations in tactics that offered renewed promise of results, as in their association with the anti-government feeling stemming from food shortages and the war in 1795/6 and in the use of mass meetings in 1795. While the escalation of conflict did threaten to impose high costs, many of those agitating for reform would also have been insulated in their perception of these costs by group norms. Furthermore, the reformers' increasing confrontation with the law, and their notable success in using the courts as a platform for their cause, would have both confirmed their sense of the urgency and legitimacy of reform and decreased their sense of the probable costs of continued agitation.

These considerations are an essential background to the analysis of radical rhetoric. It seems plausible to read stories such as Thelwall's 'King Chaunticlere' as part of a process of self-definition, involving experimentation with commitments, identities or political positions, that might subsequently be endorsed. Similarly, the juggling with Burke's phrase 'a swinish multitude' by Eaton, Spence and many others offered an opportunity to speak in a number of different characters, against which the reader can form new perceptions of his or her own. The identities experimented with, as in 'King Chaunticlere', were frequently oppositional and confrontational, and the rhetoric had its share of bravado, but that is part of its point. When challenged, reformers might prove slippery, as in the treason trials, exploiting the difference between what might have been said or written and what was really meant; but they might also be drawn into a commitment to the implications of their rhetoric. In this way, political rhetoric served to explore and reinterpret (and thereby determine) the boundaries of the politically possible and the politically desirable. Ronald Paulson, in discussing the French Revolution, suggests that '[i]f the French example made revolution possible – even desirable – it also, from the events of 1788 onward and at each new stage, served to convince many people that *anything* was now possible'.[66] Günther Lottes has suggested why British reformers might 'find their political imaginations more constrained than their French counterparts', but as the decade progressed, and the polarisation was exacerbated, those who remained committed to reform would have found the constraints less potent.[67]

Political rhetoric, then, was neither the direct expression of conviction nor just a joke. It was a way of experimenting with commitment and identity, some of which got full personal endorsement when confrontation necessitated it. But, as those commitments were elicited, actors could become successively more embroiled in confrontations that led them down paths and into activities that they would not earlier have countenanced. They were not forced to take this road, but confrontations cannot simply be assessed in terms of prudence; what was at stake for the participants was the strength of their commitments to beliefs and values that had come to play a major role in governing their day-to-day behaviour – beliefs, moreover, that had become increasingly central to their sense of who they were. Going against these commitments involved a certain loss of self; sticking with them offered confirmation.

IV

I began by looking at the role that the divisions in the reform movement have been accorded in the explanation of its failure. As will now be clear, there are good reasons for thinking that the ideological divisions among the reformers were of less significance than some writers have suggested. The movement for reform that developed as the decade progressed was not driven by high theory but by popular agitation and mobilisation against scarcity and war and in favour of reform. At this level, the diversity of reformist thinking can be seen as positively enriching the process of constructing one's radical identity. The range of radical and reformist traditions and texts, together with the practical examples of America and France, provided a context within which reformers could construct interpretations, identities and strategies. And many of the divisions that did exist, such as that between temperate reformers in parliamentary circles and the extra-parliamentary groups that, by the end of the decade, were toying with insurrection, flowed less from the intrinsic qualities of radical thought and more from the loyalist reaction and the government's

---

[66] Ronald Paulson, *Representations of Revolution 1789–1820* (New Haven, CT: Yale University Press, 1983), 2.
[67] Lottes, 'Radicalism, revolution and political culture'.

continued refusal to engage in dialogue with the extra-parliamentary groups agitating for reform.

In the final analysis, it is not clear that the fragmentation mattered very much in the debate over the prospects for Britain experiencing a French-style revolution. It is only on the most simplistic and voluntarist of assumptions that a cohesive revolutionary theory can be seen as a necessary condition for revolution. When we put the more sensible question of why reform attempts fail, we can find the answer without difficulty in the processes of polarisation and confrontation that the conservative reaction initiated, and we can see the willingness to countenance more radical aspirations and methods as an outcome of this exclusion. But the question of whether these ambitions could then have succeeded has little to do with the integrity of radical reform programmes, and much more to do with the extent to which social and economic crises associated with the war also provoked political crises and crises of legitimation – crises that mattered most not among the classes that attended the 'free and easies' of Spencian circles, or indulged in politicised millenarian speculation, but among members of the social, political and financial élites of the country. Popular discontent and a radical popular politics may be necessary conditions for revolutionary transformation, but they are not by any means sufficient.

2 Vulgar conservatism 1792/3[1]

In the fifty years since E. P. Thompson published the *Making of the English Working Class*, considerable scholarly attention has been focused on the ideological conflict that took place in Britain in the 1790s. An increasing sensitivity to the history of ideas, and to the need to place political, philosophical and literary works in their full context, has encouraged many scholars to take seriously the view that the early years of the decade witnessed something like a 'debate on France', even if they might demur at Alfred Cobban's suggestion that the decade witnessed 'perhaps the last real discussion of fundamentals in politics in this country'.[2] It was only much later, however, that the conservative 'side' of the debate received the kind of attention that the radicals had attracted since Thompson's book appeared. Although Burke had never been short of commentators, many other conservative and loyalist writers did not attract serious study till much later, not least in work by Jonathan Clark, Philip Schofield and Robert Hole.[3] In tandem with this development, there has been renewed scholarly attention to the organisational side of loyalism, to the loyalist associations, the volunteer movement, the rise of popular patriotism and the development of loyalist challenges to radical propaganda (in the form, for example, of the *Cheap Repository Tracts*).[4]

---

[1] An earlier version of this chapter was delivered at the 'Conference for the study of political thought', 'Between the revolutions', held at the University of Tulsa, Oklahoma, in April 1992. I am grateful for the various comments of the participants, to Alan Ryan for inviting me, and to David Eastwood, Jo Innes, John Stevenson, and, in particular, Iain McCalman for advice on earlier drafts.

[2] Cobban, *The Debate on the French Revolution*, 31.

[3] See J. C. D. Clark, *English Society, 1688–1832: Ideology, Social Structure and Political Practice during the Ancien Regime* (Cambridge University Press, 1985); Schofield, 'Conservative political thought in Britain in response to the French Revolution'; and Hole, *Pulpits, Politics and Public Order*. See also Claeys, 'The French Revolution debate'.

[4] Significant early work is to be found from Black, *The Association*; and Western, 'The volunteer movement as an anti-revolutionary force'. See also Ginter, 'The loyalist association movement of 1792–3'; and Mitchell, 'The association movement of 1791–3'. More recent works include Dickinson, 'Popular loyalism in Britain' and 'Popular conservatism

This new work on loyalism and conservative political philosophy has challenged the view that reformers possessed both an evident ideological superiority and a wide base of popular support and were defeated only by government repression. In contrast, it has been argued that conservative doctrine provided an impressive, deep and persuasive defence of the status quo, which spoke to the needs and interests of both the ruling élite and many of the middling sort. Moreover, the success of the loyalist associations, and the participation of the common people in Paine burnings and other loyalist activities, testify to 'the genuine popularity of the loyalist cause among all ranks in society'.[5] In the minds of the people, in this view, there was no doubt that 'the debate' was won by the conservatives. And when we turn to ask why Britain did not experience an equivalent revolutionary crisis to France, as Ian Christie did in his Ford Lectures in 1983/4, we are told that one factor, among many, was that conservative thinkers were able to summon up 'the lessons of history, of pragmatic experience, and of utility, in defence of their existing system of government', and thus to rally 'the instinctive support of the great majority of the British political nation'.[6]

While some of this work has provided a useful corrective, the broader claims that have been made are more questionable.[7] One difficulty arises from the characterisation of what took place from 1790 to 1793 as a 'debate', and the related idea that intellectual content and force of argument account for the willingness of the people to support the status quo. It is assumed that we can identify two clearly delineated sides between which some exchange took place. Neither assertion bears much scrutiny. It is

---

and militant loyalism'; David Eastwood, 'Patriotism and the English state' and 'Robert Southey and the meanings of patriotism', *Journal of British Studies* 31 (1992), 265–87; Dozier, *For King, Constitution, and Country*; Cookson, 'The English volunteer movement of the French wars'; Linda Colley, 'The apotheosis of George III: loyalty, royalty and the British nation, 1760–1820', *Past and Present* 102 (1984), 94–129, and 'Whose nation? Class and national consciousness in Britain, 1750–1830', *Past and Present* 113 (1986), 97–117; Hugh Cunningham, 'The language of patriotism 1750–1914', *History Workshop* 12 (1981), 8–33; and John Dinwiddy, 'England', in Otto Dann and John Dinwiddy, eds., *Nationalism in the Age of the French Revolution* (London: Hambledon Press, 1988), 53–70. On the later Cheap Repository Tracts dimension, see Pedersen, 'Hannah More meets Simple Simon'.
[5] Dickinson, 'Popular loyalism in Britain', 517.
[6] Christie, *Stress and Stability in Late Eighteenth-Century Britain*, 182. See also his 'Conservatism and stability in British society'; and Emsley, 'Repression, "terror" and the rule of law in England'.
[7] For works questioning the new consensus, see John Dinwiddy, 'Interpretations of anti-Jacobinism', in Philp, *The French Revolution and British Popular Politics*, 38–49; Eastwood, 'Patriotism and the English state'; and Mark Philp, 'The fragmented ideology of reform', chapter 1 in this volume. See also Harry T. Dickinson, *British Radicalism and the French Revolution* (Oxford: Basil Blackwell, 1985); and Philp, 'Introduction', in *The French Revolution and British Popular Politics*, 1–17, 13.

doubtful whether any intense political controversy is wholly, or even predominantly, intellectual in character; such controversies are complex ideological, political and social phenomena in which beliefs, objectives and what people are prepared to say or do may change radically (witness events in France in this period!).[8] To go further and to argue that Britain's avoidance of revolution can be explained by the outcome of this debate is to compound the error. Not only does this assume an emaciated view of the conditions for political stability and revolutionary change; it also moves to the centre of the analysis a counterfactual claim of doubtful relevance (the non-occurrence of a revolution). The crucial question in this period is, arguably, not why Britain avoided a revolution but how revolution came to be on the political agenda at all – if indeed it did.

This chapter proposes a partial challenge to the recent overemphasis on the intellectual vigour of conservative doctrine and the natural loyalty of the British people by looking in detail at the development of one of the key institutions of loyalism: the Association for the Preservation of Liberty and Property against Republicans and Levellers. To concentrate on the body of conservative ideas available in the period is not necessarily the best way of reading loyalist literature. One of the drawbacks of this approach is that it accords conceptual status to terms and claims that are also (and sometimes only) of rhetorical significance. To meet this point, some commentators distinguish the more populist texts from the more intellectual: Hole, for example, suggests that 'the lower the intellectual level becomes, the more the tracts depend upon various emotional devices rather than argument'.[9] This distinction ignores the fact that there were substantial rhetorical strategies at work even in the more intellectual of the pamphlets, however. More damagingly, it presupposes a distinction, between the 'vulgar' or 'popular' and the 'élite' or 'intellectual', which loyalists in the 1790s were attempting to create and institutionalise. The organisational and literary manifestations of loyalism were more multidimensional and complex in their effects than is generally recognised. By examining the correspondence directed to the London Association and by focusing on the rhetorical strategies employed by writers identifying with loyalism, we can gain a more nuanced picture of their activities – one that shows how they became committed to a project of popular instruction profoundly at odds with their original intent and their professed commitment to the status quo. The result was that loyalism found itself attempting to create a 'vulgar' conservatism.

[8] See Philp, 'Introduction' and 'The fragmented ideology of reform'.
[9] Robert Hole, 'British counter-revolutionary popular propaganda in the 1790s', in Colin Jones, ed., *Britain and Revolutionary France* (University of Exeter Press, 1983), 53–69.

For Burke, and the many who defended or imitated him, the vulgar were the object of conservative thinking, not intended participants in it; they were those who had to be ruled by a power out of themselves, those whom 'providence dooms to live on trust'.[10] In contrast, many of Reeves' correspondents in the association were prepared to argue that this exclusion could not be maintained, since the *Rights of Man* and other radical literature 'adapted to the lowest orders of the people' were persuading the vulgar 'to be dissatisfied with the government under which they live, and [to] look for something more satisfactory than they find'.[11] These conservatives believed that they too had now to address that audience. To pursue this course was to transcend Burke, for, both in forming the association movement and in subsequently developing a literature designed for the lower orders, loyalists breached the traditional boundaries of the political nation and thereby advanced a process of mass participation that they had come into existence to prevent.

Linda Colley and others have drawn attention to the mobilisation of the nation that was effected in the last three or four years of the 1790s in response to the threat of invasion.[12] Through the volunteers and the spread of patriotic propaganda, a popular movement, suffused with nationalist and loyalist rhetoric, was directed towards the defence of the country. In these accounts, the phenomenon of pre-war loyalism has received much less emphasis, however. Colley herself identifies 1797 as the key date for this strategic turn towards mass involvement, and she has no doubts as to the overriding element in its appeal: 'Between 1798 and 1805 at least, the prime incentive to volunteer was not camaraderie, or aggression, or greed, or the fear of seeming less than a man, or coercion from above, but quite simply invasion.'[13] The absence of full-scale war or the threat of invasion in the winter of 1792/3 provided a very different

---

[10] Edmund Burke, *Reflections on the Revolution in France*, ed. Conor Cruise O'Brien (Harmondsworth: Penguin Books, 1968), 151, 195. The reference to 'a power out of themselves' is ambiguous; it might be taken to refer to a power that stems from the people, but the text suggests a stronger reading: a power out of, or beyond, their control, 'not ... subject to that will and to those passions which it is its office to bridle and subdue' (152).

[11] *State Trials*, vol. xxii, case 577, 779–80. 'As the cheapness of Mr. Paine's books has put it in the power of the poorest man to purchase them, there are I believe many of them now in circulation among such people, who with great industry communicate those dangerous yet fascinating opinions of equality amongst their companions': British Library, Add. MS 16927, fo. 47 r.

[12] See Colley, *Britons: Forging the Nation*, 308–19; Western, 'The volunteer movement as an anti-revolutionary force'; Eastwood, 'Patriotism and the English state'; Clive Emsley, 'War, revolution and the nation state: the British and French experiences 1789–1801', in Philp, *The French Revolution and British Popular Politics*, 99–117.

[13] Colley, *Britons: Forging the Nation*, 305.

context for the activities of the loyalists. Mobilisation was not their initial aim, and the form of mobilisation that they brought about was of a very different character from that which occurred later in the decade. The motive Colley alludes to was simply absent. In its place, a host of other motives, ambitions and incentives drew men and women towards the loyalist associations. One result was a gradual transformation of the initial aims of loyalism and the creation of a movement that mirrored radicalism's transgression of the traditional boundaries between the élite and the common people. Moreover, in contrast to the claims that have been made for the nationalism and patriotism of the end of the decade, the commitments that this earlier loyalist movement inspired were of doubtful stability, and the eventual outcome of the associations' activities was far from certain. There are implications here for accounts of the later years of the decade. How far was the threat of invasion sufficient to transform the complex and contradictory character of earlier loyalism into patriotism or nationalism? How deep and abiding were the emotional attachments created in the later period, given their dependence on this rather rare military contingency? These broader questions cannot be dealt with here, but the detailed analysis that follows of the tensions, conflicts and ambiguities of the loyalism of 1792/3 does show both that it is premature to speak in terms of popular nationalism and patriotism prior to 1794, and that we should be extremely wary of assuming that participation in the later period was necessarily of greater depth and endurance.

I

The first nine months of 1792 saw the rapid spread of societies for political reform among the lower orders of society – 'tradesmen, shopkeepers, and mechanics' (as Hardy described them)[14] – together with assiduous attempts by the metropolitan societies, in particular the Society for Constitutional Information (SCI), to circulate the first and second parts of Paine's *Rights of Man* and other radical literature. The royal proclamation in May 1792 and the prosecution of Paine proved equally ineffective in stemming the radical tide. Moreover, events in France after the summer only increased the government's concern. The autumn saw the first major French victories in the war against the coalition. Despite the September Massacres, these were greeted by popular celebrations in Britain and by a further spate of correspondence between the various radical societies and the National Assembly. With the French abolishing

[14] Hardy, *Memoir of Thomas Hardy*, 109; see also 15.

their monarchy, offering fraternal aid to all subject peoples (19 November) and glorying in their sweeping military successes, the British government's anxieties about domestic radicalism escalated.

By December 1792, prompted by a real fear of insurgence in London, the government felt it necessary to issue a further royal proclamation against sedition (1 December).[15] The proclamation came twelve days after the foundation meeting of John Reeves' London-based Association for Preserving Liberty and Property against Republicans and Levellers (APLP). Reeves (1752–1829) was a civil servant and legal scholar, whose work for the government was extremely lucrative.[16] But he was not simply an apologist for the government, or a paid propagandist.[17] Indeed, it is clear that on this occasion he acted initially without instruction from the government, although in only a matter of days William Pitt was writing to Henry Dundas, the Secretary of State for Home Affairs, to report that the association had 'produced a great Impression, which shews that there is a Spirit and Disposition to Activity which if We give it in the outset a right Direction may be improved to important purposes'.[18] Pitt's idea of the 'right Direction' was to use the association to create 'the impression and effect of numbers on our side'.[19] In government circles there was a general sense that radicalism had grown to such an extent as to pose an increasing threat to the status quo.[20]

Reeves' association was the first, and it remained the most important in subsequent months. Founded on 20 November 1792, it announced its

[15] Emsley, 'The London "insurrection" of December 1792'.

[16] See Emily Lorraine de Montluzin, *The Anti-Jacobins 1798–1800: The Early Contributors to the* Anti-Jacobin Review (London: Macmillan, 1988), 136–8. She cites Mitchell's report of the *Star*'s assessment of £1,000 per annum.

[17] See Cobbett's account of Reeves, in William Cobbett, *The Autobiography of William Cobbett: The Progress of a Plough-Boy to a Seat in Parliament*, ed. William Reitzel (London: Faber & Faber, 1933), 67. See also 50, n. 33.

[18] Dr Michael Duffy has kindly drawn my attention to Pitt's letter to Henry Dundas of 25 November 1792, in the Pitt Papers, William L. Clements Library, University of Michigan, Ann Arbor, and provided the transcription from which the quotation is drawn. The letter establishes conclusively that Reeves was not acting on the prompting of the government. Pitt introduced the topic to Dundas as follows: 'A printed paper appeared a few days ago, which I enclose to you, and which I like in everything but its having adopted the objectionable Term of Association. It has produced a great Impression. . .' Reeves himself claimed in 1795, also in a letter to Dundas, that the association had begun without any communication with government, 'but when it was on foot, I then had some communication with persons at Whitehall. I have never had any money from Govern[men]t to carry it on.' Reeves to Dundas, 14 December 1795, Melville Castle Muniments, GD 51/1, fo. 264. I am indebted on this latter point to Dr A. D. Macintyre.

[19] William Pitt to Henry Dundas, 25 November 1792 (see note 18 above). The one thing that Pitt objected to, as we see, was the use of the term 'Association', largely, it seems, because of its connotations of an active style of organisation.

[20] See Black, *The Association*, 237–8; and Eastwood, 'Patriotism and the English state', 154–5.

existence to the public three days later in the *Sun*. The following day advertisements appeared in *The Times*, the *Morning Chronicle* and the *Sun* calling for the formation of similar societies throughout the country. At the second meeting of the APLP (24 November), it was resolved to publish *Mr Justice Ashurst's Charge to the Grand Jury of Middlesex*, and quickly agreed that a principal means by which to serve the cause of order and the preservation of the existing constitution was for the new body to 'use its best endeavours occasionally to explain those topicks of publick discussion which have been so perverted by evil designing men, and to shew, by irrefragable proof, that they are not applicable to the State of this Country, that they can produce no good, and certainly must produce great evil'.[21] To this effect, various publications were issued by the association and sent throughout the country to those soliciting them.

Reeves' association, then, did not at first see the publication of popular tracts as one of its major activities. At its first 'meeting' (which on most accounts involved only Reeves and James Moore, and on Thomas Hardy's account involved only Reeves, Moore being a pseudonym),[22] the aim seems to have been to generate further loyalist associations throughout the country and to stimulate the detection and prosecution (through ex officio information) of subversives and radical activists.[23] The decision to reprint *Mr Justice Ashurst's Charge* and the strategy of publishing and circulating the resolutions of the association were in line with the attempt to appeal to the traditional political nation. However much the circulation of radical literature among the lower orders was perceived as constituting a threat to the status quo, Reeves' response was concerned to mobilise the traditional political élite. The decision to move beyond this élite and to sanction a campaign of counter-radical propaganda directed at a popular audience emerged only gradually in the opening weeks of the movement, and the impetus for this change in strategy came (as did many of the pamphlets) from those corresponding with the association.

The 'literature' generated by the society can be divided into three categories: the correspondence to the association in London, which took

---

[21] *Publications Printed by Order of the Society for Preserving Liberty and Property against Republicans and Levellers* (hereafter *APLP, Papers*), Proceedings, I, 5–6. 'They should by reasoning, and by circulating cheap books and papers endeavour to undeceive those poor people who have been misled by the infusion of opinions dangerous to their own welfare and that of the state' (7–8). It is likely that 'poor' here means 'unfortunate', but the strategy of appealing to the lower orders was more clearly endorsed on 30 November (10). On 11 December concern was extended to print shops (15).

[22] See Black, *The Association*, 237, n. 8. Hardy was clearly mistaken; the notes on the backs of the letter to the association are in two different hands: Reeves' (which can be confirmed by other material on which we have his signature) and the very different hand of Moore.

[23] Black, *The Association*, 237.

the form of letters and copies of the resolutions of local associations modelled more or less loosely on the APLP, and forwarded with great enthusiasm (particularly after a suggestion by the latter that these resolutions might be published in a collection by Debrett, with subscriptions also being solicited); a series of such '*Publications* as the Society ordered to be printed, after they had been perused and approved by the Committee' (most of which appeared in the first volume of the *Publications Printed by Order of the Society for Preserving*...); and a series of *Tracts* that 'were put to the press, without the special direction or approbation of the Committee, by a person in whom the Committee confided'. This later group, unlike the former, was 'designed principally for the lower class of readers. The style and manner of some of these papers are, therefore, of a particular sort.'[24] Some were written by John Bowles, and William Jones also made an important contribution with his addresses from various members of the Bull family,[25] but many others were unsolicited contributions from correspondents – such as the *Dialogue between a Tradesman and his Porter*.[26]

The correspondence to Reeves and Moore over the months of December and January reveals a wide range of concerns and contains an equally wide range of suggestions as to how to manage the crisis facing the constitution. Those writing were at their most inventive in the first month; thereafter a major part of the correspondence involved little more than sending in resolutions, requests for association literature, and letters thanking the APLP for its communications.[27] It is in the first four to six

---

[24] *APLP*, *Papers*, Proceedings, preface, ii.

[25] See de Montluzin, *The Anti-Jacobins*, and Hole, *Pulpits, Politics and Public Order*, for both Bowles and Jones; and Emma Vincent, '"The real grounds of the present war": John Bowles and the French Revolutionary Wars, 1792–1802', *History* 78 (1993), 393–420.

[26] A fourth category might be made of the publications and manuscripts mentioned in, or recommended to, the association that were not adopted by it. This material is of interest because of the judgements that the committee was clearly making about how far specific publications were appropriate 'to counteract the poison that had been disseminated, and to restore the minds of the People to that tone of good sense, which has ever been the characteristic of this country' (*APLP*, *Papers*, loc. cit.). An extended examination of this literature is beyond the scope of the present chapter. It should be understood, however, that Reeves did not simply reject material that be thought too liberal or highbrow; he also rejected works that be found too 'ultra'. One correspondent enclosed a piece entitled 'To Every Honest and Open-Hearted Englishman', which Reeves rejected as 'proposing a very violent Paper against Presbyterians as a hand bill – not fit for use': Add. MS 16922, fos. 191 r–2 v.

[27] There are approximately 687 pieces of correspondence in Add. MSS 16919–28, plus three volumes of resolutions (some handwritten, some printed), totalling 245 separate resolutions: ibid. 16929–31. It is clear that, despite the belief that the resolutions would be collected and printed (which many associations found an attractive idea, and encouragement to include the names of those on local committees), there were other local associations that passed resolutions but without forwarding copies of them to Reeves. These numbers are obviously more difficult to calculate.

weeks that we find most reports of seditious activities (and most of the letters from radicals denouncing the association), and most suggestions as to how to deal with radicalism and with discontent among the poor.[28] The suggestions were extremely varied. They included rather critical accounts of the established Church, which implied that bishops and clergy might do a great deal of good simply by living in their dioceses and parishes, and others that proposed a substantial reform of the tithe system.[29] Moreover, there were proposals to boycott radical papers, and to put pressure on brewers, alehouse-keepers and the keepers of lodging houses not to admit men of seditious persuasion to their facilities.[30] There were also enthusiastic suggestions for the creation of a volunteer movement, the establishment of a loyalist uniform and loyalist oaths and petitions and the arming of the more respectable part of the community.[31] And there was a consistent concern with the pay and conditions of the army and the navy to ensure that they remain loyal.[32]

Yet, of all this activity, the most successful – that which provided the association with a continuing rationale for its existence (and in a way that gave it a degree of authority over many of the provincial associations) – was the endorsement, publication and circulation of tracts and pamphlets. Whereas just over 15 per cent of the correspondence proper related to the

[28] Letters informing on radicals include Add. MSS 16920, fos. 21 r–v, 111 r; 16921, fos. 65 r, 112 r–v, 131 r–v; 16922, fos. 34 r, 55 r, 63 r–v, 119 r–20 v, 125 r, 141 r–v, 198 r–9 r; 16924, fos. 3 r–v, 17 v, 35 r–v, 39 r–40 v, 86 r, 100 r, 126 r; 16925, fos. 137 r, 145 r–6 r; 16926, fos. 1 r–2 r, 5 v–6 r; 16927, fos. 3 r–4 r, 17 r–v, 27 r, 39 v–40 v, 41 r, 63 r–4 v, 73 r; 16928, fo. 16 r. Letters informing on radical publishers, bookshops and prints include 16919, fo. 19 r; 16920, fos. 30 r–v, 51 r; 16921, fos. 65 r, 69 r, 71 r, 80 r–1 r, 94 r, 133 r–v, 139 r–40 v; 16922, fos. 12 r, 13 r, 53 r–v, 69 r–70 r, 116 r–18 v, 167 r–v, 183 r; 16925, fos. 77 r–v*, 100 r–3 r, 129 r–v, 149 v; 16927, fo. 15 r–v (*William Wade of St John's College wrote informing on William Frend). Suggestions for new approaches to the poor include 16919, fos. 148 r–51 v; 16920, fos. 17 r–19 v; 16921, fos. 121 r–4 r; 16923, fos. 47 r–50 v, 116 r; 16925, fo. 156 r–v.
[29] See ibid., 16919, fo. 15 r; and on tithes 16921, fos.4 v, 10 r, 151 r–2 r; 16923, fo.127 v; 16927, fos. 90 r–1 v. The Church is also called upon to take a more active role at 16921, fo. 125 r, and 16927, fos. 9 r–10 r; and Sarah Trimmer gives an extremely detailed account of how the rigours of the gift relationship might be introduced in the granting of charity to the poor through the Church so as to ensure their obedience at 16921, fos. 121 r–4 r; 16922, fo. 177 r; 16923, fos. 47 r–50 v.
[30] See ibid., 16923, fo. 191 r (newspapers); 16921, fos.14 r, 73 r, 117 r; 16923, fos. 185 r–v, 189 r–v (brewers and alehouses); 16921, fo. 145 r; 16927, fo. 45 r (lodgings).
[31] Ibid., 16920, fos. 109 r, 129 r–v; 16922, fos. 133 r–4 v (volunteers); 16919, fos. 671 r–v, 142 r–v; 16924, fo. 134 r–v; 16927, fos. 63 r–4 v (loyalty test); 16919, fo.101 r; 16923, fo. 67 r–v; 16924, fo. 23 v (petitioning); 16919, fo. 144 v; 16921, fos. 139–40 v (uniform); 16921, fo. 117 v; 16923, fo. 170 r; 16928, fos. 13 r–14 r (arming).
[32] Ibid., 16919, fos. 97 r–8 r; 16923, fo. 195 r; 16925, fos. 21 v, 24 r–v, 69 r–70 v, 156 r; 16926, fos. 33 r–v, 39 v; 16927, fos. 90 r–1 v; 16920, fo. 32 r–v. For concern about the loyalty of the armed forces, see also 16919, fo. 123 r; 16920, fo. 129 r–v; 16921, fo. 90 r; 16922, fos. 69 r–70 v; 16926, fos. 33 v, 36 r; 16927, fo. 19 r.

passage of resolutions in the localities and their despatch to Reeves – the original ostensible purpose of the formation of the associations – about 20 per cent involved suggesting or sending in pamphlets, songs, handbills and, more rarely, an etching or print for the use of, or endorsement by, the committee. It is extraordinary how speedily and how substantially the publication of tracts, handbills and the rest became dominant.[33] The creation of the APLP generated a response from correspondents for which the committee was ill-prepared (hence its slowness in replying). Reeves and the government may have hoped to receive straightforward expressions of loyal sentiments by loyal subjects, but in soliciting resolutions and correspondence they opened a dialogue with their correspondents the content of which they could not wholly control.[34] The resolutions elicited letters, pamphlets and songs, some of which were substantially more moderate, and some of which were more extreme (usually linked to attacks on dissenters).[35] The various comments that Reeves and Moore made on the backs of many of the letters to the association showed that they were responsive both to suggestions and to some criticisms about the association's activities. Far from rigidly imposing a particular creed and set of aims and objectives, the London Association came to act as a clearing house for ideas about how to advance the loyalist cause, and about what issues were central to that cause.[36] For example, the divisive

---

[33] One indication of this is the fact that the collected resolutions of the loyalist associations were never printed, despite expectations, and despite solicitation of subscriptions for them, whereas the association's tracts were collected and published: ibid., 16925, fos. 3 r–4 r, 11 r , 26 r, 42 r–v, 75 r; 16928, fos. 32r, 41r. The publications were collected and reprinted despite the doubts of William Windham, the secretary of war: see ibid. 16924, fo. 92 r–v – the letter is a response to a suggestion by Reeves that he republish the tracts. Windham says that because of Reeves' desire to do so he will suppress his doubts and recommend to the 'committee' that they agree. It is not at all clear which committee this is.

[34] See Colley's characteristically shrewd comments on the broader implications of this participation in 'Whose nation?', 107–8.

[35] Add. MSS 16920, fo. 14 r; 16921, fos. 44 r–v, 100 r–v; 16922, fos. 191 r–2 v; 16925, fos. 120 r–1 r; 16927, fos. 49 r–50 r; 16928, fos. 22 r–5 r. It should be remembered that Reeves himself broached the 'ultra' line in 1795 and found his patrons disowning him when he published a libel on the constitution. See David Eastwood, 'John Reeves and the contested idea of the constitution', *Journal for Eighteenth-Century Studies* 16 (1993), 197–212; and A. V. Beedell, 'John Reeves's prosecution for a seditious libel, 1795–6: a study in political cynicism', *Historical Journal* 36 (1993), 799–824. A similar process occurred later in the decade with the establishment's attempts to rein in enthusiasts such as Henry Redhead Yorke, after his conversion, and Lewis Goldsmith – and the difficulty it had knowing what to do with James Gillray.

[36] As Mark Pottle has argued, '[E]ven at this highpoint of "loyalist" reaction the forces of conservatism were unable to monopolize the concept of loyalism. One must also consider the possibility that Reeves never intended to polarize the political nation, and by doing so attempt to distinguish the "loyal" from the "non-loyal"': 'Loyalism and patriotism in Nottingham, 1792–1816' (D.Phil. thesis, University of Oxford, 1988), 24–5.

and gratuitously anti-French character of the first resolutions evoked some constructive criticism.[37] But the major area in which the London Association was undoubtedly influenced by its correspondents was in its developing concern to address the lower orders, and in its appreciation that this required rather different methods from those used in the first of the association's publications.[38]

Fidelia, one of Reeves' female correspondents, encapsulated two distinctions central to the association when she informed Reeves:

I have had many opportunities of observing the influence of the new seditious doctrines upon the lower class of people, that class that the wicked and designing intend to use as their Engine, they are incapable of reading or understanding any good or serious address to set them right; but through the medium of popular ballads...[39]

On the one hand, we are given a distinction between the lower class of people and the rest of the nation; on the other, a distinction between responsible members of this latter class and its 'wicked and designing' members. The prosecution of publishers, booksellers and those caught peddling sedition would help to silence those of evil intent, but there remained a clear recognition that the responsible members of the nation had also to address its lower orders. Reeves' correspondents mostly worked within these categories, but many who did so were especially concerned to draw the boundaries of the responsible political nation in as broad terms as possible. As one correspondent from Scotland wrote:

[M]eantime among your friends here it is generally thought, that instead of calling yourselves Gentlemen associated, it would be more proper and engaging in these times, that your Association assumed the stile of *Independent Men* – this would be embracing the most enlarged scheme, and the more Popular, at least in this country where Pain's Books have been more Red than with you...[40]

---

[37] See Add. MSS 16919, fos. 9 v, 55 r, 101 r, 161 v–3 r ; 16920, fos. 17 r–18 v; 16923, fo. 41 r; and esp. 16926, fo. 47 r–v. See also the difficulties concerning procedure, particularly with respect to anonymous information: ibid., 16922, fos. 147 r–52 r; 16923, fos. 162 r–6 v (both concerning Thomas Law).

[38] Ibid., 16919, fos. 162 r–3 v; 16920, fos. 64 r, 113 r; 16926, fos. 3 r, 4 r, 5 v, 7 r, on concern with class composition of society; 16919, fos. 43 r–4 r, 53 r–4 v; 16920, fos. 7 r, 34 r; 16921, fos. 108 r, 148 v; 16922, fos.49 r–v, 69 r–70 r, 87r–v, 101 r, 139 r–v; 16923, fo. 168 r; 16924, fos.9 r, 53 r–v, 72 r–v; 16926, fos. 35 r–6 v, 51 r–v; 16927, fo. 471 r–v, on concern with how best to appeal to the lower orders. Concern with lower-order unrest is also expressed in ibid., 16919, fos. 35 r, 93 r–4 v, 148 r–v, 158 r–9 v; 16921, fos. 114 r–15 v; 16922, fos. 81 r–v, 129 r–30 v, 179 r–v; 16923, fos. 10 r–v, 47 r–50 v, 67 r–v; 16924, fo. 150 r–v; 16925, fos. 26 r, 77 r; 16926, fos. 1 r–2 r, 33 r–v. 39 v; 16927, fos. 5 r–6 r.

[39] Ibid., 16920, fo. 99.   [40] Ibid., 16920, fo. 113 r.

While emphasising the importance of unity among the respectable classes, the writer also identified the vulgar as potential targets for conservative propaganda. To grasp the true significance of these distinctions, we need to see them in the context of the special character of the correspondence to Reeves.

II

Commentators on the Reeves papers have noted the hesitancies of style, the tentativeness of address and the general deference of many of the letters.[41] Those writing often seemed uncertain whether their correspondence would be welcome, much of this uncertainty relating to their own social and political status. There are only a handful of letters in the collection from 'persons of quality' – peers, members of the lesser aristocracy, bishops and senior churchmen, Members of Parliament, and so on. The vast majority come from those slightly lower in the social structure: clergymen, tradesmen, merchants and men of independent means, several of whom were also local magistrates. Most of the correspondents would have been voters; many might also have been involved in the county and borough meetings of the summer of 1792, when loyal addresses were sent to the king.[42] The rarity of any reference to the events of the preceding summer in the letters suggest that those who were now writing did not see themselves as having played a significant role, however. Given this, it is not surprising to find that many of Reeves' correspondents seemed concerned to establish whether or not they qualified socially for membership of the association. P. Touch, a clergyman (a little down on his luck) who submitted a pamphlet and who had spoken to Reeves about the APLP, clearly believed he was being snubbed when Reeves failed to contact him subsequently:

Your silence, since last week, is sufficiently expressive of the Reception your generous proposal of mentioning me to Your Committee has met with. But I shall never change my political principles nor permit my public spirit and loyalty to

---

[41] My attention was drawn to matters of style in the correspondence by an as yet unpublished paper delivered to the 1790s seminar in Oxford in February 1991 by Colin Brooks.

[42] Black, in *The Association*, 232, estimates that some 360 loyal addresses were sent in before the end of the summer; the *Annual Register*, vol. 34 (1792), pt 2, 37, noted 341 by 1 September. At least some of these addresses came from meetings at which there was a significant exchange of political view, and the majorities in favour of the addresses were not always overwhelming, as Paine pointed out in his *Letter Addressed to the Addressers* (London: H. D. Symonds, 1792), 47; see also the detailed report of the Middlesex meeting in the *Morning Chronicle*, 10 August 1792.

be damped by the coldness or discouraging Behaviour of any society of men of any Rank.[43]

Moreover, the fact that so many writers drew attention to issues of rank and status – asking whether 'Inhabitants or Englishmen wou'd not be a better appellation than "the Gentlemen"', or stressing that 'persons, like myself, more in the Middle Ranks of life, know better the temper of the (*hoipoloi*) than persons of Quality can do' – underlines their sensitivity to such issues.[44] More surprising is the number of anonymous letters expressing support for the association. Some remained anonymous because they were informing on other members of the community, but there are many who wrote simply to give their backing to their association self-effacingly. It is difficult to believe that such men and, less frequently, women would have been prominent members of their local communities. Whereas the addresses of the summer of 1792 were orchestrated through local élites, the loyalist associations offered a more direct and personal form of participation in an urgent national issue. But it would not have been clear, given the apparently private character of Reeves' initiative, with whom the responsibility lay for forming local associations and for corresponding with Reeves. Because of this, those who wrote to the London Association (especially in the early stages) had to test the ground to see how far their participation would be welcome – particularly given that they were not persons of rank and quality.

Moreover, although many correspondents sought to confirm their standing as members of the responsible community, and did so by encouraging Reeves to adopt the more 'enlarged scheme', of independent men, or Englishmen, they also reinforced their own membership of this group by invoking the poor and the lower orders as the legitimate object of their concern, by insisting on the urgency of the problem of the vulgar, and by offering their services as educators of this class. Consider the judicious letter from a clergyman who, while denying pretentions of equality with the committee, equally differentiated himself from the lower orders, and did so in a way that 'enfranchised' himself within loyalism:

Excuse me, Sir, in giving my sentiments so freely, when I humbly suggest, that some recent & great compositions, tho' they convince the well-educated and informed, do not meet the understanding of the lower class of people, from whom most is to be dreaded – I have taken the liberty of enclosing a few thoughts of my own...[45]

[43] Add. MS 16921, fo. 63 r.
[44] Ibid., 16922, fo. 24 r; 16920, fo. 98 r [emphasis in original].
[45] Ibid., 16920, fo. 7 r–v. See also 16919, fo. 161 v, and the similar tone in Fidelia's letter, 16920, fo. 99 r–v.

By recognising others who had to be addressed in a particular style, the writer both distanced himself from them and identified himself as a member of the responsible political community.

This process of advancing one's aspirations through participation in loyalism did not pass unnoticed by those whose sympathies lay elsewhere:

> Now all the parish officers were burning with ambition,
> To see their names in newspapers as haters of sedition,
> These men had no vanity, but true to the blood royal,
> They eat and drink like Aldermen, to prove that they are loyal.[46]

Of course, there were different forms of aspiration served by involvement: the vast numbers of letters from minor clergymen suggest that they saw the assumption of a leading role in local associations as a route to preferment within the Church; and the sheer volume of publications sent in to the APLP suggests that loyalism could run comfortably in tandem with place-seeking or gratuitous vanity publishing. The correspondence from Sarah Trimmer and Hannah More, and one or two other women, shows us that loyalism could also provide a vehicle both for female political participation and for a continuation and extension of the 'reformation of manners' movement.[47] Moreover, the means of participation were manifold: when correspondents informed on radicals, or plied the association with proposals for preventative action, or organised local associations, they were engaging in forms of participation that, although they might have borne some resemblance to traditions of local political activity, were now linked to a national political agenda.

The concern with literary style, which many correspondents expressed when considering the lower orders, in itself implied a distinction between the rational and irrational that implicitly overrode (or, at least, conditioned)

---

[46] William Hamilton Reid, *Hum! Hum! A New Song* (1793). Its authorship lends the song added significance, given Reid's later loyalism, and his still later return to the radical fold.

[47] Add. MSS 16920, fo. 99 r–v (Fidelia); fos. 115 r–16 r (a female); 16921, fo. 76 r (Anne Kane, Woolwich); fos. 121 r–4 r; 16923, fos. 47 r–50 v (Sarah Trimmer); 16924, fo. 9 r ('A. B.' sent in *Village Politics*); 16922, fo. 69 r (a woman 'in a village bordering on Leicestershire').The last nicely captures the ambiguity of deference and a desire for participation: 'Believe me, it [the letter] does not come from a self-sufficient female, who looks upon herself as adequate to the task of instructress. I have ever thought politics a science extremely incompatible with the character of my sex; and did the question now only relate to the conduct of government, I should blush to deliver my opinion. But when every institution I have been taught to revere, and the laws which have hitherto protected me, in a peaceable enjoyment of the prosperity I possess, are threatened with total destruction, a *Mother's* feelings especially may be allowably awakened' [emphasis in original]. See Joanna Innes, 'Politics and morals: the reformation of manners movement in later eighteenth-century England', in Hellmuth, *The Transformation of Political Culture*, 57–118.

the significance of more traditional distinctions within the properly political community:[48]

Unfortunately the arguments which reason dictates are not calculated to make the same impression on the lower classes of people as those which falsehood and villainy make use of to impose on their credulity – To make an impression upon them at all very different topics must be touched on from those which would be urged to convince men of sense and understanding.[49]

Similarly, another correspondent left no doubt that he was bidding for inclusion by addressing the excluded lower orders:

If the committee should think the inclosed dialogue may be of any service, I beg the favour of them to print it. Perhaps the 10th & 11th pages savour too much of the old passive obedience. I have therefore sent also a few words which, should the former be disapproved of, may be put in their place. I confess that I think we cannot speak too highly of the subject of the monarchy to the common people, in arguing with whom we can only oppose prejudice to prejudice, and leave it to their reason to find a medium. To talk to them of the constitution is vain: they can only respect the constitution in its true representative and visible emblem, the King's person.[50]

In each case, the author claimed membership of the political community of 'men of sense and understanding' by portraying the common people as unsuited to ordinary political reasoning.

This process of differentiating the middling, responsible and reasoning orders from the vulgar did not entirely replicate Burke's exclusion of the lower orders: leaving the poor to be ruled, not reasoned with, doomed to live on trust. Even if Paine's poison was working, and 'wicked and ignorant people [were being] turned to discontent, led on by seditious publications [and] influenced by wicked men that pretend to wisdom, liberty and equality', it did not follow, for Reeves' correspondents, that the only recourse was to substitute for the decaying rule of tradition and custom a rule of naked power:[51]

Although the coercive measures of administration may smooth the surface and keep down opposition for the present, yet if the common people are not reasoned out of their pleasing hopes of general equality, and opinions circulated to make

---

[48] That is, the more the boundary of rational/non-rational is stressed, the less salient become the existing boundaries within the traditional political community. It is much harder to pull rank on those with whom you must identify to avoid a worse fate!

[49] Add. MS 16919, fos. 43 v, 44 r.

[50] Ibid., 16922, fo. 139 r–v. The publication to which he was referring was published by the association as *A Dialogue between a Tradesman and His Porter* (*APLP*, 11 [8]).

[51] Add. MS 16926, fo. 39 v; for 'poison', see 16919, fo. 53 v, and many other references.

them satisfied with Kingly government the consequences may hereafter be fatal to the constitution.[52]

The strategy advocated by those who contributed pamphlets, handbills, songs and tracts, and increasingly pursued by the association, was to find a way of speaking to the lower orders by which to secure their loyalty. This could not be simply a case of finding a more vernacular voice – a prose for the common man – in which to couch the political doctrines of conservatism, for such a project would be tantamount to democracy. On the contrary, the association and its correspondents clearly distinguished between the kinds of pamphlet that encouraged the loyalty of the middling orders and men of property and those designed for the common people, and did so in a way that signalled that a different form of inclusion was intended for the latter.

The strategy of differentiating between the lower orders and a newly swelling 'élite', and between the reprehensible and the responsible members of that élite, is obvious in the association publications that were specifically directed to the latter. It is evident in both the doctrines propounded and the tone and style of address that authors used. Good examples are the simultaneously inclusive and exclusive 'our' and 'us' in *Mr Justice Ashurst's Charge*: '[T]here is no Nation where the law is more uprightly and impartially administered, than in ours'; and 'Gentlemen, the spirit of loyalty, and love of their country, has now been raised in almost every breast (except in those rancorous hearts that have sold themselves to all mischief) and there wants nothing but perseverance to produce a general unanimity amongst us.'[53] Dr William Vincent struck the same tone:

I wish to speak a language which the meanest individual may understand; I wish to teach the poor that every plan of this sort is delusive, that even their own interest is concerned in the well-being of their superiors, and that what ever tends to dissolve the tie, instead of relieving their wants, would add ten-fold to their misery.[54]

But wishing does not make it so, and there is no doubt that Vincent was wishing to his class and not to those outside it when he insisted that 'their own interest' was also in the unspoken 'ours'. The strategy is still more evident in *A Word in Season*:

[52] Ibid., 16927, fo. 47 v.
[53] *Mr Justin Ashurst's Charge to the Grand Jury of Middlesex* (*APLP*, I [1]), 3; and *Hon. Justice Ashurst's Charge to the Grand Jury of the Court of the King's Bench. Delivered Hilary Term 1793* (*APLP*, I [7]).
[54] *Short Hints on Levelling Extracted from Dr Vincent's Discourse* (*APLP*, I [2]), 6.

There is no doubt but a perfect system of laws and government may be conceived; but to be perfect in their application and effects, they must be put into operation by beings of a superior nature to man. We are fallible creatures, *as the first and best of us know*, and the society that we compose, must partake of our imperfections...[55]

To aspire to be among the 'first and best' was, then, to recognise the unchangeability of the order. Not to do so was to acknowledge one's inferiority. Dr Watson, bishop of Llandaff, inevitably reproduced the distinction when he argued: 'That the constitution of this country is so perfect as neither to require, or admit any improvement, is a proposition to which I never did, or ever can assent; but I think it too excellent to be amended by peasants or mechanics.'[56]

This message constituted a major current throughout the publications of the association aimed at the literate and respectable. The reader was invited to recognise, as a burdensome truth, the inevitability of a class of poor, but the recognition was directly linked to an account of the organic order of society and the social and political responsibilities of the élite within this order. Of course, the wisdom to refrain from reform in a period of crisis was one of the major responsibilities. To accept those truths and responsibilities was the price of membership of this élite. It is not difficult to find similar sections in Burke's *Reflections*,[57] but the publications of the association undoubtedly extended the boundaries of Burke's intended audience and thereby simultaneously diluted the élite. These publications were widely sought for distribution by members of the middle ranks – curates, manufacturers, tradesmen and others – who could find in them a self-characterisation that flattered their social and political self-image at the cost of recognition that political reform (from which they might benefit) was too fraught with danger to be pursued.[58] At the same time,

[55] *A Word in Season to the Traders and Manufacturers of Great Britain* (*APLP*, I [1]), 13 [emphasis added].

[56] *Appendix to the Bishop of Llandaff's Sermon, Preached in Charlotte Street Chapel, April 1785* (*APLP* I [7]), 9–10.

[57] See Burke, *Reflections on the Revolution in France*: 'We know that we have made no discoveries... We have not been drawn and trussed, in order that we may be filled, like stuffed birds in a museum, with chaff and rags, and paltry, blurred shreds of paper about the rights of man. Etcetera' (181); '[W]e are generally men of untaught feelings...' (183); 'We know, and what is better we feel inwardly...' (186–7). On the extension of Burke's audience, see Reeves' note, Add. MS 16923, fo. 146, r–v. It is a striking indication of Burke's marginality to the whole movement that there is no reference to him or his work in the entire correspondence with Reeves, nor anything in the publications of the association.

[58] See ibid., 16924, fos. 154 r, 156 r–v, where the chairman of the Marylebone Association sends in the association's resolutions and then writes separately to inform Reeves that a new association headed by Lord Macclesfield is to replace his. One senses the writer's disappointment.

the incentives for such a self-characterisation were being increased by caricaturing the principles of reformers as rigidly egalitarian in all things, murderously Jacobinical and fully in favour of turning political rule over to the hands of the mob, as well as by a campaign of prosecution of radical publishers, booksellers and sympathisers.[59] Scholars who have insisted upon the relatively moderate scale of prosecutions of radicals miss the point that loyalists' arguments about the limits of legitimate discourse *were* backed by sanctions; without those sanctions, their claims would have been little more than sound and fury.[60]

This rhetoric of social responsibility and division was forged in the context of a rapid polarisation of politics, with an accompanying eradication of the middle ground. Reeves' correspondents included several whose perception of the character of reform was a nuanced and subtle one, but who nonetheless were drawn to subscribe to loyalism.[61] Indeed, Fox and many others who identified with the opposition and the cause of reform were prepared to sign some form of loyalist resolution to signify their allegiance to the constitution. It is entirely understandable that so many should have done so, given that the alternative was to be portrayed as endorsing a grossly caricatured form of radicalism.[62] It must also be emphasised that meetings that led to declarations of loyalty were not always hostile to reform – just as the meetings that had voted loyal addresses to the king in the summer of 1792 often proved fertile ground for debates on the importance of constitutional change.[63]

In eliciting loyal addresses, resolutions and declarations, Reeves and the associations pulled off a significant coup, but their success had a price. The invitation to correspond and to establish local associations provided an opportunity for direct participation in a national political issue by

---

[59] See, for example, the Coventry Association's issuing of a reward of 50 guineas for the 'discovery of persons distributing Hand Bills, pasting up papers, or giving away pamphlets of a seditious tendency' – to be paid on conviction: Bodleian Library, MS G. A. Warw. b., fo. 292 r.

[60] Emsley, 'Repression, "terror" and the rule of law in England' and 'An aspect of Pitt's "terror"'.

[61] Perhaps because they subscribe to a version of Hirschman's jeopardy thesis, which limits it to the current crisis: see Albert O. Hirschman, *The Rhetoric of Reaction: Perversity, Futility, Jeopardy* (Cambridge, MA: Harvard University Press, 1991). Add. MS 16920, fos. 9 r–10 r; 16921, fos. 4 r–v, 10 r–v, 151 r–2 r; 16923, fo. 71 r.

[62] In particular, the suggestion that any thought of reform was the grossest folly. See, for example, the endorsement of William Windham's comment 'What, would he recommend you to repair your house in the hurricane season?' in Bowles' *Dialogues on the Rights of Britons, between a Farmer, a Sailor, and a Manufacturer* (London: T. Longman, 1792): 'It must be very foolish to think of building or mending Constitutions, or doing any such nice work, in so hard a gale' (first dialogue, 15). Goodwin, *The Friends of Liberty*, 118.

[63] See Pottle, 'Loyalism and patriotism in Nottingham', 24–5. On the addresses, see, for example, *Morning Chronicle* reports throughout June, July and August 1792.

members of the middling orders – an opportunity that, once embraced, frequently handed them the initiative in their local communities. Those members of the political élite, such as Fox, who made declarations of loyalty to avoid accusations of Jacobinism and seditious leanings were often capitulating to these initiatives, and in doing so found their authority threatened.[64] When Reeves' correspondent from Wakefield informed him that with 'two other gentlemen I went from house to house for 6 days and got near 17,000 signatures to our resolutions', and then went on to mention a Paine burning and say that 'his friends, who are of some distinction are much crestfallen', it seems clear that loyalism has altered the balance of power within that community.[65] Similarly, a correspondent from Grimsby informed Reeves that, when an association was first formed, the local magistrates and justices initially refused to participate, but were shamed into doing so. When they did, they drew up a petition that was reformist in character. The town clerk even claimed to have 'red Pain' (sic) and 'found good in them'.[66] In this and other cases, loyalism challenged the established social élite in the name of the status quo.[67]

It may seem a slightly reductive reading of Reeves' correspondence to see in it a concern with social and political status rather than the heartfelt expression of loyal intent. But there is no inherent incompatibility between the two, and it appears difficult otherwise to account for the tone of much of the correspondence or for the number of letters and pamphlets sent in variously by men who had temporarily fallen on hard times but wished to play their part, by previously unpublished and untried authors who suddenly found inspiration, by those who found their fellow members of the community wanting in true loyalty and by those who,

---

[64] For the fate of someone of avowedly moderate leanings who demurred at the request to join a local association, see Add. MS 16928, fos. 32 r, 33 r–4 v. There was also concern expressed by correspondents at men of radical leanings joining associations: 'Many persons being known to join in Associations who are inimical to the Present Government, either from malignant motives, or fearing to oppose the General Voice of the Country': 16524, fo. 134 r–v.

[65] Ibid., 16923, fo. 67 r.   [66] Ibid., 16928, fo. 7 r.

[67] Similarly, loyalist prints marking the opposition also served to weaken the boundaries of the political élite. It is not difficult to find in Gillray's work an even-handedness in its overall savagery that undercut the specific polemical point a print ostensibly made. Compare R. Chartier, *The Cultural Origins of the French Revolution* (Durham, NC: Duke University Press, 1991), ch. 4. There were also a few attempts to try to restrict membership of the association and to dismiss the signatures of members of the lesser ranks as of no significance – though these might easily have been motivated by a desire that the élite status aspired to should remain exclusive in some degree: Add. MSS 16925, fo. 1 r–v; 16926, fos. 7 r, 13 r–v.

having written once without receiving a reply, wrote again to elicit whether they were in fact being snubbed.[68] Moreover, correspondence with Reeves clearly had a slightly addictive quality. Several of those who wrote did so two, three, four or more times – and did so less to impart new information than to maintain their standing as Reeves' correspondents.[69] For all the hesitancy in tone of many of the letters, there is equally a sense of satisfaction at having made a contribution to defending the established order:

That I have not been unmindful of my duty as a member of your association, I shall mention the following circumstances, which can be proved by many witnesses. Two or three nights ago, two women were singing a very loyal song out of the Harlequin Entertainment under the piazza at Covent Garden, to the tune of *Hearts of Oak* – a man whom curiosity, or a worse design had detained, cried out, It was a lie, a damned lie – which he so often repeated that the women could not go on – I asked him what part he objected to – he said to the line – 'And each man in England is sure of his own' – for he had not his own, nor could he get it – I told him, I would dare to say, he had as much more of other peoples – he said, he had none of mine, I replied putting the chain of my watch in the fob, I would take care he had none – but that if he attempted to make a riot, I would charge the constable with him; he went muttering away, but I had the satisfaction to see the crowd, which was numerous, were on my side.[70]

The writer went on to say that, while riding in Wimbledon, he had come across a public house with 'Tom Paine, No King, Damn the King' written on its shutters. He told the landlord: 'I supposed it might be done by some drunken man, but if he did not erase it, he may stand a chance of losing his license.'

---

[68] Ibid., 16920, fos. 5 r–v, 127 r; 16921, fos. 63 r–4 v, 110 r, 112 r–v; 16922, fo. 187 r–v; 16923, fo. 81 r; see also 16923, fo. 176 r, and 16924, fo. 17 r–v, in which Dr William Murray, temporarily resident at the King's Bench, expressed his concern that his potential services to loyalism were being ignored. For Reeves' reply, see 16924, fo. 18 v.

[69] An exactly similar process occurs with Home Office informers in their relations with their patrons. I am indebted to Iain McCalman for pointing to this parallel.

[70] Add. MS 16923, fo. 127 r–v. The satisfaction of reporting is evident in many of the letters to the association – both in this anecdotal, personal style and, at least as commonly, when the reporter took a distanced satisfaction in the harmonious order in which his own place was obscure. For example, at a meeting at Medlands, near Exeter, Reeves' informant identified 'a very respectable yeomanry (c 40) whom with the clergy of the different parishes, din'd together, in one Room, and in another Room were assembled a great number of considerable Masters, whilst the house was surrounded by a numerous company of that truly useful class of persons, the day labourer, who were regal'd with the wine of the county (cyder) and join'd in chorus with those singing, God Save the King and other Loyal and constitutional songs': ibid., 16924, fo. 29 r. The correspondent was, in fact, the 'only magistrate of the Hundred'.

III

Conservative and loyal political discourse in the 1790s was at one level clearly directed against the reformist ambitions of the Society for Constitutional Information, the London Corresponding Society and similar provincial organisations. Obviously, part of the point of Reeves' activities was to tarnish reform-orientated and oppositional political positions with the brush of Painite radicalism and French principles (both of which were grossly caricatured). But the correspondence to, and publications of, the APLP also constructed another group from which it distanced itself: the lower orders, potentially swayed by atheists, incendiaries, French subversives and evil men, because of the weakness of their intellectual capacities and the strength of their passions. Burke had insisted that such men had to be ruled by others, lest their passions destroy the fragile order upon which their true liberty depended. Yet, by the winter of 1792, many who wrote to Reeves sought to convince him that the state of opinion amongst them was so dangerously inflamed by talk of equality that they had to be addressed: 'They hear much about the Rights of Man; and they are taught to understand by this expression – equal division of property, no taxation – no legal control, and to pave the way for this, they are taught the doctrine of no Kings.'[71]

In response, the association published a series of tracts (many contributed by unknown correspondents) designed 'to provide for the lower class of readers'. These tracts have recently been studied for the political doctrines they advance, and for their use, and abuse, of language.[72] In her brief discussion of them, Olivia Smith emphasises their anti-intellectual character, arguing that the APLP's main aim was to persuade its audience against thinking politically: 'The tracts were designed to replace political awareness with racism, religion (of a kind), nationalism, sexual chauvinism, and, most emphatically, adherence to rigid class divisions.'[73] Similarly, she argues that, for all the appearance these tracts have of being designed for the lower orders, there is a great deal to be said for seeing them instead as a warning to the middle classes as to the risks they ran by flirting with reform and as a guide to maintaining one's authority when facing members of the labouring classes infected with a Painite distemper: 'If the pamphlets were at all effective, which they were, they

---

[71] Ibid., 16919, fo. 53 v.
[72] See Hole, 'British counter-revolutionary popular propaganda'; and Smith, *The Politics of Language*, ch. 3.
[73] Smith, *The Politics of Language*, 71.

taught the upper classes not to fear political reform so much as to fear the ignorant and violent character of their social inferiors and how to reassert control by intimidating conversations.'[74] There is much truth in both claims, and they help to support the arguments made above about the involvement of the middling orders in the loyal associations. But they risk obscuring a number of important issues raised by these more popular literary efforts – in particular, the rhetorical complexities and ambiguities of the dialogue form. There are also other factors that justify my assertion that serious attempts were being made to make the vulgar conservative.

The dialogue form was used in several APLP tracts. One, *The Plot Found Out*, involves a dialogue between three members of the Jacobin Club, in which the proliferation of characters serves no real purpose, since each does little more than continue the train of atheistical and sanguinary ruminations begun by another.[75] *The Englishman and the Frenchman* is rather more successful, because it is able to exploit national caricatures to the patriotic and stout-hearted Englishman's advantage.[76] This tract is strongest in its repudiation of the French example, however, and, despite a sideswipe at Paine, avoids tackling directly concerns with domestic reform. That issue is raised more directly in *Dialogue between a Labourer and a Gentleman*, *Equality as Consistent with the British Constitution in a Dialogue between a Master-Manufacturer and One of His Workmen*, *A Dialogue between Mr. T–, a Tradesman in the City, and his Porter, John W–* and *Village Politics*.[77] The APLP's central problem with the dialogue form was to find a voice for the representative of the labouring classes that

---

[74] Ibid., 76.   [75] *APLP*, II (3), 1–4.

[76] Ibid., 4–7. Many radicals *recognised*, although Paine did not, that the political sympathies of the populace towards reform would always be submerged once the issue became one of a conflict between Britain and its traditional enemy, the French. See Bodleian Library, MS Abinger dep. B. 227/1g.

[77] These are far from being the only dialogues associated with the loyalist movement. Others not published by the association include: *A Cordial Drop, Being the Substance of a Conversation between a Master and a Journeyman in a Large Manufacturing Town in Yorkshire* (undated broadside); *A Dialogue between Wat Tyler, Mischievous Tom and an English Farmer* (London, 1793); *Free Communing; or, A Last Attempt to Cure the Lunatics, Now Labouring under that Dreadful Malady, Commonly Called the French Disease: An Imaginary Dialogue on the French Revolution* (Edinburgh, 1793); *Principles of Order and Happiness under the British Constitution, in a Dialogue between Our Parish Clerk and the Squire* (London, 1792); *Crowns and Sceptres, Useless Baubles: A Political Dialogue* (London, 1792), republished in the same year as *Modern Madmen or the Constitutionalists Detected: Modern Politics; or, The Cat Let Out of the Pock: A Dialogue* (Edinburgh, 1793); and Bowles' *Three Dialogues on the Rights of Britons*. There is also *A Second Dialogue between a Farmer and the Curate of the Parish* (and, although I have yet to locate it, presumably a *First Dialogue* – though they both might date from slightly earlier, *c.* 1788/9). See Add. MS 16927, fo. 47 r, which expressly recommended the dialogue form.

would be both credible and compliant.[78] If the dialogue was to serve the end of persuading the poorer classes, there had to be some characterisation of them with which they could identify positively and that did not simply replicate their sense of subjugation. Similarly, the characterisation of the position of the radical had to be recognisable; if it was overly caricatured, it would miss its target. Moreover, since, as Smith points out, the readers of these publications were not to be encouraged to think for themselves, they had somehow to be depicted in a way that convincingly rendered them passive in political debate. Of all the forms of address taken to instruct the lower orders, it is easy to see why the dialogue is one of the most difficult kinds of propaganda to write![79]

These difficulties are clearly evidenced in the contrast between *Village Politics*, which is generally acknowledged to be the most successful of the dialogues, and the others printed by the APLP.[80] What distinguishes More's tract is that it is the only one to set the dialogue between two members of the labouring classes. The others, like most of those that the association did not publish, include a member of the labouring classes and a member of the middling orders (Bowles' three *Dialogues* revolve around a dialogue between a farmer and a manufacturer; the lower-class sailor provides no more than a largely humorous and wholly loyal commentary). In these inter-class dialogues, the different yet reasonably proximate social standing of the two parties – one successful, the other aspiring (albeit by political means) – allows the one to lecture the other without being associated with the hereditary system against which the latter inveighs.

---

[78] In this respect, it is worth contrasting the lack of difficulty faced by some dialogues concerning 1688 and some of those produced by radical sympathisers in the wake of the loyalist associations. See, for example, *A Dialogue on the Revolution; between a Gentleman and a Farmer* (Manchester: C. Wheeler, 1788) and Joseph Towers' *A Dialogue between an Associator and a Well-Informed Englishman on the Grounds of the Late Associations and the Commencement of the War with France* (London: Thomas Evans, 1793).

[79] I have found no earlier dialogues attempting this simultaneous appeal to, and exclusion of, members of the lower orders. For example, although his work is a likely candidate, Daniel Defoe's use of the genre in *A Dialogue betwixt Whig and Tory, alias Williamite and Jacobite* (London: S. Popping, 1693) and *A Dialogue between a Whig and a Jacobite upon the Subject of the Late Rebellion; and the Execution of the Rebel-Lords, &c Occasion'd by the Phenomenon in Skie* (London: S. Popping, 1716) was orthodox enough in being restricted to participants who were already legitimately interested and active in electoral politics. What an examination of the various dialogues catalogued as such in the British Library and the Bodleian Library underlines is not so much the absence of participants from the lower orders (there are a small number of these) as the absence of attempts to use the dialogue to exclude such characters from political discourse. This supports the view that what was distinctive about loyalist appeals in the 1790s is that they were driven by a fear of lower-order insurrection motivated by egalitarian ambitions – a fear that events in France made both more reasonable and more terrible.

[80] Add. MS 16924, fo. 9 r.

The gentleman acts as an interpreter of rich to poor, representing the order as a graded not a divided one, and one in which those who labour with a good will can assure themselves of plenty and make their fortunes.[81] But in each case there is a claim to a degree of authority and, correspondingly, a degree of trust on the part of the artisan.[82] It is easy to see why Smith reads these tracts as attempts to teach the rich how to exert authority over the poor. They must also be read as instructive instances of the difficulties of characterising the voice of the labouring man, however, and of the costs of doing so successfully.

In *Village Politics*, on the other hand, Jack the blacksmith and Tom the mason have a proper exchange of views, albeit with Jack revealed to be rather better informed on French affairs and rather better at arguing his case than Tom. Nonetheless, Tom holds to his position for much longer than do his counterparts in other dialogues; and, while his views are somewhat caricatured, and he is made to appear a little dim-witted, he does have a stab at replying to Jack. Jack makes his points by frequent references to the French and by limiting his area of concern – showing, for example, little interest (by contrast with the other dialogues) in defending the position of the wealthy:

[A]s to our great folks, that you levellers have such a spite against, I don't pretend to say that they are a bit better than they should be; but that's no affair of mine; let them look to that; they'll answer for that in another place.[83]

Jack's position is tantamount to passive obedience enjoined on religious grounds; but not wholly so. It is also argued on the basis of the blessings of the present system – and that is its strength and its weakness. It is Jack's long speech about the rule of law and the toleration of religious differences to which Tom returns in his concluding conversion speech, in which he summarises the evidence against the French and republicanism:

To cut every man's throat who does not think as I do, or hang him up at a lamp-post! – Pretend liberty of conscience, and then banish the parsons only for being conscientious! – Cry out liberty of the press, and hang up the first man who writes his mind! – Lose our poor laws! – Lose one's wife perhaps upon every little tiff! – March without clothes and fight without victuals! – No trade! – No sabbath nor day of rest! – No safety, no comfort, no peace in this world – and no world to come![84]

---

[81] Hence the emphasis on those who have risen from the ranks and are heading for the nobility in, for example, *Principles of Order and Happiness*, 16, or *Equality as Consistent with the British Constitution (APLP*, I [4]), 11.
[82] Sometimes quite crudely: 'Master: "You look on me as your master don't you." John: "Yes"': *A Cordial Drop* (and see previous note).
[83] *APLP*, II (9), 6.   [84] Ibid., 6, 10.

While Tom is rather simple, he has come to recognise certain basic political values: the rule of law, toleration, liberty of the press, support for the indigent, and so on; and, while he may have come to see France as an example not to be followed, it must also be said that Jack has unwittingly given him a set of criteria by which to judge a government. The very qualities that make *Village Politics* successful also limit its capacity to make men loyal, since it teaches them standards of assessment alongside its appeal to take the established order on trust.

As we have seen, much loyalist propaganda caricatured and parodied the position of radicals and reformers, portraying them as wild egalitarians and levellers. In doing so, it often prompted radicals further to define and defend their views.[85] But loyalists were similarly vulnerable, their tracts being open to subversive readings and lampooning by pamphleteers on the other side.[86] Of course, some loyalist products hardly required parody. One enthusiastic correspondent offered for publication a list of commands from the Gospel together with a caricatured response to each from the imagined radical:

Honour the King...
  Yes, but we have grown wiser, we don't think it right.
  We will not honour the King but will speak and write of him in the most contemptuous manner possible.[87]

Wisely, Reeves declined it; like many proposals it positively encouraged subversive thoughts while seeming to forbid them.

Indeed, it becomes increasingly difficult to distinguish parodies and propaganda. Reeves himself failed to read two pieces of correspondence appropriately. One offered a series of queries 'which I strongly recommend to you to circulate all over the Kingdom – They are in themselves so simple and intelligible that their good tendency will be obvious to the meanest capacity...':

  Is not our constitution the best of all possible constitutions?
  Is not our administration the best of all possible
    administrations?

[85] See Philp, 'The fragmented ideology of reform'.
[86] For example, the authority of the Bull pamphlets is rather undone by being taken over by more moderate voices, as in *Two Penny-Worth of Truth for a Penny; or a True State of Facts with an Apology for Tom Bull in a Letter to Brother John* [pseud. William Bull] (London: T. Knott, 1793); *More than a Pennyworth of Truth; in a Letter from John Bull to his Brother Thomas* (undated broadsheet, British Library, 1865 c. 16 [140]); and *A Few Words but no Lies from Roger Bull to his Brother Thomas* (undated broadsheet, ibid., 648 c. 26 [20]). See also the parodic song *Brother Burke to Brother Windham*.
[87] Add. MS 16927, fo. 49 r.

> Is it not impossible that there should exist a government less
> expensive, and more economical than that of this Kingdom?
> Is not our King the wisest of all possible Kings? [. . .]
> Are not the younger branch of our Royal Family the most
> discrete and virtuous members of the community and in
> every sense patterns of perfection? [. . .]
> Is not imprisonment for debt the happiest method ever
> discovered of increasing the abilities of the debtor to satisfy
> the creditor, and ultimately producing their mutual
> satisfaction?[88]

This is a brilliant parody: by mock encomiums, it implicitly proposes
criteria against which to measure the present system – and find it wanting!
Reeves made no comment on the piece, whereas he described as 'scurrilous and insolent' a trenchant piece of polemic beginning:

Bastards of Liberty
   As you have advertised for Constitutional information I would contribute my
mite to the illumination of your assinine noddles by informing you that one of the
greatest faults in the British Constitution is that it suffers such Boobies as you to
disgrace the national Character in the eyes of the rest of Europe by such lack-
adaisical proceedings as your Hackguardships have lately adopted. . .[89]

Unfortunately, Reeves failed to note that the letter was addressed to the
president of the SCI, which also met at the Crown and Anchor. But the
example is instructive, because it points to the extent to which satire and
caricature undercut the possibilities for naïve readings of texts. In doing
so, they demanded a literacy from their audience that the loyalists were
attempting to deny. This does not mean that popular audiences necessarily possessed such literacy.[90] But, while their response might have been
increasingly to dismiss printed ephemera as of no great concern to them –
and as too risky an arena to be involved in – it is equally likely that
collective practices of reading might have bridged any shortcomings in
literacy. Even if the response was to ignore the material, this only partly
served the loyalists' intentions. It hardly provided a stable, consensual
base of popular opinion; it delivered temporary compliance, not allegiance – quiescence, not patriotism.

---

[88] Ibid., 16926, fo. 29 r–v.   [89] Ibid. 16921, fo. 119 r.
[90] Although contemporary prints – and the complaints against print shops by Reeves'
correspondents – implied literacy. See ibid., 16921, fos. 125 r, 127 r; 16922, fos. 123 r,
200 r; 16927, fos. 7 r, 27 r. Moreover, when some feature of a print or pamphlet was found
perplexing (i.e. when the 'literacy' did not already exist), it is likely to have generated
questioning among its audience. A modern example of the process is the portrayal of John
Major enamoured of a bag of sand in Steve Bell's *If* series in *The Guardian* in the summer
of 1992.

It is also possible to argue that writers on popular loyalism have underestimated the complexities of the relations between script, performance
and commitment in loyalist demonstrations. The loyalist associations'
publications, both in their printed dialogues and in the 'Thomas and
John Bull' tracts and various 'catechisms', can be seen (following
Smith's argument) as 'scripting' contacts between the gentry and the
lower orders. The most prominent form of scripting, extensively used
on earlier occasions, such as the Jacobite uprising and election times, was
the popular song or ballad.[91] Equally popular in 1793 was the public
spectacle of Paine burnings. But, in every case, knowing what to say,
sing or do – being able to perform the script – should be treated as
evidence of states of mind or political disposition only with considerable
caution. The associations' publications, and the events organised by
prominent members of the local community, were attempts to determine
and impose a script on relations within the community against a background of crisis and uncertainty. With prosecutions being brought ex
officio, with local boycotts of radicals and the sacking of radical workers,
with pressure on publicans from local magistrates or committee members,
and so on, it is clear that there were substantial incentives for conforming
to such scripts – especially in the smaller communities. Behind such acts
of conformity, more often than not, lay a subtext or 'hidden transcript',
however.[92] While the loyalty of the common people has been studied by
their participation in local riots, rites, rituals, monarchical pageants and
volunteer movements, and, at a distance, in the analysis of their reasons
for contentment – the responsive poor law, the relatively high standard of
living, and so on – there is little work (probably because it is so difficult to
do) on the private and subcultural worlds that lay behind loyalist

[91] I have thus far identified several hundred different ballads published in the decade, most
of which were loyal, but it is not always easy to determine exact dating. Certainly, there
were two editions each of the *Anti-Gallican Songster* and the *Anti-Leveller Songster*, and this
barely scratches the surface of loyalist ballads extant for the period. An indication of how
clearly the power of the song was recognised by those orchestrating popular campaigns
can be seen from the list of ballads associated with the Westminster election of 1788 given
in the 'Letters from an injured man'; see Lucyle Werkmeister, *The London Daily Press,
1772–1792* (Lincoln: University of Nebraska Press, 1962), appendix V. See also Fidelia's
comment: 'I have had many Opportunities of observing the influence of the new seditious
doctrines upon the lower class of People, that class that the wicked and designing
principally intend to use as their Engine, they are incapable of reading or understanding
any good or serious address to set them right, but through the medium of *Vulgar ballads*,
surely much instruction might be conveyed and much patriotic spirit awakened, witness
Ça Ira': Add. MS 16920, fo. 99 r.
[92] See James C. Scott, *Domination and the Arts of Resistance: Hidden Transcripts* (New Haven,
CT: Yale University Press, 1990).

performances.[93] Yet there was an awareness of this underside, one that could be profoundly discomfiting to the élite – as one of Reeves' disaffected correspondents clearly recognised:

The Hampshire Sedition Hunters think it proper to acquaint their brethren at the Crown and Anchor, that last Monday their committee met – but having nothing to do – they ordered an effigy, for Tom Paine, to be made . . . [and] caused the mob to assemble to carry this effigy about the City . . . [T]he Mayor and one Alderman – being of a true Jacobite breed, gave money to the mob to Halloo – Church and King – and then to burn the effigy . . . N.B. we think it proper to inform you – that when the mob got drunk, some few did cry out – Tom Pain for ever – Tom Pain for ever, but they were very drunk. . .[94]

Reeves noted only that the report was anonymous; it is possible he did not notice the parody.[95]

IV

The formation of the loyalist associations clearly made it more difficult for many who sympathised with reform publicly to meet and discuss their views. Loyalists also made acts of conformity, such as signing petitions, participation in association activities, Paine burnings, and the like, more difficult to eschew (without turning oneself into a target). But we must avoid treating such conformity as invariably deep-rooted. Men and women who burned Paine in effigy one day might burn Pitt and Dundas in their turn a twelve-month later (more disconcertingly, they might do so for the same reasons). The vulgar conservatives who have been identified in 1792/3 may be the rioters of 1795/6 and 1799–1801. Those who smashed the king's coach on its return from the opening of parliament in October 1795 might weep at his death in 1820 and might thereafter take up the cause of Queen Caroline.

The recent emphasis on the rise of popular patriotism and nationalism suggests the emergence of new, stable forms of collective identity by which

[93] The most notable work on this subcultural world in this period, though not directly concerned with the underside of loyalism, is McCalman's *Radical Underworld*.

[94] Add. MS 16928, fo. 5 r. Compare with other 'straight' accounts in the papers of burnings of Paine: 16922, fos. 121 r–2 v; 16923, fo. 67 r; 16924, fos. 62 r (alongside Dr Priestley), 112 r; 16928, fo. 7 r.

[95] Anonymity was used by a number of radicals as a way of expressing resistance with minimal risk – and maximum enjoyment. 'My association presents their Compts to your association and beg to know how the members that compose it slept last night, they are afraid the filling up the moats at the Town, moving the money from the Bank, noise of proclamations &tc may have disturbed the peaceful serenity of their Golden Dreams': ibid., 16920, fo. 3 r. Other anonymous contributions include: 16919, fos. 49 r, 167 r–v; 16921, fos. 52 r, 53 r; 16922, fos. 13 r, 99 r–100 v, 143 r, etc. Characteristically, Hardy signed his attack on the association: see 16927, fo. 21 r.

to unite the public. But, while the loyalism of 1792/3 and the later volunteer movement undoubtedly extended a form of participation to many, and did so within a language of patriotism and conservatism, of king, country and constitution, it does not follow that those who participated fully donned the mantle of faithful loyalty that they were offered. This is true not only for those who played along to avoid the penalties reserved for radicals but also for the many who brought to loyalism their own views as to the character of the crisis and the steps necessary to meet it. As we have seen, participation was not acquiescence; those who embraced it quickly came to exercise their voice and to make demands on the system. In doing so, they further consolidated and extended the role for a broader public in the political life of the nation. In this respect, they have much in common with the radicals whom they opposed: both played an important part in creating expectations, traditions and institutions for popular participation in politics.

I have given a reading of the correspondence and publications of the loyalist associations that downplays doctrinal content and focuses on rhetorical strategies, particularly with respect to the construction of the lower orders. Although much of the published material was aimed more at the educated middle classes than at *hoi polloi*, attempts were made – albeit, on the account offered here, not wholly successful ones – to appeal directly to the people. Considerably more pamphlets, songs, handbills, and so on than could be discussed here were submitted to the APLP by correspondents who believed in such an appeal. This does not mean that they were right; but it does mean that we should take seriously their attempt to create a vulgar conservatism, not least because we can recognise thereby that, even if the more vehement and offensive of the loyalist writers, such as Jones, were savagely intolerant of the lower orders, many others, some but not all of whom were, like Sarah Trimmer, connected to the 'reformation of manners' movement, wished to see the poor and labouring classes integrated in a well-ordered society.

Their ambition went well beyond the attempt to evoke loyalist sentiment amongst the populace. Indeed, in her commitment to this project, Hannah More betrayed attitudes that were deeply critical of traditional loyalist practices. She had no truck with Paine burnings, as it smacked of intemperance, and perhaps of aristocratic politics: '[L]et's have no drinking, no riot, no bonfires; but put in practice this text, which our parson preached on last Sunday, "Study to be quiet, work with your own hands, and mind your own business."'[96] For these conservatives, there was an

---

[96] *APLP*, II (9), 10.

implicit programme of reform that reached up to the traditional élite as well as down to the common people. They provide a further example of the widely varying motives and aims that existed within loyalism. We need only compare More's comment with Cobbett's account of Reeves' motives:

[He] . . .was a really learned lawyer, and, politics aside, as good a man as ever lived. A clever man; a head as clear as spring water, considerate, mild, humane; made by nature to be an English judge. . . Among the first things that Reeves ever said to me was: 'I tell you what, Cobbett, we have only two ways here; we must either kiss their –, or kick them: and you must make your choice at once.' William Gifford had more asperity in his temper, and was less resigned. He despised Pitt and Canning and the whole crew; but he loved ease, was timid; he was their slave all his life. . .[97]

Reeves saw the choice in stark terms. In contrast, More, by writing her tracts, was looking, like many others, for a bridge between respectable and vulgar culture, through which the latter might be transformed. But, in their very willingness to take on the challenge of a printed battle with the reformers, these writers also accepted that the ideas of the latter (in however mangled a shape) had to be addressed. In doing so, they were playing their part in the formation of a popular political culture with a national political agenda. Others have argued that new forces – patriotism and nationalism – emerged to stabilise this culture towards the end of the decade and in the early nineteenth century. But, as we have seen, this was not something that the loyalists of the early 1790s could create. Despite their attempt to appeal to anti-Gallicism in pamphlets, songs and hand-bills, these bonds of national unity were forged only at the height of the war with France and with the threat of invasion. Moreover, the analysis of earlier loyalism offered here suggests that such bonds were more condi-tional and transitory than is often implied: the interest in participation would remain, but the practical consequences and ideological orientation of that interest were far from settled or stable. In this context, it is not surprising to find radicals becoming loyalists (Henry Redhead Yorke, for example), and then radicals again (as with William Hamilton Reid), or loyalists becoming radicals (as in Cobbett's case). The greater the com-plexity we recognise in the ideological terrain of the period, and the more sophisticated our account of the motives behind people's expressions of commitment, the more porous and problematic become the ideological categories of 'radical' and 'conservative'.

There is little support in this analysis for those who are convinced that conservatism won the day because of the intellectually compelling case it

---

[97] *The Autobiography of William Cobbett.*

propounded or because of its organisational capacities. Against such accounts, I have argued that simplistic formulae are unacceptable and that the example of Reeves' APLP provides ample evidence that popular loyalism was a highly complex and evolving phenomenon, which bears testimony above all to the dramatically changing character of British political culture and, in particular, the relationship between élite and popular politics in the 1790s. Although the founders of the association intended to devote their energies to persons of at least moderate substance, they were subsequently led by their correspondents to widen their brief by addressing the lower orders – albeit in different terms. Once convinced of the value of this strategy, the association, by bringing into loyalist and chauvinist appeals some discussion of political principles, inevitably contributed to the broadening of the politically literate nation. Of course, such was not the APLP's intent, but, in the context of Britain in the 1790s, Giuseppe di Lampedusa's adage 'If we want everything to stay as it is, then everything has to change' speaks eloquently of the unintended consequences of the association's actions.[98]

---

[98] Hirschman, *The Rhetoric of Reaction*, 44 – a quotation from Lampedusa's *The Leopard*.

3 Disconcerting ideas: explaining popular radicalism and popular loyalism in the 1790s[1]

This chapter examines some of the assumptions that underlie our analyses of the popular radicalism and popular loyalism of the 1790s. It is centrally concerned with the relationship between political ideas and languages and political agency, but it focuses this concern on asymmetries in the explanations given of the different movements – asymmetries that have often derived from Whiggish assumptions about the steady progress of the democratic movement for political reform, or from Marxist-influenced accounts of the rise of a working-class movement. In discussing the explanations of radicalism and loyalism in the 1790s, I also hope to shed some light more generally on the nature of radical movements, and on the relationship between political theory, ideology and political practice. Both questions turn out to be integrally related to the issue of explanatory asymmetry.

I

In the 1960s and 1970s there was a rough consensus in British political science that working-class support for Labour needed no explanation, whereas working-class conservatism did. That is an explanatory asymmetry. It arises from the view that there is a natural class constituency for labour and a natural identification of class interests on the part of members of the working class with Labour, which makes working-class Toryism exceptional. Things have subsequently changed – although scholars disagree about by how much and since when – but, leaving this aside, there is a similar asymmetry in many accounts of the 1790s. Consider, for example, E. P. Thompson's account of the development of working-class consciousness allied to the reform movement:

---

[1] My thanks for comments on earlier versions of this chapter are owed to Iain McCalman, Jon Mee and Martin Fitzpatrick, and to audiences at Hull and Cambridge Universities and the Humanities Research Centre at the Australian National University.

At the end of the decade [1820s], when there came the climactic contest between Old Corruption and Reform, it is possible to speak in a new way of the working people's consciousness of their interests and of their predicament as a class... Given the elementary techniques of literacy, labourers, artisans, shopkeepers and clerks and schoolmasters proceeded to instruct themselves severally or in groups... [H]ere and there local Radical leaders, weavers, booksellers, tailors, would amass shelves of Radical periodicals and learn how to use parliamentary Blue Books; illiterate labourers would, nevertheless go each week to a pub where Cobbett's editorial letter was read aloud and discussed... Thus working men formed a picture of the organisation of society, out of their own experience and with the help of their hard-won and erratic education, which was above all a political picture. They learned to see their own lives as part of a general history of conflict between the loosely defined 'industrious classes' on the one hand, and the unreformed House of Commons on the other. From 1830 onwards a more clearly defined class consciousness, in the customary Marxist sense, was maturing, in which working people were aware of continuing old and new battles on their own.[2]

But contrast this with his account of popular loyalism:

[T]he old pretences of paternalism and deference...were losing force even before the French Revolution, although they saw a temporary revival in the Church-and-King mobs of the early nineties, the military display and the anti-Gallicism of the wars. [T]he reciprocal relation between the gentry and the plebs ... had lasted for a century... For a hundred years they [the poor] were not altogether the losers. They maintained their traditional culture; they secured a partial arrest of the work-discipline of early industrialism; they perhaps enlarged the scope of the poor laws; they enforced charities which may have prevented years of dearth from escalating into crises of subsistence; and they enjoyed liberties of pushing about the streets and jostling, gaping and huzzaing, pulling down the houses of obnoxious bakers or Dissenters, and a generally riotous and unpoliced disposition which astonished foreign visitors, and which almost misled them themselves into believing that they were 'free'. The 1790s expelled that illusion, and in the wake of the experiences of those years the relationship of reciprocity snapped. [...] We move out of the eighteenth century field-of-force and enter a period in which there is a structural re-ordering of class relations and of ideology. It is possible, for the first time, to analyse the historical process in terms of nineteenth century notations of class.[3]

An asymmetry is implicit here. For Thompson, and for others, popular loyalism was a function of mechanisms of mobilisation and public spectacle that were a staple part of the eighteenth century, in 'Church and king' mobs or anti-Catholic riots, whereas popular radicalism represented something new, because it involved the articulate, intentional

---

[2] Thompson, *The Making of the English Working Class*, 781–2.
[3] E. P. Thompson, *Customs in Common* (Harmondsworth: Penguin Books, 1993), 95–6.

organisation of members of the artisan and lower orders into associations dedicated to the discussion of political principles and to pressing the case for parliamentary reform. Moreover, popular loyalism is seen as an essentially unstable phenomenon, at times of stress easily eclipsed by grain riots or crimp riots, whereas popular radicalism set an agenda for the participation of the lower orders in the representative institutions of British society that endured throughout the nineteenth century and provided the basis (albeit expanded to include social and economic grievances) for a radical working-class movement and an associated ideology. I have no wish to tie my case to Thompson; I think the underlying assumptions are extremely common in the literature. What I want to do, as systematically as possible in a brief chapter, is to think through whether such asymmetries are justifiable in the 1790s.

II

We should be clear about the phenomena we need to explain. Loyalist activities included the following: 'Church and king' riots in the spring and early summer of 1791; the Paine burnings and hangings throughout England and Scotland in 1791–3 (especially in the spring and early summer of 1792); the extraordinarily successful loyalist movement of 1792/3; the widespread consumption of broadside ballads and cheap political tracts written expressly for a popular audience (both in 1793, and again with the Cheap Repository Tracts in 1795); the signing of loyal petitions and the sending of addresses to the king (in the summer of 1792, but also again in the autumn of 1795 after the attack on the king's coach in October); and the participation of members from a very broad section of the British social structure in the volunteer movement in 1797/8 through (with variations) to a peak in 1803/4, but continuing into the 1810s, and in the early nineteenth-century militias. Moreover, there has been a developing literature on the spread of popular support for the monarchy and popular patriotism and nationalism, from Linda Colley and others, which sees the emergence in this period of a popular monarchy, rooted in a British nationalism that fundamentally changed the character of the relationship between the political system and the British people, and provided a popular patriotic discourse that saw Britain through the revolutionary wars and beyond as a united political nation.[4]

[4] Colley, 'The apotheosis of George III'; see also her *Britons: Forging the Nation*; Marilyn Morris, *The British Monarchy and the French Revolution* (New Haven, CT: Yale University Press, 1998); Eastwood, 'Patriotism and the English state'; and Dickinson, 'Popular loyalism in Britain'.

On the radical side we are concerned with the spread of reform societies and debating clubs, from 1791, in London and also in major provincial towns and cities; the development of an organised and articulate popular movement for reform, not least in the shape of the SCI, the LCS and other corresponding societies; the mass consumption of reform literature, especially Paine's *Rights of Man*; the petitioning of parliament, for reform between 1791 and 1793, and again in 1795 (over the 'Two Acts'); the resurgence of a popular reform movement in the summer of 1795, with mass meetings and demonstrations; and its continuation in increasingly covert activities through to the beginning of the nineteenth century. We should also include the activities of groups of those whom William Hamilton Reid referred to as infidels and political freethinkers dedicated to moral and intellectual subversion, and an auxiliary force of lower-class religious enthusiasts who also sought the overthrow of the established order and who had met in a range of popular debating clubs until government repression reduced them to all but an incorrigible remnant.[5]

There is a further dimension to these movements. Both involved the widespread circulation of political literature and ideas, both treated their conflict as, in part, a conflict of principles and both to some extent acted as forcing houses for the development of political ideas. Scholarly treatments of the political thought of this period have generally sought to show the continuities in political ideas with earlier languages and idioms of political thought – classical republicanism, country party traditions, mixed government, ancient constitutionism, both Hobbesian and Lockeian natural rights theories, Scottish political economy and even Filmerite defences of monarchy.[6] While there probably were exponents of such positions throughout the 1790s, the movements of this period cannot be seen as either straightforwardly adopting such ideas or as merely unfolding their practical implications or inherent logic. There is no unified ideology of reform or loyalism, and the commitments of those involved in popular politics, expressed in the pamphlets, statements and political activities of the period, should not be seen as relatively fixed views as to the kinds of reform or change they were concerned to bring about or resist. Rather, I have argued elsewhere both for the fragmentary character of radical thought (in particular) and for understanding the 'revolution controversy' not as rehearsing well-established political doctrines but as developing into a polarising process in which substantive political doctrine was first quickly eclipsed then ultimately transformed by the demands of political

---

[5] William Hamilton Reid, *The Rise and Dissolution of the Infidel Societies in This Metropolis* (London: J. Hatchard, 1800); McCalman, *Radical Underworld*, 1.

[6] Morris, *The British Monarchy and the French Revolution*, 62.

rhetoric, and in the course of which the agendas of the reform and loyalist movements were forged (for that generation).[7]

On this kind of account, popular radicalism in the 1790s was the outcome of a process of political contestation that began in the pamphlet press revolving largely, but not exclusively, around parliamentary circles[8] but that changed its character fundamentally into a practical political struggle for hegemony over the British people – a struggle in which they played an increasing part and during which the agenda of British politics underwent a profound change, with the traditional picture of a balanced constitution being displaced by demands for mass political participation and the elimination of political privilege. In the process, the popular movement responded to government reaction by becoming both increasingly prepared to countenance more dramatic and, eventually, more violent methods of political activity, and increasingly marginalised, losing its broad popular base. And the same evolving character to loyalist organisation and activity should also be recognised. The popular loyalist movement of the 1790s and beyond had a transformative effect on the way in which the political nation was conceived and represented in Britain. Despite its efforts to conserve a political and social order, its effect was to organise activity in a way that significantly extended the boundaries of formal and informal political participation. It is a very apt instance of Lampedusa's adage 'If we want everything to stay as it is, then everything has to change'.[9]

One feature of this account is that there is a more experimental and conditional connection between what people say and do and what they believe than is usually given in accounts of political ideology. And one symptom of this is the 'strange bedfellows syndrome' – that Paine and Burke did not see in 1787–9 that they would be violently opposed on matters of deep principle within two years;[10] that Horne Tooke was prepared to associate and work with people whose political convictions were, at bottom, dramatically different from his (such as Hardy, Paine and Godwin); that Reeves was prepared to associate himself with a very wide range of responses to radicalism, ranging from the High Church Toryism

---

[7] See Mark Philp, 'The fragmented ideology of reform', 'Vulgar conservatism 1792/3', chapter 2 in this volume, and 'English republicanism in the 1790s', *Journal of Political Philosophy* 6 (1998), 235–62.

[8] It is notable that Paine initially had thought it imperative to get the second part of *Rights of Man* published at the end of 1791, when 'the town will begin to fill' with Members of Parliament returning for the new session – although he failed for various reasons to do so. David Freeman Hawke, *Paine* (New York: Harper & Row, 1974), 238.

[9] Cited by Hirschman, *The Rhetoric of Reaction*, 44.

[10] See Thomas W. Copeland, 'Burke, Paine, and Jefferson', in *Our Eminent Friend, Edmund Burke: Six Essays* (London: Jonathan Cape, 1949), 146–89.

of William Jones and the still more virulently anti-Jacobin John Bowles through to the evangelically influenced moral reformers, such as Sarah Trimmer and Hannah More.[11] Such differences were ignored, not for tactical reasons but because they appeared less salient than the differences that existed between those favouring reform and those resisting it. A further sign of the conditional character of ideology is the often strikingly diverse intellectual trajectories that individual ideological careers took in the period: Ritson's, from Jacobite to Jacobin; Reid's, from writer of radical pamphlets and songs through to loyalist snitch on the 'infidel societies', through to a reincarnation of his initial guise; Cobbett's move from reactionary patriot to radical reformer; and Henry Redhead Yorke's reverse course, with his radicalism taking him to prison, where he was converted to the loyalist cause in the arms of the jailor's daughter (a powerful incentive, though difficult for governments to replicate on a mass scale).

The shifting ideological commitments of participants and the fragmentary character of the ideological terrain suggest both that we should not explain popular political activity as the unfolding of the implications of particular languages or discourses and that the grounds for expecting symmetrical accounts of the two popular movements may be stronger than might initially be thought.

III

It is not altogether easy to locate the precise point at which asymmetry enters accounts, but we can move towards a clearer understanding if we take components that historical accounts generally combine in a complex interplay of causal explanation, narrative, *Verstehen* interpretation and description, and press them so that they stand out more clearly than they would otherwise. This necessarily involves simplification and abstraction, but it helps us appreciate the character of the differences between accounts – even if we may later want to question the value of the categories by which we achieve this. I want to distinguish between accounts that emphasise intentionality on the actor's part and those that do not (usually by providing a causal account), and between those that see the behaviour of people participating in popular loyalism as expressive of their fundamental interests and commitments and those that do not. The distinctions are very rough and ready, but they serve their purpose. They give us the following matrix.

---

[11] See de Montluzin, *The Anti-Jacobins*; and Iain McCalman, ed., *The Oxford Companion to the Age of Romanticism and Revolution* (Oxford University Press, 1999).

Table 3.1 *Types of explanation*

	Intentional	Causal
Expressive	1	2
Non-expressive	3	4

To see how explanations might vary, compare accounts of crowd behaviour.

Cell 1. Accounts that see the crowd as the conscious agent of organised revolutionary working class, as in Georges Sorel's general strike; or as a conscious agent for a just allocation of resources, as in Thompson's moral economy.

Cell 2. Accounts that see the crowd as a process that expresses deep-seated but poorly articulated fears and anxieties – as in Lefebvre's account of the 'panics' during the Great Fear.[12] Similarly, accounts that associate crowd behaviour with objective correlates of scarcity, price rises, and so on also combine the sense that there are causal processes that nonetheless express certain fundamental concerns or interests of those who act.

Cell 3. The crowd as comprising rational individual agents within a larger process that is the aggregate of their actions (Mark Granovetter's threshold model of crowd behaviour).[13] We might also include accounts of crowds as paid mobs.[14] The behaviour in both cases is regarded as non-expressive, in the sense that the intelligibility of the individuals' actions does not add up to an intentional account of the collective behaviour of the crowd, or to an account of the actions of the crowd necessarily being expressive of the interests of its members, even if their own actions are individually rational.

Cell 4. Structural accounts of, for example, revolutionary terror. Accounts of discursive frameworks, and of the controlling force of

---

[12] Lefebvre clearly wishes to downplay the irrational character of crowd behaviour during the Great Fear, in contrast to the work of, for example, Gustave Le Bon. Nonetheless, the panics he describes are, while intelligible, at base, not rational or intentional; see Georges Lefebvre, *The Great Fear of 1789: Rural Panic in Revolutionary France*, trans. Joan White (London: New Left Books, 1973), esp. 50, part III, 137–211, esp. 156–7.

[13] Mark Granovetter, 'Threshold models of collective behavior', *American Journal of Sociology* 83 (1978), 1420–43.

[14] As discussed at points by Bohstedt, *Riots and Community Politics*; and Rogers, *Crowds, Culture and Politics*.

Table 3.2 *Classification of accounts by type of explanation*

	Intentional		Causal	
	Loyalism	Reform	Loyalism	Reform
Expressive	1a Dozier[15]	1b Thompson	2a O'Gorman	2b Wells
Non-expressive	3a Cookson	3b Christie	4a Coercion	4b Reeves[16]

languages and ideologies. In extremis, Gustave Le Bon's work on the crowd![17]

We can also categorise roughly some recent contributions to accounts of popular activity in the 1790s.

I should say something about the causal category. It includes accounts that treat the actions of agents as a result of forces – structural, economic, social or whatever – over which they have no control and from which they have little or no autonomy. Such explanations are becoming rarer and are increasingly linked to accounts of the way in which structural forces are mediated through meaningful social action. Nonetheless, there is a consistent theme in literature on popular political action that stresses either the irrationality of or the structural grounds behind popular political agency. I have also included accounts that suggest false consciousness and coercion as the ground for action. Clearly, to be coerced into doing something one must be free to do that thing, and one's behaviour might be regarded as intentional but non-expressive; while acknowledging the simplification involved in the matrix, however, I want to sustain a line between intentional action as purposive and not simply driven by exigencies that one cannot reasonably resist and behaviour in which control effectively passes to another, or is analysed as epiphenomenal of other

---

[15] The sources for this include Dozier, *For King, Constitution, and Country*; Thompson's comments on popular loyalism; O'Gorman's unpublished work on Paine burnings; Wells, *Insurrection* and *Wretched Faces*; Cookson, *The British Armed Nation*; and Christie, *Stress and Stability in Late Eighteenth-Century Britain*.

[16] I am imputing to Reeves a rather similar view to that expressed by Dr Johnson, in *The False Alarm* (1770) and *The Patriot* (1774), both in *The Works of Samuel Johnson*, vol. X, *Political Writings*, ed. Donald J. Greene (New Haven, CT: Yale University Press, 1977), 313–45, 387–400.

[17] Gustave Le Bon, *The Crowd: A Study of the Popular Mind* (New York: Viking, 1960 [1895]). For theories of crowd behaviour, see the judicious account by Rogers, *Crowds, Culture and Politics*, ch. 1; and James Coleman, *Foundations of Social Theory* (Cambridge, MA: Harvard University Press, 1990), ch. 9, esp. his distinction between panics and hostile and expressive crowds. Clearly, in the light of these works, we would be better off classifying types of crowd rather than trying to associate authors with a single type of crowd explanation. Accordingly, 'moral economy' crowds need to be contrasted with hunger-driven crowds, or panics, or élite-mustered crowds, and so on.

features of the social, economic or political environment. I say little about causal accounts; the main focus of my discussion is on the contrasting assumptions underlying intentional accounts.

Although writers such as Robert Dozier take the loyalist movement as a pure expression of the collective conservative will of the whole nation, and take expressions of loyalist sentiment at face value, loyalism was, in fact, a complex and evolving phenomenon, with the 'Church and king' riots of 1791 and the Paine burnings of 1791/2 showing different patterns of incentives from the later loyalist associations, the petitioning movements and the rise of the volunteers and militia. Moreover, Dozier tends to underestimate the range of motives people had for participating in loyalist activities and for shunning radicalism. Prior to the royal proclamation in May 1792, but with greater energy subsequently, and with renewed vigour with the development of the loyalist associations of 1792/3, members of the gentry and the magistracy were actively involved in monitoring and, when possible, either prosecuting or shutting down all radical activity. Landlords were warned not to allow their premises to be used for radical meetings; booksellers and publishers were prosecuted; and lodging house keepers were expected to screen their guests, so as to keep out incendiaries and those of evil design. In Coventry, for example, the local association issued a reward of fifty guineas for the 'discovery of persons distributing Hand Bills, pasting up papers, or giving away pamphlets of a seditious tendency' – to be paid on conviction.[18]

In collecting signatures for petitions, loyalist activists clearly intimidated many they canvassed by treating failure to sign as indicative of Painite leanings or French sympathies – hence the success in securing the signatures of leading Whigs and radical sympathisers. It is not difficult to believe that a similar process affected participation in Paine burnings. Given the structures of power within local communities, perceived non-compliance could threaten a working man with the loss of work, or custom. Moreover, the face-to-face character of petitioning and the organisation of demonstrations would have communicated a clear sense of the costs of nonconformity.

Loyalism, therefore, undoubtedly increased the perceived costs of radicalism. It also provided incentives for participation – not least food and drink, time off from work and a degree of carnival! For example: at a meeting at Medlands near Exeter, one of Reeves' informants reported that 'a very respectable yeomanry (c40) whom with the clergy of the different parishes, din'd together, in one Room, and in another Room were

---

[18] Bodleian Library, G. A. Warw. b. 292 r.

assembled a great number of considerable Masters, whilst the house was surrounded by a numerous company of that truly useful class of persons, the day labourer, who were regal'd with the wine of the county (cyder) and join'd in chorus with those singing, God Save the King and other Loyal and constitutional songs'.[19] Paine burnings also combined a judicious mixture of threats and offers. Frank O'Gorman's work on this widespread phenomenon – which takes place mainly between 1791 and 1793, and is concentrated in the provinces, particularly the county towns of England, with Paine being ritually burned in effigy on something like 1,500 occasions – has emphasised their richness in symbolic and ritualistic elements and their attendance by a great many people from the lower orders of society. In an early version of his work he suggested that they could be seen as symptomatic of a spreading panic, deriving from French subversion and radical incendiaries (a cell 2 account).[20] Where his work is incontestable is in the weight it gives to the organised character of these events; they were often organised in incredible detail, with banners, costumes, procession routes and elaborately constructed effigies. But, while this might provide evidence of the depth of the *peur* and the attempt to handle it through ritual, it also emphasises what these affairs were not – namely, they were not riots.[21] The care over their orchestration clearly indicates a desire to avoid the uncontrolled exercise of mob violence. It is not difficult to see why this was so: the experience of the Gordon riots, the example of France, long-standing experience of disruptive mob activity in elections and fears that the rioters would run out of control and turn their hands against other institutions and individuals they resented all provided ample justification. Rather than encouraging riot, the explicit target was to anathematise an imagined radical project and to make loyalism the hegemonic performance.

The balance between threats and offers would differ in individual cases, but there is evidence of a good deal of both. Indeed, among some loyalists there was a recognition that they might have so increased the

[19] British Library, Add. MS 16924, fo. 29 r.
[20] Some of this work is pending. But see Nicholas Rogers, 'Burning Tom Paine: loyalism and counter-revolution in Britain 1792–3', *Social History* 32 (1999), 139–71, and *Crowds, Culture and Politics*, 201–8.
[21] This emphasis on the controlled nature of such loyalist demonstrations – that they were not, for the most part, popular outbursts against radicals so much as carefully marshalled performances – can be recognised in reports to Reeves, such as Add. MS 16924, fo. 112: 'The last dying Speech and Confession of that infamous fellow Thos Paine who was hanged and afterwards burnt this day here, many demonstrations of loyalty was shown upon the occasion and Fox's head was fixed on Paine, with a bubble out of his mouth with these words: "I will support thy doctrine to the utmost of my abilities, I only lament that we have not the original here."'

costs of non-participation that the associations might *elicit* loyal perform-ances from committed but prudent radicals. One writer drew Reeves' attention to '[m]any persons being known to join in Associations who are inimical to the Present Government, either from malignant motives, or fearing to oppose the General Voice of the Country'.[22] This recognition was indicative of a general sense that the objective was not simply to elicit compliance but to ensure the allegiance of those involved. Indeed, it was the fear that compliance was not backed by allegiance – that it was extremely fragile – that led so many of those who wrote to Reeves to urge the APLP to direct its attention to the lower orders:

Although the coercive measures of administration may smooth the surface and keep down opposition for the present, yet if the common people are not reasoned out of their pleasing hopes of general equality, and opinions circulated to make them satisfied with Kingly government the consequences may hereafter be fatal to the constitution.[23]

Some correspondents wanted to do more than reason the poor out of their hope. Trimmer, for example, sought to give them a sense of belonging within the loyalist community: '[I]t strikes me that jealousies may arise and at least be created in the minds of many of them [the lower orders] at seeing their superiors uniting in bodies from which they are excluded.' The plan of association was incomplete insofar as it extended only to the middle orders. Involving the poor 'would give the poor a little of that *personal consequence* which is grateful to every human heart. They would consider themselves as *voluntary agents*, not as mere instruments to be used or not at the wile of their superiors – they would be stimulated to worthy actions by the idea that *individual merit* would not be overlooked.'[24]

Yet seeking their inclusion was not the same as achieving it, and, when radicals wanted to tease Reeves about his project, some did so precisely by emphasising the fragility of popular loyalist performances:

The Hampshire Sedition Hunters think it proper to acquaint their brethren at the Crown and Anchor, that last Monday their committee met – but having nothing to do – they ordered an effigy, for Tom Paine, to be made . . . [and] caused the mob to assemble to carry this effigy about the City. . . [T]he Mayor and one Alderman – being of a true Jacobite breed, gave money to the mob to Halloo – Church and King – and then to burn the effigy. . . N.B. we think it proper to inform you – that

[22] Add. MS 16924, fo. 134 r–v. See my 'Vulgar conservatism 1792/3'.
[23] Add. MS 16 927, fo. 47 v.
[24] Letter from Sarah Trimmer, Add. MS 16923, fos. 47–50 [emphasis in original].

when the mob got drunk, some few did cry out – Tom Pain for ever – Tom Pain for ever, but they were very drunk. . .[25]

The desire to bring the people into loyalism undoubtedly had an impact, however. In the 1790s popular loyalism changed the way in which political authority was exercised and supported in Britain. Participation in this movement to conserve 'enfranchised' (in a variety of ways falling short of the vote) many hitherto on the margins of the political culture or formally excluded from it. To that extent, the net effect of loyalism might be radically to change some individuals' relationship to the political (and sometimes social) world. Moreover, even if a wide range of motives might lead to initial participation in loyalism, the participation might itself have a reinforcing effect. Dundas, reflecting on the Scottish volunteers in the 1790s, commented:

> You will recollect many of the parts of this country which were most disaffected, but were insensibly cured of it by being enrolled under arms along with others of a different description. If on the other hand, they are not so associated, they become a prey to the intrigues of traitors and enemies, being debarred the privilege of bearing arms on the right side.[26]

Although Reeves' associations had a very strong middle-class membership, suggesting that such participatory benefits were largely restricted to this class, in practice loyalism, volunteering and membership of the militia undoubtedly reached down to the poorer sections of society. S. C. Smith, in a study of the militia between 1807 and 1811, found that 51 per cent of the men belonged to the 'artisan and shopkeeper' class.[27] Again, there were substantial incentives for such people to join; participation in the militia brought supplementary earnings, and provided immunity from the 'regular' militia: '[T]he clothing is a clear gain; and so is the shilling on Sunday, which forms the little sum to the poor man which may be freely

[25] Add. MS 16928, fo. 5 r. Rogers, *Crowds, Culture and Politics*, 209, treats this as a sincere loyalist account – but there are real grounds for doubt, not least the phrases 'but having nothing to do' and 'true Jacobite breed'. Compare with other 'straight' accounts in the papers of burnings of Paine: Add. MSS 16922, fos. 121 r-2 v, 16923, fo. 67 r, 16924, fo. 62 r (alongside Dr Priestley), fo. 112 r, and 16928, fo. 7 r. One of Reeves' correspondents, T Hartley of Liverpool, accused republicans of 'artfully labouring to seduce people from the king: They know themselves weak in number, and therefore act by stratagem on all occasions – They are the first of all mixed companies to drink the "King and Constitution", but it is easy to discover by their *looks* and *motions* to each other that they do it in derision only': Add. MS 16923, fos. 85–6 [emphasis in original].

[26] Cookson, *The British Armed Nation*, 67–8.

[27] S. C. Smith, 'Loyalty and opposition in the Napoleonic Wars: the impact of the local militia 1807–15' (D.Phil. thesis, University of Oxford, 1984), cited by Cookson, *The British Armed Nation*, 89, note 76. See also Gee, *The British Volunteer Movement*, esp. ch. 5, on the motivation for volunteering.

spent on happiness in any shape.'[28] As to the volunteers, '[i]ts officers were often lesser men than the gentry who built their standing out of the lesser pickings of local influence and power. Its rank and file formed from the artisan and labouring poor could derive significant material benefit from their service.'[29] The total numbers of volunteers does not look huge, initially: 116,000 in 1798, 146,000 in 1801 but 380,000 in 1804. They made up around a half of the home forces, rising to two-thirds in 1804. That gave Britain, with the militia, a total mobilised military force of over 800,000, which was more than one in five of the total population capable of bearing arms (*c.* 3.75 million) – a huge proportion of the population.[30] It was also over twice the size of the electorate![31] But does this mean that we should accept Dozier's perspective and see loyalism as an authentic expression of patriotic feeling on the part of the lower orders of society?

One complication in reaching such a conclusion is that the opposition between loyalists and reformers was an aim (and perhaps eventually an achievement) of loyalist propaganda, not a precondition for it. Patriotism had long been associated with reformist and oppositionist commitments, and it was largely during the revolutionary war that it took a distinctively conservative cast. Nevertheless, supporters of reform often continued to insist upon their loyalty to the king and constitution. Indeed, the London Corresponding Society responded to the royal proclamation against seditious writing in May 1792 by concluding that the king could not but approve of their attempt to secure a perfect representation in parliament. Moreover, in the debates held at county and borough meetings called in the summer of 1792 to send loyal addresses to the crown, there was a good deal of public dispute about what loyalism meant, with some understanding it as necessarily associated with the desire for reform.[32] What was true for 1791–4 also held true for the later episodes of volunteering. Participation undoubtedly increased, and the sympathies of the mass, armed nation that was created were enlisted for the most part against the French. The association of patriotic activity and anti-reformism, and of patriotism and mass participation, were temporary and conditional alliances, however. They required continuous promotion, and they

---

[28] Cookson, *The British Armed Nation*, 110.   [29] Ibid., 91.   [30] Ibid., 95.
[31] O'Gorman, *Voters, Patrons and Parties*, 179.
[32] See Morris, *The British Monarchy and the French Revolution*, 88. Equally, the letters to Reeves and the resolutions passed in the winter of 1792/3 hardly showed a slavish devotion to Reeves' view of loyalism. Of course, as I discuss below, there is a problem in knowing how to read such assertions and ambiguities: whether they were ways of masking radical sentiment, or whether people genuinely did not see a desire for reform as incompatible with loyalty and patriotism. That the government and its loyalist supporters came increasingly to insist on this incompatibility suggests that they were trying to draw a line that others did not naturally draw.

could, and did, break down; volunteers were unreliable when used for local policing (as during the food riots of 1800/1),[33] allegiance was often felt in strongly local terms, with a strong reluctance to serve outside the locality, and there were periodic difficulties arising from status issues between commanders and the lower officer corps. 'What was different about the national defence patriotism of the lower orders was the calculative, opportunistic attitude that was taken towards service by individuals and the collective opposition offered when service was believed to threaten general interests. Service, in other words, was overtly conditional.'[34] Indeed, the content of patriotism was 'constantly negotiable. With respect to the service that would be performed, the authority allowed officers, and the interests of individuals. On these loose terms patriotic commitment could happily coexist with all kinds of other loyalties.'[35]

On this account, it does not seem adequate to characterise popular loyalism and patriotism as the authentic expression of a secure belief in the virtues of the status quo. But is popular radicalism any more authentic or deep-seated?

IV

Some care is needed in distinguishing different types of popular participation in reform activity, such as attending public meetings, joining corresponding societies, participating in debating clubs, and so on. We need to be careful, because some activities that have implications for the direction the popular reform movement took – such as food riots and crimp riots – and certain features of mass public activities – as when the king's coach was destroyed by a mob after the opening of parliament in October 1795 – may have been driven by something other than radical intent. Behaviour may have been the inarticulate expression of anger and frustration at events or a response to people's experience of hardship. While this may have been a feature of some of the activity, however, and may have played a rather important role in some of the pressure on the government in 1795/6 and 1799–1801, it was not this activity that was seen as distinctive of the popular radicalism of the period. Rather, it was

---

[33] See Cookson, *The British Armed Nation*, 237.
[34] Ibid., 233. See also Nicholas Rogers, 'The sea fencibles, loyalism and the reach of the state'; Katrina Navickas, 'The defence of Manchester and Liverpool in 1803: conflicts of loyalism, patriotism and the middle classes'; and Jon Newman, '"An insurrection of loyalty": the London volunteer regiments' response to the invasion threat', all in Mark Philp, ed., *Resisting Napoleon: The British Response to the Threat of Invasion, 1797–1815* (Aldershot: Ashgate, 2006), 41–60, 61–74, 75–90.
[35] Cookson, *The British Armed Nation*, 237.

the organisation of mechanics, tradesmen and shopkeepers, and of members of the literate middle orders, into societies committed to the political education of their fellow members of the public and to agitation for the reform of parliament.

In understanding this activity we need to recognise, with much recent historiography,[36] that we cannot assume a direct causal connection between social location, the demand for political representation and a sense of common concerns or interests. It may be that certain social conditions would have certain natural correlates in class action, but I do not believe anyone could reasonably claim this for the 1790s. The issue, then, is whether there is some residual account that appeals to class interests.

The difficulty such an account faces lies not in its commitment to a conception of real interests (since these should not be dismissed a priori) but, instead, from connecting a story about real interests with one that shows why acting in certain ways (namely, participation in radical societies) uniquely satisfied such interests – so that the actions, statements and commitments of participants were expressive of those interests rather than being tactically and conditionally allied to them – as I have suggested is plausibly the case for popular loyalism.

The very concept of commitment involves two distinct features: it involves a certain relationship between the individual's belief set and how he/she acts, such that the action is expressive of that belief set; but, with respect to political action and organisation, we are also making the additional claim that the belief set is not simply a raw set of preferences but involves adherence to some broad principles or political ideology that guides the agent's interpretation of the context within which he/she acts, and plays a major role in the agent's sense of self and his/her associated aspirations. That means that we have to look at the way in which people's actions were mediated by representation, even if it also leaves it as a rather inscrutable matter of judgement as to how far those representations were in fact deep-seated commitments. A further dimension of activity that we must recognise concerns the individual motives that lie beneath collective action in politics. Individual acts of commitment usually take place within a broader context in which the agent identifies his/her fundamental interests both through representation and through identifying him-/herself with others who subscribe to that set of representations and with whom that commitment is shared. Certainly, this is a feature of collective forms

---

[36] Not least with Jones, *Languages of Class.*

of political action, such as the radical movement in the 1790s. But it is a dimension that adds considerable complexity to any account of there being some collective real interests underlying participation in radicalism. It does so because one dimension of the process of commitment would seem inevitably to be a sense of how widely those involved believed their commitments to be shared (and shared by those whom their political ideas predicated as those with whom they had a common interest), or how widely they believed they could become shared (among that group). And, insofar as they were not widely shared, they would need some way of explaining this apparent lack of commitment in a way that did not then lead them to doubt the value of their own commitment and the legitimacy of their aims.

One way to take the argument, at this point, would be to identify the core constituency picked out by radical reformers in the 1790s and to see how far those who espoused radical principles could reasonably be said to have had a sense of a collective identity underlying their commitments. Although this seems to offer a solution to the asymmetry problem, I suggest that it fails to do so and that we need to move to a second, more fruitful, account.

The difficulty with the idea of a core constituency, identified by the language of reform and acting as a basis for collective self-representation and commitment, is that the way the core is identified underdetermines the salience of its representation. In one sense, those pressing for parliamentary reform were pressing for the cause of the majority – those excluded from parliamentary representation. This led many to think in optimistic terms, early on, about the ease with which reform could be achieved. By encompassing the majority, the reform movement would effectively act as a voice for the people against an élite. Moreover, the fact that. after 1782, the SCI and, from 1792, the LCS and a whole host of provincial reform societies were pressing for the adoption of the principles of 'ANNUAL ELECTED PARLIAMENTS, UNBIASED AND UNBOUGHT ELECTIONS, AND AN EQUAL REPRESENTATION OF THE WHOLE BODY OF THE PEOPLE'[37] must have seemed to give them a natural majority in favour of reform – a majority that, once it realised its weight, would be able to recognise the truth in David Hume's principle that 'it is on opinion only that government is founded',[38] and through it to put into practice Paine's

---

[37] *Selections from the Papers of the London Corresponding Society*, 18.
[38] David Hume, 'Of the first principles of government', in *Essays: Moral, Political and Literary*, ed. Eugene F. Miller (Indianapolis: Liberty Press, 1987), 29–34, 32.

reading of the Marquis de Lafayette's comment 'For a nation to be free it is sufficient that she wills it'.[39]

Nonetheless, despite the apparent reasonableness of such a deduction, there were a number of obstacles, both to the achievement of the aspiration and to recognising its force as an aspiration. One set of obstacles blocked the formation of a sense of majority by dividing those who might have comprised it; another set blocked members of the lower orders from perceiving their common interests with their fellows. In the first case, although one way in which people might have recognised themselves as comprising a majority of society was in virtue of the narrowness of the franchise and their exclusion, this was a very local phenomenon, with considerable variation. Moreover, as O'Gorman has stressed, elections could be vigorous contests with extensive participation by those without the vote – and Paul Langford has suggested that some non-voters might well have had every justification for thinking of an extended franchise as a potential misfortune, involving substantial disruption of normal working activity.[40] Moreover, prior to 1792 the desire for inclusion was strongest among the more literate and educated middle classes – especially those with connections with the Dissenting community (since their exclusion was more pointed and extensive), who were practically involved in agitating for reform (and relief) both prior to and immediately after the beginning of the French Revolution. But that in itself did not create a sense of unity, since support for Dissent was not a majority issue, and those agitating for reform from a background in Dissent were by no means wholly in favour of the SCI demands for annual parliaments and universal manhood suffrage. Although those lacking the franchise were a majority, that, in itself, gave them no very strong reason for thinking and acting as a single body. Furthermore, the divisions that took place in the early years of the revolution controversy, between moderate reformers and those pressing for more extensive changes, were sufficiently clear to ensure that no sense of a simple and united majority for reform could exist. Few people could have been in a position to think that they had nothing to lose by insisting that the demand for universal suffrage and annual parliaments was strictly non-negotiable. Indeed, there is a great deal of evidence to suggest that, among members of the SCI in the 1780s and 1790s (most notoriously John Horne Tooke),[41] these shibboleths were markers in a

---

[39] Thomas Paine, *Rights of Man*, in *Thomas Paine: Rights of Man, Common Sense and Other Political Writings*, ed. Mark Philp (Oxford University Press, 1995), 83–198, 96, 172.

[40] Paul Langford, *Public Life and the Propertied Englishman 1689–1798* (Oxford: Clarendon Press, 1991), 282.

[41] See Christina and David Bewley, *Gentleman Radical: A Life of John Horne Tooke* (London: Tauris Academic, 1998).

negotiating process; few saw them as immediately attainable and many may have harboured doubts as to their ultimate desirability.

These problems were exacerbated for members of the lower orders interested in reform. For many such people, their political experience and their sense of the political order they inhabited was more a function of locality than otherwise, and they would have had little sense of the way in which their lives were systematically similar to or different from those in other counties or towns. This ignorance was recognised by the societies. Indeed, the very desire to correspond, which drove the first group of artisan reformers, was linked in part by trying to find out how far there were others elsewhere who shared, or could be brought to share, their understanding of their political condition. Although the 1790s saw the first great wave of provincial radicalism, it is plausible to argue that each local movement was shaped as much by local experience and events as by a sense that there was a broad national political agenda in which reform had to play a major part.

The lack of a clear and united majority was also partly a function of the political character of the reform movements of the period. Appeals to an economic and social base to the movements for reform were extremely rare: there was no clear, widely held sense that it was the artisan and labouring classes who produced the wealth of society, and no clear sense of exploitation that could be mobilised to create a sense of unity. Paine begins to consider exploitation only in *Agrarian Justice* – and then not in depth. Far more central for him was the engrossing of the national income through taxation by a monarchical government pursuing its private concerns through war, and although Thomas Spence made a contribution to the theme he did so to a restricted audience. There was also no immediate identification with the needy, partly because the reformers included many people with a comfortable income or wealth, and partly because the 'Treadesmen – Shopkeepers and mechanicks'[42] who formed and sustained organisations such as the LCS were neither the rural nor the urban poor. It is true that the language of exploitation was not entirely absent, nor that of need:

As our plan was *Universal Suffrage* and *annual parliaments*, the Society admitted journeymen treadsmen of all denominations into it – A class of Men who deserve better treatment than they generally meet with from those who are fed, and cloathed, and inriched by their labour, industry, or ingenuity.[43]

---

[42] Memoir of Thomas Hardy, cited in *Selections from the Papers of the London Corresponding Society*, 7.
[43] Ibid., 8 [emphasis in original].

It is notable, however, that this came from Hardy's later account. The emphasis in the opening declarations of the society was on the direct connection between representation and need:

Resolved, – that in consequence of a *partial, unequal,* and therefore *inadequate Representation*, together with the *corrupt* Method in which Representatives are elected; *oppressive Taxes, unjust Laws, restrictions of Liberty,* and *wasting of Public Money* have ensued.[44]

The languages of exploitation and need began to enter the reformers' armoury more pressingly as the cost of the war with France and the consequences of poor harvests started to bite, at the beginning of 1795.[45] There was some impetus to tackle issues of property and need earlier than this, however, in response to accusations by loyalists that the reformers were levellers in disguise. But, rather than producing a well-worked-out set of causal processes, linking wealth, exploitation, need and the labour of the poor, the most common reaction was to deny that reformers had any interest in the equalisation of property. Part of John Thelwall's *Rights of Nature* (1796), for example, was devoted to insisting that the idea of equalising property was 'totally impossible in the present state of human intellect and industry'.[46] On the other hand, the poor were occasionally used to powerful rhetorical effect, especially by the more literary radicals, to attack the combination of wealth, power and privilege among the upper classes. Consider Thomas Holcroft's incensed comments to William Windham:

Who makes the laws ? The rich – Who alone can with probable impunity, break the laws? The rich – Who are impelled by want and misery to break them, and afterwards are imprisoned, transported and hanged? The poor – Who do the work? – The poor. Who reap the fruits? – The rich. Who pay the taxes? The poor for their labours pay everything. Who impose the taxes? The rich, whose luxury devours what the labours of the poor produce. On what do the rich feed? On the product of the poor's misery. On what do the rich ride? On the bent and broken back of the poor...[47]

This was not a manifesto for revolution but, again, a series of rhetorical flourishes drawn out by Windham's suggestion that the war imposed no hardship on anyone. That the sense of exploitation was not greater was a function of the tendency to see current ills as a result of the corruptions of parliamentary representation rather than as indicative of deep-rooted

[44] Ibid., 10 [emphasis in original].
[45] See David Eastwood, *Governing Rural England: Tradition and Transformation in Local Government 1780–1840* (Oxford: Clarendon Press, 1994), 101–32.
[46] See Goodwin, *The Friends of Liberty*, 473.   [47] Ibid., 489.

structural inequalities.[48] These corruptions were sustained by 'a restless, all-consuming Aristocracy', 'treacherous and hypocritical statesmen', and by 'the venal oligarchy, (THE ONE HUNDRED AND SIXTY-TWO PROPRIETORS)' who had usurped the democratic branch of the constitution.[49] The design involved abuses in the mode of election, the duration of parliaments and the perpetuation of corrupt property in decayed corporations. But, once the problems of representation had been resolved, the other evils of society, such as poverty, would cease. Moreover, a very great proportion of the comments on the poor were comments on 'them', rather than on 'us'; that is, it was a concern that again divided the majority in terms of its self-identification, rather than uniting it. A further way in which the intensity of a collective identity and cause was vitiated was by the lack of any consistent sense of antagonism, to 'those of the higher ranks' – whom the corresponding societies welcomed but resisted putting in positions of influence, lest it prevent 'the people exerting themselves in their own cause' by coming 'to depend implicitly [as formerly] upon the mere ipse dixit of some NobleMan or great Man without the least trouble of examining for themselves. . .'.[50] The porous character of the reforming interest both gave it a degree of latitudinarianism towards those it admitted and acknowledged as its fellows, and vitiated its capacity to root their political commitments in a consistent social identity.

In many respects this simply emphasises Thompson's point about the political character of the project of poorer reformers, but in doing so it also undercuts accounts that look to the class interests of those involved. By taking a political view of the problem and of its solution, the reformers took as their allies an inherently unstable majority – unstable because, although the aggregate interest was for the inclusion of the majority, individual incentives had no such collective dimension. But this did not mean that those who perceived their political exclusion as an injustice had no reason for seeking to unite with others; on the contrary, each clearly had a prima facie, but ceteris paribus, reason for uniting with others to

---

[48] Although it has recently been claimed that we can find in this period the beginnings of an understanding of this structural inequality that does not tie it to political representation. See Noel Thompson, *The Real Rights of Man: Political Economies for the Working Class 1775–1850* (London: Pluto Press, 1998).

[49] London Corresponding Society's *Joint Address to the French National Convention, 27 September 1792*, reprinted in Goodwin, *The Friends of Liberty*, 502; William Godwin, 'Essay against reopening the war with France', in *The Political and Philosophical Writings of William Godwin*, vol. II, *Political Writings II*, ed. Mark Philp (London: Pickering & Chatto, 1993), 33–61, 37; John Thelwall, *The Natural and Constitutional Right of Britons*, in *The Politics of English Jacobinism*, 3–64, 31.

[50] *Selections from the Papers of the London Corresponding Society*, 8.

change his/her representation. In other words, it was a reason, but its force depended on a whole range of factors: the salience of that exclusion to the individual; a sense that the exclusion was shared by others in a way that gave them a common interest in challenging it; a sense that challenging it was feasible and its costs not prohibitive; and a sense that he/she could not do as well or better elsewhere.

This may seem an odd way to describe the situation, but it helps emphasise the extent to which members of 'the people' would have had a wide range of cross-cutting interests and incentives (in which locality was a consistently underestimated component). The broad convergence within the reform movement was on the wholly political character of their case, as opposed to social or economic (both of which played a central role in popular participation in the French Revolution). But, while one line between minority and majority was easy to draw (those with the vote and those without), there was little agreement on the issue of how the suffrage should be settled – no ideological consensus either on the grounds for suffrage (rights versus utility versus prescription/tradition) or on whether or how it should be extended. On this account, then, membership of reform societies, participation in public meetings, and so on might well have been as conditional for many radicals as it was for many loyalists.

Before I look at the second type of account we might give, I want to stand back a moment and look at the strategy of argument I have deployed. The preceding discussion resists the idea that a common set of real interests provided the basis for individual commitment and the unification of the reform movement, on the grounds that objective accounts of common interests are weak and difficult to connect with the way that individuals would have perceived their situation. For that reason, popular reformers' commitments might well have had the same conditional and tactical relationship to the radical ideas they were willing to subscribe to as was the case for loyalism. One possible response to this conclusion would be to claim that the failure of the project was largely a consequence of the very distinction between expressive and instrumental behaviour with which I began this chapter – that is, that we should abandon this distinction, and simply accept that expressive commitment was itself either wholly idiosyncratic or largely illusory, and that political conflict is best understood in tactical terms. Since I do not find that picture attractive, let me suggest an alternative account.

V

This alternative account of radicalism avoids the concern with class interests and focuses instead on the dynamics of contesting exclusion.

Members of the popular reform organisations that sprang up in 1791 and 1792 were largely excluded from the political system and were, in effect, making a bid for inclusion – a bid that drew forth fierce resistance. Part of the response to that resistance was a hardening of reformers' demands and attitudes, with the reaction being regarded by many as further evidence of the urgency of reform and of the need for thoroughgoing change, and, in the face of that reaction, reformers' objectives often became seen as non-negotiable. This, in turn, hardened the reaction, which, in turn, further consolidated reformers' commitments.

This story needs further development, however, not least because it implies that a process that forged commitment for the radicals, on the one hand, might equally, and for the same reasons, have forged commitments for the loyalists, on the other. I want to suggest that, in fact, there were four key elements in the process that differentially affected the reformers.

One difference between the conditional allegiance of popular loyalists and the commitments of popular radicals is that between going along with something (the status quo) and resisting it. In the opening stages of the decade these differences were not huge for many participants: voicing objections to the system of representation in the company of others might be costless, or positively rewarding.[51] The situation changed as these actions gained a salience as a result of the actions and reactions of others – especially the government and local magistrates. The prosecutions for sedition (seriously underestimated in the standard work by Emsley)[52] would have been sufficiently widely known within their localities to bring those with reforming sympathies up sharp. So too would they have been brought up by Paine burnings, anti-radical mobs, royal proclamations, county meetings for loyal addresses, and so on. Different individuals at different times found their probably rather inchoate ideas and principles challenged, and were forced to reassess them to decide how far, and in what ways, their views were dispensable, and how far they felt they had to affirm them as fundamental to their sense of themselves and their place in the world. By degrees, as they reacted to events, some came to define themselves as fundamentally in opposition to the status quo.

---

[51] As was mass participation in events celebrating French victories in, for instance, November 1792. See, for example, the *Manchester Herald*, 1 December 1792.

[52] Clive Emsley, 'An aspect of Pitt's "terror"' and 'Repression, terror and the rule of law in England during the decade of the French Revolution', *English Historical Review* 100 (1985), 801–25. The most serious challenge to date to Emsley's work is Steve Poole's 'Pitt's terror reconsidered: Jacobinism and the law in two south-western counties, 1791–1803', *Southern History* 17 (1995), 65–87. For the strategies and impact of the major trials for treason, see John Barrell's magisterial *Imagining the King's Death: Figurative Treason, Fantasies of Regicide 1793–1796* (Oxford University Press, 2000).

And, over time, they had to face the issue of how far they were prepared to go in pursuing their commitments, and how far those commitments were forced to become intellectual in character, rather than being practically motivated. Loyalists were not confronted in the same way. Evidence of radical sedition might have confirmed fears of the activities of evil and designing men, as would the correspondence between reformers and the French Legislative Assembly and, subsequently, the Convention, and the later arrests for treason. Confirming instances do not test belief in the same way as attempted refutation, however. Moreover, it is unlikely that many loyalists knowingly encountered radicals, save in the slogans they found chalked on doors, and the reports they received from loyalist pamphlets and broadsides. As a result, they were not subjected to the same challenges, and consequently did not need to press their beliefs or test their commitments.

There is also a different internal dynamic in conformist and opposi-tional social movements. In the former case, there are few costs to pro-fessing one's commitment, or to seeking to influence the direction taken by the organisation. Moreover, while those initially organising the loyalist movements sought to mobilise loyal opinion, their ambition was a forked one: they wanted to mobilise and they wanted loyalists – and, on balance, their preference was for the former. As a consequence, within loyalist associations there could be a relatively broad and tolerant attitude to the views of participants who were, for whatever reasons, prepared to espouse their loyalty to king and country. The result was a relative degree of pluralism and tolerance and a reluctance to risk alienating one's member-ship. Among reformers, once reaction began, the incentives were increas-ingly to mistrust outsiders and to shun publicity, with a corresponding tendency for individuals' commitments to harden, and for internal dis-agreements to produce faction and splitting. In this case, what remnants of popular radicalism there were within the revolutionary cells of the United Irishmen, United Englishmen, United Britons, Spencians and others hardened into unconditional commitments.

A third, related, difference between the two movements lay in the detail of their respective programmes and in the relations between leaders and followers. The points are connected. The loyalist associations, and later the volunteers and militias, relied on a high level of upper- and middle-class initiative, their organisational form was essentially laid down by the associations' leadership, and their principles and commitments were set broadly by the idea of loyalty to the crown and a willingness to follow the leadership of the government. What was asked of supporters was support in the broad endeavour: while many middle-class supporters also offered extensive advice and information, together with pamphlets, broadsheets and songs, the broader lower-order constituencies in, for example, the militia were unlikely to have been heavily involved in the ideological dimensions of their activities. In contrast, the reform organisations, as Günther Lottes stressed more than thirty years ago,[53] were less led than collectively developed, with high levels of local participation and debate over both political principles and the practical organisational details of reform. This participatory dimension to the political agenda of the reform movement meant that members of the reform societies would have had an experience of arguing through and developing the details of their political principles that would have been in sharp contrast to loyalist meetings, and would have ensured (especially given the other conditions) that those principles were forged as an ongoing process of developing commitment – a commitment that repression might silence without extinguishing.

The final difference between loyalists and radicals concerns the complications introduced by France. The popular reform movement arose, in part, out of the revolution controversy and the assiduous circulation of its central texts, and France remained a central issue for reformers – becoming a bone of contention between supporters of moderate reform, who distanced themselves from France after September 1792, and the popular organisations, whose attitudes were unaffected by the September Massacres, subsequently raising major issues of loyalty for reformers once Britain and France were at war. For many loyalists, France simply conformed to its true colours as a traditional enemy, requiring mobilisation and vigilance. But that could be achieved without thinking either that one was thereby necessarily mobilising against reform in any of its colours, or that there was any justification for linking hostility to France to denying the legitimacy of its revolution or the principles it had initially espoused. Moreover, while such a position would generate suspicion towards groups that linked themselves to this traditional enemy, and might encourage fears of fifth columnists, fellow travellers and potential insurgents in the pay of foreign powers, the connections between such characters and popular reformers were pretty tenuous and largely failed to bear detailed scrutiny once brought before a court of law.

In contrast, for reformers, France remained a complex point of identification – additionally complicated by their sense that the war against France was itself intended as a war against them. The various attempts to define the nature of the ideological links with France are evidence of the extent to which the radicals found their agenda framed by loyalism as either pro-French or pro-government, and shows the way that they

---

[53] Lottes, *Politische Aufklärung und plebejisches Publikum*; see also his 'Radicalism, revolution and political culture'.

attempted to define a path in which reform remained an option. The difficulty with this was the extent to which, as opposition to the government was faced by more vehement reaction, reformers became persuaded that their own government was engaged in a conspiracy against their traditional liberties, with France as a pretext. On the one hand, this offered an alliance with the respectable movement against the war among those whom John Cookson has called 'the friends of peace'; on the other, as the decade wore on, it persuaded many that the only chance for effective resistance to growing domestic tyranny was to seek French support. From the summer of 1792, if not beforehand, loyalism found it possible to tar radicalism with a broad French brush, and radicals were forced to work through the nature of their commitment to France and its implications, often in considerable detail. That detail often led to considerable latitude for French actions, however – not least because it was possible to explain them in terms of the exigencies faced by an embattled country, thrown into disorder by foreign interference, war, an internal history of long resistance to reform, and the continuing effects of the remnants of despotism. Furthermore, the growing sense that traditional national rivalry was being deployed against the liberties of the ordinary people gave an added dimension to the reformers' understanding of the task facing them. It increased the scale of the envisaged necessary reform, and the sense of the obstacles in its way, but it also increased the sense of urgency associated with the reform project.

In each of these four cases, we can see reformers as under pressure to work through their commitments in ways that simply did not apply to supporters of loyalism. Of course, while this account may show how initial dispositions to favour reform might be sharpened and hardened as the intellectual controversy of 1790 and 1791 became a struggle on the part of popular organisations to challenge their exclusion from the political system, it does not explain the origins of those initial predispositions. But, I would suggest, we can afford an extremely pluralist account of this; they certainly did not all come from the same source. They comprised infidels, deists, freethinkers, millenarians, Muggletonians, Swedenborgians, mystics, religious enthusiasts, Dissenters, rationalists, disaffected working men, democrats, those who had gained some political education in the American War of Independence, hacks, reviewers and publishers, dropouts from the gentry and aristocracy, literary enthusiasts for France, and so on – each of whom, in different ways, may have stumbled into the revolution controversy and found in it resonances of his/her own sense of exclusion, confirmation of the indefensibility of the aristocratic order, and intimations of the justice of his/her particular cause.

Their origins are legion. What they came to share was an experience of forging their commitments, in part in company with others, in the debating societies and political organisations of the 1790s, and in part by coming to recognise the extent to which their beliefs were anathema to the existing order and by, nonetheless, continuing to affirm them. Doing so was doubtless assisted by their sense of solidarity with others, which could be generated by organisations, meetings and membership of societies, or could arise on the back of other activities, as Hardy had relied on when the first meeting of the LCS was held: 'After the business of the day was ended they retired as was customary for tradesmen to go to a public house and after supper conversation followed condoling with each other on the miserable and wretched state the people were reduced to, merely as we believed, from the want of a fair, and equal representation. . .'[54] Even where there were such networks and a sense of solidarity, which was most likely in the larger urban areas, and principally in London – since these afforded a degree of anonymity and the opportunity for men of similar means and experiences to meet – these certainly could not insulate their members from the realisation that they were in an increasingly precarious position. But the precariousness of their position and the shared sense of exclusion, for a period at least, encouraged them to overlook their differences – most notably on the question of religion, but also on aspects of the broader radical programme. For a period, roughly 1792 to 1798 at least, there was a degree of unity on the principles of reform and the use of peaceful methods to those ends. Although membership figures for the reform societies fluctuated wildly in this period, there was a core amongst whom a sense of the justice and significance of their cause took hold, leading them to take considerable risks and incur substantial costs, which became part of the inheritance and ballast of the popular movements of the 1790s. Thereafter, in the face of unremitting government attempts at suppression, a much smaller collection of increasingly fragmented groups toyed variously with the organisation of armed resistance, the encouragement of invasion, and further forms of sedition in a radical underworld.

VI

Three aspects of this story need further emphasis and elaboration. First, the practical consequences of the war with France were huge: on the one hand, increasing suspicion of those who had tied themselves to the French Revolution, and, on the other, spreading – from 1797 onwards – a real fear

---

[54] *Selections from the Papers of the London Corresponding Society*, 6.

of potential invasion, which required extensive domestic mobilisation. For those sympathetic to reform, the war with France, and the loyalists' insistence that reformers were wild Jacobin enthusiasts, were seen as further indications that Pitt's ministry was pursuing a policy that would not only deny reform but would further load the people with excessive taxation and threaten English liberties. For loyalists, meanwhile, the reformers' continued willingness to be associated with France, and their continuing pressure for reform, confirmed their seditious intent and the dangers the constitution faced. What sustains the asymmetry between them, then, is that, whereas it was possible for a broader public to go along with loyalism because it had significant benefits and relatively few costs (as the ability of volunteer regiments to refuse to serve outside their county indicates) and was in practice a rather undemanding and tolerant creed, radicals faced the prospect of substantial costs for sustaining their commitment – and thereby had substantial incentives to review that commitment and its significance for them. Loyalists' commitments were broadly to king, constitution and country, and they were able to see reformers as tantamount to a foreign threat, which did not require refutation in detail so much as repudiation in general; in contrast, the radical societies became increasingly caught in a process of defining and defending their commitments in detail – feeling forced to tread warily to avoid prosecution for sedition, to rebut the slurs of the opposition press and to insist on their legitimate right to press for reform. And at each stage of this process a reinvestment in the commitment was required.

The second feature is the fact that this story about the forging of fundamental commitments is not harmed, in the way the class story is, by recognising the huge diversity of oppositional groups that existed in Britain in the 1790s and that were only ever loosely linked together, nor by acknowledging the considerable differences in principles and aspirations between such groups. In their different ways they had come to define themselves as oppositional, and to regard that opposition as part of a common platform – even if, in some cases, the only thing they shared was being the target of government and loyalist attack. Popular loyalists could be half-hearted, hedging their bets, but radicals had to be firmly committed – albeit not necessarily committed to the same principles or ends.

The third aspect that bears emphasis concerns the ideological diversity of the radicals, and the substantial difficulties that exist in reading some of the propaganda, ballads and squibs of the period – difficulties that arise from the local character of much propaganda, from its highly contextual nature, from the complex rhetorical techniques used to evade prosecution and from the mix of highly adept and extremely clumsy contributions.

Reeves himself mistook one of his letters as coming from a radical, not a loyalist; and failed to see that another was not a weak loyalist performance but an adept radical one. The royal proclamations, the prosecution of publishers, authors and booksellers and the hounding of chapmen and ballad singers all served to heighten tension, and, accordingly, to give publications a dramatically narrowed scope, but a correspondingly highly freighted and nuanced form. One associated feature is that much radical propaganda was increasingly dedicated to impropriety, lampooning, pornography and deriding the established political order and its members.[55] It was relatively easy to satirise and caricature the status quo, and it was often less risky and more effective – less risky because it could be more embarrassing to prosecute than ignore such publications as they parodied official and loyalist discourse and appealed overtly to values that the status quo purported to tolerate. Moreover, juries proved willing to tolerate less direct and more metaphorical attacks – as with Eaton/Thelwall's 'King Chaunticlere'.[56] In addition, it was difficult to find a common language and set of interests that would unite the heterogeneous mass of the people – especially difficult when the radicals faced loyalist appeals to popular patriotism and traditional distrust of and scorn for the French. Paine sought to do so, and in many respects had considerable success; in preparing Part Two of *Rights of Man* he claimed that he had 'so far got the ear of John Bull that he will read what I write – which is more than ever was done before to the same extent'.[57] But it is worth recognising the limits of his success. Although he achieved unprecedented circulation, he spoke in an idiom that was foreign to the traditional conception of the distinctive liberties of the free-born Englishman; his anti-monarchism was not

[55] My favourite contributions include Robert Merry's 'Wonderful exhibition!!! Signor Gulielmo Pittachio: the sublime wonder of the world', from the *Courier*, 28 November 1794; Richard Lee's *King Killing*; and the 'Admirable satire on the death, dissection, funeral procession, and epitaph of Mr Pitt', from the *Telegraph*, 20, 21, 24 August 1795. On the first, see Jon Mee's, 'The political showman at home: reflections on popular radicalism and print culture in the 1790s', in Michael T. Davis, ed., *Radicalism and Revolution in Britain, 1775–1848: Essays in Honour of Malcolm I. Thomis* (London, Macmillan, 2000), 41–55, and his '"Reciprocal expressions of kindness": Robert Merry, Della Cruscanism and the limits of romantic sociability', in Gillian Russell and Clara Tuite, eds., *Romantic Sociability* (Cambridge University Press, 2006), 104–22; on the second, see Jon Mee's 'The strange career of Richard "Citizen" Lee: poetry, popular radicalism and enthusiasm in the 1790s', in Nigel Smith and Timothy Morton, eds., *Radicalism in British Literary Culture, 1650–1830: From Revolution to Revolution* (Cambridge University Press, 2002), 151–66. See also John Barrell, '"An entire change of performances?" The politicisation of theatre and the theatricalisation of politics in the mid 1790s', *Lumen* 18 (1998), 11–50.
[56] See Butler, *Burke, Paine, Godwin, and the Revolution Controversy*, 185–8.
[57] *The Collected Writings of Thomas Paine*, ed. Philip S. Foner (Secaucus, NJ: Citadel Press, 1948), vol. II, 1321–2.

universally popular and sat uncomfortably with some reformers' emphasis on restoring a balance between constituted powers; and his proposals for welfare provision may have seemed attractive to some but it is likely that many would have resisted their non-local character, or would have preferred direct cuts in taxation. Furthermore, while his writings fuelled the leaders of popular reform and encouraged them to turn towards conventionism in pressing for reform, many among the leadership distanced themselves from substantial parts of the doctrine[58] – so much so that the willingness assiduously to circulate it seems to be best understood as on a par with the more satiric, lampooning and caricatural literature and prints circulated; they offered the frisson of thinking the unthinkable, of cocking a snook at those in authority and undercutting the pretensions of aristocracy, which, as Thompson points out, was a long-standing British popular tradition. We tend to read Paine for doctrine, but we probably understand his impact more adequately if we read him for 'attitude'. Horne Tooke found some bits of the book reprehensible, but reasoned that there were sections of the Bible 'which a man would not choose to read before his wife and daughters',[59] but his willingness to back its circulation was clearly based on his support for its effect rather than for its doctrine. Finally, Paine's standing as a potential ideologue for radical reformers was seriously complicated by his views on religion (on which there were huge divisions among reformers: Joseph Priestley described the 'age of reason' to Theophilus Lindsay as 'the weakest and most absurd, as well as the most arrogant of anything I have yet seen')[60] and, later, by his encouragement of a French invasion force (since defence of France was far from equivalent to welcoming a French invasion force).[61] Although Paine was in many respects not an extremist – certainly if compared to those to whom he nearly fell victim in the French Revolution – his universalism and his deism had a serious impact on his ability to offer a distinctive collective identity for a British radicalism.

This recognition of the difficulties facing those espousing reformist political principles invites a further conclusion. The loyalist anathematising of so-called 'republican principles' left reformers with a highly constrained form of political discourse: not that they could not think radically,

---

[58] See Parsinnen, 'Association, convention and anti-parliament'; and Black, *The Association.*

[59] Hawke, *Paine*, 225.

[60] Frank Prochaska, 'Thomas Paine's *The Age of Reason* revisited', *Journal of The History of Ideas* 33 (1972), 561–76, 566.

[61] See Alexandra Franklin and Mark Philp, *Napoleon and the Invasion of Britain* (Oxford: Bodleian Library, 2003); and Mark Philp, 'Introduction: the British response to the threat of invasion, 1797–1815', in Philp, *Resisting Napoleon*, 1–17.

but that they were confined to expressing their appeals to the public in as neutral a political language as possible. Hence the attractions of constitutionalism: to pretend a Burkean reverence for the constitution and to focus on less abstract justifications and less threatening targets within that framework. To this extent, one needs the greatest care in taking the official pronouncements of the radical societies as expressive of their fundamental commitments. There is, as I hope I have shown, every reason to think that we are dealing with an often unequivocal commitment to radical reform, but it does not follow that the language in which those aspirations were expressed fully captured the commitments of those who wrote and acted within the movement. If loyalists' lip service was not expressive, through being tentative and conditional, reformers' subscription to the idioms of constitutionalism was not expressive in a different way, because it was often tactical and rhetorical.

If this is right, then some asymmetry is permissible, but it needs to be engaged in with considerable care. It is not just a case of seeing radicalism as more expressive; we need to show in detail how the sense of fundamental interests and commitments became forged in the process of political dispute and action, and we need to recognise the refracted ways in which those commitments were subsequently expressed. In terms of our matrix, there is a further conclusion that might be drawn. The extent of popular political mobilisation in the 1790s was unprecedented; for many we are dealing with a novel experience of politicisation – one that is common to every new generation, but that in this case had no traditional forms to structure and regulate it. Events led to different experiences of this politicisation, some taking the direction of loyalism, others radicalism. But these were different experiences, with different consequences for people's sense of self and of their commitments, which suggests that the distinction between expressive and non-expressive is really one that evolved through the practical conflict of the period; it need not and should not be generated by an a priori account of real interests.

VII

Does this account have implications for our understanding of radicalism? I think a number of things follow if we think of the popular reform movement of the revolutionary period as radical.

There is little or no unity of ideology among reformers – no wholeheartedly accepted radical programme, and no sense of the implications of holding one view necessitating other views. So, if it is a radical movement it is not by virtue of a consistent ideology. This also means that the tradition of radicalism is not likely to be an ideologically consistent tradition. The 1790s may have borrowed from earlier periods, such as the English Civil War and the country party opposition movement, just as later generations borrowed from the 1790s, but the borrowings do not establish the case for a consistent tradition.

If radicalism is not a matter of ideology, is it then a question of when certain ideas and organisations, and other manifestations, are rendered radical? In other words, is what makes something radical a matter of context – perhaps a system of social and/or political exclusion, on the one hand, denying access to positions of power and influence, or, indeed, to positions of equal standing as citizens, coupled, on the other hand, with a strategy of usurpation and its ideological elaboration on the part of those excluded? And is what gives a sense of radical tradition a function of the family resemblances and overlapping memberships that existed between the groups excluded (the poor, the labouring classes, religious minorities, economically and physically exploited groups), and/or the grounds of their exclusion (denials of citizenship on the grounds of class, race, gender or sexual preference), and/or the strategies adopted for usurpation (the inversion of despised identities, the associated transformation in the sense of self and standing, the adoption of universalist principles to justify inclusion) and/or the nature and degree of resistance that they met from the status quo? Indeed, in the latter case, is it in fact a feature of movements becoming radical that their attempts to secure their goals lock them into a struggle with the existing order in which both sides become more sharply defined and more antagonistic, with the consequence that the potential costs of concessions become exaggerated? If so, is what marks radicalism its outsider status – its lack of integration in the existing political and economic system and its increasingly confrontational attitude to that system, with those involved coming to see their commitments as non-negotiable? If so – and this account seems to fit the picture of the 1790s that I have sketched – then it also becomes possible to see why some explanatory asymmetry can in fact be justified: not by an appeal to real or class interests, but by recognising the way that fundamental interests and commitments became forged in the process of political reflection and contestation.

4   English republicanism in the 1790s[1]

In the last thirty years or so there have been recurrent scholarly disputes over the question of 'method' in the history of political thought. One centrally disputed area concerns the appropriate unit of analysis for those studying classic texts. While the injunction to look to context to establish meaning is now widely acknowledged,[2] there is increasing disquiet about how to settle the content of 'context' – with proposals including reference to paradigms, discourses, ideologies, languages or cultures.[3] In the course of these debates, one major achievement has been the recovery of the republican tradition of political thought – a tradition (or paradigm, or language) that is seen as essentially continuous with classical (predominantly Roman) thought, albeit reinvigorated in the Renaissance

[1] My thanks are owed to Philip Pettit, of the Australian National University, for prompting this chapter; to Barry Hindess and others, who heard a first version at a Research School of Social Sciences conference in honour of Geoff Brennan; and to Martin Fitzpatrick, Bob Goodin, Iain McCalman, Jon Mee and Steve Small. The final version has been greatly assisted by generous comments from J. G. A. Pocock, Quentin Skinner and Philip Pettit.
[2] For a fraction of the literature in this debate, see James Tully, ed., *Meaning and Context: Quentin Skinner and His Critics* (Oxford: Polity Press, 1988); and John Dunn, 'The identity of the history of ideas', *Philosophy* 43 (1968), 85–104, repr. in his *Political Obligation in Its Historical Context* (Cambridge University Press, 1980), ch. 2.
[3] See, for example, Thomas Kuhn, *The Structure of Scientific Revolutions*, 2nd edn (University of Chicago Press, 1970); Foucault, *The Archaeology of Knowledge*; Michael Freeden, *Ideologies and Political Theory* (Oxford University Press, 1976), chs 1, 2; Pocock, *Virtue, Commerce, and History*, ch. 1; and Peter Winch, *The Idea of a Social Science and Its Relation to Philosophy* (London: Routledge & Kegan Paul, 1958). This list is not exhaustive, not least in that it does not include the burgeoning forms of holism that now beset the methodological scene in the social sciences, including postmodernism and the new historicism. Nor does it do justice (at this stage) to the subtleties of the various positions. Professor Pocock, for example, stresses the importance of languages of political theory but decidedly rejects the methodological holism that other accounts endorse: 'I am approaching a "politics of language" along a path signposted by the assumptions of classical individualism': J. G. A. Pocock, 'The reconstruction of discourse: towards the historiography of political thought', *Modern Language Notes* 96 (1981), 959–80, 961; see also his 'The language of political discourse and the British rejection of the French Revolution', in Eluggero Pii, ed., *I linguaggi politici delle rivoluzioni in Europa XVII–XIX secolo: atti del convegno, Lecce, 11–13 Ottobre 1990* (Florence: Olschki, 1992), 19–30.

at the hands of Niccolò Machiavelli and others, and surviving largely intact to influence political thought and the conduct of politics in Britain, America, France and elsewhere, at least until the end of the eighteenth century.[4]

There are two broad lines of argument recognisable in the literature on republicanism, however. The first, exemplified by the work of J. G. A. Pocock, identifies a language of republicanism operating in Anglo-American political thought, one in which we can recognise not just resemblances, patterns and continuities but also innovations and transgressions. Moreover, the plurality of languages available to speakers in the seventeenth and eighteenth centuries has become an increasingly prominent theme in Pocock's work,[5] and he has distanced himself from the use of the term 'paradigm', so as to avoid implying a monolithic or controlling structure to the 'languages' he identifies.[6] For Pocock, the historian is concerned, at a minimum,

> to discover the language or languages in which the text 'he' may be studying was written, and the parameters of discourse which these tended to impose upon its utterance; to ascertain the acts of utterance which the text or its author performed or sought to perform, and any points at which these came into tension or conflict with the parameters imposed by the languages; to ascertain any utterances which may have departed from or modified these parameters; to discover the language or languages in which the respondents can be shown to have interpreted the text, and to inquire whether these were identical or non-identical with those contained in the text or intended by its author; and to ascertain whether this process of interpretation produced any of those tensions between intention, speech act and language which we may imagine as leading to modifications or innovations in political languages and its usages.[7]

The interpretation of a text might also attempt to identify its structure and unity, and to establish what its author was trying to do in it. Not every text has such a unity, however, and unity is too often a function of philosophical or political concerns that drive the political theorist but that could not be attributed to men and women living at the time the text was produced, so we need to take great care when we identify certain components of the text as of special significance for understanding the meaning of that literary act.[8]

---

[4] For which the classic text is Pocock's *The Machiavellian Moment*.
[5] J. G. A. Pocock, 'The concept of a language and the *métier d'historien*: some considerations on practice', in Anthony Padgen, ed., *The Languages of Political Theory in Early Modern Europe* (Cambridge University Press, 1987), 19–38.
[6] See ibid., 21; and Pocock, 'The reconstruction of discourse', 966–7.
[7] Pocock, 'The reconstruction of discourse', 974.   [8] Ibid., 978.

The other line of republicanism in political theory gives it the rather more restrictive and less fluid paradigmatic status of a theoretical model. This line of argument has been used most productively by Quentin Skinner and Philip Pettit in their work on republican liberty.[9] Here, republicanism describes a normative and explanatory model that identifies a set of values and theories about the conditions for securing those values. In this sense, 'republicanism' is frequently used in contrast to 'liberal' and 'conservative' theories of politics or freedom. But the use of the term 'republicanism' is not coincidental, since its advocates freely acknowledge the influence of Pocock's work, and see their own as contributing to the recuperation of republicanism as a tradition of political thought.[10] The two lines of argument therefore retain strong affinities, but they face different challenges.

Whereas Pocock embraces the diversity of languages, idioms and rhetorics, the identification of a republican theory of politics or liberty must be far more resistant to diversity. While a historical language can be traced through exchanges and successive transformations, to the point that each element has been reworked, a theoretical model and set of values must be more robust if it is to remain *that* model, or *that* set of values. Moreover, whereas Pocock can acknowledge that republicanism is just one of several idioms or languages available, claims for the continuing influence of a republican theory of liberty imply its continuing salience in the face of such competition. Since we can identify other languages at work even in supposed exemplars of republicanism (such as Machiavelli or Algernon Sidney),[11] insofar as reference to a republican model is to help us grasp the

[9] See Quentin Skinner, 'The republican ideal of political liberty', in Gisela Bock, Quentin Skinner and Maurizio Viroli, eds., *Machiavelli and Republicanism* (Cambridge University Press, 1990), 293–309; and Philip Pettit, *Republicanism: A Theory of Freedom and Government* (Oxford University Press, 1997). Skinner and Pettit are hardly alone in emphasising the importance of republicanism as a political theory of continuing significance. I have myself engaged in a similar exercise, as have many others: Mark Philp, 'Republicanism and liberalism: on leadership and political order – a review', *Democratization* 3 (1996), 383–419; see also, for example, Cass Sunstein, 'Beyond the republican revival', *Yale Law Journal* 97 (1988), 294–326.

[10] In this respect, Skinner's 'The republican ideal of political liberty' should be read alongside his influential 'The principles and practice of opposition: the case of Bolingbroke versus Walpole', in Neil McKendrick, ed., *Historical Perspectives: Studies in English Thought and Society in Honour of J. H. Plumb* (London: Europa Press, 1974), 93–128.

[11] On Machiavelli and the competing influence of republican politics and the art of the state, see Maurizio Viroli, *From Politics to Reason of State* (Cambridge University Press, 1992) and *Machiavelli* (Oxford University Press, 1998). With Sidney, his appeal to natural rights and contractarian language is difficult to reconcile with his republican rhetoric of civic virtue: see Thomas West, ed., *Discourses Concerning Government* (Indianapolis: Liberty Fund, 1990), ch. 1, sec. 12, as against ch. 2, sec. 23.

meaning and unity of a text,[12] we need to show why it is *that* model that best elucidates what they were trying to do and say. This leaves open the possibility that texts can be furnished with the rhetoric and idioms of a range of political languages, some of which have little impact upon the unity and meaning of the text. Moreover, languages and idioms of political thought may be used, as Skinner has shown so clearly in his account of Henry St John, Viscount Bolingbroke, not so much to express an author's values as to develop arguments that political opponents find difficult to resist or dismiss – which, in turn, opens the possibility that writers may find themselves (when they get it wrong) saying things they do not mean to audiences for whom what they say has no significance! Despite their rather different agendas, then, in giving an account of a text both approaches need to show not only that there are recognisable traces of republican language but the extent to which that language contributes to the action(s) that the author performs in the text, and those that are performed *by* the text. Pocock's work encourages us to ask (with him) for how long the language of republicanism remained a significant resource for Anglo-American political discourse (thereby recognising in principle that traces might be present but not expressive of commitment, nor salient to a text's unity nor forceful within political debate). Similarly, that of Pettit and Skinner should encourage us to ask how far the republican theory of liberty that they identify contributes to our understanding of specific historical texts, and for how long that model remained a recognisable and intentionally articulated paradigm. In neither case are there grounds for rejecting republicanism as an important language or set of political values; the cases for there being a recognisable republicanism and a distinct and valuable conception of liberty are powerful. But in both cases there are grounds for asking for how long, and for how many writers, the language and/or values remained salient, thus providing us with a context for grasping the meaning and unity of specific historical texts and the contours of political debate.

I

In this chapter I argue that a fundamental shift occurred in the language of political debate in England in the last decade of the eighteenth century, and that one casualty of this shift was the language of republicanism and the associated model of liberty and politics that Pettit and Skinner, and others, have identified. While Pocock has suggested in several places that

---

[12] With Pocock, this is not the only thing with which a historian or political theorist might be concerned, but it is certainly a legitimate interest.

this was a critical juncture for political discourse and for republicanism, others have been much less circumspect.[13] In finding republicanism, as both a language and a model, to have been marginal in the 1790s, I suggest that we might also find grounds for questioning the extent of its influence in earlier decades.

I begin by characterising the republican model, distinguishing anti-monarchy sentiment from republicanism as a paradigm for political analysis that had both explanatory and normative dimensions. I indicate various ways in which it developed in the eighteenth century and suggest that many of its components might be motivated by entirely different commitments that were also available within English political culture. I go on to suggest that mid- to late eighteenth-century political controversies largely revolved around the institutional structures and practices of the English parliamentary system and that, while some elements of republican analysis and civic humanist commitments became integrated into a broad doctrine of mixed government, many others became increasingly marginal to political debate. Late eighteenth-century political debate contested in detail the interpretation of the constitution, and the customs and practices of the English state. But it did so while accepting those institutions as embodying the sovereignty of the state, which they had no wish to impugn. The result was a broadly shared tacit agreement on the

---

[13] This is a contested area, but we should contrast Pocock's recognition that the contributors central to the debate cannot be characterised as fully republican with the tendencies of others to apply labels willy-nilly. See J. G. A. Pocock, 'The varieties of Whiggism from Exclusion to Reform: a history of ideology and discourse', in *Virtue, Commerce, and History*, 215–309, where his special difficulty is with Paine, who 'remains difficult to fit into any kind of category'; see also his 'Political thought in the English-speaking Atlantic, 1760–1790: (ii) empire, revolution and an end of early modernity', in J. G. A. Pocock, Gordon J. Schochet and Lois G. Schwoerer, eds., *The Varieties of British Political Thought, 1500–1800* (Cambridge University Press, 1993), 283–317, esp. 294–317. Compare David Wilson, who argues that Paine was deeply indebted to British republican and Real Whig traditions – 'A marginal figure in Britain, where Real Whig thought was a minority outlook, Paine became an important figure in America, where it was a majority outlook': David A. Wilson, *Paine and Cobbett: The Transatlantic Connection* (Kingston, ON: McGill-Queen's University Press, 1988), 41; see also 41–8, 68–9. Reference to 'republican' or 'Old Whig' to classify the arguments of reformers more widely is also common. Claeys refers to Paine as a 'consciously modern republican' in his 'Editor's introduction' to *Thomas Paine: Rights of Man*, ed. Gregory Claeys (Indianapolis: Hackett, 1992), xi–xvii, xiv, but sees him as continuous with much earlier republicanism in his *Thomas Paine: Social and Political Thought*, 45, 75, 88, 121–2, although there is a more subtle account in his 'The French Revolution debate'. Isaac Kramnick, in his 'Republican revisionism revisited', in *Republicanism and Bourgeois Radicalism: Political Ideology in Late Eighteenth-Century England and America* (Ithaca, NY: Cornell University Press, 1990), 163–99, is deeply sceptical about republicanism – but not about bourgeois liberalism. See also Gregory Claeys' 'Introduction' to *The Politics of English Jacobinism*, xiii–lviii, and his 'Republicanism and commerce in Britain, 1796–1805', *Journal of Modern History* 66 (1994), 249–90.

basic institutional structure of the British state, which grew out of the Restoration and, subsequently, the Revolution Settlement and was increasingly stable by the middle of the century. As Pocock has suggested, 'What mattered profoundly, to the governing classes but not only to them, was the maintenance of government which protected authority, property and liberty and whose temporary dissolution had been so fearful and painful an experience.'[14]

This 'constitutional consensus' came increasingly to frame contributions to political debate, and to modify their commitments, their aspirations and the political languages that they used.[15] Republican interests and concerns got linked into and conditioned by a generally shared understanding of the Revolution Settlement as a way of protecting men's personal and religious liberty – and as a way of preserving a politically and religiously latitudinarian culture. The constitutional consensus also contributed to raising questions about the balance in the constitution and the presence of corruption. Moreover, it continued to prove an attractive political rhetoric and a flattering self-image for those who shared in the public political culture of the second half of the eighteenth century. When substantive republicanism was seen as threatening to rear its head again, however, as it was in the 1790s – prompting Burke and subsequent loyalist polemics to portray both the French revolutionaries and their English sympathisers as extremist republican 'enthusiasts' – we find the language being jettisoned. The speed with which it was abandoned certainly testifies to the violence with which it was repressed, but it also suggests that it had already become marginal to the political agenda. Although it is difficult conclusively to prove this case, the abandonment of classical republicanism in England can be contrasted with the very different experiences of France and America, which produced a vibrant eighteenth-century republicanism whose legacy can still be felt today.[16]

---

[14] Pocock, 'The language of political discourse', 26.

[15] My use of Rawls' phrase from *Political Liberalism* (New York: Columbia University Press, 1993), 158–68, is intentional, even though Rawls' concern is with fully democratic, liberal regimes. Where I see a parallel is in the acceptance within the political culture of the existing structures and institutions for settling political rivalry and a degree of restraint on outright opportunism (which is not the case under a modus vivendi), even though there is disagreement 'as to the exact content and boundaries of those rights and liberties, as well as on what further rights and liberties are to be counted as basic' (159).

[16] This is a terrain that is already deeply scarred by academic and ideological dispute. Pocock's work has been attacked by Kramnick, *Republicanism and Bourgeois Radicalism*, esp. chs. 2 and 6; the first has been dismissed as of peripheral interest, and the second as myopic Marxist rhetoric, by Clark's *English Society, 1688–1832*, esp. the postscript. The American literature is similarly contested, with the same players being supplemented by work by Bernard Bailyn, *The Ideological Origins of the American Revolution* (Cambridge,

II

Two forms of republicanism must be distinguished: a popular, non-technical idiom; and a more specialised language of political analysis. In ordinary parlance, a republic is a form of government without a monarch – and republicanism is straightforwardly anti-monarchical in sentiment. Edward Swift's outburst ('Damn the King and Queen, they ought to be put to death the same as the King and Queen of France were. I should like to see the King and the rest of the Royal Family served the same as the King of France was served. Damn and bugger the King and all that belong to him. I will always say so if I have a sword run through me for so saying. Damnation and blast the King, I would as soon shoot the King as a mad dog.') was a reasonably incontrovertible instance of this type of republicanism.[17] Yet, in contrast to Swift, a range of writers on politics whom we see as republican saw no difficulty in characterising some states with monarchs as republics. For example, the popular definition was frequently ignored in Britain by post-Restoration political theorists, many of whom believed that a mixed government, involving the combined rule of king, nobility and commons, was not just a form of, but the best form of, republican government. The claim was intelligible, because they contrasted republics with despotisms or tyrannies, not with monarchies. Republican government was a government of laws directed towards the common good of the people; despotism was arbitrary government, with the capricious will of a tyrant subordinating the political realm to his/her personal interests. The classical sources for the ideal of a mixed government of the one, the few and the many, sustaining a balance of class forces that could steer the state away from domination by any particular class,

MA: Harvard University Press, 1967); Gordon Wood, *The Creation of the American Republic, 1776–1787* (New York: W. W. Norton, 1969) and *The Radicalism of the American Revolution* (New York: Random House, 1993); Joyce Appleby, *Capitalism and a New Social Order: The Republican Vision of the 1790s* (New York University Press, 1984); Thomas Pangle, *The Spirit of Modern Republicanism: The Moral Vision of the American Founders and the Philosophy of Locke* (University of Chicago Press, 1988); Lance Banning, 'Republican ideology and the triumph of the constitution, 1789 to 1793', *William and Mary Quarterly*, 3rd series 31 (1974), 161–88, and 'Jeffersonian ideology revisited: liberal and classical ideas in the new American republic', *William and Mary Quarterly*, 3rd series 43 (1986), 3–19; John Patrick Diggins, 'Comrades and citizens: new mythologies in American historiography', *American Historical Review* 90 (1985), 614–49; J. G. A. Pocock, 'Between Gog and Magog: the republican thesis and the Ideologia Americana', *Journal of the History of Ideas* 48 (1987), 325–46; Paul A. Rahe, *Republics Ancient and Modern: Classical Republicanism and the American Revolution* (Chapel Hill: University of North Carolina Press, 1992); and J. C. D. Clark, *The Language of Liberty 1660–1832: Political Discourse and Social Dynamics in the Anglo-American World* (Cambridge University Press, 1993).

[17] Quoted by Emsley, 'An aspect of Pitt's "terror"', 157.

were Polybius's opening comments to book VI of his *Rise of the Roman Empire* and Machiavelli's restatement of the doctrine in his *Discourses*, book I, chapter 2.[18] It is this second form of republicanism that I am predominantly, though not exclusively, concerned with here. The two strands remain related because many republicans held that more danger was to be feared from the usurpation of power by the monarch than was ever likely to stem from the tumults of the people, and that, faced with a choice between kingly and popular government, the choice was an obvious one.[19]

The appeal to the common good in republicanism is subject to differing interpretations. While some commentators have stressed the Aristotelian view, that, as a political animal, man realises himself only through participation in public life, and have seen the political community as offering a distinctive form of liberty as self-realisation, some more recent commentators have suggested that the common good should not be understood as a life of political participation but in terms of the security and liberties that are achieved when a stable republic is formed.[20] On this more parsimonious theory of republicanism, republicans differ from liberals, not by virtue of a theory of 'man's' telos as a political being but in having a very clear sense of the institutional structures and types of civic culture and political motivation that are necessary to ensure a stable and flourishing regime, and in their endorsement of a conception of liberty as non-domination rather than non-interference. Civic virtue and participation are required to ensure the subordination of the pursuit of one's private interests to the common good, and to avoid the corruption of the regime and its decay into internecine struggle in which self-serving interests and the unbridled indulgence of the passions predominate. As such, civic virtue is part of an abiding concern within the tradition with identifying the preconditions for stable republican government – one that could draw on a rich tradition of classical thought, beginning with the Greeks and

---

[18] See, however, the subtle account of the relationship between ancient and early modern republicanism by Wilfried Nippel, 'Ancient and modern republicanism: "mixed constitution" and "ephors"', in Biancamaria Fontana, ed., *The Invention of the Modern Republic* (Cambridge University Press, 1994), 6–26.

[19] Niccolò Machiavelli, *The Discourses*, Bk I, 58; James Harrington, *The Commonwealth of Oceana*, in *The Commonwealth of Oceana and A System of Politics*, ed. J. G. A. Pocock (Cambridge University Press, 1992), 1–266, esp. the 'First preliminaries', 30–5.

[20] Skinner's 'The republican ideal of political liberty' emphasises the commitment that only a self-governing republic can attain greatness and guarantee its citizens individual liberty; Pettit, in *Republicanism: A Theory of Freedom and Government*, develops an account of republicanism that emphasises a 'non-domination' definition of liberty. But, for both, the liberty preserved cannot be seen as an Aristotelian form of positive liberty, and yet a high premium may be placed on the cultivation of civic virtue.

Romans (and the examples of Sparta, Athens and Rome) and revitalised within a European context by Machiavelli's *Discourses*, and during the Civil War in England by James Harrington.[21] Subsequently, many early eighteenth-century writers, most notably John Trenchard, Thomas Gordon and Bolingbroke, drew from this tradition a language with which to articulate their opposition to the dominance of Robert Walpole and his 'court' faction.[22]

The fact that the tradition was rooted in a nascent form of political sociology left it open to successive refinement and adaptation in the light of changing historical experiences. In many ways, one of the most shocking eighteenth-century innovations was to find in the conduct of commerce and the accumulation of wealth symptoms of civic health and strength, rather than of corrupt self-seeking (although the financing of the public debt remained a source of anxiety).[23] Their gradual acceptance into a tradition in which they had hitherto been condemned as inevitably corrupting resulted in the development of an ideal of a commercial republic, as celebrated by Montesquieu in a gloss on England in *De l'esprit des lois* (1748) and subsequently by Adam Ferguson (with reservations) and others in the Scottish Enlightenment.[24] A further development was a growing emphasis in the British context on the importance of the liberty of the press and freedom of speech, on broadening popular participation in elections and on particular institutional and constitutional safeguards against usurpation – including petitioning, the use of juries, and so on. These innovations both reflected and contributed to a growing tolerance for the pursuit of individual interests and a willingness to interpret the

[21] An account first outlined by Pocock in his *Politics, Language and Time*, chs. 3, 4, subsequently elaborated both in *The Machiavellian Moment* and the 'Historical introduction' to *The Political Works of James Harrington*, ed. J. G. A. Pocock (Cambridge University Press, 1977), 1–152, and revisited in the British context in *Virtue, Commerce, and History*. On the classical dimension, see Elizabeth Rawson, *The Spartan Tradition in European Thought* (Oxford University Press, 1969); Jacqueline de Romilly, *The Rise and Fall of States According to Greek Authors* (Ann Arbor: University of Michigan, 1977); and Nippel, 'Ancient and modern republicanism'.

[22] See, principally, Skinner, 'The principles and practice of opposition'; Pocock's *Politics, Language and Time*, ch. 4; and, subject to Skinner's comments, Isaac Kramnick, *Bolingbroke and His Circle* (Ithaca, NY: Cornell University Press, 1968).

[23] This theme is dealt with in several of the essays in Pocock's *Virtue, Commerce, and History*. It is discussed in relation to the 1790s by Claeys in 'The French Revolution debate'.

[24] See also Christopher J. Berry, *The Idea of Luxury: A Conceptual and Historical Investigation* (Cambridge University Press, 1995). See Ferguson's *An Essay on the History of Civil Society, 1767*, ed. Duncan Forbes (Edinburgh University Press, 1966), pt V, sects. III, IV; István Hont and Michael Ignatieff, eds., *Wealth and Virtue: The Shaping of Political Economy in the Scottish Enlightenment* (Cambridge University Press, 1983); and Knud Haakonssen, *The Science of the Legislator: The Natural Jurisprudence of David Hume and Adam Smith* (Cambridge University Press, 1981).

common good of the commonwealth in terms of the protection of individual liberty and security – which are themselves understood in terms of
common law traditions and customary liberties.

Two further developments had an important impact on English republicanism. The first was a gradual shift from the pessimism that had marked
the classical world – for which the polis was a fragile achievement, beset by
forces within and without, capable of only a brief flourishing before
decaying into corruption and tyranny, but which in that brief moment
could offer a form of life that uniquely realised man's nature as a political
animal. Between the beginning of the eighteenth century and its end,
optimism about the nature of historical change became first possible,
then commonplace. A corollary of this was the sense that reform did not
have to be seen in terms of a re-establishment of an order on its fundamental principles, as had been the case for the republican tradition (not
least for Machiavelli),[25] but could be new, innovatory and derived from
philosophical speculation and scientific study. Progress, then, could
change the way in which states were ruled. The major example of a shift
in reliance from old forms to new (albeit buttressed by the ability to appeal
to some long past examples, and in the face of a steady fear of corruption
among representatives and Jean-Jacques Rousseau's critique of representation) was the celebration of representative government as an innovation
and the increasing demand for more democratic forms of representation.

The second development concerned the franchise. Harrington and his
successors had seen landed property as a basic prerequisite for a stable
body of citizens within a state, and, although he did not restrict citizenship
to those with land, eighteenth-century theories of representation began by
limiting participation to those with immovable property within the state.
The pressure to extend the suffrage derived in part from the republican,
Commonwealthman or 'old Whig' view that the basic problem for British
politics was to diminish the potential for arbitrary power on the part of the
executive by increasing the independence of the legislature. This concern
was exacerbated by the Septennial Act, and there was growing concern
through the eighteenth century with the declining proportion of those
entitled to vote, the falling numbers of free boroughs and the existence of
substantial new urban and manufacturing areas without representation.
Many of those arguing for some extension of the franchise in the 1780s
and early 1790s had some sense that reform would ensure that the crown
did not rule unchecked and that the executive did not corrupt the

---

[25] See Machiavelli, *Discourses*, Bk III, ch. 1: 'In order that a religious institution or a state
should long survive it is essential that it should frequently be restored to its original
principles.'

legislature – and following their repeated exclusion from government several leading Whigs were prepared to court reformers with promises of limited reform, although these had come to nothing by the 1790s. But, although the demands for voting rights may have originated in concerns about the balance of the constitution, the justifications had become many and diverse by the end of the century.

The American and French Revolutions saw the issues of popular representation and democratic participation move to the centre of British political writing and controversy. From the beginning of the American Revolution we find arguments for manhood suffrage in Britain (unattached to property – or with the ownership of one's own labour being seen as a property).[26] This demand became an important component of radical politics in the 1790s, and thereafter of the popular radicalism of the early nineteenth century. This is not to say that those who favoured reform in the 1790s were persuaded of the case for universal manhood suffrage. The vast majority were not; but, from that date, the widening of the suffrage was firmly on the radical agenda, albeit supported by a mélange of claims about the original form of the Anglo-Saxon constitution, the natural rights of man, expedience, utility, and so on.[27]

In each of these cases of a gradual shift in the commitments of 'republicanism', the claim is not that every British writer with republican sentiments followed the trend but that the broad lines of debate increasingly did. In the process, the more classically inspired language of republicanism that we can find in the early eighteenth century became increasingly tangled in a variety of other indigenous strands of political and philosophical thought – Lockean natural law theory, Scottish political economy, moral epistemology, civic jurisprudence, Dissenting models of Church government, proto-utilitarianism, and so on. The slightly paradoxical result was the emergence of a wide consensus in the second half of the century that took the institutions, traditions and constitution of the British state as largely given and shared a variety of languages with which to debate their problems. The language of republicanism, rather than

---

[26] For example, Richard Price's *Two Tracts on Civil Liberty, the War with America, and the Debts and Finances of the Kingdom,* in *Price: Political Writings,* ed. David Oswald Thomas (Cambridge University Press, 1991), 14–100, 24, 80.

[27] Compare Price's view that participation in government was for the purpose of adequately defending one's natural rights (see David Oswald Thomas, *The Honest Mind: The Thought and Work of Richard Price* (Oxford: Clarendon Press, 1977), 188) with, for example, Priestley's more limited extension of suffrage – limited lest enfranchising the poor give those on whom they depended a still greater say: Joseph Priestley, *An Essay on the First Principles of Government and on the Nature of Political, Civil and Religious Liberty* (London: J. Dodsley, 1768), 19–21. See also J. Dybikowski, *On Burning Ground: An Examination of the Ideas, Projects and Life of David Williams* (Oxford: Voltaire Foundation, 1993), 166–75.

providing an integrated and sophisticated explanatory and normative paradigm for politics, became increasingly thinned and accommodated to a wide range of potentially divergent political and philosophical positions.[28] One result was the existence of a sense of shared concerns and interests between people whom we now think of as having radically divergent political positions – not least, for example, Edmund Burke and Thomas Paine.

In the late 1780s they could breakfast together contentedly; Paine later stayed with Burke at Beaconsfield; and Burke described Paine in a letter to a friend as 'the great American'.[29] What they shared was the view that England had treated the colonies poorly, that the Americans were justified in their rebellion and that the central problem in British politics was to ensure the existence of countervailing powers to that of the executive, lest the state move towards arbitrary and despotic power. Both were undoubtedly influenced by elements of old Whig or republican thought; they may also have been influenced by constitutional strands of French republicanism (predominantly Montesquieu – although he was himself heavily influenced by the English country party tradition following his stay in London from 1729 to 1731) and by its more virtue-orientated version, epitomised by Rousseau. Burke's aesthetic theory, his *Vindication of Natural Society*, his recognition of the validity of Hume's view that all government is founded in opinion (which Rousseau counselled the legislator to concern himself with most centrally in his analysis of the types of laws in a state) and his fierce hostility to corruption in government and in *mœurs* might all be seen as reflecting Rousseau's concerns. Similarly,

[28] Hence, in part, the rise of constitutionalism. See Mark Francis and John Morrow, 'After the ancient constitution: political theory and English constitutional writings, 1765–1832', *History of Political Thought* 9 (1988), 283–302; and Eastwood, 'John Reeves and the contested idea of the constitution'.

[29] Professor Pocock has suggested to me that a good deal of 'mauvaise foi' might have been present on both sides on such an occasion – but it is striking how far each clearly misunderstood how the other would react to France (Paine supplying Burke with Jefferson's letters, which the latter then used in part in his description of the revolution). It is difficult to believe that Burke would not have known the contents of *Common Sense* – not least because it was widely abused in the British press, including the opposition press, when published. See John Sainsbury, *Disaffected Patriots: London Supporters of Revolutionary America 1769–1782* (Montreal: McGill-Queen's University Press, 1987), 127–8. Another reason for resisting this explanation might be the evidence concerning Hume and Price's friendship. Of course, Hume died on the eve of the American Revolution, and this might have provided the kind of watershed to their friendship that the French Revolution provided for Burke and Paine, but it remains striking that their disagreements were not thought an obstacle to their pleasure in each other's company. See *The Correspondence of Richard Price*, vol. I, *July 1748–March 1778*, ed. W. Bernard Peach and David Oswald Thomas (Cardiff: University of Wales Press, 1994), 45–7. Godwin and Samuel Parr might be a further example.

Paine's concern with popular sovereignty, and in particular the ongoing sovereignty of the people – evidenced in his demand for periodic renewal of legislation to ensure that each generation's sovereignty was not compromised by its inheritance from earlier generations – may also have been influenced by Rousseau.[30]

But there is no point in describing such commitments, as Jack Fruchtman does,[31] as republican. While Paine embraced the term from the early 1780s, the content he gave it was, as we shall see shortly, nothing more than representative government conducted in the public good. He saw no value in kings, but he was not looking for a mobilised republic, mass political virtue and an active and engaged citizenry. By the time he wrote his *Rights of Man, Part the Second*, his concern was more expressly libertarian: to cut government and taxation, and to enable all individuals to take their place within a commercial society by providing them with support in distress and an initial capital with which to begin adult life. Moreover, his demand for simplicity in government was of long standing, and, rather than being driven by a belief in the swelling of civic virtue among the citizenry, he relied wholly on the removal of corrupt, leech-like *political* excrescences on the *social* body – the court, its web of patronage, the sinecures and pensions by which the king and his ministers subverted representative institutions to their own ends. Without these elements, society was, as he said, in almost every aspect capable of self-regulation:

[T]he more perfect civilisation is, the less occasion it has for government, because the more does it regulate its own concerns and govern itself. . . All the great laws of society are laws of nature. Those of trade and commerce, whether with respect to the intercourse of individuals, or of nations, are laws of mutual and reciprocal interest. They are followed and obeyed because it is in the interest of the parties so to do.[32]

---

[30] On Burke's relationship to the French, see C. P. Courtney, *Montesquieu and Burke* (Oxford: Basil Blackwell, 1963); and David R. Cameron, *The Social Thought of Rousseau and Burke: A Comparative Study* (London: Weidenfeld & Nicolson, 1973). For a justly sceptical account of Paine's debts to Montesquieu and Rousseau, see A. Owen Aldridge, *Thomas Paine's American Ideology* (Newark: University of Delaware Press, 1984), chs 10, 11. Slightly less sceptical on Rousseau are John Keane's *Tom Paine: A Political Life* (London: Bloomsbury, 1995), 133; and Jack Fruchtman's *Thomas Paine: Apostle of Freedom* (New York: Four Walls/Eight Windows, 1994), 6.

[31] Fruchtman remarks: 'Paine spoke the language of virtue and corruption, the distinctive vocabulary of classical republicanism. His contemporary Edmund Burke . . . also spoke that language, although quite differently from Paine': *Thomas Paine: Apostle of Freedom*, 254. See also note 11 above.

[32] Thomas Paine, *Rights of Man, Part the Second*, in *Thomas Paine: Rights of Man, Common Sense and Other Political Writings*, 199–332, 216.

The great paradox in labelling Paine a republican – in any sense of the term connected to a view of the signal importance of politics in the ordering of human destinies – is that Paine's understanding of *politics* was a very narrow one (as was John Locke's). It was *society* that Paine represented as the basis for a consensual order, linked by commerce and mutual interest, with a very minimal degree of political intervention. The scope of politics was extremely narrow: representatives pass laws that the people periodically confirm or rescind, but society can be allowed, pretty much, to get on with its business without interference. Moreover, even at his most republican, in his *American Crisis* letters, Paine suggested that the classical world was not superior in its understanding of politics and government.[33]

Similarly, any republicanism in Burke is very much overdetermined. There is no doubt that he feared the corruption of the people, saw the political order as the source and guarantor of the social order, not something that merely grew from it, and had a profound sense of the fragility of that order, beset as it was by the weakness of men's capacity for self-restraint, the strength of their passions, and their tendency to grasp at power for their own ends. Indeed, it was the fragility of the political order – and that it was absolutely essential to social peace – that led him to insist that it be insulated from change:

[I]f that which is only submission to necessity should be made the object of choice, the law is broken, nature is disobeyed, the rebellious are outlawed, cast forth, and exiled from this world of reason, and order, and peace, and virtue, and fruitful penitence, into the antagonistic world of madness, discord, vice, confusion and unavailing sorrow.[34]

But is this republicanism? Or a Protestant concern with the consequences of the Fall? Or does it bear witness to a wide range of philosophical, cultural and political influences that simply cannot be captured by a single model or tradition?[35]

Burke's and Paine's acquaintance, and their pleasure in the other's company, might best be taken as evidence that they shared elements of a language and of a set of political reflexes that might dimly have echoed republicanism but that had, in England, by the last decades of the

---

[33] Thomas Paine, *The American Crisis*, letter V, in *The Life and Major Writings of Thomas Paine*, vol. I, ed. Philip S. Foner (Secaucus, NJ: Citadel Press, 1948), 106–29, 123: 'Could the mists of antiquity be cleared away, and men and things be viewed as they really were, it is more than probable that they would admire us, rather than we them.'

[34] Edmund Burke, *Reflections on the Revolution in France*, ed. Leslie Mitchell (Oxford University Press, 1993), 97.

[35] See J. G. A. Pocock, 'The political economy of Burke's analysis of the French Revolution', in *Virtue, Commerce, and History*, 193–214.

eighteenth century, become so broad and so tenuously related to other parts of the republican tradition that neither the tradition nor its idioms or rhetoric provided any real conceptual structure to the way in which people understood politics.[36]

This is not to deny that there are ways of defining republicanism that can give a reasonably tight formulation and that might allow us to classify eighteenth-century texts as either republican or not; but that is not a game with any great intellectual pay-off. A greater pay-off comes from the identification of a distinct paradigm of analysis and value with enduring significance. This is one major dimension of Skinner's and Pettit's accounts of the republican theory of liberty – one that I have no wish to impugn, since both have rightly drawn our attention to an understanding of liberty that modern accounts of the dichotomy between negative and positive liberty do not capture. But it is another question how much the historical dimension of their accounts adds to their case, and yet another as to whether that case can be sustained in the analysis of texts from the late eighteenth and early nineteenth centuries. For the historical dimension to work, we have to show that the model is identifiable in these texts, and that those who speak in its language or are seen as deploying its concepts were in fact committed to that model. To show that they were entails showing counterfactually that there were moves they could not have accepted or made, and that they could not have done so because their intellectual commitments were to a problematic that we have independently identified as republican – that is, that the language or paradigm had a 'grip on the mind' that fundamentally shaped the individual's perception of and responses to his/her political world. Being able to identify such a paradigm would be a considerable coup, but it is not an argument that is easily brought off. The case made by Pettit is that the core commitment of the republican models was to a conception of freedom as non-domination – to be contrasted with slavery, or subjection to another's arbitrary will. Law, on this view, secured people's

---

[36] There is a judicious and careful attempt to weigh the influence of republicanism in the movement for reform in Iain Hampsher-Monk's 'Civic humanism and parliamentary reform: the case of the Society of the Friends of the People', *Journal of British Studies* 18 (1979), 70–89. This takes the view that among the Friends of the People, and especially Wyvill and Francis, the civic humanist-republican tradition was still a salient paradigm. See also Claeys' 'Introduction' to *The Politics of English Jacobinism*, which shows republican influence on Thelwall, and on his early writings in particular. In both cases it can be argued that apparent republican commitments become abandoned during the course of the decade. The debates that took place in the Edinburgh Convention in 1792 transformed the lexicon of radicalism inherited from the Society of Constitutional Information in the very process of invoking it in debates among the popular extra-parliamentary organisations. See Melvin J. Lasky, *Utopia and Revolution* (University of Chicago Press, 1976), 512–17.

freedom, rather than acting as a constraint upon it, and participation, rather than being valued for its own sake (as the self-realisation of political man), was valued as a means to ensure non-domination. Skinner's account gives more prominence to participation, but the end of participation was liberty, and he too stresses the threat to freedom arising from dependence. Both are also concerned with the eclipse of this conception of freedom by the rise of a strictly negative conception of freedom, in which the absence of interference counted as liberty, with no concern for the resilience of that absence.

Three questions need to be asked. Is this conception of freedom necessary to characterise a theory as republican? Is it sufficient? And is this a conception of freedom that we can recognise as providing a major line of fissure in the political debates and struggles of the revolutionary period – one that acted as a basic set of constraining commitments and provided a sense of common concerns and ends for some of those involved? The answer to the first question must be negative (and would be recognised as such by both Skinner and Pettit): there are other strands in the classical republican legacy in which freedom as non-domination has no real place – as in Aristotle. Moreover, Rousseau's conception of moral liberty, as living in accordance with laws one prescribes for oneself, can be read as endorsing a self-realisation, rather than a non-domination, view. The question of sufficiency is less easily answered, although we can see what the criteria would be: we would need to be able to show that someone who held a non-domination account would inevitably be driven to endorse a number of other commitments that we recognise as distinctively republican. It might be thought, for example, that two such 'entailments' from the non-domination account of liberty can be identified: that if dependence is a source of unfreedom then virtual representation will be unacceptable; and it also follows that the only sure means for securing equal rights for citizens will be by linking civic freedom to a theory of civic equality. Moreover, if we accept these two conclusions we will also want universal suffrage and equal electoral representation.[37] At this point it must be clear that the term 'republican' might best be abandoned. Clearly, republicans have not always felt the force of this deduction; moreover, while the aversion to arbitrary authority and tyranny is of long standing within the republican tradition, these 'entailments' were hardly obvious to republicans writing prior to the end of the eighteenth century. This is not to deny that they became seen as entailments by some writers in this period, but the language and traditions of republican

---

[37] I owe these suggestions to Quentin's Skinner's extensive comments on an earlier version of this chapter.

argument were not themselves sufficient for that deduction to be made. This leaves the third question: is this a conception of freedom (whether or not we call it republican) that provided a major line of fissure in the political debates and struggles of the revolutionary period – one that acted as a basic set of constraining commitments and provided a sense of common concerns and ends?

This is not an easy question to answer; and it is not just the matter of intellectual difficulty that defeats the project. The position we have identified, which links liberty as non-domination to a critique of virtual representation and an advocacy of universal suffrage and equal civil rights, does not emerge until late in the eighteenth century. There is a difficulty, however, in distinguishing defences of universal suffrage that are motivated by non-domination theories of liberty and those that are deduced from natural rights claims, utilitarian premises or arguments about the sacrosanct quality of private judgement. In these alternative theories, the conclusions linked to non-domination may be independently motivated, and non-domination may itself be an effect of non-republican concerns (such as the sanctity of individual conscience, or epistemological concerns about the authenticity of belief) or may simply not be a component of these theories. To see the non-domination, republican model as a major contributor to the controversies around the American and French Revolutions, and to see it as linked to a continuous tradition of republican thinking and language (rather than emerging for the first time in these debates), requires that we succeed in linking those developing these arguments to earlier republican accounts of non-domination. The difficulty in doing this, however, is that the terrain of eighteenth-century political debate is simply too complex to allow such connections to be demonstrable. The historical evidence shows that most late eighteenth-century writers drew freely on a wide range of intellectual traditions and mobilised rhetoric from a variety of political languages. The eclecticism of their intellectual reference points led to extremely rich and fertile political debates, but what held these debates together – what allowed these very different perspectives to cross-fertilise and cohere – was that political controversy revolved around conflicting interpretations of the constitution, its institutions and its practices that were directly influenced by ongoing struggles in parliamentary politics. In this sense, the agenda that the vast majority of political commentators and political theorists shared was framed more by the institutions and the practical exigencies and conflicts of the British political system than by any particular language or intellectual model.

It is this institutionalised locus for political argument that made republicanism in eighteenth-century Britain both a part of the landscape – since a case can be made for saying that it was instrumental in framing the political structure – and extremist, in that its full-blown classical or Machiavellian form was persona non grata, after the Glorious Revolution, as a model for British political life. Because of the civil war, substantive republicanism remained tainted with king-killing and anarchy, while the domesticated, mixed-government variety allowed those within the political culture to retain a sense of their political importance within the nation by paying lip service to a language that was only a pale shadow of the original.[38] Furthermore, the moderate model easily accommodated a very wide range of political and philosophical argument and was easily reconciled with the developing sense of historical progress. Because eighteenth-century traditions of British political thought were so powerfully linked to the practices and institutions of the British state, they were largely insulated from outside influence (such as the French Enlightenment) and any such influences were partial, being tweaked, bent, moulded and slotted into what was a highly eclectic and extremely rich culture of political and philosophical discourse.

When Burke and Paine sat down to breakfast, therefore, and when they corresponded – even when they met, as they did, after the publication of the *Reflections on the Revolution in France* and with Paine publicly committed to replying to Burke, to discuss a matter of British foreign policy – they had this broad, tolerant, one might say politically and philosophically latitudinarian culture to buffer them against the intellectual principles and inclinations that a year or two down the road were to find them implacable opponents and enemies. Time and again, in studying the flourishing of radicalism (and loyalism) in Britain in the 1790s, one is struck by the fact that people who seemed broadly to share political positions in the 1770s and 1780s would, following the revolution controversy, take diametrically opposed views on the major political issues. This apparent transformation occurred because, when put to the test in the practical politics of the 1790s – and especially during the war with France – what gave way was precisely this latitudinarian culture of the political élite. In place of this tolerance they demanded lip service to the status quo among the élite and a disciplined mobilisation of the middle orders in defence of that order. And, in pursuit of that end, those seeking reform and a greater parity of representation were represented as irresponsible revolutionists and were rhetorically tainted with French

---

[38] See Lasky, *Utopia and Revolution*, 517: 'A hundred years of hard-headed and keen-witted political analysis, from Locke and Halifax to David Hume, had proved to be a stern taskmaster for the English mind. It was as if in the century since the Glorious Revolution, it had been thoroughly debriefed.'

republicanism in its most virulent form. Between 1791 and 1803 republicanism, as a mode of political thought and expression, underwent a fatal, final paroxysm: its corpse was strung up on loyalist gibbets in the market towns of England and its rhetoric put under charge for sedition before the local magistrates. Most crucially, for the case for a republican model, from this point on republicanism is no longer recognisable as a basic language of political debate and as a source of constraining commitments and common concerns in British politics.

III

While British republicanism had been increasingly domesticated and woven into the practical politics and controversies of the Hanoverian and Georgian state, French and American writers developed more radical, and often more classically driven, reinterpretations of republicanism in the course of their struggles against absolutism (in the first case) and their sense of colonial oppression (in the second), and subsequently in their revolutions. Rousseau's *Du Contrat Social* (1762) was invoked by revolutionary ideologues in France between 1791 and 1794 to legitimate the attempt to create a republic of virtue in which citizens would subordinate their private and personal interests to the demands of active participation in the civil and military institutions of the state. The public festival and the *levée en masse* were inspired by this more Spartan, more virtue-orientated conception of the republic, which subsequently became anathematised as an integral part of the Jacobin Terror. The American case was different again. Although historians of the American Revolution once insisted on its essentially liberal character, recent scholarship has properly emphasised the presence of powerful radical republican elements within the revolutionary movement. There was a potent mixture of republicanism and millennial religious thinking, a desire to shed the corrupt influence of Britain, and a sense that the colonies offered a unique refuge for the victims of tyranny that led to some enthusiastic republicanism, albeit as often religious as secular.[39] And there is, without doubt, a strong case for recognising the influence of British opposition traditions gone native.

Nonetheless, it was in the American Revolution that an innovation of considerable importance for British radicalism was made – and it was made by writers who specifically wished to resist the more classical variants of republicanism. A common tactic that moderates adopted to temper the

---

[39] See Ruth Bloch, *Visionary Republic: Millennial Themes in American Thought, 1756–1800* (Cambridge University Press, 1985).

more virulent brands of republicanism canvassed during the revolution was to take one feature of the tradition and to give it definitional status in their account. John Adams, for example, defined republicanism wholly in terms of 'an empire of laws, and not of men', and he left it to expedience and circumstance to settle the issue of what particular form would best realise that property: 'Of republics there is an inexhaustible variety, because the possible combinations of the powers of society are capable of innumerable variations.'[40] But the most successful redefinition was one used by Paine, and given canonical status by the Federalists. Paine combined some pretty florid republican rhetoric in both *Common Sense* and his *American Crisis* letters (1776–83) with an insistence that the only republican part of the British constitution was its representative part.[41] It was a definition with which he stuck. In July 1791 he worked with a similarly lean version of the doctrine when he proposed a republican constitution for France: 'By republicanism ... I understand simply a government by representation – a government founded upon the principles of the Declaration of Rights...'[42] Similarly, in contrast to a tradition stressing mixed govern-ment, civic virtue and participation, the dangers of commerce and the pursuit of the common good, the Federalists took the term to refer wholly to the institutional form of governance and treated republican government as a synonym for representative government; as James Madison put it, in *Federalist* no. 10, 'A republic, by which I mean a government in which the scheme of representation takes place...'[43] On David Wootton's account, Paine's definitional fiat was evidence of 'the most radical available defini-tion of the term', since it meant 'government by representatives of the people, unchecked by king or House of Lords, of the sort briefly established in England after the execution of the king in 1649'.[44] But the fact that an identical definition was being used by Madison might lead us to doubt that

---

[40] John Adams, *Thoughts on Government* (Boston: John Gill, 1776), reprinted in Charles S. Hyneman and Donald S. Lutz, eds., *American Political Writing during the Founding Era: 1760–1805*, vol. I (Indianapolis: Liberty Fund, 1983), 403–9. Of course, this is also a definition that Rousseau used in *Of the Social Contract*, Bk II, ch. 6: 'I therefore give the name "Republic" to every state that is governed by laws, no matter what the form of its administration may be...' Rousseau, while open on the question of the form of admin-istration or government, was not so when it came to the social, cultural and material conditions under which such a state could come into being, however.

[41] See Thomas Paine, *Common Sense*, in *Thomas Paine: Rights of Man, Common Sense and Other Political Writings*, 1–60, 8–10.

[42] Thomas Paine, 'Letter to the Abbé Sieyès', Paris, 8 July 1791.

[43] *The Federalist Papers*, ed. C. Rossiter (New York: New American Library, 1961), 81; see also no. 14, 100, and no. 39, 240–1.

[44] David Wootton, 'The republican tradition: from Commonwealth to *Common Sense*', in David Wootton, ed., *Republicanism, Liberty, and Commercial Society, 1649–1776* (Stanford University Press, 1994), 1–41.

the statement was indicative of a radical republicanism. Rather, it was radical *with respect* to republicanism, because it challenged the commonplaces of old Whig, Commonwealthman or country party thought; but it was itself republican only in the narrow sense that it denied a role for hereditary monarchical institutions. It was, however, radical *tout court* (that is, in its general historical significance – though, paradoxically, not in the American context in which Madison wrote), insofar as the principle of democratic representation was being linked with the principle of popular sovereignty through the institutions of representative government.[45] On this account, what is important about the redefinition is not that it offers us a radical republicanism – since it was not republican in any of the technical senses of that term – but that it shifts the debate about representation out of the republican paradigm and into a dramatically democratic and politically egalitarian one.[46]

As Arthur Sheps has shown, America provided an impressive model of a representative government that could be coupled with entirely non-republican justifications for universal suffrage. One source was natural rights theory – an account Paine gave (although it was only in his *Principles of Government* (1795) that it is fully developed);[47] others referred back to a mythical Anglo-Saxon constitution, predating the Norman yoke, in which universal manhood suffrage was believed to have been a central component; and still others were prepared to rest their claims on utility or expedience. This certainly did not happen overnight, but nor was the shift one of degree. Rather, Paine, and the American example of representative government more generally, offered a powerful model for political reform (both as an objective and, through the Constitutional Convention, as a blueprint) that could draw on an indigenous tradition of natural rights thinking while simultaneously undercutting the consensus that had existed around the institutions and practices of mixed government in the second half of the eighteenth century.[48] It clearly took Paine time fully to develop the implications of his opening move against the

---

[45] The best discussion of this aspect, albeit one that (perhaps because of its North American provenance) keeps the term 'republican' very much in play, is Arthur Sheps' unjustly neglected 'The American Revolution and the transformation of English republicanism', *Historical Reflections* 2 (1975), 3–28.

[46] See ibid., although Sheps tends to overstate both the directness of the link to political egalitarianism – slaves, for example, might have found the new republic no more egalitarian than its predecessor – and the immediacy of the impact of this aspect of the American Revolution on English radicals and reformers (on which see sec. IV).

[47] Thomas Paine, *Dissertation on the First Principles of Government*, in *Thomas Paine: Rights of Man, Common Sense and Other Political Writings*, 385–408, 398.

[48] See my 'The place of America in the debate on France: Thomas Paine's insertion', *Utilitas* 5 (1993), 221–37.

mixed-government tradition in *Common Sense*, and he only slowly came to believe that the American model could be applied in the *ancien régime* states of Europe. It also took others time to realise how radical a move it was when transported back to Europe – which is why Paine and Burke were not repelled by their ideological differences before the French Revolution. In both cases a major catalyst was the French Revolution, with Richard Price's express linking of it to the dawning of a new age of liberty in America prompting Burke into a vigorous assault on the opening events and upon those who sought to base reform of the institutions of the British state wholly on abstract principle. Moreover, the divisions were further deepened by the stark opposition between ideological principles generated by the loyalist campaigns of 1792/3.

IV

I have suggested that much eighteenth-century political discourse in Britain centred around issues, framed by constitutional practice concerned with the balance between legislature and executive and with the preservation of the rights and liberties of free-born Englishmen from encroaching executive despotism or arbitrary power. For the most part, it was assumed that a parliament independent from Crown control was a necessary condition for sustaining these liberties, and arguments about parliamentary representation were couched largely in terms of the need to ensure that representatives retained a degree of independence from the patronage powers of Crown or lords. Hence the significance of the majority of eighteenth-century debates about the suffrage. These revolved around the idea of a balance, even when they appealed to other values. Thus, natural rights doctrines could be used to justify an extension of the franchise; but there was certainly no automatic deduction of universal manhood suffrage, since something substantially short of this might be presented as delivering the appropriate balance and thereby the preservation of those rights. This was the line Locke used, and it was only with Price that having a say concerning one's representative became seen as a necessary (and sufficient) condition for preserving one's liberty. But it is interesting that Paine did not make this move – saying that it was necessary – until 1795.[49] Moreover, for the great majority of writers, even

---

[49] Although this may have been a tactical silence; in his *Rights of Man* (1791), he was defending the French Revolution against Burke's attack and would have had no interest in broadcasting what he perceived as its shortcomings. In *Part the Second* (1792) he used the American example rather than that of France, and his account could be taken as implying that universal manhood suffrage was axiomatic. When he did make the move, in

in the revolution controversy, there was no sense of there being a necessary or deductive relation between natural rights and full and universal rights to participation. Rather, there was a willingness, to a greater or lesser extent, to emphasise the importance of popular participation in representative systems so as to ensure that the system remained benign – most especially, that those exercising power did not overstep the legitimate bounds of that power. And ranged against such views were theorists who believed that the balance was well protected and that the existing system could be defended in terms of general utility and the legitimate claims of its various parts.

America broke with this pattern because it faced the practical task of starting from scratch to design a form of government, and it started out without an acknowledged and credible political élite and needing to justify the form of government to semi-sovereign states and already active citizens. But quite what lesson America had for British reformers was unclear, especially immediately following the revolution. It was widely seen as an exceptional case, with few implications for established social and political orders. The French Revolution changed this. It suggested that the exceptional case could be generalised to older, *ancien régime* states, and that representative democracy could be used to ground the entire state, rather than simply act as a constraint on the executive. With this thought introduced into British political discourse, and energetically promulgated throughout the social order through the circulation of *Part the Second* of the *Rights of Man* (in which Paine's arguments for representative government drew extensively on the American example), the loose consensus that reform would seek to preserve the framework of mixed government came to be questioned. This development, coupled with widespread popular radical activity, was seen as profoundly threatening to the status quo, and led to an attempt to denigrate reformers and friends of France alike by painting them in the most lurid colours as republicans and levellers, thereby simultaneously lumping French radicalism with the English Civil War – precisely the event upon the exclusion of which the 'long eighteenth century' was founded. The two events were also explicitly

Dissertation on the First Principles of Government, it is a moot point whether the driving principle was his doctrine of natural rights or whether the non-domination view of liberty motivated his account: 'The right of voting for representatives is the primary right by which other rights are protected. To take away this primary right is to reduce a man to a state of slavery, for slavery consists in being subject to the will of another, and he that has not a vote in the election of representatives, is in this case': Paine, *Dissertation on the First Principles of Government*, 398. The sense that the real force behind the claim is a natural rights one was reinforced by Paine's evident desire to link the point to a theory of resistance: 'It is possible to exclude men from the right of voting, but it is impossible to exclude them from the right of rebelling against that exclusion; and when all other rights are taken away, the right of rebellion is made perfect' (ibid., 399).

linked in the Association for Preservation of Liberty and Property against Republicans and Levellers, founded by John Reeves towards the end of 1792 as domestic turmoil launched France into both republicanism and internationalism (with British radicals enthusiastically celebrating French victories) – an organisation that sought to delegitimate all those seeking parliamentary reform on anything but the most minute scale, by linking their preference for wider representative institutions with doctrines of popular sovereignty and egalitarianism.[50]

Of course, this was a caricature. It was rare for any but the most exceptional (and often marginal) British political writer seriously to advocate the redistribution or equalisation of property (one of the few examples being Thomas Spence, whose artisan background and autodi-dacticism helped introduce into a new plebeian, urban radicalism classic civil war texts and a new agrarianism alike).[51] There were also few clear and obvious fully fledged Jacobin republican enthusiasts – even if there were enthusiasts for France and its revolution.[52] The great majority of pamphlets written in criticism of Burke's *Reflections* in what has become known as 'the debate on France' were moderate arguments for a more nuanced and sympathetic understanding of French events than Burke

---

[50] On the Reeves associations and the loyalism of this period, see my 'Vulgar conservatism 1792/3'.

[51] See Malcolm Chase, *The People's Farm: English Radical Agrarianism 1775–1840* (Oxford: Clarendon Press, 1989); and Thomas Spence's journal *Pig's Meat; or, Lessons for the People, Alias* (according to Burke) *THE SWINISH MULTITUDE* (London, 1794–5). For example, vol. 3, 21 (December 1794): 'It is a maxim – that *"Peace is the life of the commonwealth, liberty the soul of it, and the laws its body..."* and, therefore, the hateful measure of suspending the laws, under a pretended necessity of carrying out a cruel WAR against the advocates of LIBERTY, ought to be deemed an attempt to destroy the life, soul and body, *of the republic'* [emphasis in original]. In addition, Spence reproduced a number of short sections from Harrington in the journal, along with odd extracts from Gordon's *Discourse upon Tacitus, Cato's Letters* and others.

[52] See the discussion by Richard Dinmore, an alleged Jacobin, in *An Exposition of the Principles of the English Jacobins*. There are clear cases of more classical republican influences. For example, Daniel Eaton's *Politics for the People; or, A Salmagundi for Swine* (London: D. I. Eaton, 1794), vol. I, 29–33, paraphrased Machiavelli's account of Agathocles and Oliveretto of Fermo from chapter 8 of *The Prince*. In 'Reflections of a true Briton', vol. I, 128, we find tumult unimpeached: 'The republic of Rome increased in power and greatness, amid incessant and most violent distractions. Lutheranism made rapid progress amid the vast variety of schisms that seemed to threaten its destruction. Will France prove an exception to the general rule?' On the other hand, the journal was eclectic in its radicalism, and there was hardly a consistent republican language. For example, in contrast to the non-domination definition of 'liberty', Joseph Gerrald's pamphlet *A Convention the Only Means of Saving Us from Ruin* was cited: 'Every man at the age of 21, who is neither a criminal, an idiot, nor a lunatic, has a right of voting ... from this plan the following good effect will come. First, the people will enjoy not only civil liberty, but political liberty; that is to say, they will not only be free, but have the power of keeping themselves so': Eaton, *Politics for the People*, pt 2, no. 7.

had provided, often coupled with suggestions for the partial reform of the franchise in Britain to rectify 'abuses'. Indeed, Paine, who argued deductively from principles of natural right to the unique legitimacy of representative institutions within a constitution formed by a general convention, was widely regarded by reformers as too extreme – too much outside British traditions of popular radicalism, linked as these were to a very English constitutionalist idiom – to command widespread support.[53] On the other hand, his works were recognised as a powerful weapon in the development of a popular campaign for parliamentary reform, and as a powerful antidote to traditionalist defences of the status quo, and there is no doubt that they served to introduce to a wide audience the principles of representative government and popular sovereignty. For the most part, however, those leading the reform movement until at least the middle of the 1790s shared a historical experience of parliamentary institutions, and saw popular radicalism as remaining bounded by that experience. When they wrote for a popular audience they were, for the most part, concerned with correcting deficiencies and abuses, and extending participation. Even the more philosophically extreme, such as William Godwin, when he wrote for popular consumption, did so largely within the loosely Whig tradition; and the true commitments of those more practically involved in the struggle for reform should not be equated with their more extravagant off-the-cuff remarks.[54]

In its opening developments, the French Revolution prompted a wide renewal in both élite and popular interest in parliamentary reform, even though the most common initial reaction was that the French were merely catching up with the Glorious Revolution of 1688. But the reaction to it, initiated by Burke, became driven by the belief that the demand for political reform had turned into a tool for a revolutionary movement that would convulse and ultimately destroy the political, economic, social and religious life of France. At best, one form of absolutism was being replaced by another; at worst, France was succumbing to a despotism of unimaginable proportions, a democratic despotism (as Burke put it, 'a perfect democracy is the most shameless thing in the world' – a thought that was not foreign to the ancient Greeks). Those in sympathy with France were assumed to endorse everything that followed from the initial movement for reform. And those whose sympathies were coupled with demands for reform in Britain were portrayed as designing a similar

---

[53] See Epstein, *Radical Expression*, ch. 1; and Lottes, 'Radicalism, revolution and political culture', 84.
[54] See *The Political and Philosophical Writings of William Godwin*, vol. II, *Political Writings*; and my 'The fragmented ideology of reform'.

transformation in British political life – one in which the constitutional idioms of the past century would be swept aside, destroying the very fabric of English society. We need not assume that loyalists were always sincere, nor that there were not more local motives driving the polarising of political conflict in this way, but in a country whose political, religious, cultural and social life had attained considerable stability, after an earlier century of turmoil, the French example, coupled with the rapid spread of popular societies for reform, had a powerful galvanising effect. The result was that the old latitudinarian political culture was set aside – Fox described it as 'Pitt's reign of terror'[55] – and pressure for reform was seen as straightforwardly illegitimate (this under a first minister who had introduced his own bill for reform in parliament not ten years earlier). Moreover, as part of this reaction, republicanism came to be a weapon in the hands of loyalism: a brush to tar those seeking reform or questioning the established order. Its content was wholly imprecise – as was the use of the term 'Jacobin'. It covered proto-utilitarians such as Joseph Priestley, natural rights advocates for commercial society such as Paine, perfect-ibilists such as Godwin and Mary Wollstonecraft, and agrarians such as Spence. These men and women shared a set of sympathies, and a desire for political and social change, but in no way did they share a language, or paradigm or, indeed, a programme – and the term 'republicanism' served not as a term of art but as a rhetorical ploy designed to smear those pressing the case for reform. It was one whose use accelerated after the summer of 1791 and as Britain and France edged towards war in the following year.

By the middle of the 1790s, with Britain and France engaged in an ideologically driven war with unprecedented levels of popular and military mobilisation, the old latitude and tolerance of political controversy was gone. In part it was simply held in abeyance until the end of the conflict, but in one crucial respect it was well and truly dished. In the course of the decade a fundamental shift in the character of political and ideological conflict in Britain had taken place, partly linked to the Europe-wide response to the French Revolution and partly in response to the emer-gence of the mass-based movement for parliamentary reform. Whereas the emphasis in political argument prior to the 1790s had been directed against the usurpation of power by those in public office, most centrally the king and the court, in Britain the French Revolution and the struggles over domestic reform were linked to create a profound distrust of the people among the political élite (albeit a distrust for which there were

---

[55] Goodwin, *The Friends of Liberty*, 390.

extensive existing intellectual resources and recent experience to build on – in the form of popular politics at the accession and in the Gordon riots). At the same time, the rhetoric of anti-republicanism served to delegitimate the view that the Crown posed the major threat to the liberties of the people. One consequence was that, despite the fact that Painite radicalism and a democratic platform became an increasingly integral part of the early nineteenth-century popular movement for the reform of the franchise, radicals from the 1790s onwards were generally constrained to argue their case within the older constitutional idiom, to play down democratic and egalitarian ambitions and to switch their attack from the Crown to the government and its ministers. Moreover, the fear of mass popular mobilisation divided the reform movement into two broad wings, parliamentary and extra-parliamentary, and ensured that the admission of the latter within the public political culture of the early nineteenth century was at best partial and grudging. The early nineteenth century alternated between periods of association between the two, when the reform programme was moderate and constitutional, and periods of mass mobilisation, when these links were broken. The language and aspirations of popular politics and those of parliamentary circles and the ruling élite remained permanently in tension, with a modified consti-tutionalism becoming a tactical idiom for reformist demands, and with this sitting uneasily alongside a much more democratic and egalitarian programme for political reform – including universal suffrage and annual parliaments – which formed an increasingly central part of the radical canon.[56] In the long run the popular movement became dislocated from élite and parliamentary forces, facilitating flirtations between popular radicalism and still more egalitarian, proto-socialist and utopian doc-trines, and, correspondingly, a further exacerbation of élite fears.

In both America and France the masses had stepped onto the political stage at the end of the eighteenth century, and it was accepted that they could never thereafter be wholly excluded and somehow had to be accom-modated and disciplined within representative institutions. In Britain, however, the whole tenor of political reaction to France was couched in terms of a profound distrust of the masses, and fears for the safety of the

---

[56] John Belchem, 'Republicanism, popular constitutionalism and the radical platform in early nineteenth-century England', *Social History* 6 (1981), 1–32; Epstein, *Radical Expression*. See also Philip Harling, 'Leigh Hunt's *Examiner* and the language of patrio-tism', *English Historical Review* 111 (1996), 1159–81, for a useful discussion of the balance between Painite and constitutionalist idioms in the postwar reform movement – although it makes, on the above account, too much of parallels between Hunt's patriotism and Country Party traditions.

country's ancient and venerable institutions in the face of popular sovereignty. In Britain, more than in either revolutionary case, the gradual move to liberal democratic institutions was made extremely slowly, with the élite insisting that the trade-off between those institutions and liberalism and democracy be in favour of the former. Most crucially, the masses were enshrined as the prime threat to the political order. The concerns of the previous century with shoring up the system against the potential for arbitrary rule by the executive were finessed by associating the ultimate form of arbitrary rule with populist democracy – the most shameful thing. In this development, the idioms and rhetorics of political debate open to reformers were dramatically altered. Arguments for the extension of the franchise and democratic participation were couched in terms of a reform of representation to eliminate corruption from parliament, but they were expressed alongside lip service to a Burkean sense of the organic nature and historical legitimacy of the constitution and to the sanctity of the Crown.[57] Popular radicalism nonetheless retained a democratic wing, but it found little scope for expression within the mainstream of the political culture, and the real casualties were the rhetoric and symbolism of eighteenth-century republicanism.

I have expressed doubts as to how far republicanism played a substantive political role in the second half of the eighteenth century, but its language, exemplars, symbols and rhetorical flourishes were certainly present. Moreover, they could be found not just among the political and parliamentary élite but also in the broader public culture of the country in the eighteenth century. As such, they contributed to a widely shared and tolerant political culture, with the aspirations for reform firmly linked to existing institutional practices and traditions and often resulting in a preference, in the broader culture, for an extension of the popular elements of the constitution, in particular its representation. This culture was profoundly ruptured by the American and French Revolutions. The reaction to the French Revolution made the latitudinarianism and eclecticism of British political discourse a source of weakness, and republican language a positive danger, given the need (especially pressing during the war) for a mobilised and united nation. Largely as a result of the war with France, the early nineteenth-century British state became a nation state, no longer just a fiscal-military apparatus; the people were no longer an agglomeration, but a mobilised unity with national symbols and a national

---

[57] This is linked to the dramatic rise in the popularity of the king. See Colley, 'The apotheosis of George III'. See also Peter Spence, *The Birth of Romantic Radicalism* (Aldershot: Scolar Press, 1996).

identity. Although France did not cause all this, its revolutionary and internationalist path, together with the level of mobilisation required by the war, forced the pace of existing trends. As French and Civil War republicanism were simultaneously anathematised, speakers sought (after a period of quietism) other terms in which to articulate their beliefs. Alternative principles and foundations – natural rights, utilitarianism, private judgement, economic and land reform, and so on – had coexisted for at least half a century alongside this more classical language, but in many cases these too were yoked to republicanism and 'French principles' and proved uncertain allies in the new political climate. The safest course, and one that dominated the reform movement for the first third of the century, was to adopt a Burkean reverence for the constitution and to focus on less abstract justifications and less threatening targets within that framework.[58]

This narrowing of focus should not be allowed to obscure the fact that the political culture of early nineteenth-century Britain had become sharply divided, between those linked to parliamentary institutions and those excluded, and – running parallel to this distinction – between a predominantly conservative attitude to political order, with a deep reluctance to concede demands for changes in representation, and an increasingly radical democratic movement, looking for political, economic and social reform. Above all, the old acknowledgement of the importance of popular participation was repudiated by both the political élite and many of the middle ranks, who shrank from the images of popular revolutionary violence purveyed by loyalists and historians alike. With their aspirations for democratic equality being repeatedly denied, the popular reform movement came increasingly to link political equality with social and economic equality.[59]

---

[58] Justifications that could not be denied by their opponents – as is clear from the prosecution of John Reeves for publication of an extremist loyalist pamphlet in 1795 that insisted on the primacy of the crown within the English constitution. See Eastwood, 'John Reeves and the contested idea of the constitution'. Of course, some writers, such as Richard Carlile, were prepared to avow a fully blown Painite republicanism: see Epstein, *Radical Expression*, 119–36.

[59] Pettit's suggestion, that the non-domination view of liberty was increasingly eclipsed by a negative liberty view, in part at the hands of Paley and Bentham, can certainly find support in the above argument (see his *Republicanism*, 41–50). While we may disagree about how extensively and consciously held the non-domination view was (and about what might motivate it, and whether 'republican' is the best way of describing it), his point that the turn of the century saw the rise of a negative conception of liberty seems extremely plausible and explicable in terms of the way that élite political discourse increasingly perceived the central political problem as one of sustaining state sovereignty and the rule of law against incursion by the people.

V

On this view, there is a case for English exceptionalism – a case for saying that in Britain the real flourishing of republican thought took place in the seventeenth century, and that its fruit (although it was a case of a multiple parenting) was the Revolution Settlement and subsequently the union, which helped frame a broad consensus in which its role was increasingly decorative. This consensus lasted until the American and French Revolutions, when, in formulating its resistance to that age as a repugnance for Jacobinism, republicanism and the triumph of the mob, the British state anathematised republican rhetoric and inverted the eighteenth-century commonplace so as to represent the people as the primary example of arbitrary and tyrannical authority. This inversion locked the British state into a dogged resistance to popular participation, pushed popular radicalism towards increasingly radical agendas that combined political with social and economic reform and rendered the language of republicanism unusable.[60]

How should we evaluate this outcome? On the one hand, the loss of a little republican rhetoric seems relatively harmless. We must set against this, however, the way that, with republicanism brushed aside, the patrician hegemony of the eighteenth century – which had provided a shared paradigm of politics and system of values within which to argue – was replaced by a much more resolutely elitist and exclusive state, on the one hand, and, on the other, by a popular reform movement with an agenda that found little echo of support in parliamentary circles. Furthermore, although I have been concerned with classical republicanism and its successors, we should also recognise that, while straightforwardly anti-monarchical feeling remained a current of fluctuating strength in the eighteenth century,[61] the older paradigm and rhetoric had offered a significant channel for its expression – a channel open equally to popular and élite forces. The elimination of that rhetoric – and its polemical linking with regicide, anarchy and tyranny – committed élite political discourse to a constitutional monarchism that subsequently so dominated British

---

[60] This paints the picture in broad strokes. A more detailed picture, in which we can see the Foxite Whigs as driven to pass the Reform Act of 1832 by a long-standing and unrevised conviction that the Crown remained the prime threat to the constitution, is given by Leslie Mitchell, 'Foxite politics and the Great Reform Bill', *English Historical Review* 108 (1993), 338–64. Their willingness to use the popular movement for their ends should not, however, be taken as evidence that they had any sympathy for the democratic movement; a reform bill that enlarged the electorate from 14 per cent to 18 per cent of the population needs to be treated as equivocal evidence of support for popular radicalism. Compare this account with the argument that the Crown was increasingly an object of veneration by Spence, *The Birth of Romantic Radicalism*, 7–8, 11, 15.

[61] See E. P. Thompson, 'Patricians and plebs', in *Customs in Common*, 16–96, esp. 92–3.

political culture that republicanism (both in its classical form and in its more popular form of anti-monarchical sentiment) has remained a marginal and impotent political force ever since. The French Revolution, on this view, provided the opportunity and the incentives for British political culture to turn its back on democracy and popular sovereignty and to forge a national identity around the symbols of the monarchy, the established Church and the accompanying aristocratic, inegalitarian and anti-populist institutions and commitments.

The resolutely Parliamentarist constitution hymned by Edmund Burke refused popular sovereignty in principle, but conceded many of its discrete effects in practice over a suitably immemorial timescale. Regrouped around the Monarchy and the Crown-in-Parliament mythology, this profoundly elitist structure has simply imitated the later models of democratic polity by an interminably staged and necessarily superficial process of 'modernization'. But of course, the very success and longevity of this strategy has also held populism permanently at bay. Egalitarianism in the democratic sense was partly absorbed and partly (the more important part) broken.[62]

The 'Crown-in-Parliament mythology' must not be confused with the doctrine of mixed government. It inverted the traditional suspicion towards those who rule and turned it towards those who are ruled. Seventeenth- and eighteenth-century republicanisms were not, for the most part, democratic, but they did have some conception of the people – albeit often narrowly defined – in whom they had ultimately to place their trust, for a corrupt people could never sustain or produce a non-corrupt government. Faced with the threat of a sudden broadening of 'the people' during the 1790s, such remnants of earlier republicanism were jettisoned in favour of an anti-populist construal of the political order as centred around the 'Crown-in-Parliament'. Through this inversion, the language of eighteenth-century republicanism was left behind – becoming a resource of antiquarian interest, but no longer a political paradigm or an avowable language.[63]

---

[62] See Tom Nairn's discussion in *The Enchanted Glass: Britain and Its Monarchy* (London: Hutchinson, 1988), 185; see also 134–7, 181–5.

[63] Godwin, who in 1801 described himself as having fallen 'in one common grave with the cause and love of liberty' (in his reply to Parr's Spital Sermon), attempted to revive interest in English Civil War republicanism in his *History of the Commonwealth of England: From Its Commencement, to the Restoration of Charles the Second*, 4 vols. (London: H. Colburn, 1824–8). See John Morrow, 'Republicanism and public virtue: William Godwin's *History of the Commonwealth of England*', *Historical Journal* 34 (1991), 645–64. Francis Burdett also confessed, in his letters, to an interest in the work of Harrington and Bolingbroke, as did Leigh Hunt. See John Dinwiddy, 'Sir Francis Burdett and Burdettite radicalism', in *Radicalism and Reform in Britain, 1780–1850* (London: Hambledon Press, 1992), 109–23; and Harding, 'Leigh Hunt's *Examiner* and the language of patriotism'.

5 Failing the republic: political virtue and vice in the late eighteenth century

Aristodamus, the Spartan, was one of only two survivors of the three hundred who went with Leonidas to Thermopylae. He and Eurytus were stricken by a serious eye infection and released by Leonidas from active service. Come the battle, Eurytus, although blind, had a slave dress him and guide him to the fighting, where he was turned loose to stand and die. Pantites, who had been sent with a message to Thessaly, also survived. Both returned to Sparta to be reviled as cowards. Herodotus reports that Pantites hanged himself, while Aristodamus (to whom no one would give a light for his fire or exchange words with him) redeemed himself by his bravery at Platea.[1]

These men were shamed. The culture of which they were a part understood the nature of war, the sacrifices it called for, the solidarity upon which it rested and the glory it offered those who gave their everything for their country, in such a way that, even when happenstance made it impossible for those formally committed to the body of warriors to fight, they were nonetheless seen as cowards. This judgement was one that they shared; there is no sense that they felt its unfairness, and they took steps to erase the judgement either by taking their own lives or by redeeming themselves by a display of heroism – although that redemption could have a seemingly cruel twist: Aristodamus's deeds at Platea, although magnificent, were deemed less so because it was assumed that he wished to die to expunge the stain on his name.[2] Being a Spartan was not, it seems, easy!

We find it difficult to say that Aristodamus was at fault. There are stories that he was in fact a messenger and that he dawdled on the way back to avoid the battle; and, if he had done that, then we might want to attach some blame to him, and might expect him to have a sense of guilt (perhaps that is what drove Pantites to suicide). But in most stories Aristodamus comes down to us as shamed, as seen by others in a certain way: unworthy,

---

[1] Herodotus, *The Histories*, Bk 7, paras. 229–32.   [2] Ibid., Bk 9, para. 71.

not living up to the sacrifice of his equals and falling short (which he might equally have done had he fought, been wounded and left for dead, and nonetheless survived). It is a classical case of Herbert Morris's distinction between shame and guilt: Aristodamus did not violate a rule, he did not fail to meet some minimal standard of expectation and he was not in any clear sense at fault. He was unlucky, and he was shamed by his community. His only recourse was to re-establish his standing in the eyes of others.[3]

Aristodamus is certainly not alone. In Rome, *pudor* or shame was an ever-present anxiety – something that one could bring upon oneself, but also something that might arise from a state of affairs over which one had no control, but which nonetheless implicates one's standing.[4] Robert Kaster gives the example of Quinctius Capitolinus Barbatus, who assumed the consulship as Rome's Italian enemies were at the gates of the city, and who addressed the citizens in the following terms: 'Fellow Romans, although my conscience is clear, I meet you in this place with bitter shame. . . [H]ad I known that such a disgrace was in store for us this year of all years, I should have shunned it by any means in my power – by exile or death if there was no other way of avoiding office.'[5] Again, it is through no fault that Quinctius felt shame, but shame he certainly did feel – and he could remove it only by rousing the people and defeating their enemies.

Politics comes in many forms, and the demands that it makes on its participants, and its subjects, vary considerably, from one historical epoch to another, from state to state and from tradition to tradition. There are political theories, models and languages that show a relative degree of consistency in the type of demands made of politicians and citizens, however. Indeed, one way of recognising a consistency across different texts, speeches and utterances is by identifying a core set of commitments and expectations that are common to a range of different thinkers. Republicanism offers one such example, although there are issues about what exactly is being identified: a theory, a paradigm, a tradition or a language? Aristodamus stands at the prehistory of this tradition – someone caught in the realities of the Spartan state and the expectations of its political culture. The theorisation of Sparta is something that was undertaken largely post hoc, in part by Xenephon and Plutarch, but revisited regularly through time, and in the eighteenth century becoming common

---

[3] Herbert Morris, 'Guilt and punishment', *The Personalist* 52 (1971), 305–21.
[4] See the magnificent analysis by Robert A. Kaster, *Emotion, Restraint, and Community in Ancient Rome* (Oxford University Press, 2005), ch. 2.
[5] Livy, *History of Rome*, Bk III, sect. 67, lines 1–2; cited by Kaster.

as a picture of what we have become too corrupt to sustain – and common to others as a past that has little attraction for modern man. Livy and Cicero's Rome provides a similar source of images of commitment to the public realm and an intense identification with the republic, and one that is similarly recalled throughout subsequent ages.

I

I start with Aristodamus largely to tease out something that is not often commented on in his case, or in the case of republican virtue more widely. As I have suggested, Aristodamus was shamed. But his failure was not a matter of blame, in that what he failed to do was not a function of an ill or a weak will. Nor was it something that he could have undone. Eurytus, it is true, plunged into the fray to die, but I assume that we think there was something pointless about this (not to say rather dangerous – a loose cannon in one's midst?). This suggests that Aristodamus could not have felt guilt for what he had not done and could not have done. His vice was not a lack of a quality, not the presence of an evil intent, not a case of having given in to an inclination he was expected to constrain; it was something over which he had no control (save in the sense that he could act to expunge the shame attached to him). Indeed, it would be odd to think he should repent or feel contrite, and odd to think he could in any way make amends (since it is not clear to whom amends could or should be made). All these senses seem to attach to ideas of guilt and blame, but they do not seem to comport with Aristodamus's shame. He did not violate some rule but fell short of a (truly exacting) standard; he did not cheat or break faith with others but failed himself, and by doing so he demeaned his standing in relation to others and his own worth as a Spartan. By hypothesis (since Aristodamus did not leave us his thoughts) he was shamed to the extent that he shared his compatriots' view of him and regarded himself as unworthy of a light from the fires of others or of conversation with others. His only recourse was not to make amends to others but to become a person who was not shameful, to become someone who could stand seeing himself in the sight of others – and he could do this only by a glorious death.

I make no claim for Aristodamus as a republican hero – he is little discussed – but I am interested in him as a case of republican failure, or vice. He raises an interesting question about the resources that republicanism has, as a theoretical framework or language, to understand the character of people's shortfall of virtue – not just the causes of that shortfall, but what it is to fall short. Machiavelli clearly discussed at least some people in terms that implied that they should feel shame; that it was not that Caesar broke a rule, or failed in a relationship of obligation, but that he lacked the *virtù* – failed to show the extraordinary character and ability – that would have been required to resuscitate the Roman Republic as it breathed its last. In demanding such *virtù*, Machiavelli seems to be operating against a background that implied a shame culture – that is, a culture in which conformity to rules or norms is not enough; in which obligation between agents is not the central concern; in which the focus is on what it is worthy and fitting to want and to reach for. Of course, the republican side of Machiavelli does seem to imply that settled political rule involves the rule of law and that the citizen should live under the law – constrained by it, his/her relations with others ruled by it and his/her responsibilities delineated by it – but that sounds less like a shame culture and more like a rule-based culture. But that characterisation is somewhat puzzling, because, although obeying the law is a matter of crossing a threshold, civic virtue seems to demand more than mere conformity.

I do not want to trespass on areas about which others are so much better versed, but I do want to suggest that thinking about the implied causes and experience of derogations of virtue and of vice may help us to see that a number of tensions affect attempts to construct a consistent republicanism as a political theory in the eighteenth century. These tensions are not so easily recognisable when the focus is given over to a celebration of the virtues of the republican citizen or the institutions of republican rule, which are standard fare in a great deal of the literature. Moreover, I want to suggest that the contrast between shame and guilt cultures is an illuminating one in thinking about how uncomfortably a classical picture of republican virtue sits with many of the developments in eighteenth-century political thought. That said, I am certainly not suggesting that every form of republicanism operates with a shame morality, rather than a guilt one (although I do think there is something in this, and I return to it later). Rather, the distinction that seems to me to be pertinent is that between scale and threshold moralities. In much political thought the concern is with ensuring that those in politics, and outside it, meet certain minimal (often legally defined) standards of conduct, whereby their motives for doing so are of instrumental but not intrinsic interest; this is a threshold morality. What the examples of Aristodamus and Quinctius indicate is a different set of concerns – ones in which individuals' duties go beyond any set of rules and arise from a communal sense of what it is that virtue demands given the roles they play and the dangers facing the state. What this demands may vary from the prosaic to the impossible, but that is in the nature of a scale morality. Those who are defeated in a war may fall short of the demands of virtue and be shamed, even when those demands are inhumanly high.

One central part of the classical republican inheritance is this implicit scale morality – a culture whose demands are not limited to rules and laws but that expects citizens be prepared to sacrifice all for the sake of their *patrie*. This theory may still define people's liberty in terms of the laws under which they live, and the absence of dependence; but the rhetoric that seems so central to the tradition is one that conceives of a public good, shared and identified with by all citizens, each of whose own good is dependent on the preservation of that wider good. At its best, the republic is a community of sentiment and judgement that weighs the virtues of all in terms of their contribution to meeting the demands that the political culture faces. Those who cheat and connive against the system are deemed corrupt, but so too are those who limit their commitment, who toe the line but lack virtuous motives, and those who think of their engagement with the state as delimited by the extent to which it serves their interests. Vices in this theory are not simply (indeed, may not be) derelictions of the law; they are failures of virtue, and in that sense it seems plausible to claim that a scale morality underlies much republican thinking. Moreover, for many writers, the aspiration for a republican order is an aspiration for a scale culture in which the bonds between members are such as to call forth the highest qualities of civic virtue.

The tensions in eighteenth-century thought were many, but I want to draw attention to four areas in particular that I see as contributing to eighteenth-century British political thought in a way that disturbed and muted the classical republican inheritance, and eventually led to its displacement by other models: the acknowledgement of self-interest; the recognition of legitimate opposition; the depoliticisation of virtue; and the revaluation of the nature of punishment in law. It should be obvious from such a statement that this is a sketch of an argument, and as such it is surely flawed. My concern is really to see whether there might be something other than flaws in it.

II

In contrast to the commitment to a republican virtue in which the standard of evaluation is a model of the virtuous citizen – a standard that is a scale value (not a threshold that we must cross, but a standard against which we measure ourselves, and feel shamed if we fall short of what it demands in any particular situation, even if that is barely humanly possible) – the eighteenth century came consistently to recognise that the agent is not (cannot be) wholly focused on a political identity to which everything else is subordinate, but has a range of interests and passions, many of which are private in character but that nonetheless have a legitimate claim both on the self and on the respect and forbearance of others. Indeed, following Bernard Mandeville, there was an increasing recognition that the pursuit of private interests – even rampant self-interest – has benefits for the state as a whole, through the development of an economy that is capable of meeting a diverse range of interests, passions and tastes. To have those tastes and to appreciate those refinements is not to fail in virtue, but it carves out a domain for the individual that trespasses on the traditional demands that virtue can make. Of course, the endorsement is not unequivocal; there is a sense that such tastes have bounds in polite and the civil society, within which a sense of continence is maintained. But there remains, nonetheless, a tension, between validating a sphere of private consumption and the pursuit of interests, and the sense that the demands of political virtue could be exclusive of all other claims.[6] If republican political virtue is a scale morality, then it sits uncomfortably with the acknowledgement of domains that set limits on what that scale can demand.

How can we demonstrate that the conception of morality was changing in this way in the eighteenth century? I am not sure we have to, so much as to show that there were competing languages, practices and judgements that operated on very different principles from republicanism, and that created tensions in the way that people thought about the public sphere, making the more republican claims less likely to carry authority. For example, David Hume's moral psychology was one that was centrally concerned with thresholds, with the observance of rules and propriety, with the internalisation of guilt and with the sense that blame attaches appropriately only to those who intentionally violate some standard or rule. Nor is it a case of singling out Hume or the Scottish Enlightenment in general, since they were simply instances of a more general development of threshold secular moralities in the eighteenth century that inevitably constrained the scale moralities associated with civic virtue, placing limits on the demands that political virtue can make. (My sense is that some theologically inspired moralities also do this, although they may do so either by operating a threshold account, or by having a scale account (of religious duty) that is seen as dominant over politics. Clearly, there are occasions, as in the radical reformation, when a theologically inspired scale morality dovetails with a political scale morality.) But the overall picture is one in which the very language of virtue and vice was fractured between these dramatically different perspectives, and that served to constrain the potential for the hegemony that a scale morality demands.

---

[6] In Raz's sense, of denying them weight as reasons: Joseph Raz, *Practical Reasons and Norms* (Oxford University Press, 1975), 35–48.

III

There are two related stories concerning legitimate opposition here. The first concerns the growing acceptance of political opposition and of party within the British political system, from a period in the seventeenth century when differences were tolerated only insofar as it was clear that they were temporary (not persistent factions) and concerned with the same goal: the pursuit of the public interest or good. In the course of the eighteenth century, as Caroline Robbins has argued, the language of party gradually lost its connotations as merely a cover for faction – the attempt to seize rule in the private interests of a group or section within the state – and became respectable.[7] The term 'His Majesty's loyal opposition' may not have been coined until 1826,[8] but the sense of party differences as legitimate and functional developed throughout the preceding century. There are, indeed, some markedly early examples, as John Gunn has shown,[9] in which political pluralism and religious pluralism were linked and demonstrated to be beneficial to the political health of the polity. There is a long-standing tradition of mixed government that countenances and values tensions between different social classes in the state, but the real development was the sense that groups within the same class could disagree fundamentally on issues of policy and principle, but could do so within a shared constitutional framework that these disagreements did not throw into question. This was by no means wholly secure before the nineteenth century (it is difficult not to see the Regency crisis as raising matters of fundamental and constitutional significance through partisan strife; and the extra-parliamentary reform movement in the last decade of the eighteenth century was something else entirely: being denied legitimacy as an interest or a party) but the political system did develop a substantially higher degree of consolidation than it had had at the beginning of the century, in that political and constitutional forms shaped and constrained their participants' conduct and the expression of their partisanship and differences. When the going got tough, quite fundamental issues were raised for some about how far the order had itself been subverted by those claiming to act in its defence, prompting sympathies for alternative forms of political action and political pressure, or withdrawal from the political system (as with Fox after 1797); but the party

---

[7] Caroline Robbins, '"Discordant parties": a study of the acceptance of party by Englishmen', *Political Science Quarterly* 73 (1958), 505–29.
[8] See Archibald S. Foord, *His Majesty's Opposition 1714–1830* (Oxford: Clarendon Press, 1964), 1.
[9] John Gunn, 'Party before Burke: Shute Barrington', *Government and Opposition* 3 (1968), 223–40.

system held, and by surviving the crisis it further legitimated the political process.

In many ways, the most extreme example of legitimated partisanship is provided by *The Federalist Papers*, and especially *Federalist* no. 10. In that discussion, the heterogeneity of interests, and the private character of those interests, become a central part of the theory of the political system – a system that resists falling prey to faction by its multiplication – a system united by division.

There are obvious precursors to this in theories of institutional design – in which institutions shape and constrain people's actions, and in which these are seen as having a basically passionate or interest-based character – and one such precursor is to be found in the language of republicanism. To call for the rule of good men in the expectation of getting good laws is to reverse the proper order: '[*G*]*ive us good orders and they will make us good men* is the *Maxime* of a *Legislator* and the most *infallible* in the *Politickes*.'[10] Although there is an obvious fallacy in this position (as it is not clear where the good orders and the virtuous legislator come from), the position is an important one, since it suggests a new relationship between natural feelings and motives, on the one hand, and the ends that men and women pursue in politics; no one, not even a '*nobleman*', need '*own a shame for preferring his own interest before that of a whole nation*'.[11]

Note that this suggests a threshold morality, dependent on the right rules and the right incentives, and leaving to each a sphere for his/her private concerns and morality. The point at which Harrington (and the whole neo-Roman tradition that Quentin Skinner identifies) begins to wobble, however, concerns the extent to which this threshold morality actually obscures the demand for a deeper commitment to the pursuit of the common good as a necessary prerequisite for individual liberty. I lack the space to tackle this definitively, but the following brief sketch indicates the problem. If we take individuals to be self-interested maximisers then we have two problems. First, the problem of design becomes extreme: we have to ensure that free-riding and opportunistic rule-breaking are systematically penalised, and have to ensure that those who penalise are similarly constrained, and those who regulate those who penalise are similarly constrained, and so on. The demands on the legislator are extreme, both because such intricate design seems beyond

---

[10] James Harrington, 'The model of the Commonwealth of Oceana', in *The Political Works of James Harrington*, ed. J. G. A. Pocock (Cambridge University Press, 1977), 156–359, 205; the passage is cited by Rahe, *Republics Ancient and Modern*, 412.

[11] James Harrington, 'The prerogative of popular government', in *The Political Works of James Harrington*, 389–566, 468 [emphasis in original]; cited by Rahe, *Republics Ancient and Modern*, 412.

the reach of ordinary mortals and because it assumes that those who design and implement such a programme are not themselves subject to the motives that the theory assumes drive ordinary mortals. If, on the other hand, people want republican liberty – that is, if they want their liberty as a collective, with a clear recognition that their individual liberty is conditional on and framed by the liberty of the state as a whole – then the demands of that collective liberty seem to be demands for virtue, for a willingness to put the interests of the collective before one's own; and those demands will not be a threshold but a scale demand: we must do whatever it is necessary to do if we are to preserve the liberty of our state, for our own liberty is conditional upon it.

This is a core tension for a neo-Roman account of liberty[12] – a tension that in many cases plays out in the complex relationship between interests, liberty and virtue in many of these writers. The relationship is complex, in large part, because the registers in which each dimension is discussed often differ, so that the analytic clarity about interests and design is often complemented by direct but less precise appeals to liberty, and put together with a more exhortatory emphasis on the importance of virtue. The English emphasis on republican liberty and its yoking to the rule of law are clear expressions of concern about the dangers of arbitrary political rule. But this focus does not mean that the demands placed on those who aim at republican rule are not scale rather than threshold in character. Those who advocated the neo-Roman position were well aware of more traditional concerns about the extent to which internal liberty was linked to the pursuit of *grandezza*, the dominance of one's external enemies and the acquisition of empire. These were positively linked, and also negatively, since the experience of empire would lead to the republic's fall, just as the failure to pursue it would.[13] So, while the stress on liberty indicates a partial shift in emphasis and makes the scale character of the position less obvious, it does not break from the concerns with war and expansion that underline the fact that such a morality remains essential.

In the hands of Hume, the account of interests in government takes a still more pointedly pessimistic tack in relation to the design of institutions: '[I]n contriving any system of government, and fixing the several checks and controuls of the constitution, every man ought to be supposed a *knave*, and to have no other end, in all his actions, than private

---

[12] See Skinner, *Liberty before Liberalism*.
[13] David Armitage, 'Empire and liberty: a republican dilemma', in Martin van Gelderen and Quentin Skinner, *Republicanism: A Shared European Heritage*, vol. II, *The Values of Republicanism in Early Modern Europe* (Cambridge University Press, 2002), 29–46.

interests.'[14] Hume's position has been argued to have greatly influenced the Founding Fathers in their deliberations, with much justification: 'If men were angels no government would be necessary. If angels were to govern men, neither external nor internal controuls on government would be necessary... You must first enable the government to controul the governed; and in the next place, oblige it to controul itself.'[15] As Paul Rahe has argued, while the classical republican example loomed large in the imaginations of many leading Americans at the start of the American Revolution, the post-revolutionary period saw many abandon their uncritical respect for Greek and Roman traditions of patriotic sacrifice and civic virtue, to admit a dramatically larger role for commerce, the civilised arts and, in Rahe's view, a respect for humanity in general. The post-revolutionary *Federalist Papers* position therefore started from a very different set of assumptions – and drew on a very different character of rhetoric – to make its case for a federated union of commercial republics. But it was not wholly post-revolutionary; Paine was already halfway there when he disparaged the examples of classical Greece and Rome as worthy of emulation in his *American Crisis* letters, and his formulation of the problem in 1776 was essentially the same as Hume's and as Madison's: 'Society is produced by our wants and government by our wickedness; the former promotes our happiness by uniting our affections, the latter *negatively* by restraining our vices.'[16]

Hume's position was, in fact, more complex than thus far implied; after all, he described his maxim as 'true in *politics*', though 'false in *fact*'.[17] It was false in fact because he saw the individual as more honest in private than when acting in his/her public capacity. Personal honour and a concern with integrity were a check on one's private life, while party politics served to remove this check and to insulate the individual from the criticisms of his/her adversaries: 'When men act in a faction, they are apt, without shame or remorse, to neglect all the ties of honour and morality, in order to serve their party...'[18] Such separate interests then had to be checked and balanced. In contrast, people in their private

---

[14] David Hume, 'Of the independency of parliament', in *Essays: Moral, Political and Literary*, 40–47, 42 [emphasis in original].

[15] See Rahe, *Republics Ancient and Modern*, 587; see also James Madison, *Federalist* no. 51.

[16] See Thomas Paine, *The American Crisis*, letter V, 123, and letter XIII, in *The Life and Major Writings of Thomas Paine*, vol. I, 230–5, 231; the last quote is from *Common Sense*, in *The Life and Major Writings of Thomas Paine*, vol. I, 1–46, 4.

[17] Hume, 'Of the independency of parliament', 42 [emphasis in original].

[18] Hume, 'Of the first principles of government', IV, para. 3, 33: 'When men act in a faction, they are apt, without shame or remorse, to neglect all the ties of honour and morality, in order to serve their party...'

capacity were, if not 'naturally' virtuous, increasingly socialised into the virtues through a sense of honour and reputation.[19] In 'The sceptic', Hume essentially distinguished between the man 'with a lively sense of honour and virtue, with moderate passions [whose] conduct will always be conformable to the rules of morality; or if he depart from them, his return will be easy and expeditious...' with someone 'born of so perverse a frame of mind, of so callous and insensible a disposition, as to have no relish for virtue and humanity, no sympathy with his fellow creatures, no desire of esteem and applause...'. For the latter, philosophy had no answer.[20]

This gives us four broad (non-exclusive) categories: the resolutely fallen man; the essentially private virtuous man; the public, occasionally fallen, but more or less recallable man; and the man who is swayed by faction. This last group contains elements of the others, but Hume treated all but the first as virtuous and recallable so long as the institutional design was right. But, for Hume, it was politics, and especially the opportunities it offered for party, faction and acting in concert, that threatened peace and security, by engendering passions and removing controls that would otherwise restrain the actions of men. The remedy for this was not public virtue (since, by hypothesis, in a world of party and faction, that could not be generated) but institutional design (and limits on politics). This seems to me to have gone a considerable distance from Harrington, for whom political agency and public spirit continued to play an important role.

This does not simply cease to treat politics as the sphere in which civic virtue and self-sacrifice were engendered; it takes the reverse position: that it was in politics that the most dangerous passions and interests of men were stimulated. As such, there could be no recourse to civic virtue; only institutional design and pluralism could prevent the worst excesses. The task of the legislator was to restrict the domain of politics and to protect everything outside politics from the danger that politics posed. In the eighteenth century this view was applied most strictly to concerns about the tendency to despotism amongst kings, but there was an extraordinarily long tradition of hostility to democratic forms of government that provided an undercurrent that ensured that the task at hand was seen as one of restraining and balancing monarchical and aristocratic power, rather than simply replacing it with that of the people. Hume's anxieties about

[19] See David Hume, *An Enquiry Concerning the Principles of Morals*, 3rd edn, ed. L. A. Selby-Bigge (London: W. Strahan, 1777), paras. 232–3.
[20] David Hume, 'The sceptic', in *Essays: Moral, Political and Literary*, 161–84, Bk XVIII, paras. 29, 169.

the impact of party on those in politics spoke very directly to the implausibility of that latter solution, but he faced an emerging tradition of the sovereignty of the people that would come to give a very different reading to his sense that 'all government rests on opinion', and would systematically ignore his own sense of the dangers of politics in favour of the doctrine that the people are always right.

IV

The eighteenth century also saw something like a depoliticisation of virtue. The public culture of a scale morality, which seems central to republicanism, was no longer a feasible option, except under certain extraordinary conditions. This was partly because of the increasingly plural character of the public domain(s), with the rise of social and economic life, of polite and vulgar society, of private religious observance and its failure, and of sensibility and indulgence, in each of which the central locus of activity and value lay outside the political domain, becoming an essentially private experience. The language of criticism of the conduct of others, while replete with the lexicon of classical republicanism in its emphasis on corruption and luxury, was often in fact personal and social in form (rather than directly political) and was often underpinned by a theologically inspired sense of personal sin and guilt, and the need for atonement and restitution. The commercial world threatened corruption of an essentially moral kind, as did luxury, and as did the intermingling of strata in society in sports, sex and other low pleasures. The attack on those who gave themselves over to the senses was, for most commentators, one rooted in the Bible and in a model of religious conscience. Those who sought to shame others focused on their failure to recognise their social responsibilities and duties, but the moral opprobrium was precisely that: it was for a violation of faith and responsibility; it was for their self-indulgence and their sinfulness. Their viciousness was not an absence of civic virtue; it was an absence of good faith and personal and social responsibility. James Burgh offers an interesting example of someone who moves from a wholeheartedly religious understanding of virtue and vice, in his *Britain's Remembrancer: or the Danger not Over* (1746) and *The Dignity of Human Nature* (1754) – in which prudence concerns what makes a man happy and useful, and virtue is a conformity of disposition and practice to rectitude – to his more secular and republican *Crito* (1767) and *Political Disquisitions* (1775), in which popular government demands virtue 'because nothing else will keep up the execution of the laws, and the practice of what is right'. But Burgh was travelling against a number of streams (and not all read him as travelling that far from his original position).[21]

One change that Burgh largely ignored was that the attack on conduct in the public sphere in the late eighteenth century increasingly drove a wedge between the appearance of honour and its more fundamental reality. Gabriele Taylor suggests that shame cultures cannot admit the distinction between the externals of honour and the actual possession of the virtuous qualities that they are meant to pay respect to: '[I]f a man has lost his reputation then he has lost his value in the eyes of all the members of the group, and that includes himself. So there is nothing left, no inner quality or whatever, which could be judged to be of value despite the loss of public respect. Self-respect and public respect stand and fall together.'[22] This stresses the absence of a viewpoint other than that of the group, who are at one in their understanding of motivation and conduct, which invites a distinction between those in and those outside the honour group, so that the comments and judgements of the latter have no weight or relevance to those inside, but the intensity of group membership is such that judgements from the inside are ones that the members of that group all share, even those found wanting by them.[23] In the eighteenth-century context, especially in Britain, it prompts the thought that the increasingly plural character of British society dramatically weakened the place of honour and shame except among relatively tight-knit groups. (But even here, as in the case of Admiral John Byng, the sense of public unity behind his condemnation was short-lived, even if it worked within the Royal Navy precisely as Voltaire suggested: to encourage in others a military spirit that some have claimed accounted for much of Britain's dominance of the seas.) The developing, essentially evangelical and middling-order, critique of aristocratic *mœurs* was meant to shame those who devoted themselves to their sensuality and taste, but it did not have the power to do this literally; one could be shamed, and one could feel shame, only among those whom one regarded as in some ways one's peers and equals, and the social chasm between the public culture of polite arts and letters and the life of the *bon ton* remained insuperable in the eighteenth century. Moreover, as Vic Gatrell has recently argued, from the early

---

[21] Compare Pocock, *Virtue, Commerce, and History*, 260–1, Wootton, 'The republican tradition', 29, and Carla Hay, 'The making of a radical: the case of James Burgh', *Journal of British Studies* 18 (1979), 90–117.

[22] Gabriele Taylor, *Pride, Shame and Guilt: Emotions of Self-Assessment* (Oxford: Clarendon Press, 1985), 55.

[23] You can feel shamed by being exposed to the treatment of those who have no value for you, however, if you see your vulnerability to them through the eyes of other members of your own group – internalising their gaze.

eighteenth century until the 1820s there was an increasingly tolerant, if at times bemused, detachment in the portrayal of the excesses of libertine culture, and far from it being the case that those involved could not endorse the way in which they were portrayed (at least in popular prints), it seems likely that they provided a major audience and market for such prints.[24] In stark contrast to a Spartan unity of culture, in which the social, military and political were fused in a common system of norms, values and expectations of conduct, eighteenth-century Britain offered a plurality of such domains, and in doing so worked powerfully against the unifying demands of a scale morality in politics to which all other aspects of life should be subordinate.

This wedge between the homage paid to virtue and the virtue itself – a distinction that a fully integral shame culture would find difficult or impossible to draw – was evident elsewhere. Honour was already largely separated from virtue in Montesquieu's account, with a clear sense that honour concerned the reputation rather than the qualities that this reputation purported to applaud. This position became more widely developed throughout the eighteenth century, with aristocratic honour being associated with gallantry and duelling, and a consistently misplaced concern with reputation over substance arising. On the one hand, there was fuel for this critique in the Christian contempt for such worldly values in the absence of a clear conscience. But there was also a growing middle class critique (albeit equally religiously inspired in many cases) of aristocratic *mœurs* as intrinsically false that dominated many of the novels of the last quarter of the century. To take only one example: Falkland, the representative of aristocratic *mœurs* and virtues in William Godwin's *The Adventures of Caleb Williams*. Following the shame associated with a loss of face that results from Tyrell's (a local farmer) assault on him, Falkland (who cannot challenge his social inferior to a duel) stabs him to death in the street under the cover of darkness. He then allows two innocent men to be charged, tried and executed, and hounds young Caleb Williams to the ends of the country when the latter discovers his secret. But Godwin's point was to show precisely the extent to which a concern with reputation and public honour was a chimera in comparison with what Hume would refer to as 'inward peace of mind, consciousness of integrity, a satisfactory review of our own conduct...'.[25] The critique, like that in the last six of Godwin's major novels, was driven by the view that aristocratic *mœurs*, which were once so central to the political order, were no longer relevant; that they led to violations of the most fundamental of human ties and

---

[24] Gatrell, *City of Laughter.*   [25] Hume, *An Enquiry*, para. 233.

associations; and that they destroyed emotions and sentiments that were central to the good life – a life that was seen largely in essentially private (or at most communal, rather than political) terms. The critique of aristocratic *mœurs* conducted through the novel at the end of the eighteenth century was essentially a social and personal rather than a political critique; it was directed at their irresponsibility, their wastefulness and their immorality. With the notable and intentional exception of Henry Fielding's *Joseph Andrews*, the division between the inner and outer man became a commonplace of eighteenth-century literature, and it was especially directed at the conduct of the social élite, with the critique being effected through the portrayal of the good motives that drove those whose manners did not meet the scrupulous standards of public life, or the extent to which outer forms – of politeness and manners – covered less scrupulous and attractive motives. Insofar as there was convergence on a new standard, it was that of the new man of feeling: an enlarged sensibility, and an enlarged sense of personal responsibility and social benevolence, within a personal ethic of rectitude and self-improvement, flowing from a consciousness of integrity that could withstand – and stare down – the conventional systems of honour and distinction.

This critique was in marked contrast to the representation of the debauchery and indulgence of the élite (and others) in the popular prints of the second half of the eighteenth century – a representation that was largely descriptive and partly celebratory rather than critical. But this process of representation again shows that the standards of evaluation for conduct were many and varied, and certainly did not add up to a single morality, let alone a scale morality that was warranted in asking everything from someone. The boisterous and free-spirited attitude to sex, sport, food, gaming and drink in the prints at the turn of the century suggests a freedom of manners that was rejected by the more religiously inspired reform mentalities of the middling orders and the evangelicals. But it also suggests a willingness to draw a line between personal conduct and political standing that was simply inconceivable in Sparta or in the heyday of the Roman Republic. Consider the pamphlet to which John Barrell has drawn attention by 'Hampden', *Letters to the Duke of Portland . . .* (1794), in which the author claimed not to be bothered what they did in their personal lives so long as they did the job when they turn up for work in the state: 'Our ministers may constantly be carried to bed in a state of complete intoxication without being reproved by me, while they do not stutter and reel in the Senate etc.'[26]

---

[26] Barrell, *The Spirit of Despotism*, 96.

One conclusion to be drawn is that there was no clear basis in the second half of the eighteenth century for a practical republicanism and its associated call to virtue in the increasingly plural and complex world of the court, parliament and its surrounding society and city. Republican virtue was, on this view, subject to intense competition, not simply from competing forms of self-denying virtue – industriousness, acumen, sensibility, the domestic virtues, moderation and good works – nor from competing accounts of the vices of selfishness but also from celebrations of the attractions of the pleasures and indulgences that the city and the benefits of commercial society could afford, which were there to be indulged in and which constituted at least an equally motivationally compelling view of what manhood involved as that proposed by their more straight-laced competitors.

V

At the same time, the period saw a number of serious attempts to rethink the language of punishment, and the associated concepts of guilt, blame and responsibility – whether in the writings of Montesquieu, Cesare Beccaria, Hume or Jeremy Bentham, or in the revisions to the penal systems of European states. The language of classical republicanism was a language of exhortation and encouragement – a language to inspire commitment and sacrifice in the name of the common good. Those who were deaf to it were not simply free-riders, they were its enemies (given the perpetual threat of decline or entropy), and they lost their standing as free and equal citizens – and were often treated as worthless. In contrast, Beccaria argued that punishment had to be designed to make 'the most effective and lasting impression on men's minds and inflict the least torment on the body of the criminal'.[27] Moreover, for all the emphasis on the laws, the republican exemplars concerned not so much what the law demanded but what the norms and customs of the people demanded. The turn at the end of the eighteenth century to the development of a sense of due proportion between crime, blame and punishment also pressed the question of the legal enforcement of morals. For Beccaria at least, derelictions of honour, and attacks on it, did not fall within the purview of the law; and Bentham went still further and defined duty wholly in terms of what the law demanded: 'That is my duty to do, which I am liable to be *punished*, according to the law, if I do not do; this

---

[27] Cesare Beccaria, *On Crimes and Punishments*, ed. David Young (Indianapolis: Hackett, 1986), 23.

is the original, ordinary, and proper sense of the word *duty*.'[28] He went on to suggest that political and religious duties were clear because their punishments were clear, but that moral duties were an odd middle that had no very determinate form of punishment, and so no very determinate existence.[29]

Still more corrosive to theories of vice was Godwin's determinism and his sense that crime was simply a function of error. Although the extreme to which Godwin took this picture is distinctive, the sense that vice was a form of mistake and that it could be corrected, like other mistakes, through education and reasoning was a far more widely held assumption. Moreover, it surfaced in one of the great debates of the 1790s, when Louis XVI was tried for his life. For proper republicans, Louis was a tyrant who did not deserve even the courtesy of a trial, since he was set against the republic as its irreducible other; they could not both survive, and as an enemy he had no intrinsic worth. But, while the verdict on Louis' guilt was by a sizeable majority, the argument for the appropriate punishment was considerably closer. Moreover, although these arguments were sometimes driven by prudence, they were also influenced by a sense of the king as a product of his education and experience: '[I]f Louis Capet had been born in obscure condition, had he lived within the circle of an amiable and respectable neighbourhood, at liberty to practice the duties of domestic life, had he been thus situated, I cannot believe that he would have shewn himself destitute of social virtues...'[30] In contrast to a theory in which vice, and corruption as a specific instance, were anathema to the state and indicated a degree of decay that had to be rooted out and cleansed, Enlightenment theories of crime, in which the criminal was driven by perfectly ordinary causes and remained redeemable given the right circumstances, undercut the basis for thinking that those who failed to rise to republican challenges were thereby irretrievably vicious, and thereby worthless. Furthermore, rather than generating shame and

---

[28] Ibid., 40 [emphasis in original]. See also the discussion of honour in ch. 9, in which he founds it in opinion and says: 'It is opinion ... that torments the sage and unlettered alike, that has granted esteem more to the appearance of virtue than to virtue itself, and that makes even a rascal become a missionary since he finds it to be in his own interest' (20). Jeremy Bentham, *A Fragment on Government*, ed. Ross Harrison (Cambridge University Press, 1988), 109.

[29] Ibid., 109–10: 'Moral duty is created by a kind of motive, from which the *un*certainty of the *persons* to apply it, and of the *species* and *degree* in which it will be applied, has hardly yet got the name punishment: by various mortifications resulting from the ill-will of persons *un*certain and variable, – the community in general: that is, such individuals of that community as he, whose duty is in question, shall happen to be connected with.'

[30] Paine's speech to the National Convention, in Michael Walzer, ed., *Regicide and Revolution: Speeches at the Trial of Louis XVI* (Cambridge University Press, 1974), 209.

isolation within the community, the fallen warranted intensive conversation (given its most extreme form in Thomas Holcroft's *Anna St Ives* (1794)) and efforts at reformation. This sense that the fallen could be reclaimed went powerfully against a sense that their corruption was something that had to be cleansed from the state.

Paine, whose plea for clemency for the king is cited above, can also be identified with the other philosophical dimensions that I have identified. The emphasis on commerce and its pacific effect in the letter to the Abbé Raynal (1782) and thereafter, and the tendency to assign the causes of misery and oppression to the rule of monarchy and aristocracy (in conspiracy with the Churches) that was increasingly explicit in his writings after July 1791, were coupled with a corresponding pastoral and commercial utopianism. In the second part of the *Rights of Man*, America was described as subsisting almost without government for the best part of the revolution. Paine was not immune to federalist concerns about the potentially dangerous influence of government, but he became increasingly strident in his insistence that it was monarchy and aristocracy that were responsible for the evils of government – and for the evils among those who rule. And he coupled this with a peculiar combination of a basically libertarian position, in which the only proper role for government was, through law, to secure to the individual his/her natural rights, and a gradually expanding conception of what those rights might demand from government. In contrast to those who sat in the Federal Convention in Philadelphia in the summer of 1787, Paine never really explored the potential for democratic or representative politics to give rise to a distinct species of political problems, and only rarely engaged with the kinds of issues that kept his adopted countrymen at their work of design. He clearly shared a good deal of the language and some of the commitments of his friends and colleagues, but his re-encounter with Europe after 1787, and his new sense (since it was certainly not there in 1776) that Europe could free itself from the shackles of monarchy and oppression, derived from a position that was, at base, strikingly different from Madison and others – different, most fundamentally, in the optimism that underlay his commitment to the common sense and capacity for reason of the ordinary man, and in that sense different for his depoliticisation of the nature of virtue.

VI

What I take these different trends in eighteenth-century political thought to show is that substantial changes were taking place, at a theoretical and philosophical level, but also in the institutions of commerce, civil society and the public sphere, the practices of religion and the family, and in the expectations that people had of each other and of themselves. These changes undermined the basis for a language of classical republicanism that captured anything of real political substance. As we have seen in the case of James Burgh, this does not mean that such positions were never advocated, but they increasingly sat against a background – both intellectual and practical – that was increasingly in tension with them, especially with respect to their underlying conception of the demands of morality and politics.

I do not expect all those echoing classical republican themes and language to operate with a shame morality. The constructions of the classical exemplars of republicanism did rely on key aspects of a scale morality, however: a commitment to the common good was demanded that was not about simply meeting a basic threshold but that demanded civic virtue, coupled with a sense that the absence of such virtue was an indication of corruption and a decay in civic *mœurs*. There were many accounts of such virtues in the eighteenth century that did not all have the same structure or commitments and in which virtue was not conceived wholly in this way. This diversity and pluralism in conceptions of republican virtue was fuelled to a considerable extent by the developments I have discussed. I take that diversity as evidence of the decay or evolution of a tradition, one that took it a considerable distance from its past and that, by the beginning of the nineteenth century, was almost wholly eclipsed and replaced by a modern republicanism, which shared a name with classical republicanism but was of a dramatically different character. A central element of the rhetoric of classical republicanism is that it articulates a scale morality, and my sense is that there were increasing tensions between this rhetoric in the eighteenth century and the various developments to which I have drawn attention. Above all, things that were vices became more widely accepted as a natural element of human society, and became understood and represented as areas in which the individual should be left free to choose; when that freedom to choose in itself placed constraints on the demands of a scale morality calling for civic virtue, I should emphasise that I am more than aware that others, many of whom continue to use the language of republicanism, have drawn attention to such developments in the past, and have seen them as providing the basis for an evolution of republican concerns. I differ in understanding the republican constructions of virtue and vice as relatively systematically scale rather than threshold in character. Insofar as a range of elements that are threshold in character were introduced into people's thinking, were coupled with a widening plurality of ways of thinking about the demands of virtue and the nature of vice, and became systematically endorsed and integrated into political and social practices, then appeals to the older republican framework became less coherent and compelling. One consequence was that the republican rhetoric increasingly parted company with people's everyday experience, or retained a connection only by the interposition of mediating elements, such as Christian doctrines of sin and redemption, which have a very ambivalent relationship to republicanism. Another is that the language ceased to have normativity for those it addressed, and possibly those who deployed it, in that it no longer engaged people's sense of how it was that they should conduct themselves in relation to politics and the state. A further consequence was that elements of the tradition become split off and developed semi-autonomous lives, free from the normative implications and conclusions of the original theory.

But these possibilities are not quite the whole story. There was a flourishing of pure republican virtue at the end of the eighteenth century, and there were occasions on which some of the ancient cultural apparatus returned, and that deserves comment. In Britain the development of a number of these various lines of argument and perspectives on individual conduct, partisanship and institutional design were linked to processes of state consolidation and took place against the background of the development of commercial society, the acceptance of political conflict and opposition and the development of a procedurally stable legal system. By 'consolidation' I mean the willingness of people engaged with the political process to accept the process as sovereign over them, irrespective of the direct outcome for their particular preferences or position. This was a long and slow development, and it was an uneven one, even in eighteenth-century Britain. It was uneven because it remained a potentially unstable achievement. Consolidation depended to some extent on the attitude of 'win some, lose some', but that was conditional on winning some, and on the issues under negotiation not being too central to individuals' well-being – enabling them to treat the outcomes with equanimity even when they went against them. It assumed that people had a reasonable degree of confidence over the long term, so that a setback today would be redeemed by gains tomorrow. In Britain there were points when this does not seem so self-evident, the war with France and the repression of the radical societies in the 1790s being one example – not just because there were organisations for reform that denied the legitimacy of the status quo and whose exclusion from the political process may well have generated a 'lose today, lose tomorrow' attitude, but also because those who took the order for granted came to see it as fundamentally threatened and were prepared to rouse themselves in its defence, through the loyalist associations and the volunteer movement. In this context, aspects of classical republicanism were mobilised, albeit in often starkly contrasting ways, with Burke deploying elements in defence of the status quo, and radical reformers such as Thelwall and Vicesimus Knox adapting different elements to rather different ends.[31]

In Britain, as people reflected on the existing order and what would serve to stabilise it and legitimate it, many reformers appealed to touchstones of ancient constitutionalism, the rights of free-born Englishmen and a sense of the corruptions of the parliamentary order following the introduction of septennial parliaments and the subsequent withering of the franchise. Moreover, many found in Paine's writings a language and a model of political reform that, even if it ran contrary to domestic traditions, provided a powerful weapon of critique and ridicule to be used against the increasingly resistant political élite. And some found in the republicanism of the past, and in the models of past republics, inspiration for rejection of the existing order and tools for itemising its corruption. But it is when under pressure, when driven into relatively secretive and exclusive groupings, that the language of republican resistance and of liberty or death came to seem more natural: '[W]hen a faction is formed upon a point of right or principle, there is no occasion, where men discover a greater obstinacy, and a more determined sense of justice and equity.'[32] As John Barrell has argued, however, a considerable body of people (certainly more than turned to rebellion) were increasingly affected by what is effectively a new set of invasions of privacy by the state and its agents in the 1790s – one that I think we should understand as evidence of the state's new willingness to demand from its subjects evidence of crossing a threshold of conformity that it had not previously felt necessary. For many, such demands encouraged a resistance that was more defensive than expansive, and encouraged a switch to a language of rights, privacy and arbitrary rule that drew on a wider and more eclectic set of languages than classical republicanism.[33]

In France, following the financial crisis brought on by the American War, a different dynamic unfolded as the *ancien régime* began systematically to collapse. A similar process of mobilisation took place, but with radically different results. It was less ordered, less clear in its sense of what was to be won or lost, but it reached more systematically down through society to touch vast numbers with no previous political experience or

---

[31] See the use of Thermopylae in *Report of the Committee to the London Reforming Society* (London: J. Bone, 1795), 12 – invoking the inspirational character of the example, without the associated shame for failing to rise to the challenge (although those who do thus fail are described as no better than the 'ox which grazes on their plains').
[32] Hume, 'Of the first principles of government', IV, para. 3, 33.
[33] Barrell, *The Spirit of Despotism*, 166 and throughout.

expectations. Moreover, the close links in Paris between the clubs – the Jacobins, Cordeliers and others – the Paris Commune and the Legislative Assembly (and subsequently the National Convention) produced an atmosphere in which a relatively small group of men and women played out their struggle to consolidate the state in front of, and by orchestrating the responses of, the people of Paris and the National Guard, and against the background of an increasingly threatening international order that soon degenerated into war. In this struggle, categories were forced into simplified antonyms: citizen or enemy, a sovereign people or an enslaved one, the people's virtue or aristocratic corruption. And in this simplification, at its most intense, something like a scale culture developed and took the driving seat of politics, ushering in demands for an essentially immoderate, unconditional commitment to the republic and calls for the highest sacrifice, in which those who were unwilling or unable to commit were as nothing.[34]

There were theoretical resources that aided this process – Rousseau, for one: '[E]very wrongdoer, in attacking the rights of society by his crimes, becomes a rebel and a traitor to his country. By violating its laws he ceases to belong to it, and is even making war on it. The preservation of the state becomes incompatible with his own; one of the two must perish; and when a criminal is put to death, it is as an enemy rather than as a citizen.'[35] And that rhetoric was replayed in the public forum:

And I say that the king should be judged as an enemy; that we should not judge him so much as combat him... Louis is an alien among us... [T]here was nothing in the laws of Numa by which to judge Tarquin; nothing in the laws of England by which to judge Charles I; they were judged according to the law of nations. Force was used to repel force, to repel an enemy, an alien. [...] A people does not judge as does a court of law. It does not hand down sentences, it hurls down thunderbolts; it does not condemn kings, it plunges them into the abyss... Louis must die because the nation must live.[36]

This added a further dynamic to the identification of vice, corruption and enmity among those whom one opposed. 'The soul of the republic is *vertu* – that is, the love of the fatherland and the high-minded devotion that resolves all private interests into the general interest. The enemies of the republic are those dastardly egoists, those ambitious and corrupt men.

---

[34] This is not to disagree with Keith Michael Baker's more precise allocation of individual responsibilities in 'Classical republicanism in eighteenth-century France', *Journal of Modern History* 73 (2001), 32–53, but I would frame that attribution by institutional factors (not least a quasi-'dual power') and the pressures caused by war and mass mobilisation.

[35] Rousseau, *Of the Social Contract*, Bk II, ch. 5; see Walzer, *Regicide and Revolution*, 72.

[36] St Just, quoted by Walzer, *Regicide and Revolution*, 121, 125–6, 133, 138.

You have hunted down kings, but have you hunted out the vices that their deadly domination has engendered among you?'[37] Rapid social and political change produces winners and losers whose gains and losses are long term in their effects – thereby upping the odds. Winners find it hard not to regard those who resist them as perversely motivated – and in late eighteenth-century France this meant sticking to privileges, forms and practices that oppressed and excluded the people. Losers see the winners in similarly venomous terms, with revolutionaries being depicted as threatening to undo the intricate order of society motivated by a politics of envy and by greed. Faced with change or the threat of it, we find a snowballing of political rhetoric that, in itself, increased the tension and the stakes, threatening institutional consolidation and the practices and manners that had thus far sustained it.

Late eighteenth-century England, France and America all betrayed evidence of rapid political change in which the terms of political discourse and the protocols of political exchange were subjected to massive strain. In that process, older assumptions and expectations, and more visceral reactions, came to frame people's understanding of those to whom they were opposed. Moreover, people's sense of their own position demanded some support, so that they saw their struggle not as a personal one but as linked to a group or cause or movement, which took their motives to a less personal, more exalted plane. As these conflicts developed, the languages of enmity also evolved, often echoing older or more stable political and moral languages, but often adapting these opportunistically to meet particular exigencies and often cutting them off from the deeper layers of assumption or argument that once underpinned that terminology.

Furthermore, there is a problem of spheres. In attacking Warren Hastings, Burke's rhetoric of corruption, decline and the public good played to a House, a legal tradition and a political élite fully familiar with the language and conventions on which he drew. In many respects it was a bravura performance – to shame and expose the seedy underbelly of the pomp and pretensions of colonial administration. That arena was one that was increasingly under pressure to admit a range of other voices and demands, through petitioning and the work of the reform associations and the extra-parliamentary movement. While there was a relatively stable language of parliamentary exchange, in the late eighteenth century there was no real sense of how to deal with these extra-parliamentary demands – above all, no sense of how they might be integrated into the process: the options seem reduced to concession or resistance. And that led to

---

[37] Maximilien de Robespierre, quoted by Ruth Scurr, *Fatal Purity: Robespierre and the French Revolution* (London: Chatto & Windus, 2005), 209.

repeated iterations of obstinacy and struggle between parliament and those outside it, with the latter occasionally driven to see the existing regime as fundamentally obdurate and calling for more dramatic measures. In France, which faced very similar dynamics but with an almost complete absence of parliamentary and deliberative conventions and practices, and with the added pressure of foreign war and fears of monarchist plots against the republic, in the iterations of contestation, certain languages gained ascendancy. And they did so with devastating effects, in part because of their distance from the experiences and practices of the recent past, so that the elements of modernity – a bill of rights, constitutions, industry, bourgeois society, the pursuit of private interests – were suddenly both acknowledged, and subordinated to a political head that was modelled 'in the manner of antiquity'.[38] In this manner, few, if any, of these elements had a place, as the rule of the Committee of Public Safety demonstrated and which Louis de Saint-Just brusquely abbreviated: 'There are three sins against the republic: one is to be sorry for State prisoners; another is to be opposed to the rule of virtue; and the third is to be opposed to the Terror.'[39]

What does this mean for republicanism, in both its classical and its modern forms? One view is that we need to think of them not as stable conceptual frameworks or languages but as resources that coexist alongside other resources, and that are drawn on in the interpretation of events and in formulating people's responses to events. Their relevance and power is in large part determined in their use, rather than by their reference. Moreover, given the myriad tensions and ambiguities that exist in and between these political and philosophical, and religious, discourses, we should not expect to see them applied in anything other than a selective and often opportunistic way, with some tensions ignored, some repudiated, some positively embraced. But, to temper this view, we should acknowledge that there remains a need for a sense of surface and depth – to couple the sense that the precise rhetoric used is influenced by what people are trying to do with particular audiences[40] with the recognition that at times they draw on and refer to deeper foundations and commitments that give a greater degree of coherence to people's thought and practices. At other times, though, the rhetoric so parts company with the practices, institutions and expectations of a society that, should it, under particular and extraordinary conditions, come to dominance in politics, it

---

[38] See Patrice Higonett, *Goodness beyond Virtue: Jacobins during the French Revolution* (Cambridge, MA: Harvard University Press, 1998), 1, citing as an epigram from Karl Marx and Friedrich Engels, *The Holy Family*.
[39] Scurr, *Fatal Purity*, 276.   [40] With Skinner, *Visions of Politics*, chs. 4, 6.

will result in a fundamentally despotic and draconian form of political rule. My suggestion is that the scale morality of virtue and vice in the republican tradition is one such deeper element, a basic commitment that provides coherence to much of the republican tradition, but one that, by the end of the eighteenth century, had become increasingly fragmented as it contended with a range of newer developments that sat very uneasily alongside it. Whereas, in the English Civil War and afterwards, the language of republicanism articulated a sense of the responsibilities of a ruling class, united by virtue and their commitment to liberty and the public good, the French Revolution, through a concatenation of events, raised this classical language to ascendancy alongside a rhetoric of popular sovereignty, democracy and the people's will, with lethal results.

I have tried to suggest that a whole range of traditional republican failings become an accepted part of the eighteenth-century body politic: faction became party; corruption ceased to be synonymous with the pursuit of self-interest; libertinism became liberty; and wrongdoers, rather than being seen as at war with society, were recognised as its potentially educable victims. Above all, we lose the possibility of Aristodamus's fate – to be shamed for a less than complete identification with the republic; and we gain a more confusing and less attractive indulgence for people's freedom to choose, and to indulge themselves. With that we get the beginnings of a truly modern sense of negative liberty, which is not moralised but is essentially a doctrine of non-interference and has only threshold constraints on its exercise, leaving an equal liberty – indeed, licence – for all.

6   Paine's experiments

I

In the last ten or twenty years much has been written about Thomas Paine. But the vast majority of this work, my own contributions included, tends to treat Paine's more scientific writings as of little intrinsic interest. Indeed, they are seen as symptomatic of his view that the world is an easily legible text, open to one's common sense, the reading of which could only be obscured by the fraudulent doctrines of organised religion and the hereditary system. For Paine, men established society to meet their wants and harmonise their interests, but these benign origins became lost through the corruptions of hereditary government and the attempt to establish authority over individual beliefs. The example of the American Revolution, and the shock it sent through the states of Europe, demonstrated, he believed, that it was only a matter of time before this system of imposture would be unmasked and the order overthrown, to be replaced by a system of open, republican government. Once freed from predatory kings and courtly politics, commerce would mediate between nations to harmonise their interests and produce a global order of enlightenment and reason.[1] Science and its progress are clearly *symptomatic* of this process of enlightenment, but there was nothing in Paine's political writings to suggest that it has a special role.

This reading is often associated with a tendency to treat Paine's comments on scientific matters with a certain amount of condescension. The man was an autodidact, he had little formal training and he was largely ignorant of scientific method and mathematics; his scientific interests were superficial, and he adopted scientific terms and models as metaphors – not because he wanted to convey the conceptual content of their original use but because he wanted to reap the cachet of their scientific status with

---

[1] See Paine's letter to the Abbé Raynal, in *The Life and Major Writings of Thomas Paine*, vol. II, 211–62. Note that this view post-dated Paine's writings on the American Revolution, which were marked by a sense of American exceptionalism. See my *Paine*, ch. 2.

an audience whom he sought to persuade, by appeals variously to science, reason and common sense, to sweep aside the old orders of superstition and imposition.

Indeed, his interests in science might easily be dismissed as driven by more deeply held theological commitments, not least because his most extended treatment of the central concerns of eighteenth-century science came in part one of his *Age of Reason*, where it provided a deist text of nature as an alternative to the biblical tradition of Christianity, against which Paine inveighed. For Paine, 'God speaketh universally to man' – not in a particular natural language, but in a universal language of nature:

The Creation speaks a universal language, independently of human speech or human language, multiplied and various as they be. It is an ever existing original, which every man can read. It cannot be forged; it cannot be counterfeited; it cannot be lost; it cannot be altered; it cannot be suppressed. It does not depend upon the will of man whether it is published or not; it publishes itself from one end of earth to the other. It preaches to all nations and to all worlds; and this *Word of God* reveals to man all that is necessary for man to know of God.[2]

He went on to appeal to the eternal principles of the world, which we have come to recognise through geometry, trigonometry and astronomy as the true 'soul of science': 'It is the structure of the universe that has taught this knowledge to man. That structure is an ever-existing exhibition of every principle upon which every part of mathematical science is founded.'[3]

The Almighty Lecturer, by displaying the principles of science in the structure of the universe, has invited man to study and imitation. It is as if He had said to the inhabitants of this globe that we call ours, 'I have made an earth for man to dwell upon, and I have rendered the starry heavens visible, to teach him science and the arts. He can now provide for his own comfort, AND LEARN FROM MY MUNIFICENCE TO ALL, TO BE KIND TO EACH OTHER.'[4]

What need do we have, on Paine's account, for a text, cobbled together from the mythological scribblings of past pretenders to knowledge, when we have before us the order of the universe that reason and science reveal to us? This picture is reiterated in his *Discourse Delivered by Thomas Paine, at the Society of the Theophilanthropists, at Paris, 1798*:

The universe is the bible of the true Theophilanthropist ... Contemplating the universe, the whole system of creation, in this point of light, we shall discover, that

[2] Thomas Paine, *The Age of Reason*, in *The Life and Major Writings of Thomas Paine*, vol. I, 463–604, 482, 483.
[3] Ibid., 489.   [4] Ibid., 490 [emphasis in original].

all that which is called natural philosophy is properly divine study – It is the study of
God through his works.

The good book of nature is the text, science is the lens through which we
must read it, and the works of God are what is revealed through such a
reading. Seen in this way, Paine's science seems wholly driven by his
theological interests: it is an expression of faith rather than expressing
the objective detachment of the true scientist.[5]
    Paine's deism might equally be linked to his commitment to common
sense.[6] He was a man who knew his own mind and had a secure sense of
his place in the world, and who applied his common sense to matters of
politics, economics, religion and the study of nature, and came up with a
coherent – though perhaps not always very subtle – body of belief about
the given order of the world. His confidence in his common sense seems
unshakeable; as he announced in his *Age of Reason*, 'My mind is my own

---

[5] We can recognise this kind of reductionism in I. Bernard Cohen's comment, in his work on
the place of science in the political thought of Thomas Jefferson, Benjamin Franklin,
Madison and Adams, *Science and the Founding Fathers* (New York: W. W. Norton,
1995), 59, that '[p]olitical creeds are always ultimately based on religious beliefs or political
or social philosophies, a set of general beliefs or axioms from which particular deductions
are derived'. From this premise, it would be tempting to jump to the conclusion that, for
Paine at least (a man whose scientific activity was too negligible for Cohen's notice), the
basic axioms were religious, and that science had neither a foundational place in Paine's
thought nor even the role of an independent variable – being wholly reducible to the
religious motives that drove his creed. Indeed, this is the line that Jack Fruchtman
essentially takes in his *Thomas Paine and the Religion of Nature* (Baltimore: Johns Hopkins
University Press, 1993), in which Paine's scientific interests are almost wholly ignored.
Paine's deism might explain his interest in and enthusiasm for science (although he was
largely out of his depth, since he lacked any formal training), and it would also explain his
more general understanding of the role of reason and his belief in the progressive enlightenment of mankind and the growing pressure towards rationally ordered political and
economic systems that could coexist harmoniously.
[6] There are considerable difficulties in grasping quite what Paine meant by 'common sense'.
These are well illustrated in Fruchtman's discussion of the concept in his *Thomas Paine and
the Religion of Nature*. Fruchtman argues: 'Common sense was the means by which the
mind understood the way that the heart felt about reality. It had nothing to do with abstract
reasoning or metaphysical concepts. It was wholly empirical because it was based on
sensory perceptions' (21). Given this account, it is not surprising to find that Fruchtman
nowhere discusses Paine's scientific interests, the impact of Newtonianism on his thought
or even the lectures of Benjamin Martin and James Ferguson. Another way of construing
common sense, following the eighteenth-century writer and divine James Beattie, would be
to see it as signifying 'the power of the mind which perceives truth or commands belief, not
by progressive argumentation, but by an instantaneous, instinctive, and irresistible
impulse; derived neither from education, nor from habit, but from nature' (*Oxford
English Dictionary*, citing Beattie, 1772). In other words, the intuitive grasp that we have
on natural and moral truths fit together in a harmonious whole unless distorted by some
external force or corruption. If Paine's common sense was Beattie's, rather than
Fruchtman's, we have a considerably more demanding job on our hands to understand
Paine's position and the role played by science in it.

church,' and '[I]t is necessary to the happiness of man that he be mentally faithful to himself...'[7] But this belief, and his sense of its sacrosanct quality, seems to be still more deeply grounded in a faith in God's beneficent construction of the world. Drawing on a loose understanding of the Newtonian system as evidence of a beneficent order, he appropriated scientific evidence and argument, and, more generally, the study of nature, as confirming instances of this faith. Moreover, this sense of the naturalness and 'givenness' of the order of the universe allowed him to interpret deviations from this order as a function of ignorance and superstition – results of the imposture of established religion and the hereditary system. In such a system there was little room for refutation, since every deviation at the level of politics and society had an explanation, and every feature of creation was treated as evidence of a 'first cause' and His design:

The only idea man can affix to the name of God is that of a *first cause*, the cause of all things. And, incomprehensible and difficult as it is for a man to conceive what a first cause is, he arrives at the belief of it from the tenfold greater difficulty of disbelieving it... [E]verything we behold carries in itself the internal evidence that it did not make itself ... and it is the conviction arising from the evidence that carries us on, as it were, by necessity to the belief of a first cause eternally existing, of a nature totally different to any material existence we know of, and by the power of which all things exist; and this first cause man calls God.[8]

This belief can be seen as the unifying theme throughout Paine's work, providing a consistent, simple and unsophisticated touchstone for his commitments, and allowing him a clarity of vision that is able to sweep away – mentally, if not practically – the old order of ignorance and superstition, priestcraft and hereditary dogma. His deism, his confidence in an ordered universe and his insistent appeal to the judgement of the common man personify a populist version of the rationalism and optimism that it has been traditional to associate with the Enlightenment.

Why buck such trends in the interpretation of Paine's scientific activity? One reason for doing so is the fact that few commentators have attempted to take Paine's scientific interests seriously.[9] One explanation for this is that the evidence we have of his activity is not extensive; there are a few papers, mainly concerning his bridge, and a number of letters, and there are the comments in his *Age of Reason*, and other religious writings, but little more. There is also, however, a more general problem in knowing

---

[7] Paine, *The Age of Reason*, 464.   [8] Ibid., 484 [emphasis in original].
[9] Although this needs moderating for Moncure Conway and A. Owen Aldridge, and especially for Harry Hayden Clark. On the other hand, in the case of scientists who have attempted to do so, there has been a conspicuous lack of historical sensitivity: see, for example, J. G. James, 'Thomas Paine's iron bridge work 1785–1803', *Newcomen Society Transactions* 57 (1987), 189–221.

how seriously to take his scientific pretensions, since we need to have both some understanding of what he was trying to do and some sense of how what he was trying to do related to the standards of thinking and experimentation practised by his contemporaries. Only once we have reached that point can we really make much estimate of the weight of his activity and, more centrally, of its relationship to his political (and religious) thought. Since those writing about Paine have often been most attracted by the democratic and egalitarian thrust of his writing, it is easy to see why these more complex contextual judgements might be skirted, and his scientific writing rather ignored. Moreover, there are, I argue, a number of more subtle methodological problems concerning the nature of belief and the relationship between experience, experiment, axioms and foundational commitments, which complicate inquiry into Paine's scientific understanding and its relationship to his other beliefs.

I have no wish entirely to overturn the picture I have just sketched of Paine's beliefs. But I do want to suggest that we might profitably refine it; and I also indicate why we might be advised to pay more attention to Paine's scientific interests than has been customary. In doing so, I hope I can claim to be following the recommendation of at least one of Paine's friends and contemporaries, Joel Barlow, who issued the injunction: 'The biographers of Paine...should not forget his mathematical acquirements and his mechanical genius.'[10]

II

We know rather little about Paine's early years and his formal education. He attended a local grammar school until the age of thirteen, but left to work as a staymaker with his father. He had a pretty firm dislike of his trade, and, although he practised for periods when he could not afford to do otherwise, he also tried a variety of jobs, including setting himself up as a schoolmaster on one occasion. Like much of the rest of his first thirty-seven years, Paine's activities here were conspicuous only by their failure. He eventually became an exciseman and tobacconist, and in 1772/3 went to London to present a petition to parliament asking for an increase in excise wages. In doing so he neglected his profession, his business and his wife, and when he returned he found that he had been sacked by the customs service and bankrupted in business, and that his relationship with his wife had irretrievably broken down. Having settled his affairs, he returned to London in 1774, obtained letters of recommendation from

[10] Moncure D. Conway, *The Life of Thomas Paine* (London: Watts, 1909), 99.

Benjamin Franklin and boarded ship for the New World. Although there is not much in this to impress us with Paine's education, the period he spent in London stands out as a major turning point in his life, both practically, because it was at this time that he made Franklin's acquaintance, and intellectually, because it was the period in which he received what scientific education he had. In his *Age of Reason*, Paine described himself in the following terms:

The natural bent of my mind was to science. I had some turn, and I believe some talent, for poetry; but this I rather repressed than encouraged, as leading too much into the field of imagination. As soon as I was able I purchased a pair of Globes, and attended the philosophical lectures of Martin and Ferguson, and became afterwards acquainted with Dr Bevis, of the society called the Royal Society, then living in the Temple [one of the four Inns of Court, or legal associations, in London], and an excellent astronomer... After I had made myself master of the use of the Globes and the Orrery, and conceived an idea of the infinity of space and the eternal divisibility of matter, and obtained at least a general knowledge of what is called natural philosophy, I began to compare – or, as I have before said, to confront – the eternal evidence those things afford with the Christian system of faith.[11]

---

[11] Paine, *The Age of Reason*, 496, 498. Paine did not date this connection. Following Clark, John Keane's biography *Tom Paine: A Political Life* suggests it must have been when Paine returned from one of his sea voyages, having run away from his father's business – dating it to the middle of the 1750s. But Keane admits that Bevis was not then resident in the Temple, and it is equally likely that the whole of this experience in fact belonged to the later period of residence when representing the excisemen's cause. Both Martin and Ferguson lectured in London, in 1757/8 and 1772/3. See John R. Milburn, 'The London evening courses of Benjamin Martin and James Ferguson, eighteenth-century lecturers on experimental philosophy', *Annals of Science* 40 (1983), 437–55; and A. Q. Morton, 'Lectures on natural philosophy in London, 1750–1765: S. C. T. Demainbray (1710–1782) and the "Inattention" of his countrymen', *British Journal of History of Science* 23 (1990), 411–34. Moreover, Paine also mentioned, elsewhere, the influence of George Lewis Scott (an eminent amateur mathematician and one-time tutor to George III), whom he most likely met when Scott was a member of the Board of Excise and when Paine was in London in 1772/3. It was Scott who introduced him to Franklin. I doubt if much rests on exactly when Paine first attended the lectures, but most of the evidence points to the later rather than the earlier period. What we do know is that the impact of Paine's scientific interests can be detected in even the earliest pieces written on his arrival in America in 1774/5, and they remained a common theme subsequently throughout his life; see, for example, his 'Useful and entertaining Hints', signed 'Amicus' (10 February 1775), which used the collections of minerals and fossils in the Philadelphia Library Company as the starting point for a peroration on the interconnection between science and industry, and on the largely untapped potential for mineralogical exploration and exploitation in America, coupled with a proposal for using the intellectual resources of the American Philosophical Society to examine samples of earth and minerals so as to facilitate knowledge of their potential – supplementing 'the defective knowledge of the individual' from 'the common stock' – and giving a new spring to agriculture and manufactures; *The Life and Major Writings of Thomas Paine*, vol. II, 1024–5.

In what follows, I am assuming that Paine attended the lectures while in London serving the excisemen's cause. This is contentious; many other biographers suggest that he received his education in 1757/8. Bevis was not then in the Temple, however, and George Lewis Scott, who introduced Paine to Franklin, is most likely to have come across Paine in connection with the excise case when he was a member of the Board of Excise (and that would not have been relevant for Paine in 1758, while it was in 1772/3). On the other hand, Bevis died in 1771, which suggests that it may well have been between Paine's periods as an exciseman that he attended the lectures, and met Bevis and Scott (i.e. 1766, when his plea for reinstatement may have brought him the acquaintance of Scott). But I do not think – in this case at least – that the exact timing matters so long as the facts are right!

What does Paine's scientific education mean in practice? What was involved in mastering the use of 'the Globes' and 'the Orrery', in conceiving an idea of the infinity of space and in obtaining at least a general knowledge of natural philosophy?

Benjamin Martin lectured in the winter of 1772/3 at his premises, 171 Fleet Street, on Mondays, Wednesdays and Fridays at 6:30 p.m. Admission was one shilling per lecture (rather than having a course fee).[12] The lecture course ranged over electricity, and its application in medicine; the nature, properties and generation of air; the air pump; the properties of light, optics; the orrery; hydrostatics and hydraulics; pendulums and clockwork mechanisms; geography and the globe; the celestial globe; and magnetism. James Ferguson also lectured that winter, though his lectures were somewhat disturbed by family difficulties. He lectured daily (except Sundays) at 7:00 p.m. for a course of twelve lectures, also at a shilling a lecture. The course was roughly similar, with more emphasis on the use of the orrery, and with a more systematic approach to the topics than Martin. Martin, the more entrepreneurial of the two, also sold equipment, but both men designed their own equipment for the experiments they performed. They also published various works on the use of globes, on Newton's astronomy, on mechanics, and so on. Ferguson was a Fellow of the Royal Society (and of the American Philosophical Society), and was granted a small annual pension by George III in 1760.

In his major work on *Science and the Founding Fathers*, Bernard Cohen distinguishes two central types of scientific activity handed down from Newton: the study of mathematical laws and principles and their application to rational and celestial mechanics, including the study of the motions

[12] See Milburn, 'The London evening courses of Benjamin Martin'.

of the planets; and the experimental and largely non-mathematical study of the world, covering material such as Newton's own work on optics, but also including any form of practical experimentation or the collection and classification of phenomena. The lectures given by men such as Martin and Ferguson were almost entirely concerned with the non-mathematical side of rational and celestial mechanics, with occasional incursions into experimentation. There is little evidence that the lectures covered the mathematics of mechanics. Ferguson described himself as having been taught arithmetic, decimal arithmetic and algebra, and the elements of geometry, but shaved that this education had been disrupted after a short while, and he was described by a contemporary as being ignorant of geometry and incapable of recognising a geometrical proof – requiring for his own proof the construction of a machine for the replication of movement. Clearly, mathematics was central to Newton's work on celestial mechanics; the development, for example, of the mathematics of the *Philosophiæ Naturalis Principia Mathematica* was centrally concerned with the analysis of tangents to circles, areas under curves and points in motion on a curve – all fundamental tools for measuring ellipses and planetary motion. But none of this appeared in Ferguson's or Martin's popular works, nor in their published lectures. Rather, their account of planetary motion was given largely in mechanical terms, together with some account of forces that act on matter, such as gravitation, attraction and compulsion. Moreover, as far as can be ascertained, Martin similarly lacked a grasp of the complexities of Newtonian geometry and calculus.[13] Their forte lay much more centrally, in the practical demonstration of rational and celestial mechanics.

Paine clearly invested a good deal, not just intellectually but also practically, in these lectures. Attending them was not cheap, and he also purchased a 'pair of Globes'. Martin advertised a range of such equipment. Manual orreries were £2 12s. 6d, those with wheel work, £8 8s. 0d. Large orreries sold for as much as £150. Globes ranged from Senex globes of 28" diameter in mahogany frames for £35 through to smaller globes with cheaper frames, to 3" globes in a case for 10 shillings – though these latter would have been the least useful for the more precise type of calculation an aspiring student of astronomy would have wished to attempt. To have attended enough lectures to have reached a degree of familiarity with the concepts and methods of the new natural philosophy would, then, have involved a significant outlay on Paine's part. It is

[13] Benjamin Martin, *The Philosophical Grammar; or, View of Modern Philosophy* (London: J. Noon, 1735), vii: 'Sir Isaac's *Principia* are all inveloped, not only from the common Ken, but from the general Tribe of mathematicians themselves.'

possible that he came to London with some reserves derived from his tobacconist business and from his excise work; it is also possible that he drew on the money allocated as expenses by the excisemen whose case he was representing.[14] But, certainly, he seems to have been prepared to devote a significant sum to his interests.[15]

What evidence is there that he retained anything he learnt in these lectures? The purchase of the globes might be thought to be little more than a scientific affectation, but this ignores the extent to which the globes were seen as providing problems for resolution. Martin's own *An Essay on the Nature and Superior use of Globes* (1758) ended with a range of problems for resolution, and, while these were clearly aimed at the education of young minds, they give a good indication of the kinds of exercises that Paine could have undertaken with them: finding the longitude and latitude of a place; calculating distance and bearing; calculating the place of the Sun, and its declination, ascension, altitude, and time of rising and setting; setting comparative times for different places; identifying the length of the night in different parts of the globe; and so on (see Figure 6.1).[16] Although the same type of problem was not set for the celestial globe, the text covered similar types of issues with respect to identifying the visible constellations and planets. Very similar problems were also discussed in Ferguson's lectures; but Ferguson also included a detailed account of, and sets of problems designed for, the celestial sphere.[17]

The orrery was a good deal more complex. The more sophisticated forms could cost a great deal of money, but Ferguson also developed a simpler version for showing the diurnal and annual motions of the Earth and the Moon and Sun. The more complex versions sought also to demonstrate the movements of Mercury and Venus in relation to them. It is unlikely that Paine would have purchased an orrery, but he doubtless had access to one during the lectures, and they would have played a central part in describing the motions of the planets within the Solar System; most crucially, they sought to *show* how the planetary system

---

[14] James, 'Thomas Paine's iron bridge work', claims that Paine squandered £500 that the excisemen had collected for their campaign, but there was no evidence that Paine received that sum, and Francis Oldys, his hostile biographer, could rise only to accusing him of having secreted £30. See Conway, *The Life of Thomas Paine*, 12–15.

[15] Which also supports the later dating of his attendance at the lectures.

[16] James Ferguson, *Astronomy Explained upon Sir Isaac Newton's Principles and Made Easy to Those Who Have Not Studied Mathematics*, 2nd edn (London: J. Ferguson, 1757), 79–81.

[17] James Ferguson, *Lectures on Select Subjects in Mechanics, Pneumatics, Hydrostatics, and Optics: With the Use of the Globes and the Art of Dialling* (London: W. Strahan, 1760). See esp. 278–306, 312–29 and material on rectification of the globe (including the harvest moon, for which Ferguson was renowned). See also the discussion of the armillary sphere, 329–33.

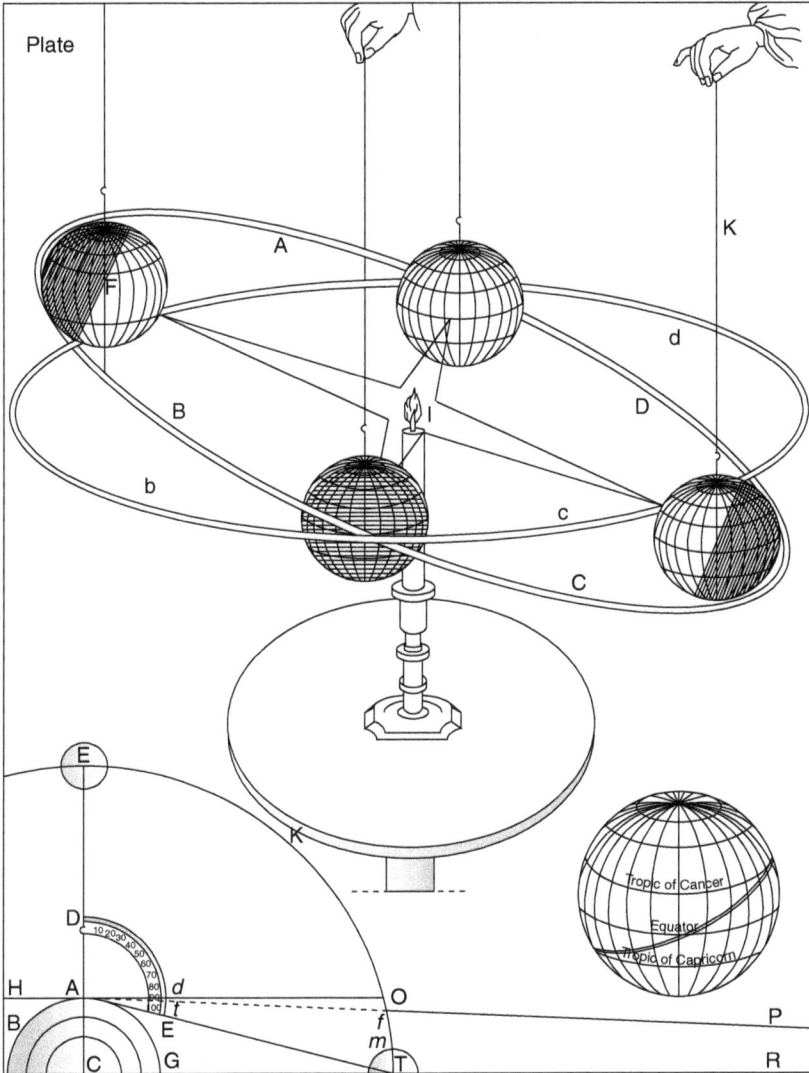

Figure 6.1 Exercises in globes: the use of candle and globes to demonstrate the motions of the planets
Source: James Ferguson, *Astronomy Explained upon Sir Isaac Newton's Principles and Made Easy to Those Who Have Not Studied Mathematics,* 2nd edn (London: J. Ferguson, 1757), 72–3.

worked, by reproducing its motions and relations mechanically. The development of a facility, through the use of an orrery, mechanically to reproduce the motions of the planets might not have been necessary for an understanding of celestial mechanics, but it might have been a sufficient to demonstrate the basic principles. Moreover, it would have done so in a way that dispensed with the more mathematical foundations developed in the *Principia*. There is some evidence that Paine saw things in this way from his comments in his *Age of Reason* about the way that the use of mechanical apparatuses substituted for the 'invisible agency by which all the component parts of the immense machine of the universe have influence upon each other and act in motional unison, without any apparent contact, and to which man has given the name attraction, gravitation and repulsion ... [and] the humble imitation of teeth and cogs...'.[18]

The mastery of the globes and orrery should, then, be associated with a pretty good understanding of the principles of astronomy and celestial mechanics. Indeed, since it is doubtful that he had access to Ferguson's or Martin's work when writing *The Age of Reason* (Paine always claimed that it was written without access to the Bible – and it is doubtful that other books would have been easier to obtain),[19] his recall of the basic principles of the Solar System is impressive. His account centred on astronomy, especially in the section on 'The plan and order of the Universe',[20] in which he detailed the character of the Solar System, the tilt of the Earth, the relation of the planets and the distances between them, the extent of the known Solar System, the nature of the stars and the probability of the existence of a plurality of worlds.[21]

There is also evidence that Paine had some independent grasp of the system. On Ferguson's account, not only was the Solar System evidence of God's beneficent design, but God remained an active interventionist

---

[18] Paine, *The Age of Reason*, 489.
[19] See Paine's account of the circumstances under which he wrote part one in the preface to part two: ibid., 514.
[20] Ibid., 500–3.
[21] While the last might be thought to be an eccentric addition to a comparatively conservative science by Paine, it is worth comparing Ferguson's comments in his *Astronomy Explained upon Isaac Newton's Principles*, 5: 'What an august! what an amazing conception, if human nature can conceive it, does this give of the works of the creator! Thousands of thousands of suns, multiplied without end, and ranged all around us, at immense distances from each other, attended by ten thousand Worlds, all in rapid motion, yet calm, regular, and harmonious, invariably keeping the paths prescribed them, and these Worlds peopled with myriads of intelligent beings, formed for endless progression in perfection and felicity. If so much power, wisdom, goodness, and magnificence is displayed in the material Creation, which is the least considerable part of the Universe, how great, how wise, how good must HE be, who made and governs the whole' [emphasis in original].

agent. He suggested, for example, that the Moon was nearer the Earth than formerly, and that its orbit of Earth would diminish over time, 'and therefore, she must come to earth at last; unless that Being, which gave her a sufficient projectile force at the beginning, adds a little more to it in due time'.

Here we have a strong philosophical argument against the eternity of the World. For, had it existed from eternity, and been left by the Deity to be governed by the combined actions of the above forces or powers, generally called Laws, it had been at an end long ago. And if it be left to them it must come to an end. But we may be certain that it will last as long as was intended by its Author, who ought no more to be found fault with for framing so perishable a work, than for making man mortal.[22]

Paine's position diverged from Ferguson's on this point. *The Age of Reason* did not envisage a continually interventionist God so much as a single first cause, whose design of the celestial order was such as to require no further intervention. In this respect, Paine's reading of Newtonian mechanics is one that was substantially more rationalist and deist in its implications than was that of many of his contemporaries (Anglican circles, for example, seem to have avoided drawing deist conclusions from their interpretation of Newton's account!). But this variance does suggest that Paine was not simply parroting the arguments of those who lectured to him. He advanced a view of the order of the system of the universe that had mathematical realism at its core:

Man cannot invent anything that is eternal and immutable; and the scientific principles he employs for this purpose must be, and are of necessity, as eternal and immutable as the laws by which the heavenly bodies move... The scientific principles that man employs to obtain foreknowledge of an eclipse, or of anything else relating to the motion of the heavenly bodies, are contained chiefly in that part of science which is called trigonometry... In fine, it is the soul of science; it is an eternal truth; it contains the *mathematical demonstration* of which man speaks, and the extent of its uses is unknown... It is the structure of the universe that has taught this knowledge to man. That structure is an ever-existing exhibition of every principle upon which every part of mathematical science is founded.[23]

In contrast to Ferguson, then, Paine seems to have been working with a conception of the natural order as governed by immutable mathematical principles. Within that system the development of human knowledge was

---

[22] Ferguson, *Astronomy Explained upon Isaac Newton's Principles*, 61–2; see also his *Lectures on Select Subjects*, lectures 44 and 45, on the importance of God's intervention as a result of a combination of planets in the same quarter of the heavens disturbing their motions through mutual influence.

[23] Paine, *The Age of Reason*, 488–9 [emphasis in original].

a function of the discovery of those principles and their rigorous application to phenomena in the world. While God was attributed the role of creating this immutable order, Paine was working with a more Platonist conception of that role and the creation than was Ferguson.

This suggests that Paine learnt a good deal on the celestial mechanics side. But there is also evidence that he attended to the details of their accounts of the nature of matter and so on. In a note to Thomas Jefferson, in which Paine referred to a conversation of the previous evening when Jefferson had argued that Newton's principle of gravitation would not explain, or could not apply as a rule to find the quantity of the attraction of cohesion, Paine's response was certainly not poorly informed. In his *Lectures on Select Subjects*, Ferguson identified five properties of matter, the fifth being attraction, of which there were four kinds: cohesion, gravitation, magnetism and electricity. Ferguson defined the attraction of cohesion as that by which small parts of matter were made to stick and cohere together, and he cited a range of implausibly connected examples of cohesion, including sugar or sponge drawing up liquid, flat oiled surfaces of marble sticking together and drops of mercury running together. Paine tried to distinguish between attraction and cohesion and to suggest that cohesion was best understood as a mechanical interlocking of parts of matter, leaving attraction as a quality of matter acting at a distance from the visible presence of matter. Although Paine's similes for explaining the difference were rather quaint, and tended to the anthropomorphic, the thrust of his point was one about qualities of matter, and, in eighteenth-century terms, he made an intelligible stab at an important concept.

On balance, then, although there is not a huge amount of evidence concerning Paine's grasp of the material covered by Martin and Ferguson, what evidence there is suggests that Paine probably did have a pretty good grounding, less in the mathematical principles of mechanics than in arguments concerning celestial motion; although Joel Barlow clearly did rate his mathematical understanding, there is nothing in his writing to demonstrate the extent of this grasp.[24]

This does not settle the issue of the nature of the relationship between science and religion for Paine, to which I return in my concluding remarks. But, as an interim comment, we can recognise that Paine, like many of his scientifically informed friends and contemporaries, found in

---

[24] Although there is also little to justify James' claim that Paine's pretensions to mathematical knowledge were 'mere window dressing': James, 'Thomas Paine's iron bridge work', 209. James' uncritical reliance on Gouverneur Morris's diary, which was markedly hostile to Paine and keen to belittle his achievements, is unfortunate.

the axioms, methods and principles of Newtonian astronomy a system with which they could make coherent sense of the order of the universe they inhabited. This understanding included a number of straightforward factual claims about the movements of the planets, together with explanatory accounts that linked those factual statements in a way that secured them as robust elements within an overall framework. For some, the framework remained heavily influenced by traditional theology, but this was not the case for Paine. Rather, he seems to have taken the framework as a form of complex orrery – a system that required a first cause but that, once in motion, provided an order that allowed us perfectly to predict and understand the fundamental elements of the natural world, with no further reference to God. Within this frame, then, the activities of observing and recording evidence and explaining phenomena could be done wholly in accordance with the principles of that science. To this extent, it was able to hold religious and mythological explanation at the borders of what was a practically and conceptually rich paradigm. That God still appeared at the edges of the scheme does not mean that Paine's scientific interests were driven by his religion. Indeed, the impression that God played a prominent role in his understanding partly arises from the fact that his comments on science and the Solar System were made in the context of his deist attack on the Christian religion – an attack that was, nonetheless, motivated by a concern that, 'in the general wreck of superstition, of false systems of government and false theology, we lose sight of morality, of humanity and of the theology that is true'.[25]

In many ways, it seems much more likely that his scientific education might have had some effect upon his religious thinking, since it provided him with a core of evidence, factual claims and propositions that carried their own authority by their predictive and explanatory power. To be introduced to this way of experiencing the world, and to be taught how to make the explanation work for himself (through the exercises for globes and orrery), was to be taught a method for arriving at certainty against which neither opinion nor authority could stand. It was an appeal to the authority of reason, experimentation and evidence. If this is the true kernel of Thomas Paine's education, rather than the knapsack of homespun philosophy picked up while being buffeted by the experience of repeated failure in mid-eighteenth-century England, we might expect that it would have a powerful impact both on his thinking and his subsequent writing. Not least, it might have given a degree of rigour and an evidential grounding to the core of his 'common sense'. It might have

---

[25] Paine, *The Age of Reason*, 464.

done this, but it is worth reflecting, first, that there is no evidence that Paine's understanding was any more sophisticated than the average member of the educated middling orders, and, second, that even if this is what Paine got from the paradigm it is clear that a great many of his contemporaries did not – finding it eminently possible to remain committed Christians *and* Newtonians! Moreover, as I discuss in my concluding remarks, we need to be extremely careful about the assumptions such claims make about the interconnection between scientific and other types of activity.

III

Thus far I have discussed Paine's interest in the more theoretical parts of science or natural philosophy, but eighteenth-century science was not just a set of particular beliefs; it also involved a set of practices and methods that embodied principles by which true and false statements were distinguished, proofs established and evidence gathered. Moreover, there were many different areas of scientific activity within which individuals might specialise. Paine was actively involved in practical experimentation, the construction of models, the testing of hypotheses and the building of tools and machinery. Although he corresponded and met such eminent scientists of his day as his lecturers, Sir Joseph Banks, George Scott, Franklin, Jefferson, David Rittenhouse, and so on, he did not, for the most part, discuss with them the intricacies of infinitesimal fractions and the fundamental theorem of the calculus. But this does not seem to have mattered greatly. Paine's letters to Jefferson, the person to whom the great bulk of his extant correspondence on scientific matters was addressed, only rarely concerned the more abstract aspects of natural philosophy (such as the attraction of cohesion), and more commonly focused on practical experimentation and the design of machines – and, of course, his bridge.

One way of viewing the difference between the more mathematical and astronomical side of science, on the one hand, and the more experimental, on the other, is that between the deductive and the inductive. The deductive, for which the more mathematical and geometrical work provides the model, begins with certain axioms and sets out to establish, by logical means, certain conclusions. Its paradigm case in the eighteenth century is Newton's *Principia*. The inductive uses experience and experimentation and seeks to derive generalisations that can then be subject to further testing; and it is more Baconian in form (although Newton's *Opticks* is equally a good example). Although it is important to recognise these two elements in the scientific activity of the middle of the eighteenth century, it would be a mistake to think of them as clearly and consistently distinguished in the manuals of popular science. Compare, for example, Benjamin Martin's discussion of the use of hypotheses in science with the entry on 'Hypotheses' in Temple Croker's *Complete Dictionary of the Arts and the Sciences* (1765). Croker held that only axioms and propositions derived from the nature of things were acceptable as the basis for scientific activity, and that the hypothesis had no role to play. Martin, on the other hand, in *The Philosophical Grammar; or, View of Modern Philosophy* (1735) defended their use against those 'who will receive no system of philosophy, but what is wholly founded on Mathematical Experiments and Demonstrations'. Nevertheless, there is a good deal of slippage in the terms with which experimental activity was discussed, and it is not surprising that, despite these seemingly disparate positions, the two works were in full agreement on the four fundamental rules for the construction of explanations for phenomena (probably because, as Croker acknowledged, the propositions derived from the third book of Newton's *Principia*):

I We must take Care to admit no more Causes of natural Things, than what are true, and sufficient to explain their Phaenomena.

II We must observe always to assign the same causes for the same Natural Effects.

III Those Qualities which cannot be increased or diminished, and agree to all Bodies in which Experiments can be made, must be adjudged the Properties of all Bodies in general.

IV Propositions and Conclusions, deduced from actual Experiments, must be esteemed true and accurater, notwithstanding any *Hypotheses*, or received *Suppositions*, to the contrary, and must be insisted on 'till some other phaenomena, either render them more accurate, or liable to exception.

It is not difficult to recognise these principles at work in Paine's own activities. In 1783 he was in Princeton with George Washington, close to a creek reputed to be capable of being set on fire. Paine, Washington and one or two others rowed out into the river and, holding lighted cartridge paper over the surface of the water, disturbed the mud at the bottom of the river, thereby releasing bubbles to which they set fire. The next time Paine was in Philadelphia he mentioned the experiment to Rittenhouse. The two hypothesised that combustible matter (vegetable or otherwise) that underwent decomposition either by fire or water in a confined space and in a manner so as not to blaze would be inflammable whenever it came into contact with flame. Paine and Rittenhouse then conducted a series of experiments to test the hypothesis that the destruction of flammable material by heat (sawdust in a sealed gun barrel, placed in a furnace), without flame, would result in the production of flammable gas.[26] This was by no means a trivial or eccentric discussion. In 1774 Benjamin Franklin had written to Joseph Priestley about the raising of a flame on the surface of water, and his account was not dissimilar to Paine's; moreover, it recorded that a letter on the issue was read to the Royal Society in England in 1765.

Franklin and Paine's experimental and scientific interests met on other occasions. There was correspondence between Franklin and General Charles Lee in 1776 about stockpiling arms in case of war, in which Franklin hoped that bows and arrows would also be laid up, since these had numerous advantages. A little over a year later Paine wrote to Franklin suggesting the development of 'fire arrows', of an iron construction, and he claimed that he and Rittenhouse were collaborating on a test model. Similarly, in 1785, Paine wrote to Franklin to describe his experiments to produce a smokeless candle, created by a bore running through the centre of the candle (Franklin had experimented when in Paris with a number of others on producing a smokeless lamp, without great success).[27] And on 1 January 1786 John Hall, the craftsman and mechanic whom Paine employed on his bridge, wrote in his diary: 'Mr Paine went to dine with Dr Franklin today; staid till after tea in the evening. They tried the burning of our candles by blowing a gentle current through them. It greatly improved the light. The draught of air is prevented by passing through a cold tube of tallow. The tin of the new lamp by internal reflections is heated and causes a constant current. This is the Doctor's conjecture.'[28]

It is worth comparing this process of testing and experimentation with Paine's occasional bouts of inductive generalisation. In a letter to Jefferson in Paris in September 1788, he proposed a method for estimating the loads of timber that may be gained from a tree. He started his calculation by drawing a parallel between a tree and a fountain (see Figure 6.2):

It is evident that no more water can pass through the branching tubes than pass through the trunk. 2nd, that admitting all the water to pass with equal freedom the sum of the squares of the diameters of the two first branches must be equal to the square of the diameter of the trunk ... etcetera [so that] the solid content of the whole will be equal to the cylinder of the same diameter of the trunk and height of the fountain.

By considering a tree as a fountain, with 'the sap ascending in capillary tubes like the water in a fountain [so that] no more water will pass through the branches than pass through the trunk', Paine was asking us to

---

[26] *The Life and Major Writings of Thomas Paine*, vol. II, 1062, 1063.   [27] Ibid., 1025.
[28] Conway, *The Life of Thomas Paine*, 340.

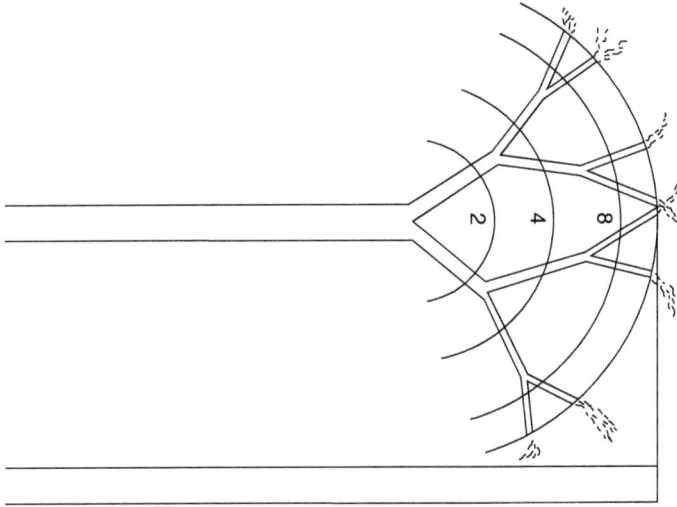

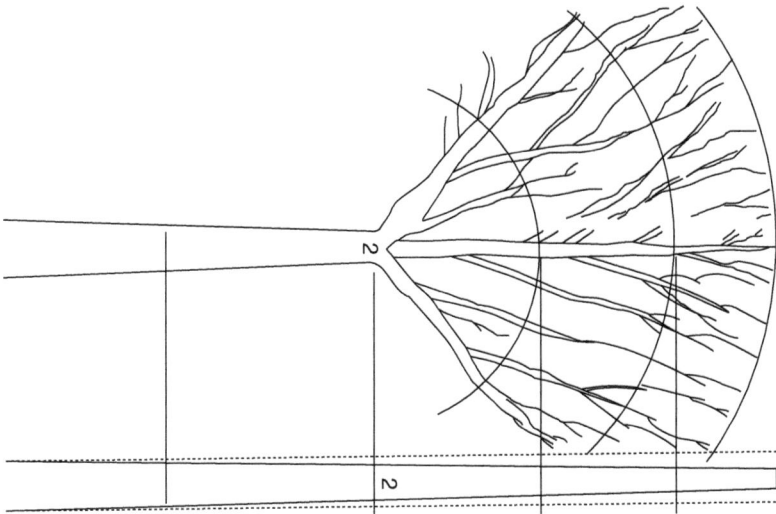

Figure 6.2 Tree and fountain
Source: The Life and Major Writings of Thomas Paine, vol. II, ed. Philip S. Foner (Secaucus, NJ: Citadel Press, 1948), 1036–7.

consider the branches as so many sub-divisions of the trunk as they are in the fountain, and their contents are to be found by some rule with the difference only of a pyramidian figure instead of a cylindrical one. Therefore to find the quantity of timber (or rather loads) in the tree... Draw a pyramid equal to the height of the tree ... taking for the inclination of the pyramid, the diameter of the bottom, and at any discretionary height above it which is as 3 and 2.

As sensible men should never guess, and as it is impossible to judge without some point to begin at, this appears to me to be that point, and by which a person may ascertain near enough the quantity of timber and loads of wood in any quantity of land, and he may distinguish them into timber, wood and faggots.[29]

The letter might seem surprising, as, if we follow Paine in comparing the areas of the circles created by dissecting the trunk and the branches, we might expect him to use the formula πr^2. The calculation works equally well with the diameter squared, however. This is not to say that the calculation is flawless; it makes a number of assumptions, not least that the rate of capillary action is the same throughout, and that the proportion of the trunk and branches through which water passes are in ratio to their size, and are invariable across types of tree. But, while Paine's account might seem rather bizarre, it is in many ways a perfect example of inductive reasoning. There must be some proportion between the size of a trunk and its branches, just as there must be some proportion between the width of a trunk and the height it can support. What Paine did was to make this assumption of a set of ordered and proportional relations and then apply the model of a fountain (thereby making the assumption that the single most important activity of the trunk and branches is the dispersion of moisture). It might seem that the account was seriously flawed, since, although it was designed to indicate the proportions of different qualities of wood, Paine nowhere explained at what point the trunk began branching, nor why there should be a constant ratio of length between the different parts of a tree. But, in fact, Paine made no such assumption. The observer has to measure the ratios, but Paine's method indicated not the length of different qualities of wood but, once we know or estimate the length, the quantity of that type of wood. As such, it is a perfect example of Paine's use of induction, based on a mechanical model of a natural phenomenon, filled out with additional empirical detail.[30]

---

[29] *The Life and Major Writings of Thomas Paine*, vol. II, 1035.

[30] I suspect that it is also an excellent example of Paine's ability to make use of other people's ideas – and his tendency not to credit them. Compare, for example, Paine's picture with the Leonardo da Vinci diagram given in Martin Kemp's *Leonardo* (Oxford University Press, 2004), 138–41. This too was drawn to demonstrate that in branching systems there is a degree of proportionality between the thicker and thinner branches. But it was drawn as an analogy with the lungs, and the concern was with the proportionality of the fluid passing through the tube to the area of the cross-section of the tube. Again, there was a

In 1801 Jefferson was also treated to letters concerning the possibilities of driving mechanical power by the use of gunpowder;[31] on the finishing of walls to make them secure against the weather; and on Paine's success in constructing carriage wheels on the basis of concentric circles, as opposed to cutting the rim across the grain: 'They are equally as firm as if they were a natural production and handsomer than any wheels ever yet made. But the machinery I have invented, and the means I used, to bring them to this perfection I cannot describe in a letter.'[32] In 1805 he was writing about his design for improving his new house; the following year he was proposing an explanation for the incidence of yellow fever; and at the end of his life he produced pieces on fortification, the use of gunboats and the difficulties in proposals to prevent the harbour of New York being reached by enemy ships.

Moreover, and most importantly, he spent the best part of seven years of his life designing and then trying to bring to realisation his iron bridge project, first in America and then in Europe. The bridge was distinctive first in being constructed from wrought iron, second in the design drawing in the shape of a spider's web, and third in being designed to span large distances without the use of piers. The bridge dominated Paine's life between 1785 and 1792; he designed various models, making several in wood. One was constructed from 1" square wood, with each piece 12.5" long, from which he constructed a model of 13 feet: '[W]hat weight it will bear, as it cannot be ascertained without breaking it, I am unwilling to put to an experiment. Four men have been on it at one time, without the least injury to it, or sign of any.'[33] Paine then hired the English forgeman, mechanic and inventor John Hall to help him make a sizeable metal model with which he hoped to persuade the Pennsylvania Assembly to build a 400 ft bridge across the river Schuylkill. When the Pennsylvania Assembly proved reluctant to build the bridge (it would have found it extremely costly to do so, as no existing ironworks was capable of producing the quantity of metal the design required), he took the models over

recognition that trees are not perfectly symmetrical, but the general rule seems to hold good – and, as with Paine, there was an argument that the total sum of the cross-sectional areas across the arc would be the same as the areas at any other arc drawn from the centre. It seems unlikely to me that Paine would have come up with the proposal wholly independently of this other version, but it is not easy to tie Paine to this version and to demonstrate his knowledge of it. The pictures came originally from the Codex Ubrinas in the Vatican. Thus far I have been unable to find any eighteenth-century copies of the diagram that Paine could have had access to, but it seems possible that Paine might have seen copies made by or ordered by Philip Mazzei, an intimate of Jefferson in Paris who arranged to have copies of various Florentine pictures and who had a small vineyard in Colle in Tuscany. The parallel is certainly striking.

[31] *The Life and Major Writings of Thomas Paine*, vol. II, 1047–50. [32] Ibid., 1425.
[33] Ibid., 1027.

to Europe and showed them to the French Academy of Science (although not to the Corps des Ponts et Chaussées, reputedly a much more demanding body, with considerably greater expertise than the academy), which was very much interested, in part because of a spate of proposals for iron bridges in France and the development of a range of models, some similar to Paine's, by French engineers.[34] He also applied successfully for a patent in England and collaborated with one of the foremost ironworks in England (that of Thomas Walker, in Rotherham) to produce a substantial model of the bridge with a 90 foot arch, constructed with 3 tons of iron and bearing a load easily of double that weight. On Paine's account, the bridge attracted a good deal of attention, not least from Sir Joseph Banks and members of the Royal Society, 'who appear as much pleased as if they had an interest in it',[35] and from those who paid to walk across it when it was finally erected in a field between Paddington and Marylebone in the summer of 1790.

More sceptical accounts have pronounced the exercise a flop, however, with the bridge seeming flimsy, subject to rust and having to be taken down prematurely because the wooden abutments gave way. J. G. James, a leading expert on early iron bridges, is openly hostile to Paine's attempt, suggesting that he borrowed many ideas from the French and that his bridge was 'ill-conceived and represented a retrograde step in the erratic advance of iron bridge technology'. On the other hand, he does concede that this 'should not be allowed to obscure the equally incontrovertible fact that he played an important role through his publicity of the topic and his ability to persuade backers to erect a full-sized example from which others better qualified than he could draw practical lessons'.[36] Despite James' technical expertise, there is a sense that he operates with a wholly teleological account of technological progress, in which the heroes are those whose work is justified ex post facto, and the villains are those whose work is not. More especially, with respect to Paine, even if we do not believe that he made a major contribution to progress in bridge-building, we should still recognise that there is ample evidence that it was an area of interest and expertise within which he made a contribution *by the standards of that practice*. In other words, while his financial arrangements may have been maverick, his enthusiasm rather amateurish and his design, in the last analysis, flawed, we need to acknowledge that he was recognised as a

---

[34] See J. G. James, 'Iron arched bridge designs in pre-revolutionary France', *History of Technology* 4 (1979), 63–99.

[35] Cited by W. H. G. Armytage, 'Thomas Paine and the Walkers: an early episode of Anglo-American co-operation', *Pennsylvania History* 18 (1951), 16–30, 27.

[36] James, 'Iron arched bridge designs in pre-revolutionary France', 218.

serious contributor to the field. James both asks too much and is prepared to concede too little. Although Paine's bridge never forged a river, there seems little doubt that he contributed to demonstrating the value of iron as a material for bridging large rivers without the use of piers. To do so, it seems clear that he would have had to have at least some basic mathematics and geometry. What he lacked, because everyone else did, was a science of materials to allow him the better to assess the weight of the iron he would need to use. On the other hand, it is also true that the systematic production of high-quality iron on a large scale, allowing a precise knowledge of its weight-bearing capacity and susceptibility to uneven expansion and contraction, was still in the future.

There remains an issue about how seriously to take all this activity. Is it significant that Paine wrote about scientific matters predominantly in his correspondence with Franklin and, more frequently, Jefferson? Is this a case of Paine trying to sustain his standing with two central figures in America by appealing to a common interest in scientific inquiry? I doubt it. One reason we have these letters is that Jefferson and Franklin kept them; we can only speculate about others written and lost (although we do know that there are more than we have to Joseph Banks, George Scott and others). Moreover, there is nothing I have found in the correspondence with Jefferson, Franklin or others to suggest that they had anything other than a genuine interest in, and respect for, Paine's proposals; (Gouverneur Morris, on whose judgement James relied, was more sceptical, but he clearly had an axe to grind). Jefferson was certainly critical of some of them. He wrote to Paine expressing doubts about some aspects of the design for alterations to his house, but he did so in a manner that we cannot regard as condescending.[37] And there is no evidence that Franklin, Washington, Jefferson or other senior figures of the revolution and the scientific community in America, with the exception of Morris, had anything other than a genuine interest in Paine's ideas. On the methodological principle of charity we have, I think, to believe that they took Paine's ideas every bit as seriously as he did.

IV

What, then, can we say about the relationship between Paine's scientific activities and interests and his politics, and his religion? Should we see his scientific understanding as shaped by his religious beliefs, and, above all perhaps, by his sense of the sufficiency of individual conscience in

---

[37] *The Life and Major Writings of Thomas Paine*, vol. II, 1057.

religion, politics and science? Should we play down Paine's knowledge and expertise in astronomy and celestial mechanics, and play up his experiments and inventions, so as to indicate that science was, for Paine, an extension of common sense rooted in experience? We might feel justified in doing this, but there are at least three other ways in which Paine's activities might be read.

In the first, science becomes much more central to understanding Paine's politics. The account begins with celestial mechanics and induction. For all the theist conclusions drawn from the movements of the planets – with respect to the providential ordering of nature, and the role of God as a first cause – the idea of a systematic order to nature knowable through human reason, and subject to practical demonstration and mathematical proof, can be seen as having an extraordinarily powerful effect on Paine, showing him the power of inductive reasoning. On this view, his reading of common sense was one shaped by his belief that nature provided the basis for a moral geometry, which began from the axioms of the equality of individuals and the absence of divinely ordained authority. This sense of moral geometry is best captured by Jefferson:

> We hold these truths to be self-evident: that all men are created equal; that they are endowed by their creator with *Inherent* and inalienable rights; that among these are life, liberty, and the pursuit of happiness: that to secure these rights, governments are instituted among men, deriving their just powers from the consent of the governed; that whenever any form of government becomes destructive of these ends, it is the right of the people to alter or abolish it...[38]

This inductive pattern of reasoning, which we can see in evidence in Paine's writing throughout his life, worked in a very different way from the traditions of political discourse in England in the 1790s. Hence the radicalism of the *Rights of Man*, and hence the reluctance among those attracted to radicalism wholly to endorse Paine's principles, which were recognised as foreign to the free-born rights of Englishmen to which it was customary to appeal. Paine's position on rights was axiomatic and universal, not empirical and local; in this he was clearly drawing inspiration from outside the conventional sources of English political argument, and it seems plausible to think that a major inspiration was the model of reasoning he found in the lectures of Ferguson and Martin and among the scientists with whom he worked in the New World.

A second way of understanding the impact of Paine's scientific interests is to see scientific activity as giving him a purchase on the world that was of

---

[38] 'A declaration by the representatives of the United States of America, in general congress assembled', in *Jefferson: Writings*, ed. Merrill Peterson (New York: Library of America, 1984), 19–24, 19 [emphasis in original].

a fundamentally different order from that gained in politics. The rigorous formulation of propositions and their testing, in some cases against evidence, in others through the deployment of models and machines, allowed the development of a set of propositional attitudes that were fundamentally orientated, on the one hand, to states of affairs in the natural world and, on the other, to criteria of consistency and coherence between propositions. In contrast, political discourse was saturated with semi-propositional beliefs; the distinction is Dan Sperber's:

> Propositions are either true or false. Sets of propositions are either consistent or inconsistent. Propositions, as opposed to sentences or utterances, cannot be ambiguous and hence true in some interpretations and false in others. Yet some of our so-called beliefs have several possible interpretations and we can hold them without committing ourselves to any of their interpretations... Many of our thoughts are what we might call semi-propositional, they approximate but do not achieve propositionality.[39]

Sperber's suggestion (albeit advanced in a rather different context) is that, rather than treating all beliefs as of equivalent standing, which is the route that relativism takes, we can distinguish between beliefs made up from factual statements and true and consistent propositions and beliefs whose content is semi-propositional because it is ambiguous, unclear and subject to a variety of interpretations, and thus cannot be said to be either true or false. Paine's scientific 'education', and his practical experimentation, would have offered him a rigorous method for formulating and testing propositions. To put science at the core of Paine's later life would be to bring to the fore his rootedness in a way of understanding the world that is propositional, evidentially established and insistent upon coherence – one that, as a result, cuts through an understanding of the world based on authority (religious or secular) and on force and fraud. Throughout Paine's writing, one consistent device was the debunking of symbolic practices and the rhetoric and illusion around authority, in favour of simple propositional statements:

> Mr Burke talks about what he calls an hereditary crown as if it were some production of Nature; or as if, like Time, it had the power to operate, not only independently, but in spite of man; or as if it were a thing or a subject universally consented to. Alas! It has none of those properties, but is the reverse of them all. It is a thing in imagination, the propriety of which is more than doubted, and the legality of which in a few years will be denied.[40]

---

[39] Sperber, *On Anthropological Knowledge*, 50–3.
[40] Thomas Paine, *Rights of Man* [1791], in *The Life and Major Writings of Thomas Paine*, vol. I, 244–458, 322–3.

Can we take this as evidence that natural science drove Paine's thinking, or should we just see it as a rhetorical strategy (even if that rhetoric was itself driven by an understanding of the character of evidence, reasoning, ideas and grounded belief that derived from a model of scientific understanding)? What is a king but a man; and what is the Bible but the product of men? Statements need to be purged of their illusion and muddling, and distilled into a rational kernel of factual propositions. As a way of proceeding among his contemporaries in late eighteenth-century political discourse – not least as a way of proceeding against Burke – the method was extremely powerful; clear thought revealed that the emperor had no clothes.

On this second view, the methodological training that encouraged Paine to break down ideas into sets of coherent factual propositions played a much more formative role than the experimental side of his various scientific inquiries.

The third position I want to discuss recognises that this second account has its limits, and it resists the view that Paine should be understood as trying to found a political science. The axiomatic propositions upon which his political creed was based were hardly straightforwardly factual; the view that all men come equally from the hand of God was not an obvious candidate for a straightforward factual proposition. Did Paine realise this? Was he attempting to apply standards of rigour and clarity in dealing with the social and political world that mirror those with which he worked in the scientific? Or had he a sense of the different character of the activities, so that his application was knowingly metaphorical? This is a difficult judgement to make, but there are grounds for thinking that Paine did know the difference between a factual proposition and a rhetorical move. His scientific thinking may have informed his political rhetoric, but what drove that rhetoric was, above all, the desire to dethrone religious and political authority by appeals to the experience and aspirations of the middling ranks and artisan classes of society. The essential equality of individuals, then, could be seen both as a type of axiom and as a powerful rhetorical weapon against the status quo. But we need not think that Paine saw the axiom as having the status of a scientific proposition.

What about Paine's experiments? One thing to which we should be alert is the multiplicity of areas of inquiry in which he worked; indeed, one source of the impression that Paine was a dabbler is precisely his apparent willingness to have a go at whatever attracted his fancy. There is something in this: when we look in detail at the relatively sparse remains of his scientific work, it appears to be eccentrically diverse in character. In fact, we might also be drawn to the conclusion that, whatever his education in Newtonian science, his practical approach lacked any unifying methodological principles. This would be a mistake. There is a great deal of variation in his writing – and variation in the level of expertise and in the extent to which he relied on induction or deduction in approaching a subject. But two factors may have contributed significantly to this. One is the extent to which such methodological eclecticism was present in a good deal of the work of Paine's acquaintances; the other is that methods must by necessity be adapted to their objects of study. Different features of the natural world and universe are differentially open to empirical inquiry, inductive generalisation and the formulation and testing of hypotheses. Eighteenth-century science is best understood, then, not as a single activity but as a loose group of activities, which hung together with varying degrees of tightness because of a shared attitude towards establishing statements as factual by reference to inductively generated models, supported by evidence, by appealing directly to states in the world and by their consistency with other statements. Seen in this way, one implication for the translatability of Paine's scientific interests to the world of politics or religion is that, although we can detect a general disposition to establish an axiomatic base for generalisation together with an insistence on clarity and determinateness of propositional content, the connection between the very different areas of activity was likely to be a loose one. In other words, in contrast to the tendency to reductionism in the study of Paine – bringing his science down to an extension of common sense, or treating it as a function of his religious commitments or treating his scientific activity as foundational – I am suggesting that there may have been no single foundation for Paine's thinking. His beliefs in politics, religion and science might have had elements in common because of the extent to which he was impressed by the way that a broadly scientific approach could open up the natural world to coherent understanding, but, rather than insisting on linking everything back to this common core, we should recognise that the impact of his scientific education on his other inquiries was of a limited character. There are strict limits on the extent to which a scientific attitude can clear up the terminology and practice of politics, and perhaps still stricter limits on the extent to which it can resolve theological issues – and there is nothing in Paine's work to suggest that he believed otherwise. If this is the case, then we should expect there to be only limited possibilities for generalising from one field of activity to another – a view that helps explain how it was that many others who wrote on science in this period might have held quite markedly different beliefs on politics or religion. The determinateness of scientific knowledge and practice simply does not spill over directly into other areas of activity; indeed, even within science there are quite marked differences in the type of knowledge achievable.

The drive in scientific activity is towards unambiguous statements of testable content, albeit with different areas of science drawing on induction and deduction to different degrees. This is not to say that all scientific statements are true; only that truth in the form of unambiguous factual content and consistency is what they track – and what they tracked in the late eighteenth century. As I have suggested, one way to identify connections with Paine's politics would be to recognise a similar type of pressure in his political writing. Clearly, such an interpretation can be given: the desire to disambiguate, to clarify, to work inductively from axiomatic principles, and, equally, a sense of experimentation in political affairs, by which ideas might be tested (albeit the real experiment was always America for Paine, and he had real doubts about its translatability, though fewer between 1789 and 1798). But, on the account I have sketched, there are strict limits to the extent to which this recognition allows us to explain Paine's political or theological writings in relation to his scientific work, because of the inherent recalcitrance of the subject matter to the type of rigorous analysis and testing that Paine rightly believed could be applied to the natural world.

On this reading, what Paine wrote at the opening of *Rights of Man* ('What Archimedes said of the mechanical powers, may be applied to Reason and Liberty: *Had we*, said he, *a place to stand upon, we might raise the world*. The revolution in America presented in politics what was only theory in mechanics')[41] does not mean that we should take him to be using science as a model; rather, it functioned as a metaphor or analogy. When he used thirteen sections in his bridge (the number of states that took part in the American Revolution) we should not think that he was politicising his science so much as adding a rhetorical flourish or garnish to what was essentially a mechanical experiment. Clearly, in some cases the connections seemed closer, as in the attack on established religion in his *Age of Reason*. Here, though, the account of the order of the universe was offered as an alternative to the pretensions to authority upon which the religious world view is founded. And the attack worked as a confession of faith based on reflection on nature and experience, rather than as a claim about the inevitability of deism for anyone holding a Newtonian view of the world.

Science may have afforded Paine's thinking a certain methodological rigour, but it would be greatly to exaggerate to claim that this method was unproblematically translatable across the wide range of subjects on which Paine wrote – politics, economics, theology, and so on – or, indeed, that

---

[41] Paine, *Rights of Man* [1792], 353–4 [emphasis in original].

Paine believed it was translatable. We are left, then, with a much more fractured picture of his activity than is customary; a view in which science had its own domains, but did not determine his religious, political or other beliefs. This more fractured view can be discomfiting. It is easy to see why commentators are attracted to the idea that there must have been some common core that held all these different beliefs and activities together. But, in refusing to endorse views that reduce all Paine's activity to science, or that identify deism as the underlying force behind his oeuvre or that insist on the fundamental character of Paine's common sense, I am also rejecting the idea that such a common core of method, ideas or beliefs has to exist (whether for Paine or for us). Men and women, more generally, process information differently in different contexts, demand higher or lower standards of rigour and assess their responsibilities differentially between activities. Although there are indications that Paine's scientific understanding had some influence on his political and religious thinking, through the use of analogies, similes and models and through the application of certain methodological principles, the differences between the various types of activity must be recognised, and the allusive and metaphorical character of the references must be acknowledged. If we worry about what held these different practices and knowledges together and made them cohere, the best answer we can give is that it was their shared, social character that allowed their social reproduction and that enabled men and women to negotiate those boundaries and hiatuses by which we are now sometimes shocked.

With respect to Paine, when we encounter his conviction of an afterlife in which virtue will be rewarded and vice punished,[42] or his complete silence on women and his relative silence after 1776 on the issue of slavery,[43] his failure to discuss the Irish or the Indian questions, or his apparent lack of comment on the US federal constitution and the federalist debates, save for the gloss given in *Rights of Man, Part the Second*,

---

[42] Thomas Paine, 'My private thoughts on a future state', in *The Age of Reason*, ed. John M. Robertson (London: Watts, 1910), 123.

[43] See Thomas Paine, 'Letter to anonymous, March 16, 1789', in *The Life and Major Writings of Thomas Paine*, vol. II, 1285–6, in which he despaired of seeing an end to the infernal traffic in 'Negroes'; there were also two comments about the immorality of slavery in a long letter written to Jefferson in 1805, in which he reserved his greatest wrath for Liverpool and its conduct of the slave trade and referred to a plan of Jefferson's for making slaves tenants on plantations: ibid. 1458, 1462, 1464. His very early piece in the *Pennsylvania Journal*, 'African slavery in America', has now been rejected as authentically Paine's by Aldridge in *Thomas Paine's American Ideology*, 289–91. Indeed, although Aldridge insists that Paine did speak out on the subject, he also claims that the most explicit defence is in an obscure poem written during the French Revolution.

chapter IV,[44] in each case we are encouraged by his other works to expect something different, but in each case we make the mistake of thinking that Paine's intellectual, emotional, social and political worlds were seamlessly connected, and that he too made such apparently obvious connections.[45] These points at which we sense a fissure or gap in Paine's beliefs do not indicate that his thought was incoherent. Rather, they show that he did not share our world view, nor our way of holding together the different bodies, types and subjects of belief that he held. In his own time, among his contemporaries, many of these fissures may have been unrecognised, because the boundaries between the various domains of belief and practice were tacitly shared, and, as such, negotiated unproblematically. But this tacit sharing also allowed for moments of transgression, as when Priestley, for all his rationalism and his scientific work, was recorded by John Adams commenting that 'the ten crowned heads of Europe were the ten horns of the Beast in *Revelation*', and 'the execution of the king of France is the falling off of the first of those horns'.[46] Paine similarly exploited the rhetorically powerful move of transgression, in which, for example, the tacit conventions concerning the religious implications of the Newtonian world view could be challenged. But transgression can work in either direction: by deploying scientific language to attack religious belief, or vice versa; while Paine seems to have drawn on the more rigorous types of knowledge to construct his critique of politics, Burke might be said to have worked the other way.

For all the apparent unity and simplicity of Paine's position, we fail to grasp his world unless we recognise the multiple and fragmentary character of his knowledge and commitments. The significance of his scientific activity, then, is not that it allows us more fully to appreciate the core of rationalism that drove Paine's political and religious thought but, on the contrary, the fact that it can help us see the complexity of his intellectual world and the multiple character of its domains of knowledge. And, in recognising this, we can also recognise that the world in which men and women thought and acted was a substantially more complex and fragmented one than is captured by our conventional picture of the period as one of Enlightenment.

---

[44] See Chapter 7 below, though.
[45] This is not to suggest that we cannot find ways of explaining these silences. We might, for example, suggest that Paine avoided discussing slavery because the institution sat badly with his endorsement of the American system of government. But we need to be very careful not to allow our interpretation of Paine's beliefs to press us into thinking that there were implications of his doctrine that he should have recognised and that, consequently, require explanation.
[46] Clarke Garrett, *Respectable Folly: Millenarians and the French Revolution in France and England* (Baltimore: Johns Hopkins University Press, 1975), 133.

7   Revolutionaries in Paris: Paine and Jefferson[1]

> Be encouraged all ye friends of freedom and writers in its defence...
> Behold the light you have struck out, after setting America free, reflected
> to France and there kindled into a blaze that lays despotism in ashes and
> warms and illuminates Europe.[2]

Richard Price's stirring celebration of the cause of liberty seems to
endorse a view that became widely held between 1789 and 1792, namely
that the principles of the American Revolution had laid the foundation for
a similar revolution in France that might also extend to Britain. Modern
commentators have almost entirely resisted this view: some have treated
the French Revolution as a modern, socially transformative and progressive revolution (rather than as a classical revolution, involving the returning of political society to its original principles); others have seen America
as a limited political revolution in sharp contrast to the French, in which
social issues derailed political reforms to produce a depth of political
intrusion into the private world that opened the road to totalitarianism.
But these contrasting perspectives have developed with the benefit (and
the blinkers) of hindsight, and few who responded positively to the opening events of the French Revolution grasped that this might be a radically
different set of events from those of America in 1776. Hence, in part,
people's confusion over Burke's reaction.

This sense of America's contribution to France's revolution was important for both Thomas Paine and his friend Thomas Jefferson. Nevertheless,
while the American experience exercised a powerful influence on Paine, I
argue that his experiences in Paris (in Jefferson's circle) and in London, in
the late 1780s and early 1790s, had an independent impact both on his
understanding of America and its revolution and on his expectations for

---

[1] My thanks are owed to the editors and to audiences in London and Warwick for their
comments, and to Jonathan Clark for his careful reading of the chapter, which corrected a
number of errors.
[2] Richard Price, *A Discourse on the Love of our Country*, in *Price: Political Writings*,
176–196, 196.

France and Britain. I focus here on the changes in Paine's position in the opening years of the French Revolution, the implications that these have for his understanding of the nature of democracy, and his subsequent re-evaluation of America's implications for Europe in 1791/2. The main focus of the chapter is on Paine rather than Jefferson, who left France in the autumn of 1789, but their intellectual kinship in the two years they overlapped in Europe helps us to understand why Paine's thinking took the direction it did in the aftermath of Jefferson's departure. Linking the interpretation of the writings of the two men in this period allows a clearer appreciation of the ways in which their affinities derived in large part from their interpretation – and reinterpretation – of America.

The argument of this chapter touches on broader issues concerning political ideas in the American and French Revolutions at the end of the eighteenth century. On the one hand, it gives grounds for resisting the rather teleological account that drives a certain amount of American historiography, in which the movement for independence and the institutions of representative democracy are seen as the natural and inevitable outcome of the self-determination of the American people. For a number of writers on France, the French Revolution demonstrates a similar conceptual determinism, in which the events of 1792–4 are the unfolding of the logic inherent in the claims by the National Assembly to embody the general will. Whereas the American tendency is to see the institutions of democracy and representative government as the necessary consequence of commitments to rights and popular sovereignty, however, in the French case the language of the people, the nation and its sovereignty open the conceptual space for the emergence of the Terror.[3]

---

[3] On the American front, see, for example, Edmund S. Morgan, *Inventing the People: The Rise of Popular Sovereignty in England and America* (New York: W. W. Norton, 1988); on France, this line has been developed and pursued by a number of interpretations, including the later work of François Furet. But see the closing remarks to what is one of the most important works on the discourses of political theory in the French Revolution: 'To the extent that their acceptance of the suspensive veto implied a repudiation of Sieyès's arguments for a theory of representation based on the division of labour, the assembly was setting aside a discourse of the social, grounded on the notion of the differential distribution of reason, functions and interests in modern civil society, in favour of a discourse of the political, grounded on the theory of a unitary general will. In the most general terms, it was opting for the language of political will, rather than that of social reason; of unity, rather than of difference; of civic virtue, rather than of commerce; of absolute sovereignty, rather than of government limited by the rights of man – which is to say that, in the long run, it was opting for the Terror': Keith Michael Baker, *Inventing the French Revolution* (Cambridge University Press, 1990), 305. See also Kenneth Margerison, *Pamphlets and Public Opinion: The Campaign for Union of Orders in the Early French Revolution* (West Lafayette, IN: Purdue University Press, 1998), 77–82, for comments on the similar position of Furet and Ran Halévi. Some of these ideas link to Hannah Arendt's reading of the two revolutions in *On*

In contrast to such perspectives, this chapter emphasises the contingent development of ideas, and the underdetermination of events by language and theory. French and American historiography have both emphasised the power of political language and discourse, but they have not, in my view, sufficiently acknowledged that, in this period at least (1776–1830), the Atlantic world underwent massive political and social upheaval, in which political discourses were dramatically transformed, and re-emerged in often unpredictable and contradictory ways that were not, for the most part, driven by any internal conceptual necessity or logic. The analysis undertaken here of Paine's developing position argues that his understanding of his world changed, but that there was nothing predetermined about the process or the direction of these changes. I suggest that historians need to recognise that historical actors changed their minds for reasons that were not always apparent to them, and that we should not assume that what seems an obvious entailment to us would also have been evident to them. Between 1787 and 1792 Paine's political vision broadened dramatically to encompass the possibility of a political transformation for Europe on the American model. In that process, however, his French and British experience led him dramatically to revise his understanding of America's past and of its relationship to the future, and that, in turn, subsequently transformed his expectations of Europe's future.[4]

I

In 1774, after a history of successive failures in Britain, Paine secured letters of introduction from Benjamin Franklin, whom he had met in London, and using the money he had received under the articles of separation from his wife he bought himself a passage to the United States.[5] In America he blossomed, becoming one of the most influential pamphleteers of the American Revolution and playing a part in both federal and Pennsylvanian politics. He accompanied John Laurens on a short visit to France in 1781, but seems to have had few contacts among the French, associated chiefly with Laurens and Franklin and returned to America with Laurens several weeks later. In the aftermath of the American Revolution, and with the financial security to pursue his scientific interests, Paine developed a design

---

Revolution (London: Faber & Faber, 1964), and the themes are also picked up in Antonio Negri's *Insurgencies: Constituent Power and the Modern State*, trans. Maurizia Boscagli (Minneapolis: University of Minnesota Press, 1992).

[4] In these notes I suggest that a similar case can be made for Jefferson, although I lack the space to do so fully.

[5] For the articles of separation, see the document acquired by the East Sussex Records Office in November 2009.

for a single-span bridge made of iron, but, finding it difficult to attract sponsors in America, he determined to take his model to Paris.

Paine arrived back in Paris in May 1787. He was quickly in touch with Jefferson.[6] While the full extent of his day-to-day contact with Jefferson is not wholly clear, we do know that he associated with the Marquis de Lafayette and others of Jefferson's circle.[7] Indeed, between 1787 and 1789 various discussions and exchanges took place involving Jefferson, Paine, Lafayette, and others, which covered a number of major political issues: they examined and responded to the proposals of the Federal Convention of 1787; they deliberated over the basic principles underlying the institutions and practices of popular government; they engaged in a pragmatic discussion of the constitution of France and how it might

---

[6] Paine was resident in Paris principally in the spring and summer of 1787; between December 1787 and February 1788; in the spring of 1788; in the winter of 1789/90; from April to July 1791; and from August 1792. He also corresponded with Jefferson and Lafayette (not always directly) when in England. It is also important to recognise the significance of Paine's earlier trip, and of the letters of introduction he secured from Franklin (with whom Paine seems to have become intimate only on that visit), which brought him into a range of circles he would have otherwise found difficult to reach. This issue is poorly discussed in most secondary sources), but see Philipp Ziesche, 'Thomas Paine and Benjamin Franklin's French circle', in Simon P. Newman and Peter S. Onuf, eds., *Paine and Jefferson in the Age of Revolutions* (Charlottesville: University of Virginia Press, 2013).

[7] There is a question of when Paine met the Marquis de Condorcet. Paine's correspondence mentioned a number of major figures, such as the Duc de La Rochefoucauld, General Chastellux, Guillaume-Chrétien de Malesherbes, Jean Baptiste Le Roy, the Comte de Buffon, Abbé Morley, M. Terenet, and others (see *The Life and Major Writings of Thomas Paine*, vol. II, 1262–3), but not Condorcet. Does this mean they did not meet until 1789 or 1790? It should be noted that those listed appeared in a letter to Franklin in which Paine was noting particular friends of Franklin. There is no firm evidence of contact with Condorcet, although he would have been aware of Paine's bridge project and he was closely associated with Jefferson, which makes some contact likely. See Jean-Paul Lagrave, 'Thomas Paine et les Condorcet', in Bernard Vincent, ed., *Thomas Paine; ou, La république sans frontières* (Presses universitaires de Nancy, 1993), 57–65, which suggests they were acquainted from 1787: 'Paine et les Condorcet s'étaient connus dès 1787 et avaient pu s'apprécier. Mais ce n'est réellement qu'à partir de 1791 que l'action allait la souder de façon indéfectible' (57); and Elisabeth Badinter and Robert Badinter, *Condorcet, 1743–1794: un intellectuel en politique* (Paris: Fayard, 1988), 227–28. Certainly, by 1789–91, Paine and Condorcet were close (see A. Owen Aldridge, *Man of Reason: The Life of Thomas Paine* (London: Cresset Press, 1960, 145), but it is difficult to identify the starting point of their relationship; Paine's first mention of him in a letter that survives dated 16 April 1790. Foner attributes Paine's writing of *Prospects on the Rubicon* (1787) to the influence of Lafayette, Condorcet and Loménie de Brienne: *The Life and Major Writings of Thomas Paine*, vol. II, 620. Paine's contact with Lafayette is much clearer; he knew him from America, and gravitated to him partly because of his fluency in English. One reason that Paine and Condorcet may have been less close in the initial stage of the French Revolution was that Condorcet was a supporter of de Brienne's reforms, and did not see the need for calling the Estates General: Keith Michael Baker, 'Condorcet', in François Furet and Mona Ozouf, *A Critical Dictionary of the French Revolution*, trans. Arthur Goldhammer (Cambridge, MA: Belknap Press, 1989), 204–12.

navigate through the difficulties that increasingly beset it from 1787; and they analysed the relative merits and disadvantages of the British constitution as a potential model for France and America.[8] For example, on 4 February 1788 Lafayette reported that 'Mr Jefferson, Common Sense and myself are debating [the proposed constitution] in a convention of our own as earnestly as if we were to decide upon it'.[9] Through these discussions, Paine and Jefferson both began to rework and rethink their principles in ways that produced major developments in their positions, and, in Paine's case, had a powerful subsequent effect on the development of his views between 1789 and 1792.

Paine's biographers have tended to see him, at this point, as obsessed by concerns relating to his bridge but his correspondence demonstrates his involvement in a number of other domains. In the absence of an American minister in London, he affected to play the role himself, and sought out for discussion a number of leading Whigs, including Sir George Staunton, Charles Stanhope, James Fox, Edmund Burke, the Duke of Portland and William Petty, the Marquess of Lansdowne.[10] His correspondence shows that his attention was engaged by events in Britain, France, and elsewhere. Indeed, his concern over the possible war over the Dutch revolt led him to write *Prospects on the Rubicon* in August 1787.[11]

That Paine was engaged in thinking and deliberating about politics and its principles is also clear from the fact that at least three major themes, which were central to the first part of his *Rights of Man* (1791) but were largely absent from his earlier writing, emerged for him in discussions in France in the late 1780s. The first concerns the language of rights.

No fully worked out account of natural right was published by Paine until the first part of *Rights of Man* in 1791.[12] A draft of his distinction

---

[8] The evidence, discussed below, relies on a various letters and texts – including the French edition of John Stevens' *Observations on Government: Including some Animadversations on Mr Adams's Defence of the Constitutions of Government of the United States of America and on Mr De Lolme's Constitution of England* (New York: W. Ross, 1787), the two parts of Paine's *Rights of Man* (1791, 1792) and a number of letters written by Jefferson, Lafayette and Paine. On Stevens, see below, notes 15 and 16.

[9] Louis Gottschalk, *Between the American and the French Revolution (1783–1789)* (University of Chicago Press, 1950), 374.

[10] See, for example, *The Life and Major Writings of Thomas Paine*, vol. II, 1265, 1270–1, 1283, 1300–1.

[11] On Russia, see ibid., 1271; the Austrian Netherlands, 1288; the Turks, 1301.

[12] It may seem surprising that there is no discussion of rights earlier in Paine, given that we associate the practice of drawing up a bill of rights with America. But, in fact, the language of rights had a rather uncertain place within American debates (enabling a generation of scholars to dismiss Locke's influence) until crystallised in the debates on the bill of rights in relation to the federal constitution in 1787 and 1788. Clearly, in one sense, an awareness of rights claims was a powerful current in American thought, but, in the process

between types of rights appeared in a letter to Jefferson written in 1788/9, however, well before Burke's *Reflections on the Revolution in France*.[13] In this letter (referring to a discussion the previous evening at Jefferson's), as in *Rights of Man*, natural rights were distinguished into those that we have the power to execute (as in the right to think for ourselves) and those that we need a civil power to support (as in the right to property). Although the discussion was fuller in *Rights of Man*, this earlier letter shows that, rather than responding to Burke's attack on 'natural rights' by developing a new set of distinctions, Paine had already largely worked these out. Moreover, the impetus for doing so was a discussion of a pamphlet defending the federal constitution by James Wilson, in which Wilson saw individual natural rights in terms of the right to 'act as his pleasure or his interest may prevail', which rendered the state of nature 'insupportable', requiring us to give up these rights in order to preserve our liberty.[14] Paine accused Wilson of muddling liberty and security, and the position he advanced was one in which natural rights were entrusted the better to be exercised, rather than given up or alienated. It is this that disposed Paine to the idea of an enumeration of rights: in his view, all civil rights had at their basis a natural right that they sought more effectively to secure. This position was one shared by Jefferson and Marie Jean de Caritat, Marquis de Condorcet. All three men regretted the omission of such a statement in the American case and argued for its inclusion, doing so in circles that

of bringing them to the fore and grounding a wider political argument on them, those earlier commitments became reworked and reinterpreted, not least because they had traditionally been thought of as rights against a potentially tyrannical political power and there was widespread uncertainty as to whether such rights were required by, or legitimate in, a political order deriving from the sovereignty of the people. See, for example, Alexander Hamilton's resistance to a bill of rights in *Federalist Paper* no. 84, in *The Federalist: The Gideon Edition*, ed. George W. Carey and James McClellan (Indianapolis: Liberty Press, 2001), 445. There was a widespread sense that such a bill would have a different function – one that 'delimited certain areas of individual behaviour over which the sovereign majority relinquished control': Willi Paul Adams, *The First American Constitutions: Republican Ideology and the Making of the State Constitutions in the Revolutionary Period*, 2nd edn (New York: Rowman & Littlefield, 2001), 143. As late as the 1780s only half the American states had bills of right, and they were not used as the basis for judicial decisions. It seems plausible to claim that, while a sense of rights against an oppressive colonial power were clear, the place and meanings of rights within a republican polity were slow to emerge – as, indeed, the discussion on the bill of rights in 1787/8 demonstrates. See also Keith Michael Baker, 'The idea of a declaration of rights', in Dale Van Kley, ed., *The French Idea of Freedom: Origins of the Declaration of the Rights of Man and of the Citizen* (Stanford University Press, 1994), 154–96.

[13] Reprinted in *The Life and Major Writings of Thomas Paine*, vol. II, 1298–9. The letter referred to a meeting at Jefferson's house in Paris, which he left to return to America in October 1789.

[14] James Wilson, *The Substance of a Speech Delivered by James Wilson, Esq., Explanatory of the General Principles of the Proposed Federal Constitution* (Philadelphia: T. Bradford, 1787), 7. See below note 20.

subsequently influenced debates in France in the Estates General and the National Assembly prior to August 1789, and it is clear that we should treat Paine's discussion in his letter as part of wider deliberations on the federal constitution.[15]

The second issue concerns the nature of constitutions and their relationship to government. The discussions of constitutional matters in relation to America, Britain and France became increasingly linked in Paine's circle in Paris. There was a growing polarisation between anglophiles, who hoped that the failure to resolve the French state's financial problems would produce a political reform that would move the French constitution closer to that of the British, and those who despaired of any constitution that retained the independent power of the nobility in a system of checks and balances. The American case became central to one influential group of French thinkers, deriving originally from Anne-Robert-Jacques Turgot but subsequently associated with Condorcet, the Comte de Mirabeau, Lafayette, La Rochefoucauld, the Abbé Sieyès, Pierre-Louis Roederer and Charles Talleyrand.[16] Curiosity about America had been fuelled by French involvement in the American Revolution, and in 1783, during Franklin's period as special minister to France, he persuaded the Comte de Vergennes to allow him to translate and publish in France a complete set of constitutions from the American states, which had sparked further interest. What united those in the anglophobe group was a resistance to the idea of distinct orders within the state. They embraced the principle of the sovereignty of the people, without intermediary orders of political privilege, and they depicted America as a perfect example of a sovereign legislature and as a dramatic departure from the aristocratic order of England. One striking example of this commitment was their translation and extensive annotation of John Stevens' account of America as *Examen du gouvernement d'Angleterre comparé aux constitutions des états unis* (1789), which attacked Jean Louis De Lolme's and John Adams' laudatory accounts of British government and the principle of mixed government.[17] James Madison sent the pamphlet to Philip Mazzei, a close associate of Jefferson's, who worked with

---

[15] See Jefferson to Madison, 15 March 1789, in *Jefferson: Writings*, 942–6; Marquis de Condorcet, 'Letters from a freeman of Newhaven to a citizen of Virginia (1787)', in Fiona Sommerlad and Iain McLean, eds., 'The political theory of Condorcet II', Social Studies Faculty Working Paper no. 1/1991 (University of Oxford, 1991), 26–73.

[16] Joyce Appleby, 'America as a model for the radical French reformers of 1789', *William and Mary Quarterly*, 3rd series 28 (1971), 267–86, esp. 274. Paine sent his regards to Mazzei via Jefferson on 16 December 1788: *The Life and Major Writings of Thomas Paine*, vol. II, 1273.

[17] See Appleby, 'America as a model', Stevens, *Observations on Government*; Jean Louis De Lolme, *The Constitutions of England* (London: Debrett, 1777); and John Adams, *A*

Pierre Samuel du Pont, Condorcet, Jean Antoine Gallois and the Abbé Piattoli to turn it into a weapon for the anglophobe view.[18] Jefferson did not mention the pamphlet, but he owned an annotated copy, and Joyce Appleby suggests that he played a part in diverting the printer employed to work on a French edition of John Adams' *Defence of the Constitutions of the Governments of the United States* (1786) to the task of publishing a translation of Stevens with an additional 200 pages of closely argued notes.[19] We do not know if Paine read it – we do not know what Paine read! – but it seems very likely that he did. Indeed, it seems likely that the evening Jefferson and Paine, and possibly others, spent in Paris in 1788 discussing James Wilson's pamphlet on the federal constitution informed the notes of the highly annotated edition of Stevens' *Examen*.[20]

Although Stevens ended his pamphlet by broadly endorsing the two-chamber system of the federal government, he expressly rejected the idea that bicameralism was rooted in or reflected some fundamental distinction between orders within society.[21] He attacked, that is, the idea of mixed government as a balance of different social orders in the states (which he associated with the British model), but he was open to the possibility of a bicameral legislature (a topic on which Paine usually argued for unicameralism, but often with the added idea of splitting the legislature in two so that one part should debate and the other decide).[22] This distinction tended to be overlooked by those in France who were concerned to reject mixed government and to advocate a unitary assembly in the subsequent debates on the formation of the Estates General. As a result, Stevens' discussion of bicameralism was wholly ignored in the additional notes to the French edition.

Defence of the Constitutions of Government of the United States of America (Philadelphia: Hall & Sellers, 1787). See also Keith Michael Baker's discussion of Stevens' pamphlet in the French context in 'The idea of a declaration of rights'.

[18] Philip Mazzei, *Memoirs of the Life and Peregrinations of the Florentine Philip Mazzei, 1730–1816*, trans. Howard R. Marraro (New York: Columbia University Press, 1942), 278.

[19] Joyce Appleby, 'The Jefferson–Adams rupture and the first French translation of John Adams' "Defence"', *American Historical Review* 73 (1968), 1084–91.

[20] See above, note 12. Stevens, *Observations on Government*, 231, n. 28, concerned itself with James Wilson's argument that a declaration of rights was superfluous. That argument was not in fact made in *The Substance of a Speech* but did appear in Wilson's *Substance of an Address to a Meeting of the Citizens of Philadelphia* (Philadelphia: T. Bradford, 1787), delivered on 6 October 1787. It is possible that Paine's 'Letter to Jefferson' (*The Life and Major Writings of Thomas Paine*, vol. II, 1298–9) referred to this earlier pamphlet, but the phrasing does not quite fit. The editors of the Stevens book do seem to have been drawing on the (earlier) October speech, however; but the focus on Wilson does seem likely to have been something mediated through Jefferson and Paine's circle.

[21] See Stevens, *Observations on Government*, 51.

[22] *The Life and Major Writings of Thomas Paine*, vol. II, 525–8.

Stevens also seems to have engaged the imagination of the French reformers on the principles underlying the construction of the state, with his distinction between the people, the constitution and the government subsequently making an appearance in the first part of Paine's *Rights of Man* (1791):

The constitution of the state ... is that original compact entered into by every individual of a society, whereby a certain form of government is chalked out and established unalterably, except by the people themselves: thus by a constitution then, when applied to civil society, we do not mean government itself, but the manner of its formation and existence. [...] The governments in these states are in fact nothing more than social compacts entered into for the mutual advantage of the individuals of whom the society is composed.[23]

This distinction between the constitution as an act of the people and the government as 'the creature of a constitution' was a central part of Paine's position in the first part of *Rights of Man*: '[A] constitution is a thing *antecedent* to government, and a government is only the creature of a constitution. The constitution of a country is not the act of its government, but of the people constituting a government.'[24] But this was a new development for Paine. In his *Dissertations on Government* (1786), in which he gave one of his fuller discussions of political principles, the people were conceived of as the sovereign power, but their sovereignty was exercised in 'electing and deputing a certain number of persons to represent and act for the whole...'.[25] In other words, it was expressed in their electoral, rather than their constitutive or legislative, capacity. Moreover, in his discussion of the character of the social compact, there was no discussion of constitutions. What was missing from the earlier position, but was present in 1791, was the view that the people's sovereignty was expressed in the creation of the constitution, rather than either directly in legislation or by proxy through their representatives. Nonetheless, we can see Paine grappling with the idea in his insistence in *Dissertation* that '[t]he sovereignty in a republic is exercised to keep right and wrong in their proper and distinct places... A republic, properly understood, is a sovereignty of justice, in contradistinction to a sovereignty of will.'[26]

What Paine did not have in 1786 was the distinction between a constituent power and the constituted power of government. Although the

---

[23] Stevens, *Observations on Government*, 44, 50. See also 50–3, where Stevens addressed the issues of democracy and stability.
[24] Paine, *Rights of Man*, 278 [emphasis in original].
[25] *The Life and Major Writings of Thomas Paine*, vol. II, 369.   [26] Ibid., 375.

distinction is widely attributed to Sieyès, it figured substantially earlier in the debates on the formation of the state constitutions of America after 1776, with 'the phrase and the thing' first emerging in the struggles to establish statehood for Vermont.[27] Although there were suggestive comments in *Common Sense* that implied something like the distinction, this was not something that Paine had worked out. But it was a principle and a distinction that he had firm control of by the end of February 1789, when he argued that William Pitt ought to have held a national convention over the king's illness, 'for if government be permitted to alter itself, or any of the parts permitted to alter the other there is no fixed Constitution in the country'.[28] This suggests that it was the example of the creation of the Federal Convention itself, with, possibly, the theoretical defence of the distinction in Stevens, that convinced Paine of the point and gave him the terminology to articulate it. It also suggests that Stevens, the federal constitution and Paine's Paris circle may subsequently have had an impact on French views as to the proper relationship between the people, the constitution and the government, furnishing Sieyès with the distinction with which he is so often associated. Certainly, the group with whom Jefferson was most closely associated combined resistance to giving independent weight to any social order within the constitution with the view that the constitution should be understood as the expression of an original compact that established a form of government that could be changed only collectively by reference back to the people. Moreover, these views were central to some of the debates about unifying the three estates into a single National Assembly and arguing for a founding act of constitutional design for France.

The impact of the 'American' argument is hard to tell, but it was certainly feared by many in the Estates General, for whom the English model seemed self-evidently appropriate. Norman Hampson quotes Stanislas, Comte de Clermont-Tonnerre, elected president of the Assembly in mid-August 1789, on the threat to the British model: 'One cannot pretend to do better than that nation [Britain]. Not long ago, on the credit of several writers, people professed the most exaggerated admiration for the British constitution. Today they affect to despise it, following the opinion of an American writer who is full of contradictions.' Hampson suggests the 'American

---

[27] On the attribution of the distinction to Sieyès, see Arendt, *On Revolution*, 162–3; on the Vermont distinction, see Adams, *The First American Constitutions*, 63. Adams attributes to John Adams and Paine attempts to formulate the principle, in Paine's case referring to the discussion in *Common Sense* (1776), in which Paine suggested the formation of a continental conference to frame a continental charter: Arendt, *On Revolution*, 28–9.
[28] *The Life and Major Writings of Thomas Paine*, vol. II, 1280.

writer' was Paine, but there is a greater probability that it was Stevens (although the uncertainty between the two is itself revealing).[29]

The issue of rights and the nature of constitutions were two central elements to Paine's attack on Burke, on which Paine's views developed in this crucial period between 1787 and 1789. The third was the issue of the sovereignty of each generation, which Paine later deployed to undermine Burke's claim that the British people unconditionally and in perpetuity willed their subjection to William of Orange and his successors. This claim can be linked to principles of natural right, but a link is not a deduction; natural rights theorists over the previous two centuries had failed to draw the implications that Paine and Jefferson did. Moreover, it seems clear that both men developed an interest in the issue and developed the principle around the same time. In Jefferson's case, he developed a set of arguments about the sovereignty of each generation in his correspondence with Madison in September 1789, with no evidence of such a commitment earlier in his writing. Paine gave the argument considerable prominence only eighteen months later in the first part of *Rights of Man*. Furthermore, rather than thinking that the principle somehow originated without prompting in Jefferson, it is much more plausible to think that Jefferson was drawing on discussions he had had with others, that Paine was cognisant of these discussions and that he was probably a participant in some of them between 1787 and 1789. Certainly, it is too much of a coincidence to think that Paine hammered out the principle wholly independently in responding to Burke's *Reflections*, while Jefferson (if one follows the editors of his collected papers) picked it up from his doctor, Richard Gem, and then restricted its discussion to his correspondence with Madison.[30] Moreover, Iain McLean's claim that the principle was in fact derived from Condorcet's work simply adds to the sense that this was an idea that was being generated in discussions that centrally involved the Parisian group that Paine and Jefferson were closest to. Indeed, it seems highly likely that such discussions were in turn drawing on Adam Smith's discussion in *Wealth of Nations*.[31]

---

[29] Norman Hampson, *Prelude to Terror: The Constituent Assembly and the Failure of Consensus, 1789–1791* (Oxford: Basil Blackwell, 1988), 73.

[30] See *The Papers of Thomas Jefferson*, vol. XV, *March 1789 to November 1789*, ed. Julian P. Boyd (Princeton University Press, 1958), 384–99. The complete series (hereafter *PTJ*) consists of thirty-nine volumes so far.

[31] Iain McLean, 'Thomas Jefferson, John Adams, and the Déclaration des Droits de l'Homme et du Citoyen', an unpublished manuscript in the author's possession. On Smith, see *An Inquiry into the Nature and Causes of the Wealth of Nations*, ed. Roy Harold Campbell and Andrew S. Skinner (Indianapolis: Liberty Press, 1976), Bk III, ch. 2, sect. 6, 384–5.

Those troubled by the suggestion that Paine used Jefferson's and others' ideas without attribution should recognise that Paine adopted whatever ideas he found useful in the causes he promoted and was not at all troubled by taking them from others without attribution. *Rights of Man* (1791) included Jefferson's description of Marshal de Broglio (i.e. the Duc de Broglie) as a 'high-flying aristocrat, cool, capable of every mischief'; and there is a letter from Paine to Jefferson describing a method for measuring the amount of wood in a tree that appears to have borrowed from Leonardo da Vinci![32] Similarly, Jefferson did not attribute the thought of generational sovereignty to Dr Gem or Condorcet or Smith in his letter to Madison; his concern was with the idea, its validity and its ramifications, not with who might claim to own it. For both, ideas were no man's property, and these ideas were very much in general circulation, with each writer developing them in distinctive ways, having drawn from the common stock.

II

Paine and Jefferson shared a revolutionary American experience, and they also shared a number of points of doctrine about the nature of political systems, the ultimate sovereignty of the people and the importance of a bulwark of rights by which to protect the people from those who governed them. They shared, I believe, two further positions, at least until Jefferson returned to America at the end of 1789. The first was a sense of American exceptionalism; the second was a hesitation over how to describe the kind of order they hoped for in France. The exceptionalism is clear: before 1789 neither Paine nor Jefferson saw events in France as heading for an American system of government. They responded to the events of 1789 as a limitation of arbitrary power, within a constitutional and representative system headed by a monarch. It is difficult to be wholly sure what Paine envisaged, partly because we do not have much evidence other than letters prior to 1791, and partly because we cannot be sure how far the first part of *Rights of Man* fully expressed his beliefs about French developments, as against emphasising its positive dimensions as a rhetorical contrast to the picture he drew of the British constitution. Certainly, what he said about changes in Britain was largely compatible with a constitutional monarchy with a reformed House of Commons, and what he said about France was not hugely different.[33]

---

[32] See Paine, *Rights of Man*, 261; on Leonardo, see Kemp, *Leonardo*, 138–41; and Paine to Jefferson [May? 1788], *PTJ*, vol. XIII, *March 1788 to October 1788*, 225–6.

[33] Paine's letter to Thomas Walker in February 1798 talked of the 'Majesty of the Nation' being 'collected to a centre and residing in the Person exercising the Regal Power', which

Jefferson was similarly limited in his expectations of the revolution in France. What united them was the view – captured by Paine in *Common Sense* – that America was exceptional and that the popular institutions that marked the American case were inappropriate for the substantial, luxurious and corrupt commercial states of 'Old World' Europe. In this respect, it is striking how reticent Paine was in his comments on monarchy until the very end of *Rights of Man*, and it is important not to underestimate how his position on Europe was transformed after the late spring of 1791, and especially after Louis XVI's flight to Varennes. (Even in his letter of June 1791 he argued: 'Monarchy signifies in its primary meaning, *the despotic rule of one individual...* In this relation France is not a monarchy...')[34]

In January 1789 it is clear that he still thought that America was dramatically different from Europe:

A thousand years hence ..., perhaps in less, America may be what England is now! The innocence of her character that won the heart of all nations in her favour may sound like a romance, and her inimitable virtue as if it had never been. The ruins of liberty that thousands bled for, or suffered to obtain, may furnish materials for a village tale or extort a sigh from rustic sensibility, while the fashionable of that day, enveloped in dissipation, shall deride the principle and deny the fact. [...] [W]hen the empire of America shall fall ... it will ... be said ... here! a painful thought! the noblest work of human wisdom – the grandest scene of human glory, the fair cause of freedom ROSE and FELL.[35]

Paine did occasionally refer to the American example having an impact on Europe, as when he sent the key of the Bastille to Washington as 'one

---

followed a similar French view that the king was the representative of the nation as a whole: *The Life and Major Writings of Thomas Paine*, vol. II, 1279. Nonetheless, the suggestion that Paine was a monarchist, wildly inconsistent or an opportunist, made in Hazel Burgess's *Thomas Paine: A Collection of Unknown Writings* (Basingstoke: Palgrave Macmillan, 2009), with respect to an attributed pamphlet of 1791, misses the extent to which, until then, Paine had had rather different assumptions about America from those about Britain. Burgess bases the attribution of the pamphlet (addressed to the king) on the fact that it is signed 'Common Sense' ('the name no other would dare assume': 149) and on the grounds of phraseology and wording. Although there is no space here for detailed refutation, neither claim really stands scrutiny. It is doubtful that Debrett would have published a pamphlet by Paine; the use of 'Common Sense' throughout the pamphlet was not a mark of Paine's British writings, whereas we know that James Perry used the signature (see his DNB entry); the defence of mixed government went against Paine's remarks in his letter to Walker; and the direct address to the king was not Paine's practice. Moreover, the database 'Making of the modern world' contains seven pamphlets published under the signature of 'Common Sense' between 1780 and 1830, only one of which Burgess attributes to Paine (and that, in my view, wrongly).

[34] *The Life and Major Writings of Thomas Paine*, vol. II, 1316 [emphasis in original].
[35] Ibid., 1276 [emphasis in original].

of the first ripe fruits of American principles transplanted to Europe', but this does not mean that he held the view that American principles could be systematically applied elsewhere. This suggestion did not appear until the second part of *Rights of Man*, and Paine was clear that this work was a departure from the first.[36] Jefferson's position was hardly different: he was attracted to France, but it bore no comparison to America; he compared an American education with a European one, with the later corrupting the former's love of equality; and, in a letter to George Wythe, he predicted:

If all the sovereigns of Europe were to set themselves to work to emancipate the minds of their subjects from the present ignorance and prejudices, & that as zealously as they now endeavour the contrary, a thousand years would not place them on that high ground on which our common people are now setting out.[37]

Like Paine and others, Jefferson thought that the American Revolution had 'awakened the French nation' (or, at least, the thinking part of the nation) 'from the sleep of despotism in which they were sunk' – but, again, this did not mean they should or could imitate America. The end was a liberal constitutional monarchy, a stop to arbitrary power and a place for a nobility of talents rather than birth.[38]

Paine and Jefferson also shared the language they used to describe the systems of government that they advocated. In his *Condition of the Working Class in England*, Engels referred to Paine as 'the famous democrat', and that is a description that few today would hesitate to apply. But it was not a term Paine used. Indeed, there was no European use of the term prior to 1790 (and its use in America was rare and complex, being used by some interchangeably with 'republican' – and, in the hands of most, it signified support for the popular self-government of small states, which tied in with a classical set of ambitions for a virtuous people).[39] When it was used in Europe it was initially used pejoratively. People in eighteenth-century Europe saw democracy as referring to small city states, governed by the people, with a tendency to instability and succumbing to the control of demagogues; or (with Adam Smith) they used the term as a description for primitive forms of government for undeveloped societies; or, finally, but

---

[36] Ibid., 1303, 1321.

[37] Jefferson to James Monroe, 17 June 1785, in *PTJ*, vol. VIII, *February 1785 to October 1785*, 227–35; to John Banister, Jr., 15 October 1785, in ibid., 635–8; and to George Wythe, 13 August 1786, in ibid., vol. X, *June 1786 to December 1786*, 243–5.

[38] Jefferson to George Washington, 4 December 1788, in ibid., vol. XIV, *October 1788 to March 1789*, 328–32; and to Richard Price, 8 January 1789, in ibid., 420–24.

[39] Adams, *The First American Constitutions*, 103: Patrick Henry described himself as 'a Democrat on the plan of our admired friend J. Adams'.

most commonly among reformers, they saw it as one component of government, arranged in a balance between monarchy and aristocracy. In the first two cases it was seen as wholly inapplicable to modern commercial societies of any size; in the latter case it was an element of popular representation within a balanced constitution, but it was not one that necessarily demanded universal suffrage, secret ballots or frequent elections. Later, in 1816, Jefferson insisted that 'a democracy is the only pure republic, but impracticable beyond the limits of a town'. At the same time he acknowledged that

[t]he full experiment of a government democratical, but representative, was and is still reserved for us... [T]he introduction of this new principle of representative democracy has rendered useless almost everything written before on the structure of government...[40]

That clarity was not present in the late 1780s, however, when he was in France; and Paine was no clearer. Paine was an outspoken critic of mixed government in *Common Sense*, referring to the king as the remains of monarchical tyranny and the House of Lords as the remains of 'aristocratical' tyranny. But he made no positive case for democracy there. Much like *The Federalist Papers*, he preferred the language of 'republic' to that of democracy. In 1786 he wrote:

In republics... the sovereign power, or the power over which there is no control, and which controls all others, remains where nature placed it – in the people; for the people in America are the fountain of power... This sovereignty is exercised in electing and deputing a certain number of persons to represent and act for the whole, and who, if they do not act right, may be displaced by the same power that placed them there, and others elected or deputed in their stead...[41]

Prior to the discussion in part two of *Rights of Man* there was no explicit reference to democracy as the appropriate political form. Moreover, if we ask who put 'democracy' on the map of debates in the early 1790s, the answer is Burke, for whom the term formed a central plank of his attack on France, even though he attacked them for something they embraced only later. Neither Paine nor Jefferson advocated 'democracy' for Europe or America in the late 1780s, and only later (in 1791/2) did Paine argue that representation had enabled a new democratic form to be applied in countries of any extent.[42] At the end of the 1780s that thought was still

---

[40] Jefferson to Isaac H. Tiffany, 26 August 1816, in *The Writings of Thomas Jefferson*, ed. Andrew A. Lipscomb and Albert Ellery Bergh (Washington, DC: Thomas Jefferson Memorial Association, 1904), vol. XV, 65–6.
[41] Thomas Paine, *Dissertations on Government*, in *The Life and Major Writings of Thomas Paine*, vol. II, 367–414, 369.
[42] Ibid., 368–75.

being worked out. And, while Stevens did argue that the American states were 'approaching nearer to perfect democracies than any we have accounts of', and denied that such governments would inevitably collapse, what drove his position was the view that 'MAN IS ACTUALLY CAPABLE OF GOVERNING HIMSELF'.[43] In other words, what they agreed on in the 1780s was something like a principle of popular sovereignty, not as something to be exercised continuously through a general will but as a basic principle underlying the formation of constitutions and thus, indirectly, of governments. Both insisted, borrowing the phrase from Lafayette, that 'for a nation ... to be free it is sufficient that she wills it'.[44] As Jefferson put it in 1792, it was '[t]he catholic principle of republicanism, to wit, that every people may establish What form of government they please and change it as they please; the will of the nation being the only thing essential'.[45] Sieyès would have wholly agreed, but that demonstrates that it was possible to secure unanimity on *this* fundamental principle when thinking about the people of America, France and Britain without anything necessarily following in terms of government forms, including the presence or absence of monarchy, or the extent of popular participation in government. My sense is that this captures precisely the positions of both Paine and Jefferson in the late 1780s: that they took from the American Revolution a principle of popular sovereignty, but did not apply it identically in Europe and America, and in Europe they did not see it as opposed to the institution of monarchy. What did stick in their craws was aristocracy and arbitrary power.

III

Jefferson returned to America in the autumn of 1789, but Paine's thinking developed further in significant ways, most notably in the second part of *Rights of Man* (March 1792), in his *Letter Addressed to the Addressers* (August 1792) and in his *Dissertation on the First Principles of Government* (July 1795).

The second part of *Rights of Man* was not a reply to Burke. It was a freestanding account of the nature and principles of government. It started

---

[43] Stevens, *Observations on Government*, 53 [emphasis in original]. See also Wilson, *The Substance of a Speech*, 10, in which he essentially backed away from subscribing to the view that the Federal Convention was recommending a democratic system, ending by an appeal to it being 'a form of government founded on and by the PEOPLE' [emphasis in original].

[44] Paine, *Rights of Man*, 255, 322.

[45] Jefferson, *The Anas*, 1792, available at www.history1700s.com/etext/html/texts/jefferson/jeff1a.txt.

with the example of America, as the only place where the reform of government and man could begin and as having introduced a revolution in the principles and practices of government. In 1791 he had defended the French reforms that produced a moderate constitutional monarchy; in 1792 he conceded that this was no longer relevant. Instead, the American Revolution became the fulcrum on which the political world could be made to turn, eradicating not simply the order of the nobility but the very principles of monarchical and hereditary government, and replacing them with representative democracies: 'Government founded on a *moral theory, on a system of universal peace, on the indefeasible hereditary Rights of Man*, is now revolving from west to east... It interests not particular individuals, but nations, in its progress, and promises a new æra to the human race.'[46] The contrast he had drawn in *Common Sense*, with liberty fleeing from east to west and with the principles of the New World being of little relevance to the corrupt orders of the Old, was transformed by coming to see the American example as the instigator of a revolutionary change to wholly representative government throughout the Old World. The evidence strongly suggests that he did not hold this view before the spring of 1791 (shortly after 14 July 1789 he was predicting that the whole thing would be settled), but it is absolutely clear that he did thereafter.[47] Accordingly, he developed a much more thorough account of representative government than had appeared earlier in his work.[48]

In doing so, he returned to the contrast between governments founded on reason and ignorance drawn in the 'Conclusion' to part one of *Rights of*

[46] Paine, *Rights of Man*, 356.
[47] See Paine to Thomas Walker, 26 February 1789, in *The Life and Major Writings of Thomas Paine*, vol. II, 1278–81; to Anonymous, 16 March 1789, in ibid., 1285–6; and to Washington, 31 May 1790 ('complete and triumphant'), in ibid., 1304.
[48] Jefferson's views on French affairs are discussed by Conor Cruise O'Brien, *The Long Affair: Thomas Jefferson and the French Revolution* (London: Sinclair Stevenson, 1996), esp. ch. 2. O'Brien misses the point that Jefferson had dramatically different expectations of Europe compared to America, and so interprets the letters very unsympathetically. But there seems little doubt that Jefferson, like Paine, started with limited expectations; that he thought the French king a good man (Jefferson to Edward Carrington, 16 January 1787, in *PTJ*, vol. XI, *January 1787 to August 1787*, 48–50); that he saw the existing regime as constructed on a despotic model (to Madison, 30 January 1787, in ibid., 92–7); that he believed that de Brienne could give the people 'as much liberty as they are capable of managing' (to John Adams, 13 November 1787, in ibid., vol XII, *August 1787 to March 1788*, 349–51); that he had doubts as to whether they would get a better constitution than the English (to Richard Price, 8 January 1789, in ibid., vol. XIV, 420–4); that he anticipated that reform would leave the king 'possessed completely of the Executive powers' (to Diodati, 3 August 1789, in ibid., vol. XV, 325–7); and that it was only after his return to America that he believed that the new regime would be a fundamental change that would affect the whole of Europe (to George Mason, 4 February 1791, in ibid., vol. XIX, *January 1791 to March 1791*, 241–3). Essentially, his train of thinking ran remarkably parallel to Paine's.

Man, arguing that all hereditary government was in its nature tyranny, treating a people as hereditary property, as if they were flocks or herds.[49] In contrast, representative government was a new departure, one that was not to be equated with democratic government, which he took to be direct popular government appropriate only to the small city states found in the ancient world.[50] The principle of representation was unknown in ancient democracies, with the result that as those states grew they collapsed into tyranny. In contrast, modern states engrafted representation onto democracy, ensuring its suitability for any state, as America demonstrated.[51] In *The Federalist Papers*, Madison referred to states with representative government as 'republics'. That was a position close to Paine's own in his *Dissertations on Government* (1786) through to (and including) his letter to the Abbé Sieyès in July 1791; but in *Rights of Man* (1792) Paine denied that republics were a type of *government*. Indeed, 'what is called a *republic* is not any particular form of government. It is wholly characteristical of the purport, matter, or object for which the government ought to be instituted', and government that did not make this the end of its activity was neither republican nor good. Many governments claimed the title, but 'the government of America, which is wholly on the system of representation, is the only real republic ... that now exists. Its government has no other object than the public business of the nation, and therefore it is properly a republic...' It was naturally opposed to the word 'monarchy', which essentially signified 'arbitrary power in an individual person; in the exercise of which *himself*, and not the *res-publica*, is the object'.[52] Only representative democracy, then, could claim legitimacy. Hence the introduction of a sustained critique of monarchy at the end of chapter 3 of part two.

Gary Kates sees Paine as having been influenced by those more radical than him in France, and believes that his definition of 'republic' – as 'wholly characteristical of the purport, matter, or object for which government ought to be instituted ... RES-PUBLICA, the public affairs, or the public good; or, literally translated, the *public thing*' – was 'lifted practically verbatim from his friend Bonneville's daily newspaper, Bouche de fer'[53] in July 1791. In fact, Paine used this phraseology in his 'To the authors of "Le Républicain"', written on 11 June 1791 to Condorcet and others planning to establish a republican paper, and in doing so he was effectively reworking

---

[49] Paine, *Rights of Man*, 364.   [50] Ibid., 369.   [51] Ibid., 371.
[52] Ibid., 370, 369 [emphasis in original].
[53] Paine's definition is in ibid., 369–70 [emphasis in original]. Gary Kates, 'From liberalism to radicalism: Tom Paine's *Rights of Man*', *Journal of the History of Ideas* 50 (1989), 659–87, 581.

commitments from his *Dissertations on Government* of 1786, nearly two years before his major stay in France.[54] Kates is right that we should pay attention to Paine's involvement with reform circles in France, and is absolutely justified in thinking that the vast majority of Paine scholarship, with the notable exception of Owen Aldridge's, is almost entirely innocent of any such attention.[55] But the evidence for seeing Paine as simply absorbing the intellectual innovations of his French friends does not seem strong, especially given the way Paine's thinking was evolving. Moreover, we also need to consider Paine's value for his French friends; they were attracted in large part to his American experience and, in their turn, they reinforced in him a sense of the importance of that experience and its significance as a basis for reform in Europe – something that is evident even in the first part of *Rights of Man*.[56] Kates emphasises the place of Sieyès in *Rights of Man* (1792), but it is crucial to realise that in 1791 and 1792 Paine was writing for a British audience, rather than a French or American one, and, much as he was prepared to debate with Sieyès, he recognised that a British audience would have little interest in the detail of their disagreements and that he should focus directly on the principle of monarchy rather than giving Sieyès the detailed rebuttal that Burke had earned in 1791. Kates also points out that Paine parted company with Lafayette (as did Condorcet in July 1791), but in Paine's case he seems to have seen this as largely a matter of the pace rather than the destination of reform (he was probably aware of Lafayette's letter to Washington, written in January 1790, that talked of preparing the nation for a convention in ten years or so to remedy the remaining defects of the constitution), and there is evidence much earlier in his correspondence that he saw a divergence in judgement between himself and Lafayette.[57]

---

[54] Thomas Paine, 'To the authors of "Le Républicain"', in *The Life and Major Writings of Thomas Paine*, vol. II, 1315–18; I have rehearsed some of these points in 'Political theory and history', 143. Kates also sees Sieyès as the real foil for Paine in the second part of *Rights of Man*, although it is striking that he made only a brief appearance (being mentioned three or four times in a matter of a few pages in the third chapter in relation to the dispute over monarchy), and his appearance was briefer than that of Burke (in the second part, and, indeed, even in this chapter).

[55] See Aldridge, *Man of Reason*, esp. chs. 7–15. See also A. Owen Aldridge's 'Condorcet et Paine', *Revue de littérature compare* 32 (1958), 47–65. Subsequent to Kates, see Richard Whatmore's Kates-influenced account in 'A gigantic manliness: Thomas Paine's republicanism in the 1790s', in Stefan Collini, Richard Whatmore and Brian Young, eds., *Economy, Polity, and Society: British Intellectual History 1750–1950* (Cambridge University Press, 2000), 135–57.

[56] Paine, *Rights of Man*, 300: 'The American Constitutions were to liberty, what a grammar is to language: they define its parts of speech, and practically construct them into a syntax.'

[57] *The Letters of Lafayette to Washington, 1777–1799*, ed. Louis Gottschalk (Philadelphia: American Philosophical Society, 1976), 346 (12 January 1790), 349 (23 August 1790); the same sentiment for deferral was echoed in a further letter of 23 August 1790. On Lafayette's response to the federal constitution, such as his comments on the need for a

These various signs require careful, contextual reading. Paine's increasing confidence in the potential for change in Europe was partly a function of his reading of French events, in which his newer French friends were playing a significant part, but it was also probably influenced by his contacts in England, where the reform movement was spreading.[58] Moreover, the evidence suggests that it dated from the early months of 1791, when he was in England writing the concluding sections of the first part of *Rights of Man*, in which he settled on the contrast between government by reason, election and representation and that by ignorance and hereditary succession, with America epitomising the former. Difficult as it is to establish influence, it is important to recognise that Paine's attitude to Britain (and France) changed dramatically in this period, and the factors that might have influenced him, such as the rise of an extra-parliamentary radical movement, were ones in which he also played a significant role; in this sense, his own success may have proved deeply persuasive!

Even if we doubt that Britain is the source of his anti-monarchism (in the sense that it was Britain that persuaded him that a fuller move to a republican (American) model was possible in the spring and early summer of 1791), it does seem undeniable that it was the British context that encouraged him to make the move from natural rights and popular sovereignty, which were present in *Rights of Man* (1791), and from the advocacy of the representative system and American conventionism in the second part of *Rights of Man* (March 1792) to the demand for universal manhood suffrage that he made in his *Letter Addressed to the Addressers*, written in the summer of 1792:

As every man in the nation of the age of twenty-one years pays taxes ... out of the product of his labour ... so has every one the same equal right to vote, and no one part of a nation, nor any individual, has a right to dispute the right of another.[59]

This move really does seem to have derived not from France, which he had not visited for a year, but from his involvement with the Society for Constitutional Information and the London Corresponding Society, associated with and buttressed by his new sense that a fully representative form of government was possible for the *ancien régime* states of Europe.

---

bill of rights, see letter of 1 January 1788: 334. On Lafayette, see Paine's comments in his letters to William Short, in *The Life and Major Writings of Thomas Paine*, vol. II, 1306 (1 June 1790), 1309 (22 June 1790).

[58] Having been initially dismissive of the political possibilities of the British people when he returned to Europe.

[59] Thomas Paine, *Letter Addressed to the Addressers on the Late Proclamation*, in *Thomas Paine: Rights of Man, Common Sense and Other Political Writings*, 333–84, 377.

IV

My central contention is that Paine's intellectual position was a changing one, and that we should understand these changes in part in relation to his experiences in Paris with Jefferson and his circle, where he was involved in debates in which the American experience became gradually universalised. In the process, it also became reinterpreted and reinflected with meanings that would not have been obvious to, or recognised by, these men a few years earlier. Paine's and Jefferson's European experiences reshaped their understanding of the American Revolution and of its fundamental principles – encouraging the elaboration of a theory of government based on the sovereignty of the people, distinguishing between that will and the constitutions and governments through which it was expressed, validating a set of natural rights claims to set limits to government action, increasingly coming to see these as demanding generational sovereignty and (eventually) universal manhood suffrage and, finally, coming to espouse the language of representative democracy that, over the next twenty or thirty years, began to take root in America and in Britain.

One piece of evidence that underlines the danger of reading the radicalism of 1791 and 1792 back into earlier understandings and claims is Price's 'effusion of zeal in the cause of human liberty and virtue' with which I opened this chapter – the light struck out in America reflected to Europe.[60] What is rarely noticed is that Price himself insisted that it was not a clarion call for republicanism or democracy, and in that sense it was not an understanding of the achievement of America that called for the kind of transformation of government that Paine came to see as essential by the spring of 1791:

I cannot help taking this opportunity to remove a very groundless suspicion with respect to my self, by adding that so far am I from preferring a government purely republican, that I look upon our own constitution of government as better adapted than any other to this country, and in Theory excellent, etc... I know not one individual among them [Protestant Dissenters] who would not tremble at the thought of changing into a Democracy our mixed form of government, or who has any other wish with respect to it than to restore it to purity and vigour by removing the defects in our representation, and establishing that independence of the three states on one another in which its essence consists.[61]

---

[60] Price's own description, in a letter to John Adams, 1 February 1790, in *The Correspondence of Richard Price*, vol. III, *February 1786–February 1791*, 271.

[61] Price to William Smith, 1 March 1790, in ibid., 273, quoting his *The Evidence for a Future Period of Improvement in the State of Mankind with the Means and Duty of Promoting It* (London: T. Cadell, 1787), 30.

The account that I have given, which sees an inching forward on the part of Paine and Jefferson, in a course they shared with their French friends into 1790 and 1791, is intended in part as a caution against seeing such changes as inevitable. The language of politics changed dramatically in France during the revolution, but, rather than seeing this as in some way conceptually driven, it seems to me to make more sense to see it as a chaotic and complex process in which language was as much at the mercy of change as driving it. One example is the use of 'democracy'; secondary literature does not hesitate to use the term, but it was not widely used at the time, and when it was used, either positively or negatively, it was almost entirely rhetorical and contentless. Moreover, insofar as it was used, it was because it was a negative term that became revalorised by being turned against the emergent enemy, the aristocrat (albeit that too was a relatively late manufacture, in the summer of 1789 and afterwards).[62] This was clearly no more than a gesture, but there is a school of thinking on the revolution that elevates its events into a battle of ideas and language, and in my view underplays the extent to which they were as much victims of a progressive collapse of order as they were its drivers.

A second issue concerns America. I have offered an account of American assumptions, about their gradual Europeanisation. If we follow the story through to 1793–6 we can see that events in France, paradoxically, eventually began to reconfirm for Paine and Jefferson a sense of America's difference. But this is not a stable conception of America at work. The existing literature fails adequately to recognise the way in which positions that sounded the same in 1805 as in 1785 had come to be attended by a host of new assumptions and implications; and that, in often very different ways, the French Revolution made Americans in Europe (and many at home) think differently about their revolution so that the future they drew from it in the early nineteenth century was not one immanent to it but, rather, involved considerable retrospective reinterpretation – much as, I have suggested, Paine's and Jefferson's sense of America was changed by their experience of France.

In the account I have given, Paine clearly changed his position, but not just as rhetorical sallies against opponents in pamphlet debates. The reading of *Rights of Man* that I have offered sees his position changing prior to Burke's *Reflections*, arising from discussions of America influenced by developments in France and, later, in the light of his acquaintance with the British reform movement. In these developments we have a process that included experiences, intellectual exchanges, conceptual

---

[62] See William Doyle, *Aristocracy and Its Enemies in the Age of Revolution* (Oxford University Press, 2009).

reworking, reactions to others, the reading and rereading of events, and so on. In this process, it seems to me, we see people's thinking change and their intellectual commitments and positions take on new significance for them, and they drew conclusions that they had not seen as there to be drawn earlier. And I emphasise this because, while it is possible to read Paine wholly as a powerful rhetorician and pamphleteer, responding to circumstance and using whatever arguments he thought would work with his audience, I hope that I have established that a great deal more was in play in his work.

8   Godwin, Thelwall and the means of progress[1]

On 21 November 1795 William Godwin published his *Considerations on Lord Grenville and Mr Pitt's Bills Concerning Treasonable and Seditious Practices and Unlawful Assemblies*, signing it 'by a Lover of Order'. A week later the second edition of Godwin's *Enquiry concerning Political Justice, and its Influence on General Virtue and Happiness* appeared. The latter had been undergoing a process of revision for the previous twelve months; the former was written at pace between 16 and 19 November, following the introduction of the bills between 6 and 9 November. Both publications have been seen as indicating that Godwin had, to some degree, lost his radical nerve.[2] The second edition of the *Enquiry concerning Political Justice* is seen as a more generally cautious and reserved text than the first edition, although there are disagreements about just how much more cautious, and *Considerations* reveals Godwin taking a critical stance towards the activities of the reform societies in the wake of the treason trials and the subsequent development of the popular protest movement against the war, recruitment practices and shortages of food. Although there were a number of incidents of food and crimp riots in the summer of 1795, the public meetings organised by the London Corresponding Society had been remarkably well ordered. At the opening of parliament, however, two days after a mass meeting organised by the

[1] My thanks are owed to James Grande, Robert Maniquis, Jon Mee, Victoria Myers and David O'Shaughnessy for their comments on an earlier draft of this chapter.
[2] The classic example of someone taking the revisions to Godwin's *Enquiry concerning Political Justice* as indicative of recantation is Thomas de Quincy's comment 'The second edition, as regards principles, is not a re-cast, but absolutely a travesty of the first, nay, it is all but a palinode...': see Don Locke, *A Fantasy of Reason: The Life and Thought of William Godwin* (London: Routledge & Kegan Paul, 1980), 93. Locke characterises Godwin's treatment of Thelwall as a 'stab in the back' and reports a rumour that Godwin had been won over by a government pension: 102. On this, see Jon Mee, '"The press and danger of the crowd": Godwin, Thelwall and the counter-public sphere', in Robert M. Maniquis and Victoria Myers, eds., *Godwinian Moments: From the Enlightenment to Romanticism* (University of Toronto Press, 2011), 83–102, 101, n. 35, in which Amelia Alderson teases Godwin about a pension for *Considerations on Lord Grenville and Mr Pitt's Bills*.

LCS, the king's coach was allegedly fired on, and when it left parliament after depositing the king it was altogether destroyed by a mob. The government, still smarting from the failure to secure verdicts in the treason trials of 1794, was increasingly concerned about the prospect of popular unrest fusing with the reform societies' attempts to create a politicised, perhaps revolutionary, popular movement. Accordingly, it sought to tighten the law on treason and to restrict the activities of the reform societies through the 'Two Bills'. In doing so, the government faced serious extra-parliamentary opposition, much encouraged and aided by the Foxite Whigs, who maintained that the bills prepared the way for Pitt's own 'reign of terror', although the government also received considerable support in the form of loyal addresses organised throughout the country.

Godwin's changes in *Political Justice* are often explained in terms of his having bent before the blast of reaction, but it is *Considerations* that gives rise to claims of apostasy. And the particular object of his supposed betrayal was his friend, the political activist and writer John Thelwall. This chapter takes issue with this analysis and argues that part of our failure to understand Godwin's position in these two publications derives from the tendency to read the political positions of those in the 1790s largely in terms of the highly polarised positions represented in the debate on France.

I

In periods of intense political dispute people's positions become increasingly extreme and more forcibly stated. The 'debate on the French Revolution', the 'Burke–Paine debate' or the 'revolution controversy', as it has latterly and more felicitously been titled,[3] provides ample evidence of an increasing polarisation between the forces of order and those of reform; between those defending the constitution and its practices, as if in a last-ditch struggle to preserve immemorial things from subversion, and those accusing the government of wilful and tyrannical designs on the liberties of the ordinary person, as if to make reform still more urgent and justify more extreme methods of organisation and campaigning to achieve their ends. Between 1793 and 1798 the pamphlet debate sparked by Edmund Burke's *Reflections on the Revolution in France*, and accelerated and made manifestly more popular in character by the publication and mass circulation of Thomas Paine's *Rights of Man*, evolved into a practical

---

[3] See Cobban, *The Debate on the French Revolution*; and Butler, *Burke, Paine, Godwin, and the Revolution Controversy*.

struggle for and against the political status quo. By the last years of the decade the radical societies had been effectively suppressed by the government and by loyal associations hunting purveyors of sedition and insurrection in every corner. These actions left only minor underground outposts, largely influenced by the Irish insurrection, which now contemplated armed resistance.

We should not think that this polarisation was a process whose path was charted from the beginning, however, with lines of engagement laid between reformers and reactionaries in the opening salvos of the discussion. Even if attitudes to France and the opening events of its revolution did become increasingly polarised, especially after the September Massacres of 1792, this was only one dimension of the controversy, and those who contributed to it did not line up systematically in a way that allows us to identify a fundamental fault line running through the polity. If there was a fault line by the middle of the 1790s, it was an artefact of the way that the controversy had been handled by those who resisted and those who sought reform. In different hands, things might have been different.

This claim might seem perverse: Painite radicalism was never destined to sit easily with Burkean conservatism. Neither author left room for legitimacy in his opponent: Burke became a defender of the indefensible, the institutions of hereditary succession, aristocracy and monarchy; Paine became the purveyor of revolution and republicanism.[4] Indeed, so alien was the work of each to the other that it is easy to see why commentators have often demurred at the thought that they were ever in any sense engaged with the arguments of each other.[5] That position is overstated: true, Burke did not attempt to respond to Paine to any degree; but Paine did make an effort in the first part of *Rights of Man* to address Burke's claims about the French and their proceedings and he did address a series of central claims that Burke made in his *Reflections*, such as those concerning the nature of rights and the capacity of one generation to contract away the rights of subsequent generations. But the overstatement has a point: the second part of *Rights of Man* made only passing reference to

---

[4] We should note, however, that their disagreements were not clear to them until relatively late in the day, since there was considerable mutual respect in 1788, and Paine wrote to Burke as late as 17 January 1790, giving an optimistic account of the way in which things were proceeding in France and offering to show him, when they next met, Jefferson's letter of 11 July 1789 describing the events of the early part of the revolution. See *The Correspondence of Edmund Burke*, vol. VI, *July 1789–December 1791*, ed. Thomas W. Copeland (Cambridge University Press, 1967), 67–75.

[5] For example, R. R. Fennessy, *Burke, Paine and the Rights of Man: A Difference of Opinion* (The Hague: M. Nijhoff, 1963).

Burke, and it moved the debate onto a terrain that Burke had no intention of addressing.

The claim that other paths were possible is more appealing once we recognise that, especially with respect to the issue of reform in Britain, the two protagonists did not clearly divide the field of opinion. This is not only because there were more moderate and conciliatory loyalists than Burke (it is striking, for example, that Burke was not reprinted or edited for popular consumption in the tracts published by the Association for the Preservation of Liberty and Property against Republicans and Levellers, and he was largely ignored by those developing brands of more popular loyalism) but there were also far more conciliatory and less extreme reformers than Paine. Indeed, there were few in the British context, as I read it, who had any clear sense of what a wholly representative form of democratic government might look like, so that most positions tended to assume that a reform of the suffrage was to be undertaken within the existing frame of government.[6] There is some evidence of 'king-killing' republicanism with the republication of civil war pamphlets and the use of stories, songs and images such as 'King Chaunticlere', 'Bob shave the king' and some of Richard Lee's cartoons in the mid-1790s, but much of this was heavily arch and rhetorical in character – cocking a snook, and baiting the government with material the prosecution of which would make the government look silly and which all but the most hand-picked of juries would fail to find seditious.

While aspirations for republican and democratic institutions may have been real enough for a few, there is little evidence that the more prominent radicals who remained in Britain should be understood as dyed-in-the-wool republicans, Jacobins or democrats. This is in part because these terms themselves become so freighted that their use, both negative and positive, did not have much concrete reference: they were positions

---

[6] A relatively extreme case is that of Thomas Cooper, whose *A Reply to Mr Burke's Invective* (London: J. Johnson, 1792) was very much influenced by Paine and Sieyès – even if the basic principle that all power is derived from the people can be found in his paper to the Literary and Philosophical Society of Manchester dated 7 March 1787, well before the publication of Paine's book. But many writers assumed that latter principle without feeling the necessity of questioning the doctrine of mixed government that holds sway over the vast majority of the proponents of reform. Major Cartwright was certainly an important, and the predominant, example in this period, but so too was Thelwall in his *Tribune*, in which he argued that the constitution of Britain was a democracy having 'some mixture of aristocracy in its legislature, and adopting an hereditary chief magistrate to be responsible for the execution of the laws and who is called a *King*'. But the institutions were subject to 'the grand object, the welfare of that great body *from whom all power is derived, and for whom all power ought to be exercised*': see John Thelwall, *The Tribune, a Periodical Publication, consisting chiefly of the Political Lectures of J. Thelwall: Taken in Short-hand by W. Ramsey, and Revised by the Lecturer* , vol. II (London: J. Thelwall, 1796), 213 [emphasis in original].

parodied and pilloried in the attack.[7] And they were either exaggerated or minimised in their defence depending on whether the aim was to shock or conciliate. This makes it very difficult to say who really stood for what – a difficulty compounded by the fact that few, it seems, had a secure grasp of the varieties of republican or democratic government that the French had experimented with or advanced, and few had clear ideas of what government might look like in England if substantial inroads were to be made into hereditary privilege in terms of parliament and the Crown.[8] People might have sensed that these institutions trespassed on their claims to competence in political matters and on the principle of equal rewards for equal talents. They might have also agreed with their French cousins that the antonym of democracy was aristocracy, and therefore directed their ire towards that group, but they lacked the particular issues that gave such an animus to the French hostility to that class.[9] In this sense, the 1790s witnessed a politicisation of both middling and lower orders that took a more organised and articulate form than had previous incursions of popular politics onto the national political scene, but it was not yet a unified and coherent movement for democratic government, as those imply who see it as the precursor to the reform organisations of Chartism and the later nineteenth century.

One indication that we are in danger of misreading the polarisation as having ideological, rather than political, origins can be seen in the case of William Godwin. Godwin's foray into the public debate on France was relatively elevated and oblique. His intentionally monumental *Enquiry concerning Political Justice* of 1793 leaves no doubt that he wanted to stand above the particular details of the debate, and that he also wanted to contribute at a more abstract level to the development of the political and moral principles that he saw as implicated in the debate. As a result, he paid close attention to the pamphlet controversy, read and reread the works of its principal contributors and sought out many of them as acquaintances. He

[7] See Anne Plumptre's clear-sighted comments on the polemical character of disputes, in *A Narrative of a Three Years' Residence in France, Principally in the Southern Departments, from the Year 1802 to 1805*, vol. II (London: J. Mawman, 1810), 97; and my 'The fragmented ideology of reform'.

[8] This was true equally for Paine, whose experience on the National Convention's committee on the constitution in 1792/3 and whose friendship with Condorcet, the chief architect of the proposals for a new constitution in 1793, did not produce any detailed discussion of constitutional arrangements for either France or Britain.

[9] See Amanda Goodrich, *Debating England's Aristocracy in the 1790s: Pamphlets, Polemics and Political Ideas* (Woodbridge: Boydell Press, 2005), ch. 2, for the argument that it was Paine and his followers in particular who sought to rake up hostility to aristocracy. Nonetheless, it is striking how enduring the model of mixed government was among radicals, and how far they continued to assume some degree of leadership from the political élite.

was also well aware that his own work might be received as a contribution to the discussion that Burke and Paine had largely initiated. Subsequent generations have made a similar judgement, and have sought to assess how far the radicalism of the first edition of the *Enquiry concerning Political Justice* was subsequently toned down as a result of the ferocious reaction against the reformers and activists with whom Godwin is identified. Godwin's later political writings, especially *Cursory Strictures* and *Considerations on Lord Grenville and Mr Pitt's Bills*, are also read in this spirit, the former as an eloquent defence of his friends and associates from the charge of high treason levelled at them in 1794, the latter as signal evidence of his betrayal in 1795 of his friend Thelwall and of the radical movement more widely, in favour of a conservative desire to prevent disorder and to place security before progress and individual liberty. Having had a sense of Godwin's being on the side of the radicals, many readers see him, in *Considerations*, as a slightly pompous, self-serving renegade.

This characterisation treats the divisions of the 1790s as altogether too polarised, and too natural and obvious, however. One was either for reform or not, for Paine or for Burke, and in making this judgement we echo and compound the experience of those in the decade who found the middle ground being rapidly eroded in favour of a still starker choice between insurrectionary activism and some position between quietism and loyalism. The inappropriateness of treating the Burke–Paine division as directly parallel to the loyalism–reformism division can be recognised at two distinct levels. The first, which is not my target here, involves recognising that the rhetorical tactics of reformers and loyalists alike should not be confused with substance.[10] Pocock's wholly apposite comment, that it is difficult to know quite what tradition of British political thought to fit Paine into, indicates how far his work was in a real sense foreign to domestic British traditions of agitation for reform.[11] Paine's work was taken up and distributed widely partly because it was so very different, partly because its shock value was rather gleefully recognised and partly because Paine was well connected and assiduous in promulgating his ideas. But we should not think either that loyalist rhetoric against reform fairly represented Paine's work or that the rhetoric against Paine's work fairly represented the positions of those who favoured parliamentary reform. Instead, loyalist rhetoric covered elements of representation

---

[10] On this theme, see my 'The fragmented ideology of reform' and 'Disconcerting ideas: explaining popular radicalism and popular loyalism in the 1790s', Chapter 3 in this volume.

[11] Pocock, *Virtue, Commerce, and History*, 276.

with a healthy layer of misrepresentation and tarred reformers with 'French principles'. But the second level, at which we can recognise a much more complex set of issues and commitments beneath the apparent polarisation, comes from the careful analysis of the texts written by those sympathetic to and aligned with the radical cause. Godwin's writings of the 1790s provide one such example, with his piece on the 'Two Acts' being a particular case in point.

II

Godwin was certainly linked to the debate on France. Although we do not know when he first read Burke's *Reflections*, because he did not begin noting his daily reading in his diary until September 1791, we do know that he read it (probably reread it) in January 1792, and again in June 1794. He was also attentive to Paine's work, having read the first part of Paine's *Rights of Man* between the first printing of February 1791 by Joseph Johnson (who then withheld the text from publication for fear of prosecution) and the eventual 'first' edition, published on 13 March by J. S. Jordan (as indicated by Godwin's borrowing the book on 3 March 1791).[12] But there is no evidence to suggest that Godwin ever contemplated contributing a pamphlet to the debate, despite being well informed about affairs in France from his work on the 'European history' section of the *New Annual Register*.[13] That he was not so minded is clear from the fact

[12] The story that Holcroft and he were involved in a committee to organise its publication holds little water, however. Holcroft's famous note seems, on balance, to have referred to the first part of *Rights of Man*, but there is nothing to suggest that Godwin had any involvement in the publication of the text: 'I have got it – If this do not cure my cough it is a damned perverse mule of a cough – The pamphlet – From the row – But mum – We don't sell it – Oh no – Ears and Eggs – Verbatim, except the addition of a short preface, which, as you have not seen, I send you my copy – Not a single castration (Laud be unto God and J. S. Jordan) can I discover – Hey for the New Jerusalem! The millennium! And peace and eternal beatitude be unto the soul of Thomas Paine': cited by Charles Kegan Paul, *William Godwin: His Friends and Contemporaries*, vol. I (London: Henry S. King, 1876), 69. It is clear from his diary that Godwin read both the first and second parts of Paine's *Rights of Man* in advance of publication, but it was the second part that had the most to fear from 'castration', because of the dispute with its first printer, who was a closet loyalist: see Thomas Paine, *Rights of Man: Part the Second* (London: S. Jordan, 1792), appendix, 175–8. Nonetheless, the 'we' in 'we don't sell it' seems to have alluded to Joseph Johnson, and that would imply that it referred to the first part. See Mark Philp, 'Godwin, Holcroft and the rights of man', *Enlightenment and Dissent* 1 (1982), 37–42; and Jenny Graham, 'The publication of part one of the *Rights of Man*', *Enlightenment and Dissent* 12 (1993), 70–7.

[13] Godwin had written pamphlets in the 1780s and was to do so again in 1793 ('Essay against reopening the war with France'), 1794 (*Cursory Strictures*) and 1795 (*Considerations on Lord Grenville and Mr Pitt's Bills*). The 'Essay against reopening the war with France' remained unpublished, probably because it was overtaken by events. It was published for

that, when he turned to the task of *Political Justice*, he had a much grander plan than simply to contribute to a debate that, at the time of proposing, might have seemed likely to be as ephemeral as most.[14] It is fair to say that he had a sense of the scale of the issues raised by these events, and by their representation by Burke, Paine and others, and he recognised that they touched on the fundamental moral and political questions that he wished to address. But, when he began the project, it seems likely that he believed he would contribute, in large part, by acting as a conduit for various aspects of French political thought that were not widely known in England.

This much is evident from the way in which the first draft of *Political Justice* begins.[15] Setting aside so-called Tory and Whig positions on the nature of government and its imperfections, he aims to consider arguments of moral and political philosophy that treat government not simply as an instrument to protect liberty but as a powerful machine – an 'omnipotent engine' with the 'human as its pliant material' – discovering in it 'the great desideratum for advancing mind to courage, justice, virtue and perfection'.[16] Godwin's starting point was that 'the moral character of the species is in a considerable degree the result of the institutions of their political government'.[17] Once started, however, Godwin clearly found it difficult to sort out his chosen path of argument. In the opening chapters of the first edition, Godwin quickly loses confidence in the power of institutions positively to transform people's experiences. Hints remain of that potential, but by the beginning of Book II he seems to have adopted a largely negative view of government, and one that is very much indebted to Paine: 'The necessity of constraint grew out of the errors and perverseness of a few. An acute writer has expressed this idea with peculiar felicity. "Society and government," says he, "are different in themselves, and have different origins. Society is produced by our wants, and government by

the first time in vol. II (*Political Writings II*) of *The Political and Philosophical Writings of William Godwin* (hereafter *PPW* 2). Godwin also wrote a series of political letters between 1791 and 1794, also included in *PPW* 2. While this activity demonstrates his awareness of contemporary debates, it also underlines the fact that his concern was to pitch *Political Justice* at a level that was largely above these debates.

[14] It must also be said that he had negotiated a relatively lucrative arrangement with George Robinson for *Political Justice*, and it is unlikely that a pamphlet could have paid such returns.

[15] The manuscript of the first draft is at the end of the volumes of manuscripts of *Political Justice* in the National Art Library at the Victoria and Albert Museum, London. A transcription of the major part of the first draft is published at the end of vol. IV of *The Political and Philosophical Writings of William Godwin* (hereafter *PPW* 4).

[16] References are to the first edition, published as vol. III of *The Political and Philosophical Writings of William Godwin* (hereafter *PPW* 3), with variants published in *PPW* 4. See *PPW* 4, 367.

[17] Ibid., 376.

our wickedness. Society is in every state a blessing; government even in its best state but a necessary evil.'"[18] From this point, once Godwin has decided that there is nothing immutable in people's characters and passions, the argument increasingly turns to the ways in which the progress of knowledge and understanding can liberate individuals from the constraints of government through the increasing perfection of character and mind.[19]

In *Political Justice* Godwin at first emphasises the impact of social and institutional structures on the formation of character, asserting that political institutions outweigh literature and education, while innate endowment, national character, luxury, and so on weigh neither as given nor as unchangeable. This perspective does not sit comfortably with the quotation from Paine regarding the wholly negative and remedial function of government, nor does it sit well with the pastoralism of Paine and Jean-Jacques Rousseau, who both influenced the opening three books.[20] Godwin was effectively straddling two positions, one emphasising that the development of society and government is deeply linked to human progress, the other seeing government as an instrument solely for managing our tendency to pursue our interests beyond the point of what is fair and reasonable. The latter position emphasises that government's proper function is marginal and remedial and should leave people (and society) to their own, essentially natural, devices to the fullest possible extent; this position often links to the view that, once established, government often overreaches itself so far that it becomes a source of corruption.

These positions are not essentially those of Tory and Whig. Both the Scottish and French Enlightenments advanced a progressive view of human and social development from relative barbarism to civilisation, a view that offered a powerful and potentially optimistic alternative to arguments that rested on apparently more primitive claims about the state of

---

[18] *PPW* 3, 48; the quotation follows loosely the first lines of Paine's *Common Sense* (1776).

[19] And this turn in Godwin's argument raises the problem of the appropriate methods of reform. Although I address a part of that issue in this chapter, much more can and should be said: see, for example, Victoria Myers, 'William Godwin and the *Ars Rhetorica*', *Studies in Romanticism* 41 (2002), 415–44; Mee, '"The press and danger of the crowd"'; and the discussions in Godwin's *Enquirer* (1797), reprinted in *The Political and Philosophical Writings of William Godwin*, vol. V, *Educational and Literary Writings*, ed. Pamela Clemit, esp. pt. 1, chs. 1, 9, 11, each of which points to the different ways in which Godwin successively grappled with this issue.

[20] Rousseau is a difficult influence to track, since the arguments for simplicity of *mœurs* and politics in the *Social Contract* are not easily reconciled to the powerful sense of historical development and the interdependence of culture and institutions in *A Discourse on Arts and Sciences* and *A Discourse on the Origin of Inequality*.

nature and the original contract. It is very difficult to deduce exactly what influenced Godwin's position, and the diary's late start is tantalising.[21] In addition, while some of the reading he lists as he wrote *Political Justice* clearly influenced the particular angle that he took on a topic, it is evident that the architecture of the book as a whole (and the design of his reading material) had already been largely set. We do not have access directly to the influences that shaped his conception of that task, although his report on his Dissenting education at the Hoxton Academy and on his discussions with Frederick Norman, one of his parishioners in Stowmarket who persuaded him to read Baron d'Holbach, Claude-Adrien Helvétius and Rousseau, provides some guidance.[22] Nonetheless, for the first edition of *Political Justice* probably the French influence was most important for him. One intriguing set of suggestions is the list of French writers given at the beginning of the diary (which opened in 1788), but, while it is plausible to think that these represented either an achievement (texts read) or a set of aspirations (texts he wanted to read), it is clear that they are far from being an exhaustive catalogue on either side; at most they identify the literary and philosophical writers in French that he considered important.[23] We do know, however, that he failed to appreciate the economic writings of Adam Smith and that he makes no mention of the work of either Ferguson or Millar. But he read David Hume reasonably consistently while writing *Political Justice*, working with his *Essays* early on and later turning to the *Enquiry* and the work on causation and the human understanding when he was nine months or so into the project. It is clear, however, that his 'conversion' to Hume as an epistemologist had occurred only incompletely by the second and more systematically by the third edition, although his sympathy with Hume's position on the interrelationship between government and opinion is clear from the beginning of *Political*

---

[21] The diary began in 1788, and listed his reading only from September 1791. Godwin's diary is part of the Abinger Collection held by the Bodleian Library. A digital resource, backed by a Leverhulme-funded project and including a complete scan of the diary and a searchable database, has been available as part of the Oxford Digital Library since September 2010; the editorial team is Victoria Myers, David O'Shaughnessy and Mark Philp, with the assistance of Kate Barush, James Cumming and James Grande. See http://godwindiary.politics.ox.ac.uk.

[22] On Godwin's background in Dissent and the influence of Frederick Norman, see his 'Autobiographical fragments', in *The Collected Novels and Memoirs of William Godwin*, vol. I, ed. Mark Philp (London: Pickering & Chatto, 1992), 39–51, 44.

[23] The list is set out as follows [emphasis in original]:
Malherbe, <u>Corneille</u>, <u>Racine</u>, <u>Molière</u>, <u>Boileau</u>, <u>Quinault</u>, La Fontaine, Rousseau, de la Motte, Chaulieu, Gresset, Crebillon, Voltaire, Destouches, Regnard.
Rollin, Vertot, Bossuet, Voltaire, Raynal, Saint Real.
Malebranche, Rousseau, Helvetius, Montesquieu, Mirabaud, Pascal, Nicole.

Justice.[24] Montesquieu and Rousseau, on the other hand, featured as reading right at the beginning of his work, albeit in a way that suggests that Godwin was essentially revisiting texts he knew well.

What is less expected, however, is the prominence of Burke in Godwin's reading. Burke's work turned up regularly in the diary, with *Reflections* being reread on a number of occasions: on 27 October 1791 he began the *Appeal from the New to the Old Whigs*; in January 1792 he reread *Reflections*; in March he was reading 'Burke on Ireland'; April saw him return to the *Reflections* and 'Nat. Society'; in June he was comparing Burke and Paine on 'Property' and reading Burke on 'Oeconomy'; in July he looked at Burke's speech to the electors of Bristol and the *Essay on the Sublime*; in September he returned to the *Reflections*; and in November he was noting '6 October' – a reference to Burke's account of the *journée* that brought the French royal family back from Versailles to Paris. This attention to Burke is important, because it illustrates the extent to which Godwin remained heavily influenced by Burke and, correspondingly, suggests that his own work was never going to line up clearly on anti-Burkean lines.[25] Godwin may have felt the distance politically between himself and Burke, but he remained powerfully drawn to the more organic picture of the social and political world that Burke had developed; and several of those by whom he was clearly influenced, such as Montesquieu and Hume, had also been influential on Burke.

Commentators need to understand that, while Godwin was attracted to the idea of eradicating government and increasing the individual's independence from all forms of cooperation and coercion, he was also strongly drawn to the view that progress is itself a collective enterprise. It is collective in that only under appropriate circumstances can people develop their capacities so as to be emancipated from institutions that initially nurture but can come to constrain those capacities. Rather than thinking of progress as stripping away the corruptions of government and society, Godwin conceived it as increasing rational capacities that are themselves influenced by and linked to political and social institutions and that need to be guided by those more enlightened in the pursuit of truth. This in part accounts for the uncertainties that dog the drafts and opening books of *Political Justice*; they are driven by the view that government does have an immensely

---

[24] See my *Godwin's Political Justice*, chs. 7, 9. Hume's pronouncement 'It is therefore, on opinion only that government is founded', in 'Of the first principles of government', 32, is clearly echoed in Godwin's assertion 'All government is founded in opinion', in Bk II, ch. 4, of *Political Justice*; *PPW* 3, 63.

[25] In his *The French Revolution Debate in Britain*, 130, Gregory Claeys recognises the echoes of Burke's work in the revisions to the second edition, and especially in *The Enquirer* (1797). We differ in the extent to which we see the Burkean elements as evident, and as influential from the first edition, and beforehand.

powerful impact on the way people develop, think and behave, and by the sense that there is a way of gradually emancipating people from this tutelage so that they can stand on their own reason and judgement. The doctrine of necessity that drives the second half of Book IV also underpins the picture of progress throughout the work, and is central to Godwin's sense that positive and permanent change is possible and that emancipation is not simply a matter of throwing off chains but must involve a progressive unpicking of them, through the exercise of reason and the development of truth (as is clear from his comments about Helvetius's despair of the situation in France).[26] Truth and discussion become forces for development that drive the component parts of society forward and render increasingly super-fluous the imposition of government.

This is not Paine's story, that hereditary government has, by force and fraud, usurped the judgement of the people and needs to be swept away to allow them to exercise their original capacities freed from arbitrary inter-ference. It is a narrative of historical change in which truth plays a central part, but it is one that is linked to broader changes in government and society. The hesitations over the start of *Political Justice* need to be seen as Godwin trying to combine a story of interlinked social, political and cultural change with an account of emancipation from force and fraud. And this combination, which was a common one in the second half of the eighteenth century, remains through successive revisions, generating a series of anxieties and concerns that help account for a number of appa-rent changes in Godwin's position in subsequent years.

III

My concern here is with one set of changes in particular that address the role of political associations and the nature of resistance. These fill a section of *Political Justice* with three chapters largely rewritten for the 1796 edition, and the issues also resurfaced in his pamphlet *Considerations* in November 1795. In both cases, we can see Godwin working away at this more profound set of issues about whether we should understand progress as simply a removal of fraud or recognise the role that political and social institutions play in determining the conditions for truth to develop. Although there is a tendency in both cases for commentators to accuse Godwin of simply bending to political pressure and turning conservative in

---

[26] *PPW* 3, 126–7: Godwin reports Helvetius lamenting 'in pathetic strains the hopeless condition of his country' and suggesting that the moment was past when a book could turn the people to reform, when in fact (Godwin says) reform lay close at hand thanks to the work of those, Helvetius included, who were at the vanguard of French thought.

the hostile political atmosphere of 1795, I want to suggest that it is more plausible to see him as returning to mine a vein in *Political Justice* that had been problematic from the start and that represents, in a fashion, both sides of the debate between Burke and Paine: Burke in his account of the fragile interconnectivity of social and political institutions and the dependence of the arts and sciences on their stability; Paine with his account of the extent to which these institutions increasingly rested on fraudulent claims to authority.

The doctrine of the opening chapters of the 1793 edition of Book IV of *Political Justice* is clearly stated: 'The revolutions of states, which a philanthropist would desire to witness, or in which he would willingly cooperate, consist principally in a change of sentiments and dispositions in the members of those states. The true instruments for changing the opinions of men are argument and persuasion.'[27] Godwin did admit the possibility that self-defence may call for action in extremis, but the thrust of his case was unmistakably that such occasions were very much the exception and that progress could not be made by means other than the development of knowledge and understanding. His attitude to political associations was in keeping with this: revolutions derived from the progress of mind made by those with the capacity and leisure for study and reflection. The truths that issued from these sources would diffuse themselves, but not until they were fully disseminated and understood could they command universal assent and enable society to move forward. This division of labour was inevitable, even if Godwin's longer-term aspiration was for all to partake in the same opportunities for reflection. But the process of dissemination was a slow one, and 'he that begins with an appeal to the people, may be suspected to understand little of the true character of mind. A sinister design may gain by precipitation; but true wisdom is best adapted to a slow, unvarying and incessant progress.'[28] Godwin has no doubt that associations can easily feed the passions rather than the intellect: 'There is nothing more barbarous, cruel and blood-thirsty, than the triumph of a mob.'[29] What he does concede is that, although the progress of truth needs to be taken slowly and 'in all possible tranquillity', an association might be acceptable as a means of providing the 'early and unequivocal display of opinion' that new encroachments on liberty may warrant. And, while Godwin allows the importance of clubs for discussion, 'they cease to be admissible, when united with the tremendous apparatus of articles of confederation and committees of correspondence... Truth disclaims the alliance of marshalled numbers.'[30]

---

[27] *PPW* 3, 115.   [28] *PPW* 3, 118.   [29] *PPW* 3, 118.   [30] *PPW* 3, 119, 122.

This doctrine was substantially the same in the 1796 edition. The argument is more carefully developed, picking away in the opening chapter at the preconception that majorities appreciate the truths they often espouse; he makes more of stoic values, so that the freedom of the wise consists not in their physical liberty but in their knowledge; and, instead of praise for the American and French Revolutions,[31] he takes the view that the philosopher has a responsibility to delay events, if he cannot entirely prevent them, until they are entirely consensual. But the principles are essentially similar, if developed at greater length. They are, however, more explicitly tied to a view of progress that rejects the idea that change is a process of flux in which *carpe diem* is the watchword, and that sees the invention of printing as central to the development of human intellect and the progressive advance of knowledge. That innovation has made possible the uniting of all the members of the community and has made inevitable the progress of political truth.

It is easy to see *Considerations* as another matter entirely – a direct attack on friends and associates for their involvement in political action in a context of government repression and intolerance. But this reading overlooks the deeper principles Godwin found in the issue at hand. *Considerations* falls more or less cleanly into three parts: a critique of the activities of the radical societies; a critique of Baron Grenville's bill on treasonable and seditious practices; and a critique of Pitt's proposal on unlawful assemblies. The first part is the most shocking for most readers. It can seem deeply quietist: '[P]ublic interest and security require from men, to a certain degree, an uniformity of action, and an uniformity of submission... Reason and expostulation here are not sufficient: there must be an arm to repress; a coercion strict, but forbearing and mild.'[32] And it can seem deeply disloyal. Referring to Thelwall's lectures and their protestations of non-violence, Godwin writes: 'It is lord [sic] George Gordon preaching peace to the rioters in Westminster-Hall. "Commit no violence," said his lordship, "but be sure you do not separate, till you have effected your purpose." It is Iago adjuring Othello not to dishonour himself by giving harbour to a thought of jealousy.'[33] In contrast, the section on Grenville is a good piece of forensic work, pointing to the catch-all definition of sedition as inciting the people to hatred or 'dislike'; to the way that even the mildest of political speculations, such as Hume's 'Idea of a Perfect Commonwealth', might, in the wrong hands, give rise to a prosecution for treason; and to the tendency of the bill to give employment to an army of spies and informers who will effectively destroy the

---

[31] *PPW* 3, 116.   [32] *PPW* 2, 126.   [33] *PPW* 2, 133.

conditions for confidence between men.[34] Pitt's bill is denounced for its capacity to intimidate and to silence those who address any sort of meeting and for the draconian punishment annexed to the offence (the death penalty). In driving home his point, Godwin uses an image that Benjamin West was to immortalise in his popular print *A Lock'd Jaw for John Bull* two days later and that Spence was to commit to coin in the following year: '[T]he master clasps a padlock on his lips and he must be silent.'[35]

Godwin goes on, moreover, to argue that the bills were modelled on legislation that had been passed to cope with temporary difficulties in the reigns of Elizabeth and Charles II – both, significantly, *before* the Glorious Revolution. He suggests that Grenville, Pitt and others – he cites Lord Macdonald, the chief prosecutor in Paine's trial – were treating the history of Britain as if the revolution was not a defining moment for its constitution. The precedents, then, came from a time when the liberty of the House of Commons had not been established and when politics was disfigured by wars of succession and religion. Godwin then goes on to show, drawing on Hume's *History*, that the occasion for the precedents that Grenville cites for the treason bill was a parliament so effectively intimidated by the queen that she openly avowed her unwillingness to tolerate any questioning of her will. Far from drawing on the established constitution, these 'precedents' might just as well have been drawn from France and Spain – two classical despotisms. In implicit alliance with Burke, Godwin treated the 1701 Act of Settlement as the occasion for the establishment of the constitution, rendering nugatory any appeal prior to that period for precedents.

What Godwin does not do in *Considerations* is to question the principles upon which the agitation for reform drew. The issue entirely concerned the means of progress, not the ends: 'No infatuation can be more extraordinary than that which at present prevails among the alarmed adversaries of reform. Reform must come. It is a resistless tide; and, if we endeavour to keep it out too long, it will overwhelm us.'[36] But, as to means, 'we must both accommodate ourselves to the empire of old prejudices, and to the strong and decisive influx of new opinions'. He criticises the London Corresponding Society for setting up a system like the Jacobin Clubs, which, by collecting together large numbers,

---

[34] *PPW* 2, 143, 145–6.
[35] *PPW* 2, 148. West's print, published by S. W. Fores, is dated 23 November 1795 (British Museum Catalogue, 8693). For Spence's political token, see Franklin and Philp, *Napoleon and the Invasion of Britain*, 44 (West's print, 42).
[36] *PPW* 2, 159.

threatened to repeat the Gordon riots of 1780. Although Godwin expresses concern that the LCS lacked the ballast of property in its membership,[37] it was mainly its mass public meetings that he thinks warrant the attention of the government – irrespective of the intentions of those who organised the society – on the grounds that the consequences of their actions were not wholly within their control and that the best intentions might produce deeply regrettable outcomes. He does not say, however, what attention they deserved, although clearly he thinks that they did not deserve these bills and that the existing legislation concerning assembly and riot was sufficient to handle the danger.

The case against the public lectures of Thelwall, which Godwin had himself attended on 12 June 1795 (and on 17 February 1794, before the treason trials), was more mixed. He asks that the lecturer 'have a mind calmed and ... consecrated by the mild spirit of philosophy', and recommends that he 'have a temper unyielding to the corrupt influence of a noisy and admiring audience'.[38] Godwin's strictures on Thelwall are severe, but the records that we have of the lectures suggest that his comments had some justification. According to Hazlitt, Thelwall was,

[i]n speaking, like a volcano vomiting out *lava*... He was the model of a flashy, powerful demagogue – a madman blessed with a fit audience... The lightning of national indignation flashed from his eye; the workings of the popular mind were seen labouring in his bosom: it writhed and swelled with its rank 'fraught of aspics' tongues' and the poison frothed over at his lips. Thus qualified, he 'wielded at will the fierce democracy, and fulmin'd over' an arena of souls, of no mean circumference.[39]

And Thelwall's response to the 'Two Acts' was certainly less restrained than Godwin's:

I am not very careful, citizens, about my words tonight: for I declare no death is so terrible to me as living to see the day in which this bill is accepted. I have two infants, the joy of a father's heart, whose innocent smiles furnish my only relaxation... But I protest sooner would I see those infants strangled before my face, sooner would I have my body pierced like a culender ... than live under the reproach of suffering this bill to pass without all the opposition I have the power of making...[40]

---

[37] *PPW* 2, 130. [38] *Considerations on Lord Grenville and Mr Pitt's Bills*, *PPW* 2, 132.

[39] William Hazlitt, 'On the difference between writing and speaking', in *The Complete Works of William Hazlitt*, vol. XII, ed. P. P. Howe (London: Dent, 1931), 262–79. Partially cited by E. P. Thompson, in 'Hunting the Jacobin fox', *Past and Present* 142 (1994), 94–140, 96–7.

[40] Cited by Thompson, 'Hunting the Jacobin fox', 97.

As Jon Mee has shown, however, Thelwall in many respects also aspired to be a true disciple of Godwin, and was himself anxious about the corruption of his judgement by the applause of the crowd, and the need to avoid the inflammation of the crowd by passion and rhetoric.[41] Indeed, the lecture that Godwin attended on 12 June 1795 exhibited Thelwall in sober mood – conscious that before a crowd 'the mind is sometimes apt to become inflamed, to lose sight of principles, and dwell too much on personalities; – to suffer passion to snatch the reins from reason and to foster prejudice and resentment when truth and justice ought to be the only objects'.[42] But, for Godwin, this confession seems to have been inadequate, perhaps because it became clear from the reports of others that the lectures were resumed in a more combative spirit, and perhaps because Godwin was also anxious about Thelwall's participation in the mass public meeting of 26 October 1795, at which, for all Thelwall's expressly pacific purposes, Godwin would have feared a pandering to the opinions of the mob. The difficulty in assessing how fairly Godwin treated Thelwall cannot be settled solely in the light of Thelwall's pro-claimed principles, since Godwin firmly believed that there was many a forum in which truth simply could not be advanced, and he condemned the lecture theatre and the mass meeting alike on these grounds. Thelwall's own insistence that he was concerned in the pursuit of truth and virtue would have rung hollow to Godwin, demonstrating that Thelwall failed to grasp Godwin's point about the importance of the rational communication of truth and the sanctity of private judgement. It is also true, however, that insistence on rational communication as the basis for change meant that Godwin's strictures on reform condemned the vast majority of political activity on the grounds that it was not a proper vehicle for the dissemination of truth. One consequence of Godwin's position is that he was in danger of following the loyalists in lumping together the broad range of radical groups and activities as equally danger-ous, rather than recognising the attempts made by people such as Thelwall to tread a distinctive but essentially judicious line.

For Godwin, 'reform is a delicate and an awful task. . . It must be carried on by slow, almost insensible steps, and by just degrees. The public mind must first be enlightened; the public sentiment must next become unequivocal; there must be a grand and magnificent harmony, expanding

---

[41] See Mee, '"The press and danger of the crowd"', which makes clear Godwin's doubts about the extent to which it was possible for a lecturer to maintain the philosophical calm that was seen as essential to the cause of truth, given the effects on him of the reactions of the audience.

[42] Thelwall, *The Tribune*, vol. I, 335. My thanks are owed to James Grande for drawing the details of this lecture to my attention.

itself through the whole community. There must be a concert of wills, that no minister and no monopolist would be frantic enough to withstand.'[43] There had to be these things because, without them, the social fabric would be ripped apart, men and women's security would be surrendered and the development of human society would be set back. On the grounds of the sanctity of private judgement, on the grounds of utility and on the grounds of the intricate set of relations and causes that link together the social and political fabric and the liberty of its subjects into a seamless garment, precipitate change had to be resisted. This attention to the cloth of historical inheritance and the slow nature of enlightenment and reform was central to Godwin's world view in *Political Justice*, and it formed the key to understanding his mature novels, with their painstaking delineation of the causal conditions, expressed through the acts of men and women who incompletely understand their situations and their emotions and whose capacity for reason too often leads hubristically to their downfall. *Caleb Williams*'s Falkland was one such flawed character: the product of his class and circumstance, capable of greatness but subverted from within by the norms and *mœurs* of his caste, which made it impossible for him to treat Williams as his equal and which led him to sacrifice his virtue through a concern with the public bubble of his honour. This was not a picture that Godwin shared with Paine; it was one that he drew in part from Montesquieu and Rousseau and from Hume and Burke, and he did so from the beginning of *Political Justice* – indeed, from the very first draft.

This reading places Godwin in the centre of the debate on France, not in the sense that he was the major contributor, but in the sense that what became a set of polarising forces around him increasingly left him with a position that was both sympathetic to and critical of Burke and Paine and that he occupied more uneasily as the debate became progressively a pamphlet and print war. Godwin's response to Thelwall was a response to his sense that he was facing a dual extremism – both of the government in its panic, and the reformers, who shut their eyes and 'believe, while everything is auspicious, that everything is desperate'.[44]

It is possible, of course, to read the pamphlet as a considerable rhetorical success: Godwin adopted the position of someone aloof from the reform societies and from the governmental panic, calmly picking off the arguments and errors of each side and demonstrating that the bills were unnecessary and the panic unfounded. That the pamphlet should have been so favourably reviewed might similarly suggest that Godwin had

---

[43] *PPW* 2, 132.   [44] *PPW* 2, 162.

managed to hit the right rhetorical note, not showing enough of his hand by denouncing the government for despotism and irrationality to be deemed a radical and condemned accordingly, nor appearing uncritical of those who sought reform. But Godwin's own views on candour would make it difficult for him to acknowledge that his position was driven wholly by polemical purposes rather than by his sincere commitments – and his reaction to Thelwall's outrage suggests that he believed he was acting with perfect candour, not simply instrumentally.[45] Moreover, while the political context really had made polemic the order of the day, Godwin must be understood as sincerely trying to rise above it, to reason in measured tones about the appropriateness of the conduct of the two sides and of the government's remedies. That some reviews, such as those in the *Monthly Review* and the *Monthly Mirror*, were able to recognise this is, I would suggest, evidence that middle ground continued to exist and was probably occupied by many, but it was ground that was increasingly whittled away as the contest between government and its opponents intensified – and it was ground that was more secure at the level of the monthly reviews than at the level of the pamphlet and broadside controversy.[46]

What Godwin wrote about Thelwall does look pretty close to betrayal, but only if we accept, as Godwin did not, that the process of political change involves sharp contrasts, organised struggles and high levels of partisan conflict. That picture is not an eighteenth-century picture – a century in which party was accommodated increasingly, but did not

---

[45] For Godwin's correspondence with Thelwall, see Charles Cestre, *John Thelwall* (London: Swan Sonnenschein, 1906), appendix 1; and Thelwall, *The Tribune*, II, vii–xvii, III, 101–5. In Godwin's diary, for 10 January 1793, he reported discussing the preface to his *Enquiry concerning Political Justice* with William Nicholson, who praised his 'dissimulation'. The comment suggests that Godwin might not have been committed to perfect candour, but we have no way of knowing how far Nicholson's praise was welcomed or acknowledged as just.

[46] The *Monthly Review*, new series 18 (December 1795), 451–2, praised Godwin's 'moderate, candid, and judicious' opening remarks, and pointed to the way that the beginning of the pamphlet might lead the reader to suppose that he was in favour of the legislation, only to demonstrate that, 'after a strict and ample scrutiny', the measures were 'totally condemned as in the highest degree unjust, arbitrary, and dangerous'. The reviewer judged that the pamphlet had been written with 'uncommon energy and animation'. The *Monthly Mirror* 1 (December 1795), 104, gave a very brief review that admitted to taking a position widely opposed to the author's, but nonetheless conceded: '[W]e must, in justice to him, allow a considerable portion of praise for the manly manner in which he has treated the subject.' The *Analytical Review* 22 (November 1795), 541–3, quoted extensively from the pamphlet and refrained largely from judgement, save in its conclusion: 'The pamphlet is written with great ability, but the author, doubtless from a "conciliating spirit", adopts facts and inferences, that have hitherto been proved only by the bold and unqualified assertions of men, whom he loudly condemns.'

wholly dominate the political landscape (certainly not the extra-parliamentary landscape), and in which the struggle for parliamentary reform
was in the process of formation rather than already established. Paine's
powerful polemics may easily mislead us into thinking that the lines of
battle (and thereby of loyalty) were clearly laid down. In practice, they
were not. On the contrary, there was a good deal of confusion and
uncertainty about where to stand and about what was implied in practice
by one's intellectual commitments. One result is that various individual
careers tacked between reforming and loyalist positions. Moreover, this
process was hugely complicated by the pressure increasingly put on
people to declare one way or another and to face the consequences that
an increasingly repressive regime, backed by local prosecutions and the
intimidation of those sympathetic to reform, sought to impose. Under
these conditions, Godwin took the courageous step of attacking the government's bills, but he did so while attempting to avoid partisan polemic.
His wish to stand above the fray was absolutely at one with the position he
took up in *Political Justice*; his concern was impartially to conduct the
arguments, not to descend to the polemics of the pamphlet literature. It is
true that he did not sound very courageous when he told Thelwall that he
was not entitled to make public use of the knowledge that Godwin had
authored the pamphlet and when he suggested that Thelwall would
probably 'contribute, as far as your power may extend, to consign me
also to the lamp-post'.[47] But writing the pamphlet was nonetheless evidence of his courage, because he had every reason to think that he could be
a target for a government concerned to root out sedition (and, indeed, he
did soon become a target of a government-sponsored press, even if he
avoided prosecution – which others did not).[48] However aloof his tone, it

[47] See Cestre, *John Thelwall*, appendix, 203. The letter was dated 28 November 1795.
[48] Godwin's associate Edward Henry Iliff was less successful. His strident attack on the
army, Church and political institutions was accompanied by a very Godwin-like insistence
on the progress of reason and opinion and the utter repudiation of recourse to violence,
but the pamphlet was prosecuted nonetheless. See Edward Henry Iliff, *A Summary of the
Duties of Citizenship! Written Expressly for the Members of the London Corresponding Society*
(London: Richard Lee, 1795). We should also bear in mind that Godwin was well
acquainted with many radicals who were prosecuted for their actions or publications
(and visited many of them in jail) – including those involved in the Scottish Convention
trials of 1794 and the London treason trials of the same year, and others, such as Thomas
Muir and Thomas Fyshe Palmer, and Henry Redhead Yorke (whose sentence he discussed on 29 November 1795). He was also an occasional associate of Colonel Despard,
who was executed for treason in 1803. Note also that Godwin expressed his fear in
relation to 'lamp-posts' – the gallows of the popular *journée* – as if his fear was of
Thelwall galvanising the crowd against him. Moreover, for all Thelwall's accusations of
quietism, Godwin seems to have been moved to some sort of political action during the
campaign against the 'Two Acts'; on 22 November 1795 he entered in his diary 'Write
petition'.

is clear that he regarded the government's actions as little better than contemptible and as bordering on despotism. He refused to take a stand with the reform organisations, then, not because he rejected reform but because his conception of reform was a relatively traditional, élite-led form of enlightenment that moved forward from the order from which it sprang. His more utopian hopes aspired to a progressive liberation from the different European paths and towards an increasing convergence on reason and truth, but for that process to happen private judgement and sober discussion were essential, and for these to be realised people had to be secure from arbitrary rule, either by governments or by crowds.[49]

Godwin was on the losing side in this debate. Not only were the 'Two Acts' passed but there was also a growing recognition amongst those favourable to reform that the scale of the government's backlash against the popular movement would severely damage the conditions for the development of truth and the progressive enlightenment of society. The position of the enlightened intellectual came under increasing attack. Much the same indignity that Godwin inflicted on Thelwall was visited upon him in turn by James Mackintosh – to whom he responded with much the same indignation – and by a host of anti-Jacobin novels and squibs. Moreover, his historical reputation has always been marred by Thelwall's assertion that Godwin's 'visionary peculiarities of mind', which 'recommend the most extensive plan of freedom and innovation ever discussed by any writer in the English language', were coupled with a conviction that it was necessary 'to reprobate every measure from which even the most moderate reform can rationally be expected'.[50] Thelwall's attack had some force: Godwin's position threatened to lapse into a form of passive obedience, and it threatened to have nothing practical to say to any who looked for positive change in the state.

What makes this judgement overly harsh is that it needs to be correctly framed, but not by a view that saw the interests of the people and the political establishment wholly at odds and necessitating a practical struggle to force the powers that be to make concessions to the masses. That view was only gradually and with difficulty recognised by many who wrote in the opening phases of the debate on France; and it only became clearly articulated as options in the contrast drawn, from the second and third decades of the nineteenth century, between moral and physical force

---

[49] See *PPW* 3, 467, on violence and the imposition of a revolution; but also see ibid., 468, where he appeals to the dislocated limb analogy. Godwin sets out the responsibilities of those who were to be precursors to the rest in the discovery of truth: 469–70. See also *PPW* 4, 317.

[50] *The Tribune*, II, vii.

reformisms. Rather, the judgement on Godwin needs to be framed by an eighteenth-century Enlightenment that saw in the development of science and knowledge a vehicle for the progressive emancipation of mankind from want. In this frame, those of more enlightened understanding played the key role in developing and diffusing the truths of morality and science that their researches uncovered, while recognising that existing contexts had a powerful grip on people's minds, limiting their understanding and calling for patience in the educative process. Framed in this way, what is extraordinary is less Godwin's position and more that of Paine and those who followed him, who sought a direct and urgent emancipation from the status quo, with little sense of the potential costs of such a rupture with the cultural, social and political context. With hindsight, we might think that Paine got it right in terms of the ends to be pursued and the necessity of confrontational means. Godwin did not deny those ends, however. He merely suggested that their pursuit was in itself a complex task of achieving intellectual emancipation from the system of dependence upon the political and social élite that European societies had inherited and that their practices continued to promote.

9   Politics and memory: Nelson and Trafalgar in popular song[1]

John Harkness, a Preston printer in business between 1840 and 1866, published a ballad sheet, probably in the middle of the 1840s, containing two songs. *The Comforts of Man* retails the story of a young man who, thinking he ought to have the comforts of a wife, asks young Betty, his sweetheart, to marry him. She consents, but the marriage turns sour as our hero is subjected to repeated spousal abuse. His final verse rues 'the day that ere I was married', and concludes 'What a plague is the comforts of man'. The other song is entitled *Grand Conversation on Nelson Arose*. It lists Admiral Horatio Nelson's achievements, at the Nile, Copenhagen and Trafalgar, and it recounts his fearlessness and the loyalty of his officers and men. The later verses suggest that the song was written soon after the completion of Nelson's column (1843) and Trafalgar Square. The most striking feature of the song, however, is the fact that the title and the implied tune are borrowed from a slightly earlier and better-known song that achieved wide circulation and that has lodged itself in the oral tradition: *The Grand Conversation of Napoleon*. As in life, so in death: Nelson and Napoleon remain locked in an engagement in which their posthumous reputations contest for ascendancy. Moreover, they do so in popular song, one of the most important but largely neglected channels for

[1] I owe thanks to Alvero Herrero, who acted as a research assistant in a critical phase of this project; to Alexandra Franklin, who guided me through the ballad collection at the Bodleian Library; to the Department of Politics and International Relations at the University of Oxford, for its support; and to Derek McCulloch, the director of Café Mozart, a group of musicians specialising in the songs and music of the period, for his expertise and access to material covering the more élite songs of the period. The sources of material for this chapter are diverse, but the bulk comes from the Bodleian Library, especially its Curzon and Harding collections and the essential searchable web-based ballads database, which is available through the Bodleian's website (www.bodley.ox.ac. uk/ballads). I have also drawn on material in the British Library and on the resources of the Cecil Sharp Library (and its enormously helpful librarian) in London. In addition, there are a number of printed sources that are cited whenever they are the source for a particular song.

information and public memory in the eighteenth and nineteenth centuries.

I want to go some way to correcting this neglect by examining the range of songs we have about Nelson and by setting them in the context of the intense ideological mobilisation that took place in England in the mid-1790s and again at the height of the invasion threat in 1803–5. The chapter is primarily concerned to indicate the sheer volume and range of Nelson songs, to go some way towards an analysis of the provenance of the songs and to consider the role they played in the memorialising of Nelson. I return, in conclusion, to reflect on the contrast between Nelson and his implicit antagonist, Napoleon Bonaparte.

I

Although *Rule Britannia* is still widely sung and it is possible to find the words and music for *Hearts of Oak*, *Roast Beef of England* or *Britons Strike Home*, and although there is some general awareness that these songs would have been sung in ships, at dinners and at public entertainments during the military campaigns against, first, Revolutionary and, subsequently, Napoleonic France, there is substantially less acknowledgement that Nelson himself was directly celebrated and commemorated in song, and that such songs formed an important part of a much wider campaign to rouse British resistance to Napoleon and to encourage public support for the navy and the military. There are a number of reasons for the neglect of this aspect of Nelson's reputation: many songs were ephemeral, their provenance and subsequent histories are not easy to track, and it is not easy to grasp their significance without having a sense of the other songs being written, sung and circulated in the period and a sense of the political context in which such songs figured. To address the neglect we must address these obstacles.

In the winter of 1792/3 the Association for the Preservation of Liberty and Property against Republicans and Levellers was set up, and it encouraged all loyal persons to correspond with the association, to inform on local subversives and to send in copies of material to be published so as to sway the minds of the lower orders against the surge in popular radicalism spreading through the country. One of the APLP's female correspondents shrewdly drew attention to the importance of popular song in the political struggle:

I have had many opportunities of observing the influence of the new seditious doctrines upon the lower class of people, that class that the wicked and designing intend to use as their Engine, they are incapable of reading or understanding any good or serious address to set them right; but through the medium of popular ballads surely much instruction might be convey'd and much patriotic spirit awakened.[2]

The suggestion was taken up with enthusiasm, with the association and its sympathisers initiating the prosecution of ballad sellers caught selling works with more insidious and subversive messages and positively encouraging the writing, printing and circulation of songs and ballads supporting king and constitution, and attacking the ideas of the reformers and some of their principle supporters – especially Thomas Paine.

From the beginning of 1793 until the end of the decade the ideological and political confrontation between the government and reformers ratcheted up in intensity, with the government launching a series of prosecutions of leaders of the reform movement in 1794 and with some reformers becoming prepared to countenance more radical opposition to what they saw as Pitt's tyranny. The insurrection and subsequent landing of a French invasion force in Ireland, and growing demands at home for peace, coupled with rioting over food shortages and recruitment practices, only strengthened the government's intransigence. In parallel, as contestation over the public's loyalties intensified, the government, loyalists and local magistrates increasingly silenced popular songs and singers that were critical of the government or supportive of France, and published street ballads become more consistently loyalist in character. There were one or two ballads sympathetic to the Spithead and Nore mutinies in 1797, and some ballad writers with reformist leanings did remain at work throughout the period – such as John Freeth, Robert Burns and Robert Anderson – but there was very little published in popular broadsides in England that was openly critical of Pitt or of the handling of the war, or that was expressive of the widespread unrest that marked the country in 1798/9 and 1800/1801. In contrast, in Ireland the circulation of popular songs with political content (both radical and loyalists) was widespread until the insurrection of 1798, and songs from that insurrection circulated widely throughout the country thereafter, even if many were expressly proscribed in an attempt to extinguish them.[3] Indeed, as the Irish case shows, even if repression could largely eradicate printed songs sympathetic to reform, it did not mean that such songs did not exist; ballad and song collectors early in the nineteenth century found many songs traceable to the period preserved within the oral tradition, which made their way into print forms only when government repression relaxed and political opposition

---

[2] BM Add. MS 16920, fo. 99.
[3] See the excellent collection of Irish songs given by Terry Moylan, *The Age of Revolution in the Irish Song Tradition: 1776 to 1815* (Dublin: Lilliput Press, 2000).

again began to flourish, tentatively in England after 1805, and more vigorously after 1815.

That loyalist sentiment became the only acceptable script for popular politics did not mean that this sentiment was entirely manufactured. Sympathy for reform did not necessarily entail an unwillingness to defend one's country or hostility to those who did. And some with sympathies for reform certainly contributed to celebrations and commemorations of British victories and British heroes. John Thelwall, the leading radical and the third major defendant in the treason trials of 1794, ventured into print after Trafalgar with a poem on Nelson's death, *The Trident of Albion*; and Freeth, for all his Whig and reformist sympathies, wrote several songs celebrating British victories, including 'From the mouth of the Nile, flush'd with glory behold' ('All shall yield to the mulberry tree') *On Admiral Nelson's* Victory, *Britannia Triumphant*, to celebrate the battle of the Nile.[4] One dimension of this relative silence for reformers, therefore, may well be that their hostility to Pitt and to the political system was leavened by their suspicion of the French and their sense of the importance of national self-defence; wanting an end to the war was not the same as not being concerned about losing it. Nonetheless, although loyalists and the government had every interest in ensuring that people saw support for national defence as entailing support for the administration and for the constitution, we have considerable evidence at the end of the 1790s of widespread unrest over the continuation of the war, recruitment, the price of bread and the unresponsiveness of the government to demands for political reform. What is striking is how far this unrest was absent from the broadsides and popular songs of the late 1790s and early 1800s, despite the fact that these normally provided one of the key conduits for public commentary on events and for the expression of concerns and grievances.

In contrast, loyalist songs flourished, especially around the invasion threats of 1797/8 and 1803–5. Loyalist and government-sponsored presses pumped out songs and broadsides to meet every occasion.[5] This investment in popular song was certainly not new: election songs were common throughout the eighteenth century, and there is evidence of

---

[4] All songs are referred to by: 'first line' (tune) *title*. Where no tune is identified, no bracket appears; where the tune is printed with the words, '(printed)' appears. This method of reference is not without difficulties, as a number of versions of essentially the same song may have different first lines, but differences in titles are still more common, and it is the standard method. On Freeth, see note 8.

[5] Interestingly, when Freeth produced a collection of songs during the peace of 1803 the Nelson song was not included, but an earlier version hymning Admiral Edward Russell's victory at Cape Barfleur in 1692, with the same tune and chorus, was reprinted; although it is difficult to be certain, it seems likely that the peace genuinely resulted in a desire to seek a rapprochement with France, leading to a downplaying of recent, more nationalist, songs.

massive spending on the part of the Treasury to secure the election of
certain candidates in London in the elections in the late 1780s and early
1790s and thereafter.[6] But, in such cases, there were usually two or more
sides to the controversy, each having its say. What is distinctive about the
time of the Revolutionary War, and especially the opening of the
Napoleonic War, is the degree of dominance that loyalist forces secured
over this dimension of popular culture, and the consequent lack of
contestation.

The intense politicisation of songs and singing in this period has implications for the broader understanding of the significance of popular
culture in this period. Many scholars examining the published material
of the period 1793–1815 have been tempted to speculate about the
creation of a sense of national unity and national spirit in response to
the threat of French invasion, suggesting, for example, that the massive
enlistment in the volunteers in 1803–5 (when some half a million men
joined volunteer regiments) was a function of their ideological commitments against the French. There are, in fact, more prosaic explanations,
not least the immunity from impressment and militia duty that it gave
those who volunteered.[7] Such accounts also understate the complexity of
popular attitudes to politics, their leaders and the enemy. Popular songs
and ballads offer one window on this suggestion of a national unity in the
face of French invasion, although it is a complex one. There are many
songs, but we need care in how we read them, because many were the
products of members of a social and political élite concerned to generate,
reinforce and express a sense of unity in their audiences and to achieve
dominance over potentially contending voices.

I emphasise 'printed' material but this was not the only vehicle for the
transmission of popular song. The literature in general draws a distinction
between popular ballads, sustained and transmitted through the oral
tradition; popular broadsides, which were published, usually singly or in
pairs in a strip sheet; popular songs that originated in music hall performances and then might also be sold in broadside form, or were collected
together in cheap collections of songs; and more élite forms of song that
were performed in public by recognised singers of the day and published
with music and orchestration for several instruments. Moreover, these
categories were not hard and fast, perhaps especially in this period. In part

---

[6] See the chapter on the spending of George Rose in Werkmeister, *The London Daily Press*,
1962), 317–80.

[7] See the discussions in Colley, *Britons: Forging the Nation*; Cookson, *The British Armed
Nation*; Gee, *The British Volunteer Movement*; Rogers, 'The sea fencibles, loyalism and the
reach of the state'; Newman, '"An insurrection of loyalty"'; and Navickas, 'The defence of
Manchester and Liverpool'.

because of the intensity of loyalist pressures, and partly associated with an interest among the middle and upper classes with more popular traditions of song, material moved across such boundaries, with music hall songs being transmitted into oral culture and being collected a century or more later in the oral tradition, and popular songs being appropriated (both music and words) by composers at the end of the eighteenth and beginning of the nineteenth century who drew on 'folk' elements for their compositions – a transmission repeated at the end of the nineteenth century with Vaughan Williams' appropriation of folk songs and ballads to form the basis for some of his own work.

This background is important for appreciating some of the aspects of the songs that emerged about Nelson. A considerable number were written expressly for loyalist purposes, to celebrate his victories, but also to demonstrate and to rouse others to show their attachment to their country and their hostility to Britain's enemy, the French (and, after 1803, to Napoleon in particular). This is not true of all the songs, but the dramatically heightened ideological stakes of the period without doubt influenced what was written, what was circulated and what survived the immediate crisis.

II

The survival of popular songs relies heavily on printed material – in the form of strip sheets of ballads sold in the street by peddlers (who would advertise their wares by singing them), cheap garlands of collected songs that also sold to a popular but slightly wealthier audience, songs that appeared in journals, newspapers and periodicals of various kinds, and songs published with music for performance in public and at home. We also have sources drawing on the oral tradition from the beginning of the nineteenth century, however, so it is also possible to identify ballads and sometimes to date them to a particular period. As to who wrote the songs, here the information varies considerably. At one end we know of local ballad writers, such as John Freeth in Birmingham, Robert Burns in Scotland and Robert Anderson in Carlisle, and we have publications and manuscript material from them that allows us to identify their loyalties and to date some of their material.[8] But none of them offer a great deal in relation to Nelson in particular. For example, Freeth, a publican with reformist leanings, wrote songs to existing tunes to entertain his customers and periodically published collections of his material; despite

---

[8] See Mark Philp, Roz Southey, Caroline Jackson-Houlston and Susan Wollenberg, 'Music and politics, 1793–1815', in Philp, *Resisting Napoleon*, 173–204.

his generally reformist outlook he wrote several songs celebrating British victories.[9] Clearly, sympathy for reform did not entail antagonism to the Royal Navy or a lack of concern with the country's military defence.

At the other end of the scale, we know the composers and the lyricists for a number of songs written for Covent Garden, the Theatre Royal and other large-scale, public occasions, and we know in detail the musical entertainment output of Charles and Thomas Dibdin, the former a prolific writer and performer of songs and entertainments in which the sturdy British 'tar' in particular was celebrated, the latter his son, who also turned to composition and wrote several pieces on Nelson.[10] Otherwise, though, a great deal remains anonymous, ranging from traditional street and naval ballads, which were a major conduit for reporting battles and British victories, to a considerable bulk of material clearly written by educated members of the public and designed for performance in loyalist and volunteer organisations and at local events. This last group is significantly more insistent in ideological tone and message, lauding Britannia, her king and constitution, and celebrating stout British tars in general while generally lacking much of the specificity that many of the more apparently popular ballads exhibit.

We need now to indicate the scale of this material. Quantification is difficult, because apparently different songs sometimes turn out on closer inspection to share the same core, because it is impossible to cover every possible source of material (and I make no claims to having done so), and because of the diverse locations in which such material is to be found. But, accepting these caveats, I have thus far identified around ninety songs from the period that feature Nelson in some way. I am certain more exist, but this is already a very substantial group, dwarfing, for example, those in praise of Admiral Richard Howe or other contemporaries of Nelson. The only major contender getting equivalent (and possibly more) attention is Napoleon, but the great bulk of that is critical, at least until the end of the war! In marked contrast to that material, I have been unable to identify anything that would count as a critical or hostile song (even in relation to his less successful endeavours) in all the Nelson material. I have also failed to find a single scurrilous ballad about him – an even greater source of surprise, since he was not exactly spared on this front by James Gillray and other caricaturists.[11]

---

[9] See John Horden, *John Freeth (1731–1808): Political Ballad-Writer and Innkeeper* (Oxford: Leopard's Head Press, 1993), 166–7, 197–8 (the earlier song in praise of Admiral Rodney in 1783 has been adapted largely wholesale to celebrate Nelson).

[10] See *Songs of the Late Charles Dibdin, with a Memoir*, ed. George Cruikshank, 3rd edn (London: Henry G. Bohn, 1852).

[11] See especially Gillray's *A Cognocenti Contemplating ye Beauties of ye Antique* (1801) and *Dido, in Despair* (1801). There is a later song, based on a very famous Napoleon ballad but

The scale of the outpouring of songs on Nelson is certainly linked to the demand for popular songs as a means to interpret, commemorate and, in a sense, complete the events of the day in a period of major national anxiety and crisis. The absence of any later revisionism or emerging counter-interpretation reflects the extent to which the material and messages penetrated deep into the public culture, fixing certain elements of a national historical memory and folklore. His victories, at the Nile, Copenhagen and Trafalgar, restored British confidence in a navy (and its leadership) that had been racked by the Spithead and Nore mutinies of 1797. For the political élite, and for ordinary members of the public who feared the collapse of British naval resistance to France, Nelson's successes (following Admiral Adam Duncan's at the battle of Camperdown) struck a major chord, and it is not difficult to read considerable relief in the accompanying lyrics. When the political climate again became more con-tested after 1805, with the emergence of new political opposition, events had moved on, and Trafalgar and its hero were securely past – and in many respects remained a monument to military heroism with which the rest of the war found it hard to compete (John Moore's death in the Peninsular Campaign of 1809 might have contended for heroic status, but the controversies over the war, namely the corruption in its equipping and the incompetence in its leadership, meant that there was – in contrast to Nelson – little sense of unanimity in his commemoration).[12] A further indication of Nelson's standing is that some of the songs continued to be printed and sold until the late nineteenth century. There was clearly a

reworked for Nelson as *The Grand Conversation on Nelson arose*, that probably first appeared in the 1820s and that does have some lines about the end of the war bringing poverty and hardship, but it is essentially uncritical of Nelson. So is the one song that is preserved about the attack on Boulogne, a fragment of which was collected in the oral tradition by Patrick Shuldham-Shaw and Emily B. Lyle, eds., *The Greig and Duncan Folksong Collection*, vol. I (University of Aberdeen Press, 1981), 353. While my comments are restricted largely to material published between 1789 and 1815, the lack of criticism held true throughout the nineteenth century. There were occasional later songs, some printed around the centenary of Trafalgar, that are not markedly different from the earlier songs; see, for example 'For England love and beauty' *The Hero of Trafalgar*, composed expressly for the centenary by Sarah Swain, 'Poetess laureate of the West Indies'. In the late 1880s John Parnell also published a long ballad to Nelson, '"Tis of a little Norfolk boy' *The Battle of Trafalgar*, which adds little – save length – to the loyalist hymning of Nelson eighty years earlier. There is also, for those interested, a not so clean twentieth-century ballad (*A Ballad of Good Lord Nelson*) written by Lawrence Durrell, which begins: 'The Good Lord Nelson had a swollen gland; Little of the scripture did he understand; Till a woman led him to the promised land; Aboard the *Victory* O, *Victory* O.'

12 Indeed, Nelson is used as an example to follow in the campaign in '"Twas on a Thursday morning that from Cadiz we set sail' *Barrosa Plains*: 'Look back to Cape Trafalgar, boys, where Nelson bled before: the blood that conquered on the sea shall conquer on the shore' (referring to the Battle of Barrosa, 4 March 1811). See Moylan, *The Age of Revolution*, song no. 177.

market for material in his own lifetime, although some was clearly 'supply-led', with loyalist organisations paying for the cheap or free publication and circulation of songs; there is no doubt that the songs also responded to popular demand, however, and that his reputation remained marketable for a number of years.

III

Of the ninety or so songs, there were a number of productions clearly designed for élite circles, such as the piece by William Shield and T. Goodwin of the Theatre Royal in Covent Garden, 'When the *Victory* weigh'd anchor' (printed) *Lord Nelson's* Victory. Two similar contributions from John Braham were 'In death's dark house the hero lies' (printed) *The Victory and Death of Lord Viscount Nelson* and 'Cease vain France, ill-manner'd railer' (The storm) *The Death of Nelson*; Upton and Schroeder contributed 'Genius of Britain, why that down cast eye' (printed) *The Hero of the Sea, or Nelson Immortal*; and Charles Frederick Horne produced 'A navy, colonies and trade, the tyrant cried' (printed) *Trafalgar: An Heroic Song*. These songs were, for the most part, too intricate and verbally convoluted to move easily into the street ballad or oral tradition. The one exception was Braham and Samuel James Arnold's *Death of Nelson* ('O'er Nelson's tomb,/With silent grief oppress'd,/Britannia mourns her hero,/Now at rest:/But those bright laurels/Ne'er shall fade with years;/Whose leaves, whose leaves are watered/By a nation's tears'), which was reprinted on ballad sheets throughout the nineteenth century. Although I have quoted the recitative, the actual verses are con-siderably more robust, and singable, beginning: ''Twas in Trafalgar's bay/We saw the Frenchmen lay/Each heart was bounding then;/We scorned the foreign yoke/Our ships were British oak,/Hearts of oak were our men', and in some cases the song was reprinted without the recitative. There were also several songs by Charles Dibdin, including 'I say my heart' *Nelson and the Navy*, 'Be the great twenty-first of October recorded' *The Death of Nelson*, and 'Ah, hark the signals round the coast', *The Arrival of Nelson's Corpse*. Dibdin was an energetic composer and performer who took his one-man shows of songs around the country to considerable public acclaim, and whose work consistently appropriated, and subsequently re-emerged in, popular song. His son, Thomas, though less renowned, also added to the Nelson canon.

Not all the more élite songs were concerned with Nelson's death, though this certainly was a major focus. There were also earlier pieces: Charles Dibdin celebrated a succession of naval heroes in 1799 with 'Why I'm singing' *Naval Victories*; William Shield produced a piece on

Copenhagen, 'For glory, when with fav'ring gale' *The Danish Expedition*; Dussek wrote an instrumental celebrating Copenhagen; Haydn composed his *Battle of the Nile*; and a celebration of the Nile, 'Never yet in ancient story did more gallant deeds appear' (printed) *Welcome Nelson Home Again*, was 'set to music by a lady of fashion'.[13] And, of course, there were similar pieces celebrating victories by Howe (1794), Duncan (Camperdown, 1797) and others. The Nelson songs, though considerable in number, were probably outweighed numerically (albeit not by much) by a host of generic anti-Napoleonic songs, and songs in praise of volunteering and of bold British tars, both of which were largely for the more élite audiences. Indeed, one feature of many of the loyalist songs of the period was their more general character; they did not focus on detail or narrative, they sketched broad positions of support for king and constitution and they attacked their enemies. There was also a good deal of repetition, with songs being adapted by a phrase here or a word there to suit one volunteer regiment rather than another.

An indication of the transmission between the popular ballad and the music hall is Charles Dibdin's work. A number of his songs, such as *A Salt Eel for Mynheer* (on Duncan and Camperdown – but appearing also as *A Salt Eel for Monsieur*, celebrating the Nile) and *Nelson and the Navy*, were published as street ballads until well after the end of the war, as well as in collections of popular songs – something that is evident in relatively few other cases. This is partly because they are lively songs, written in clear and idiomatic English, which themselves drew on popular material and tunes. Dibdin's son Thomas also followed suit, with a song written for the music hall with a theatrical setting and sung by Mr Fawcett with 'unbounded applause in the interlude of the musical entertainment, *Nelson's Glory*, at the Theatre Royal, Covent Garden': 'Of our Island we've sung til the welkin has rung' *The Great Nation*, a song that, essentially, compared the aspirations to be a great nation on the part of France with the British: 'John Bull like a fool, says he wont go to school/From home, for a French education...'. (A more fanciful song, not by one of the Dibdins but betraying a similarly musical entertainment origin, is 'The watry god, great Neptune lay' *The Watry God* (written by Wagnell), which has Neptune expostulating over the number of naval heroes that Britain has – so many that the ruler of an island producing such men must himself be a god!) Many of Charles Dibdin's songs, some of Thomas Dibdin's and

---

[13] There are a considerable number of musical pieces named after Nelson and/or various battles, such as Joseph Dale's sonata for pianoforte *Nelson and the Navy*, published in 1798, and a host of dance and folk tunes that incorporate 'Nelson' in their title (such as the *Nelson Hornpipe*), though they may well be earlier tunes that have been renamed.

several of those of others formed parts of whole programmes of musical entertainment. This may also have been the case with a song by Mr J. Stawpert of Newcastle, linked to the Theatre Royal, about *John Diggins*, in which Diggins is bullied by his father into coming to town (to 'Buy myself a blue jacket, and put off the clown, and fight for my country and king'), where he hears a poor beggar boy singing

> He sung how that Nelson had lately been shot
> O – I verily thought I'd have died on the spot,
> For father told I that lead, e'en boiling hot,
> Wou'd ne'er take the life of this man.
>
> At length the boy prov'd e'er he ended his song,
> That nature and valor however so strong
> Must still bow to fate, so poor father was wrong,
> And Nelson's gone, – dead – after all.

with the conclusion that he vows to write to Admiral Cuthbert Collingwood, straight for a place, 'So I may chance to revenge Nelson's wrongs'.

Charles Dibdin also contributed 'Now listen my honies a while if you please' *The First of Sweet August* (also published in broadside) and his son Thomas wrote a whole musical entertainment called *The Mouth of the Nile or the Glorious 1st of August*, loosely arranged around the Nile (although the final section is pretty much the only explicit reference), including two untitled songs that feature Nelson in one way or another: 'When the world first began' and 'In the midst of the sea, like a tough man of war'. Charles Dibdin's 'I say, my heart, why, here's the works' *Nelson and the Navy* also commemorates the victory, and gives most prominence to Nelson, whereas 'Our anchors weighed to sea we stood' *Warren Triumphant* gives greater prominence to Commodore Warren (for the dispersal of the French invasion fleet near Ireland), and Nelson gets only a minor mention.

There are a number of songs that refer to Nelson only in passing, for example, alongside a range of other naval and/or military leaders: 'Come now heroes of this war' *Heroes of This War* hymns Howe, Viscount John Jervis, Duncan, Mitchell and Abercrombie: 'Says gallant Nelson at the Nile,/Egad I'll have the day –/And so he had a glorious spoil –/But two could run away'.[14] 'What matter your ditties, your jokes and narrations' *The Tars who've Lathered the World* also links Nelson and Duncan as finishing off a job started by Howe and Jervis. Similarly, *Dumplings for*

---

[14] See also the later song 'The trumpet sounds, the valiant troops are form'd' *England's Queen and England's Glory*, probably written in the late 1840s, in which Nelson and the battle of the Nile are cited as an exemplar of English heroism.

Bonaparte has a chorus that praises the admirals in succession. Nelson's 'turn' is as follows:

> But let us sing of the great Buonaparte,
> Of that wonderful hero I'll something impart,
> They say that bold Nelson has stopt him awhile,
> And has dish'd his great fleet at the mouth of the Nile,
> *Huzza for brave Nelson, for brave Nelson huzza, and*
> *Like them lets be ready and steady, boys, steady.*
> On the first of August, let us never forget,
> 'Twas that proud day they engag'd at sunset,
> And of their supper Nelson gave them enough,
> But the dumpling from Norfolk they found rather tough,
> *Huzza for brave Nelson, etc.*

Charles Dibdin's *Naval Victories* does much the same, ending:

> But as if British tars, to their country so hearty,
> Was determined still honour on honour to pile,
> Ninety-eight, first of August, did up Bonaparte,
> By the wonders that Nelson performed at the Nile.
> But Lord how I talk, ain't the nation bestowing
> A pillar to tell about tars and their lives?
> And 'tis gloriously done, for to them 'tis all owing,
> That we've laws and religion, and children and wives.[15]

A slightly different form of inclusion is exemplified in the adaptation of more traditional songs and themes to link them with Nelson. For example, *A New Song Called the Victory* is, for all its title, essentially a simple ballad story: 'I am a youthful lady, my troubles they are great'. Her lover, of whom she dreams each night, is too poor to satisfy her parents; he is then press-ganged into the navy and comes to serve on the *Victory*, and – in the final verse – we get the first mention of Nelson, along with the denouement:

> Here's a health unto the *Victory* and crew of noble fame,
> And glory to the noble lord, bold Nelson was his name,
> In the battle of Trafalgar the *Victory* cleared the way,
> And my love was slain with Nelson upon that very day.

Another version was collected that does not get beyond the verses on the press gang, suggesting that this is an earlier ballad adapted for the occasion. Nonetheless, it clearly becomes a part of the oral tradition, being collected in the 1840s, and it is still around in 1951 in Nova

---

[15] See also Freeth's 'As Englishmen finding our rights are at stake' (Hearts of Oak) *The Sailor's Rouse*, which declares that Nelson is now on his way.

Scotia.[16] 'As early one morning in the groves I was walking' *The Damsel in Tears* is a similarly traditional song about the loss of a lover alongside Nelson at Trafalgar. A more maudlin connection between the two is established in the sentimental 'Stay lady stay for mercy's sake' *The Orphan Boy*, in which a boy sings to a stranger of his father's death at Trafalgar, followed quickly by his mother's of a broken heart, but even this is more persuasive than the pastiche in 'It was early one morning' *The Widow's Lamentation*, in which the narrator comes across a widow and child and offers her (rather unconvincing) comfort that her husband died with Nelson. There are also songs in which the narrative is more directly about a sailor (unmediated by the lover) who dies alongside Nelson, such as 'Tom Splice was a tar in whose bosom was blended' *Nelson and Victory*.

There are also a range of other songs, such as 'Oh my comrades...' *The Sailor's New Leg*, that have a much more tenuous connection with Nelson. This is a quasi-comic song (of a type much exploited by Charles Dibdin)[17] about a sailor having his leg blown off by a cannonball during Trafalgar (although in reality it could have been set anywhere), its opportunism evident in the lack of any mention of Nelson's death. A still more extreme version of a traditional song that has been fitted to the occasion is *Crippled Jack of Trafalgar*, in which neither Nelson nor Trafalgar is mentioned in the body of the song, but which is clearly designed for the ballad peddler to sell his wares as highly topical.

Perhaps the largest single category of songs relating to Nelson (often with a popular pedigree, and lasting well into the nineteenth century) is the battle narrative ballads, essentially similar to those celebrating Howe's 1 June 1794 victory, or Duncan's victory over the Dutch at Camperdown in October 1797 or many other naval battles throughout the centuries.[18] In Nelson's case the boundaries of the category were somewhat blurred, since, while there are several songs commemorating each battle, there are also a number of others that smack of élite attempts to pastiche more traditional songs but that generally lack the detail and incident that mark the more narrative ballad.

---

[16] See Roy Palmer, *Boxing the Compass: A Guide to Traditional Shanties and Working Songs of the Sea*, rev. edn (Todmorden: Herron Publishing, 2001), 184–5.

[17] See, for example, 'My name, d'ye see,'s Tom Tough *Yo Heave Ho*, which ends with the narrator having lost an eye and a toe, and singing old songs.

[18] See, for example, *A New Song on the Sea Engagement 1st June 1794*; *A Copy of Verses on the Glorious Victory Obtained by Lord Howe, over the Enemy, in a Long Engagement*; *Howe Victorious; or, The French Defeated*; *Duncan and Victory*; and so on.

IV

The first group of songs to feature Nelson consists of those celebrating his victory at Aboukir Bay, or the battle of the Nile. The core of these songs (of which there are some thirteen) are traditional battle narratives that give a basic account of the events of the battle with a degree of objectivity in the commentary.

'Come all you valiant heroes and listen unto me' *Defeat of the French Fleet* (alternative title: *A New Song of the Total Defeat of the French Fleet*) details the chase across the Mediterranean and the onset of the battle.[19] It is not sanitised, as many songs are, but refers to the many who were slain – 'While the blood it poured from the decks and stained the watery main' – and it refers to Nelson and some hundred others being wounded. It also emphasises, as do most of the songs, the number of French ships captured or destroyed and the very few that escaped. 'Come all you British sailors bold, and listen to my song' *The Battle of the Nile*, of which Firth gives only an incomplete version, is one of the most detailed of the battle narratives relating to Nelson.[20] It gives an account of being unable to find the French fleet until they caught up with the *Reguli*, which gives news from Malta and sends them on to Alexandria. When they catch the fleet the ships are named in order, and the battle described, with the destruction of the *L'Orient* as a centrepiece:

> Now the glory and the pride of France the *L'Orient* was called,
> And in the centre of their line she got severely mauled;
> Gave her a dreadful drubbing, boys, took fire and up she blew,
> With fourteen hundred souls on board which bid this world adieu.

'Now ye sons of Britannia, attend to my strains' *Capture of the French Fleet* provides a basic narrative, saying 'Some hundreds were wounded and many were slain,/Still Britons are masters and lords of the main', but it ends with a direct bid for charity: 'May a blessing attend those that give some relief,/To the widows and children that now are in grief,/For the loss of their husbands are now in distress,/And left with their children to moan fatherless'. This is certainly not unusual and is probably linked to the use of the songs as a way of raising money through street performance. In the case of ''Twas on the ninth day of August, in the year ninety eight' *The Battle of the Nile* the battle narration is provided (implicitly) from the

---

[19] In broadside ballad, but also in Palmer, *Boxing the Compass*.
[20] See Charles Harding Firth, *Naval Songs and Ballads* (Ithaca, NY: Cornell University Press, 1908), 288–9.

perspective of the *Majestic*, whose captain, Westcott, was killed early in the action and replaced by Mr Cuthbert:[21]

> Full fifty seamen we had slain, which grieved our hearts full sore;
> Two hundred more were wounded, lay bleeding in their gore.
> But early the next morning most glorious for us to see
> Our British ships of war, brave boys, were crowned in victory.

The dating to the 9th might suggest a degree of authenticity, as does the still later dating in ''Twas on the twenty-second we fought in Aboukir Bay' *The Battle of Aboukir Bay*, in *The Greig and Duncan Folksong Collection*, which centres around 'little Jim', a powder monkey who sings the chorus 'Soon we'll be in London town, sing my lads yo ho!', only to be picked off by a musket bullet in the last verse, leaving not a dry eye on board.[22]

In 'It was in the forenoon of the first day of August' *Mouth of the Nile*, the explosion of *L'Orient* is celebrated but the narrative is muddled. There is a detail, however, that is absent from other songs:

> As the night came on, we formed a plan
> To set fire to one hundred and twenty guns;
> We selected with skill, and unto them did thrill,
> We secur'd our shipping, and laugh'd at the scene.

Freeth's song 'From the mouth of the Nile, flush'd with glory behold' (All shall yield to the mulberry tree) *On Admiral Nelson's* Victory, *Britannia Triumphant* is a reworking of an old song written to celebrate the naval victory of Admiral Edward Russell and adds little in terms of detail. Much the same can be said for 'Never yet in Ancient story did more gallant deeds appear' *Welcome Nelson Home Again*, which is a more élite song; it is brief, lacking in battle details and concludes with the verse 'Eager crowds around him pressing', welcoming back the hero of the Nile. In a similar vein, 'Fame let thy trumpet sound' *The Voice of Fame* mentions the battle off Egypt's coast and Vice Admiral François Brueys, the French commander, being sent to the shades, but it is a typical loyalist song, sung to *God Save the King*.

'Arise, arise! Britannia's sons arise!' *The Battle of the Nile* is, in many respects, a typical loyalist effusion – overconvoluted in style, and lacking detail, objectivity and distance: 'For the genius of Albion, victory proclaiming/Flies throughout the world, our rights and deeds maintaining

---

[21] See W. Roy Mackenzie, *Ballads and Sea Songs from Nova Scotia* (Cambridge, MA: Harvard University Press, 1928), 203–4.

[22] This offers a contrast to Felicia Heman's 1829 poem 'The boy stood on the burning deck', dealing with a boy from *L'Orient*!

[...] Mars guards for us what freedom did by character gain'. Surprisingly, it is also available as a street ballad, and while, in some versions, the chorus is sometimes simplified, the ballad is basically unchanged. Nevertheless, it cannot be described as a narrative song, and its aim seems wholly laudatory. Its tune was reused on a number of occasions, however (in one case in the Peninsular War, when the brave sons of Spain are enjoined: 'Drive hence, the Tyrant's minions back to France'), and there is no doubt that it entered into popular and folk memory, although it is interesting that on more than one occasion it was paired on broadsheets with 'Ye gods above protect the Widow' *Death of Parker*, the major ballad on the execution of Richard Parker, the leader of the mutineers at the Nore in 1797.

'Arise, muse, arise, assist me to sing' *Britannia's Triumph; or, Nelson Honoured* is similar but does have slightly more detail ('At the setting of the sun, the battle it begun./Broadside for broadside for fourteen hours long;/We sent them cruising in the air,/Which made the Frenchmen all to stare,/They struck their flags their fate to share,/With bold Nelson'), but it does not expressly mention the Nile and it is, most likely, a loyalist song, written directly afterwards to celebrate the victory. The same applies to 'With strains melodious make the heavens ring' *The Conqueror: On the Glorious Victory Obtained by Lord Nelson*, whose verses remain as convoluted as the opening lines – 'With strains melodious make the heavens ring/Ode – sovereign lyre – this noble action sing' – and in which the location is mentioned entirely en passant: 'Majestic Nile beheld the bloody fight/And rear'd his sovereign head to view the knight'. It is not a great success as a song!

Charles Dibdin's 'I say me heart why here's your works' *Nelson and the Navy* (also known as *Nelson and Warren*) is a piece directed to celebrate the English successes in Egypt more generally: 'Between the English and the Turks they'll lose both their army and their Navy'. His 'Now listen my honies a while if you please' *The First of Sweet August* is another typically eulogising song, celebrating the British victory but lacking any detail of the battle. These are classic Dibdin territory: cheery and lively songs, short on detail and the realities of the encounter, but plugged into the need to reflect national pride in the achievements: 'Nelson went out with determined view to keep up our nation's glory;/So of thirteen large ships he left Mounseer two; Just to tell the Directory the story'. Finally, the ubiquitous sailor's girl, Nancy, features in a widely published ballad 'Near a clear chrystal stream, where sweet flowers do grow' *Nancy's Complaint for the Loss of Her Sailor, Who Was Killed by the French on the First of August*, in which she mourns for his loss. Although it shares many of the tropes of a traditional lament it does seem to have been written for the occasion, with Nelson being mentioned in three of the five verses.

The Nile ballads were, on the basis of internal evidence, written up quickly after the event. As we have seen, the dates given for the battle vary and the details of the battle remain local to each song, and, while most of the songs mix description with a certain amount of eulogising, this was not exceptional in comparison with other battles and other heroes. The several more élite songs tend to lack the detail and they also focus on Nelson far more (while the battle narratives often tell the story from the perspective of a particular ship), and they add considerably more reference to the defence of Britain and its liberties. Those that have been collected in the oral tradition tend to be those with more detail and 'locality'; those that we find published and reprinted in the nineteenth century tend to be Dibdin's and the more élite 'Arise, arise! Britannia's sons arise!' *The Battle of the Nile*. Being confident about the later publishing history of popular songs is extremely difficult, but few others seem to have been reprinted, probably because later events would have rendered these songs less relevant, both for immediate purposes, when new victories were being added, and for subsequent generations, for whom Trafalgar partially eclipsed the Nile.

V

'Of Nelson and the north, sing the day' *Copenhagen/Battle of the Baltic* is a twenty-seven-verse account of the battle, which mentions Nelson only in the opening line and focuses largely on the action and on the celebrations that will greet the news.[23] It has the hallmarks of a more élite song, possibly written by one of the officers, in the complexity of some of its phrasing, which is only marginally less present in the other version we have – 'Of Nelson and the North sing the glorious day's renown' *The Battle of the Baltic*. For example,

But the might of England flush'd	Three cheers of all the fleet,
To anticipate the scene	Sung Huzza!
And her van the fleeter rush'd	Then from centre, rear, and van
O'er the deadly space between.	Every captain, every man,
	With a lion's heart began
'Hearts of oak,' our captains cried,	To the fray.
When each gun	
From its adamantine lips	Oh, dark grew soon the heavens –
Spread a death-shade round the	For each gun

---

[23] See Firth, *Naval Songs and Ballads*, 290–5. The alternative version is from a broadside ballad dated 27 January 1855 in the Bodleian collection.

ships,

Like the hurricane eclipse
Of the sun.

From its adamantine lips
Spread a death-shade round the
   ships,
Like the hurricane eclipse
Of the sun.

'You undaunted sons of Britannia lend an ear' *Action off Copenhagen/The Siege of Copenhagen*, although briefer, manages more detail and is less complex; it also accords a greater role to Nelson, not so much in the battle as in the wrapping up (which was, of course, seen by many as an integral part to the battle and to the claiming of a victory).[24]

'The Russians, Swedes, and Danes combine' *Nelson's Thunder or the Danish Submission* treats Frederick, the Danish Crown prince, as ambitious for British territory and the capture of Hamburg but being seen off by Nelson's tactical skills, but there is little detail of the battle. 'Nelson the Great he is the man' *Nelson and Victory* provides a narrative but, like *Nelson's Thunder*, this really revolves around Nelson, who features in several verses for his courage in taking on the Danes, his joining in the attack and, finally, his clemency in rescuing drowning Danes: 'Nelson the Great he form's a plan/to snatch from death each hostile Dane;/The boat was mann'd without delay/To save each Danish seaman'. 'Draw near, ye gallant seamen, while I the truth unfold' *A New Song on Lord Nelson's Victory at Copenhagen* is similarly laudatory, but links Nelson with his tars in the final stanzas:

> Now drink a health to gallant Nelson the wonder of the world,
> Who, in defence of his country his thunder loud has hurl'd;
> And to his bold and valiant tars who plough the raging sea,
> And who never were afraid to face the daring enemy.

Finally, Shield's 'For glory, when with fav'ring gale' *The Danish Expedition* is a typically rousing élite song, lacking in detail and with resounding patriotic conclusions to each verse. It does, however, pay due respect to Admiral Parker as the commander of the fleet, acknowledging that it was Parker who sent Nelson to the Danes to negotiate, thereby conveying a sense of protocol and authority that is not entirely in keeping with the events of the battle!

The battle of Copenhagen was relatively under-sung, in comparison with the Nile. There are several good-quality battle narratives, however, although the line between these and the more loyalist effusions, which is relatively clear in the case of the Nile, is less easily drawn here. In this case,

---

[24] See Firth, *Naval Songs and Ballads*, 295, but there are also several copies in the Bodleian ballad collection.

the brief invasion scare in England in 1801 following the battle, the general war-weariness and perhaps the apparent distance of the Danish concerns from the more pressing demands of the French may have led to less attention being paid to the victory.

The only song I have been able to identify that tackles one of Nelson's less successful sallies concerns the attack on Boulogne in August 1801, 'On the second of August, eighteen hundred and one' *Second of August*, but this seems to be both well informed (except about the date, which was 4 August) and well disposed to the commander of the attack:

> On the second of August, eighteen hundred and one,
> As we sail'd with Lord Nelson to the port of Boulogne
> For to cut out their shipping, which was all in vain:
> But to our misfortune they were all moor'd and chain'd
> Our boats being well mann'd at eleven at night
> For to cut out their shipping, excepting they fight:
> But the grapes from their batteries so smartly did play
> Nine hundred brave seamen killed and wounded there lay.
> [. . .]
> Our noble commander with heart full of grief
> Used every effort to afford us relief,
> No ship could assist us, as well you might know;
> In this wounded condition we were toss'd to and fro
> And you who relieve us, the Lord will you bless
> For assisting poor seamen in the time of distress.
> May the Lord put an end to all cruel wars,
> And peace and contentment be to all British tars.

As Roy Palmer, who includes a full (marginally different) version of the song in his *Boxing the Compass*,[25] acknowledges, the song was partly an appeal for financial aid for seamen, which may account in part for its restrained tone towards Nelson's enthusiasm for the task and the failures of intelligence that wrecked the attack.

VI

There are at least eight traditional battle narratives of Trafalgar, although several of them also have different versions. 'Arise, arise brave Britons, perform your loudest lays' *Nelson's Glorious Victory at Trafalgar* is essentially the same as 'Come all you jolly sailor's bold, in chorus join with me' *A New Song Called Nelson's Victory*; 'The twenty-first day of October'

---

[25] A fragment of the same song is also recorded in Shuldham-Shaw and Lyle, *The Greig and Duncan Folksong Collection*. I have taken the verses from a broadside in the Bodleian ballad collection.

Brave Nelson (but with significant variation);[26] and 'We got ready for battle, to face the daring foe' *Nelson's Victory at Trafalgar*.[27] The versions all emphasise the smaller number of British ships, Nelson's death and the number of ships taken (although the numbers given vary between these songs).

'Come all you gallant heroes and listen unto me' *N[elson's] Glorious Victory* emphasises the chasing of the French fleet from 19 October, the formation of two columns of attack and the engagement, which lasted four hours and ten minutes, with Nelson being slain on the point of victory. 'Come all you gallant seamen that unite a meeting' *A New Song Composed on the Death of Lord Nelson* is a classic narrative that also includes reference to his past glories. It features a verse of the 'Then up steps the doctor' variety, but the focus is essentially on Nelson asking how the battle had gone, and on commemorating his memory.[28] 'It was daylight the next morning' (alternative first line: 'Great deeds of former heroes') *Nelson's Fame and England's Glory* focuses on the detail of the battle – the first engagement with a French eight-four gunner, manned by 900 French boys, the sinking of the *Trinidad* and the numbers taken (although these vary between the versions). Interestingly, neither version mentions Nelson's death.[29]

'You true sons of Britain, give ear to my ditty' *A New Song Called Lord Nelson* is a curious song, which interweaves a battle narrative in classical form with a whole range of biblical references:

> As we sailed from Moab to the plains of Jericho
> Where Joshua was praised and trumpets did sound,
> Seven times there we sounded, surprised their city
> Our foes we destroyed and their walls tumbled down.
> Seven broad sides that immortal Lord Nelson
> Pour'd in on those Frenchified traitors with might,
> They all struck their colours, were forced to surrender,
> Unto him as he was a true Israelite

In many other respects it is a straightforward battle narrative, with many similar details to others. 'Come list you lads where ere you be' (Arethusa) *Nelson's Victory and Death* is distinctive in mentioning 'While he was contending with his foes/Was oft implored to change his clothes/No, No, said he, I'll stand in those/As Admiral of my squadron./As they, his

---

[26] See John Ashton, *Modern Street Ballads* (London: Chatto & Windus, 1888), 298–9.
[27] MacKenzie, *Ballads and Sea Songs from Nova Scotia*, 203–4.
[28] There are several broadside editions, and the song also appears in Ashton, *Modern Street Ballads*, 300–1.
[29] See, in the oral tradition, Shuldham-Shaw and Lyle, *The Greig and Duncan Folksong Collection*, vol. I, 354; and, for the street ballad, see John Holloway and Joan Black, *Later English Broadside Ballads*, vol. II (London: Routledge & Kegan Paul, 1975), 174–5.

captains, he addressed/A ball smote him fatal on the breast'. 'I'll sing of famed Trafalgar if you'll listen to me' *Trafalgar* misses that detail but includes 'We marked the man that did the deed, that aimed the fatal ball/And picked him from the rigging, riddled through with English lead'. 'Ye sons of Britain in chorus join and sing' *Nelson's Death and Victory* is essentially a narrative ballad, but ends with the hope that the battle will bring peace and a restoration of trade![30]

In addition to these eight and their variations, there are a number of others that appear to have been written directly for loyalist purposes. The contrast is tentative and the lines somewhat blurred but, unlike the former group of battle narratives, these songs seem not to be trying to convey anything distinctive about Nelson or about the experiences of the battle. They also lack objectivity and distance, tending to insist on a moral and an assertion of patriotism. For example, there are several songs in which the narrative is essentially swamped or excluded by the glorification: 'Britons! You heard Trafalgar's story' *Nelson and Collingwood* is one such instance – and the opening – 'Britons! You heard Trafalgar's story,/You triumph in your country's glory;/Mourn o'er the relics, pale and gory;/Of brave immortal Nelson' – has some of the better lines! But, while such songs seem clearly linked to loyalist propaganda, there are several others that combine narrative and effusion more subtly: 'Britannia musing o'er the deeds' *Britannia's Revenge for the Death of Her Hero*, although it has elements of narrative, is essentially a call to avenge Nelson's death, as is 'When Neptune first at love's command' *When Neptune &c.* 'Ye sons of old Albion for valor renown'd' *The Departed Hero* gives a potted summary of Nelson's various victories, combined with an effusive commemoration, as does 'Since the birth day of Britain a period long fled' *Chapter of Victories*.

'When Nelson saw off Trafalgar' (Rule Britannia) *England Expects Each Man Will Do His Duty* is certainly effusive – 'Weep, sons of Britain the godlike Nelson's dead/With victory crowned, he nobly bled' – but it lacks any real detail. 'When Nelson first at Britain's call' *Britannia Mourn the Hero Slain* has essentially similar problems, whereas 'From the direful scene returning, where grim carnage stalk'd around' *The Fight off Trafalgar* provides an odd combination of an overconvoluted beginning followed by increasing narrative style, with first-person narrator. Similarly, *Death and Victory* starts in typically loyalist style: 'When the navy of Gaul, our inveterate foe, called the valour of England their rage to

---

[30] See Palmer, *Boxing the Compass*, 182–3.

oppose/Brave Nelson who never in battle would yield/For Britain and George nobly enter'd the field/To be true to the true land of freedom he swore;/As the blue that adorn'd the proud standard he bore'. But this is followed by a verse on his death in battle, and the final verse has a sentimental, but not unballad-like, twist, with the flagstaff being planted beside his grave – 'Where as gratitude's tear wou'd the spot oft bedew/ Thus moisten'd – at length to a laurel it grew'.

The songs that focus directly on mourning Nelson's death, rather than seeing it as integral to the action in Trafalgar, are almost entirely of the more élite form. That there should be so few popular songs expressly on his death and commemoration of his deeds is not, I think, surprising, since the natural context for popular songs would be the narrative of Trafalgar, rather than a more abstract concern with a contribution to his country. Charles Dibdin provided two such songs: 'Come messmates rejoice' and 'Ah Hark, the signals round the coast'. There are also two that were sung by Charles Incledon, the renowned Covent Garden tenor: 'Cease vain France' (The storm) *The Death of Nelson* and 'Fate uncontroll'd by human prayer' *Nelson's Tomb*. The equally well known Braham song 'In death's dark house' (printed) *The Victory and Death of Lord Viscount Nelson* was 'received with unbounded applause at the Theatre Royal, Drury Lane, in the melodramatic piece commemorative of that remarkable event' (written by R. Cumberland). Two similar pieces are 'In the temple of fame, where the ghosts of the brave, ascend from the mouldering tombs' (printed) *Britannia's Hero; or, Nelson Eclipsing the Heroes of Yore* and 'Let Britons Nelson's valour sing' (Arethusa) *A Small Tribute to the Memory of the Late Gallant Lord Nelson* (written by J. Pratt and containing the thought that, as Nelson was dying, Victory caught him in her arms, and, to the sounds of success in battle, he soared to heaven).

Perhaps the most striking group of songs consists of those that effectively enjoin us to move on, thereby both celebrating Nelson as a hero and preparing us to recognise others who will do the same for their country. There is some indication of a wish to draw a line under the war during the peace after the Treaty of Amiens in 1802, when the *The Newcastle Bellman* was written; the first verse begins 'Talk no more of brave Nelson, or gallant Sir Sydney,/'Tis granted they're tars of a true British kidney/And people are curious, such heroes to see/But neither are half so much follow'd as me [the town cryer]'. But in the case of the post-Trafalgar songs the motive was not war-weariness so much as a need for closure to the mourning of Nelson, and for reassurance that his loss would not expose the country to the French: a good example is *Admiral Strachan's Victory* (chorus: *Hearts of Oak*), whose first two lines are 'Though with tears we lament our great Nelson's demise, Let the nation rejoice that more Nelsons arise'.[31] And, 'In a battle you know we Britons are strong' (Chapter of kings) *Trafalgar's Battle*, the sole purpose of the song seems to be to introduce and underline the importance of Collingwood. Indeed, many of the Trafalgar songs were keen to reference other naval leaders: see the last verse of 'Arise, Arise, Brave Britons' *Nelson's Glorious Victory at Trafalgar*, which hymns Collingwood and Vice Admiral Thomas Masterman Hardy; and 'Britons, you've heard Trafalgar's story' *Nelson and Collingwood*, which ends with the lines 'Mourn for Nelson in his grave;/Rejoice and cheer the living brave/With modest, gallant Collingwood'. 'Come all you gallant seamen' *A New Song Composed on the Death* ... similarly concludes 'Here's God bless all seamen that speak for his good/May the heavens go with you, and ten thousand blessings/Still rest on the fleet and brave Collingwood'.[32] While 'Old England's long expected heavy news from our fleet...' *Nelson's Death* does not go so far, Collingwood is also central,[33] and, in 'We got ready for battle' *Nelson's Victory at Trafalgar*, Hardy and Collingwood again feature in the final verse.[34] In contrast, 'Where now my dear Boney is your grand combined fleet' *Lord Nelson's Victory* brings on Admiral Sir Richard Strachan to sweep up the remainder of Napoleon's fleet. (See also Dibdin's manuscript 'When Nelson fell, the voice of fame' *When Nelson Fell*). Although there are variations here, it is clear that many of these songs were about shoring up national confidence in the wake of Nelson's death and providing a positive form of closure.

More unusual is 'Britons all attend, while I sing of your friend' *Gallant Lord Nelson*, to the tune of *God Save the King*, which is, essentially, a song about Nelson's funeral, the last three verses basically detailing the attendance of captains, lieutenants, admirals and sailors:

> Lords, Dukes and Judges there
> So grand the sight
> Did appear,
> And great was the throng,
> Princes, Earls and Squires too,
> Lord-Mayor and Sheriffs also,
> The body followed its true
> Of Admiral Nelson.

---

[31] Firth, *Naval Songs and Ballads*, 304.
[32] See ibid., 302–4; and Ashton, *Modern Street Ballads*, 302–4.
[33] See Roy Palmer, *A Ballad History of England* (London: Batsford, 1979), 88–9. There are also broadside ballads of this song, some beginning 'Britain's long expected great news'.
[34] Mackenzie, *Ballads and Sea Songs from Nova Scotia*, 203–4.

The picture is of a unified nation paying homage to Nelson. If it was unusual to have a penny ballad written for your funeral, it was doubly so to be able to match this with two whose occasion was the creation of the national memorial to your last battle. 'Old England/Britain's long expected...' *Nelson's Death/Nelson's Monument* announces the intention to build a monument to his victories – 'A monument for Nelson, and a sword for Collingwood' – while 'As some heroes bold, I will unfold' *Grand Conversation on Nelson Arose* in part celebrates the building of Trafalgar Square and Nelson's column in the 1840s. This later ballad has features that distinguish it from almost all the other material on Nelson, however, even if it is not a particularly successful song. Nelson is depicted as committed to liberty, yet in the following verse Nelson, Hardy and Collingwood are credited with causing 'some thousands to be slain, while fighting on the raging main', and this is followed by a middle verse that has considerably more objectivity and ambiguity in it than most of the other songs connected to Nelson:

> Many a gallant youth, I'll tell the truth, in action have been wounded,
> Some left their friends and lovers in despair upon their native shore,
> Others never returned again, but died upon the raging main,
> Causing many a mother to cry, my son, and widows to deplore.
> When war was raging, it is said, men for their labour were well paid,
> Commerce and trade were flourishing, but now it ebbs and flows
> And poverty it does increase, tho' Britons say they live in peace,
> This grand conversation on Nelson arose.

It is not difficult to find fault with the song as a song, but it is markedly different from the songs of 1797 to 1806 – indeed, different from anything else about Nelson in the nineteenth century: it is complex, ambiguous, open to interpretation and partly critical, and it comments on contemporary affairs and, at least by implication, government. In fact, those qualities were pretty standard fare for many street songs and penny ballads in the eighteenth and nineteenth centuries, but they are qualities that were effectively silenced in relation to Nelson by a combination of repression, prosecution and propagandising, especially when the government was fiercely embattled by internal dissent and threats of invasion from 1796 to 1799 and when it was most threatened by Napoleon between 1803 and 1805. It is not that songs about Nelson were singled out for such censorship, but Nelson's ascendancy coincided with the key period of loyalist dominance and government resistance to radicalism, and, by the time the political context again became more contested and pluralist, Nelson's exploits were a matter of past record and new issues existed to task the ballad writers.

VII

Songs were also performances, and most of these songs were written for public performance, and in some cases for public participation. For loyalists, the performance was part of the process of bringing together and uniting in sentiment an audience. Earlier in the 1790s there were instances of rival clubs meeting in the same taverns and singing songs that borrowed each other's tunes but put them to new purposes, so that many performances were multi-layered processes of ideological contestation and confrontation. For loyalists, those early lessons had certainly been learnt by 1803–5: both the value of the medium for arousing public participation and commitment, and the importance of silencing the opposition. To encourage participation many loyalist songs were written to existing tunes, with existing choruses, thereby facilitating identification with the cause espoused (using especially *God Save the King, Rule Britannia* and *Hearts of Oak*). That so many of these songs (especially those relying on established tunes) proved ephemeral would not have been thought significant by their writers and those who circulated them; their fundamental purpose was to contribute to and help to manage the historical moment, rather than to provide a lasting tribute. Nonetheless, some songs did endure, and it is in their endurance that they helped play a deeper part in the creation of a popular cultural memory.

The outpouring of material on Nelson was, I have suggested, partly a function of the loyalist dominance of the presses, linked to a sense of relief associated with naval success in the wake of Spithead and the Nore, and an élite sense of the importance of commemoration and celebration of the achievements for maintaining the support of the wider British public – an issue that the 1790s had brought to the centre of the political stage. It was also informed by more traditional practices of celebrating battles in narrative songs. The absence of any counter-Nelson songs, associated, for example, with his less successful endeavours (such as the failure of the attack on Santa Cruz de Tenerife), or any songs containing a whiff of scandal or scurrility, is, I am suggesting, partly a function of the extent to which popular culture, by the middle of the 1790s, had become tightly policed and, by 1803, had become wholly dominated by loyalist forces. This dominance also seems to have had the effect of pressuring the market for songs and ballads in a way that melded together genres and types of song, and bridged earlier patterns of circulation; it is as if songs were squeezed into circulation by whatever means available. Moreover, a number of these songs – a mix of battle narratives and songs coming from popular entertainments and the loyalist presses – live on as the nineteenth century's inheritance of songs about Nelson. The most popular songs about Nelson in the last half of the nineteenth century seem to have been: 'O'er Nelson's tomb' *Nelson*, the élite song by Arnold and Braham and 'Old England/Britain's long expected...' *Nelson's Death/Nelson's Monument* (both of which are centred on Nelson's death); 'Come all you gallant seamen that unite in a meeting' *A New Song on the Death of Lord Nelson* and 'The 21st day of October...' *Brave Nelson* (both battle narratives of Trafalgar); 'Arise, Arise, Britannia's sons arise' *The Battle of the Nile* (an élite song about the Nile); and, especially in the 1830s and 1840s, 'The second of August eighteen hundred and one' *The Battle of Boulogne*. Through this legacy, loyalist dominance had an enduring impact on the way Nelson was celebrated in popular public memory in the nineteenth century, and, in that sense, is evidence of its more lasting impact on the creation of national unity and national myth.

This success seems to be linked to a broader failure, however. The picture is a complex one, and it is one about which it is difficult to generalise on the basis of the evidence I have been able to collect thus far, but, while there were printings of some of the Nelson ballads throughout the nineteenth century, there were fewer late in the century and little or nothing in the early twentieth century. It also seems that very little of the Nelson material survived in the oral tradition. Interestingly, even in collections of Dibdin's work, except when these aim to be comprehensive, the Nelson songs fare less well than his more generic sailor and soldier songs. Moreover, although the nineteenth century remained alive to some Nelson songs, they generated few new songs, and none that added any depth or colour to the characterisation of Nelson.[35] One reason is that the strongly loyalist character of many of the songs sits uncomfortably with popular ballad traditions, which take a more objective and critical view of war and its costs; but it may also be that the continuing élite celebration and commemoration of Nelson, combined with the lack of an independent narrative voice in songs from the period, came to act as a deterrent to their continuing salience for popular audiences and ballad singers. The Nelson of the popular songs of his day was the untarnished national hero; there was no ambiguity to exploit, no flaw in the marble, and, as a result, no room for some independent purchase on him. That this is so is, I have argued, largely a function of the intensity of the loyalist

---

[35] See above, note 11; later songs that mention Nelson include 'O will you buy my images' *Images*; 'All you that are low-spirited I think I won't be wrong' *Sportsmen*; 'The trumpet sound, the valiant troops are form'd' *England's Queen and England's Glory*; 'Oh Britannia! The gem of the ocean' *Nelson's Last Sigh; or, the Red, White and Blue*.

attempt to dominate and determine the way that people understood and responded to the war and the threat of invasion, but the result is a tradition of singing about Nelson that never gained the objectivity and distance that characterises so many of the popular ballads, which have endured and remain an essential part of a popular cultural memory.

This chapter does little more than scratch the surface of the world of popular song and its relationship to popular politics and cultural and national memory. As should be clear, there is considerably more material than I have been able adequately to discuss here, and I have been able to say only very little about the broader context of song and its place within Georgian political culture and society, despite insisting on the importance of setting this material against that background. Nonetheless, the aim has been to draw attention to material relating to Nelson that has been largely forgotten in the scholarship on him. I have argued that this material should be read against the background of the intense struggle to secure the loyalty of ordinary Britons and to mobilise them against the substantial and serious threats of invasion by France. The very scale of this activity has led some writers to see the period as a watershed in the building, or forging, of the British nation, but, while there is much that is instructive about such a claim, the material I have discussed here suggests more tentative conclusions – confirming the state's ability to ensure a uniformity of expression of sentiment but not wholly to determine that this sentiment was deeply held.

The unalloyed heroism of Nelson that emerges in the songs contrasts strongly with the more nuanced and subtle songs about Napoleon, Waterloo and the wars that appeared after 1815, which suggest a more complex and critical attachment to the country and its enemies than is evident from the Nelson material.[36] In such ballads, Napoleon is represented as a man of passion, as flawed and tragic, but as someone who achieved much and whose standing as a hero is in many respects enhanced by his humanity and his weaknesses. In contrast, in the representation of

---

[36] I am thinking of 'It was over that wild beaten track, a friend of bold Bonaparte, did pace the sands and loft rocks of St Helena's shore' *The Grand Conversation of Napoleon*; 'By the dangers of the ocean, one morning in the month of June' *Bonny Bunch of Roses O*; 'One night sad and languid I lay on my bed' *Napoleon*; 'I am Napoleon Bonaparte the conqueror of nations' *Napoleon Bonaparte*; 'Bony is gone from the wars of all fighting' *Napoleon on the Isle of St Helena*; 'Napoleon is no more, the French him did adore' *Napoleon the Brave*; 'Attention pay both young and old, unto these lines I will unfold' *Napoleon's Remains*; 'Arrah Muther, but times is hard' *Boney's the Boy for Kicking up a Row* (among others).

Nelson in popular songs, there is no flaw. It is difficult to demonstrate unequivocally that it is the sanitised and untarnished portrayals of Nelson that undermined the chances of survival for songs about him, but it is striking both how far they have been lost in traditions of popular song and that this fate has not been shared by some of the later songs about Napoleon.

10   The elusive principle: collective self-determination in the late eighteenth century

The self-determination of states is central to conceptions of state sovereignty in the early modern period, but it is not a conception of *collective* self-determination. In the course of the eighteenth century something like a sense of collective self-determination developed, but its implications have not been thought through primarily in the context of international relations and the standing of a state with respect to other states. Rather, the principal focus has been an internal-to-states account of the nature of the sovereignty that the state embodies. In the course of this development, a range of issues have arisen that complicate the force of claims for self-determination.

One central issue concerns the normative standing of the concept of self-determination. The principle of self-determination for states in a realist world of conflicting state interests stands as a principle of prudence, but it does not necessarily have any deeper normative foundation: 'might' may become 'right', but it is not entirely clear why the interest each ruler has in pursuing his/her own interests has *moral* weight to constrain the similar claims of another ruler. Self-determination as a principle, then, looks as if it might simply be a gloss on the facts of competition between states in the assertion of the interests of those who rule.[1] To the extent that 'collective' self-determination could be realised, this might add substantial normative weight to the principle of self-determination.

The case I want to make is that we can recognise many of the conceptual components that are required to make up a doctrine of collective self-determination, and we can see eighteenth-century political thought as grappling with many of these elements, even if it is anachronistic to see it as attempting to develop this doctrine. But the way thinkers tackled these elements reveal many of the difficulties and inherent tensions that the doctrine faces. It is not an accident that these principles were being

---

[1] On the history of some of these lines of thought, see Richard Tuck, *The Rights of War and Peace: Political Thought and the International Order from Grotius to Kant* (Oxford University Press, 1999).

experimented with and advanced in the eighteenth century, especially in the last two decades. Traditional doctrines of the nature of relations between states were undergoing a dramatic change, and the understanding of the internal character of states was changing – essentially, from a position in which international affairs were the legitimate concern of the Crown to the view that the Crown in all its concerns acted on behalf of the people, so that the legitimacy of state policy became a function of its relationship to the body politic whose will it represented or embodied. A central component of this development was the rise of the sovereignty of the people – both in theory and in practice – and the validation of the principle of representation.

I

What is it that makes the polity a unity? What unites a multitude into a single order? What validates that order's claims to sovereignty over a particular territory and a people? And what validates the particular terms of contractual arrangements? These questions raise issues about the nature of a people, and the extent to which a people should be understood as a political entity or nation that then sanctifies the claims of national sovereignty and nationhood. This way of thinking has a history, but it is not a very long one. In many respects its most eloquent initial exponent is Thomas Hobbes, and the Hobbesian tradition remains powerfully influential, perhaps especially in France, and perhaps most in the work of Jean-Jacques Rousseau.

In *De Cive* and *Elements of Law*, Hobbes distinguished between a multitude and a people, the former lacking unity, the latter being, in effect, one person with one will, which 'included and involved the will of every one in particular'.[2] The sovereign and the people are, in these earlier writings, one and the same for Hobbes. This meant that, in all governments, including monarchies, the people rules – 'for the people wills by the will of *one man*'. The multitude and the people are mutually exclusive, but the people comes together out of the multitude, not by assembly and contract, so much as by a collective willing of the city – 'one in which the sovereign was the assembly of all the people deciding by majority vote'.[3]

In *Leviathan*, the 'radical differentiation between people and multitude disappears':

---

[2] Murray Forsyth, 'Thomas Hobbes and the constituent power of the people', *Political Studies* 29 (1981), 191–203.

[3] Ibid., 194 [emphasis in original].

The multitude becomes one person through being represented by one person: A multitude of men, are made *one* person, when they are by one man, or one person, represented; so that it be done with the consent of every one of that multitude in particular. For it is the *unity* of the represener, not the *unity* of the represented, that maketh the person *one*: and *unity*, cannot otherwise be understood in multitude. And because the multitude naturally is not *one*, but *many*; they cannot be understood for one; but many authors, of every thing their representative saith, or doth in their name...[4]

For Murray Forsyth, whereas *De Cive* and *Elements* see the sovereign and the people as one, 'in *Leviathan* the sovereign represents the person of the commonwealth'.[5] Hobbes' 'formulation of the relationship between represented and represener brilliantly catches the logic of absolute monarchy under the *ancien régime* in claiming that unity in multiplicity could inhere only in the person of the monarch, whose sovereignty derived from the fact that the unity and identity of the state resided nowhere but in his individual person'.[6]

The puzzle with the Hobbesian picture is how the normative argument works. It seems entirely plausible to read Hobbes as having a horizontal picture of a covenant of association, coupled with a vertical picture of the transfer of rights or the authorisation of a representative as sovereign:

[I]t is a reall *Unitie* of them all, in one and the same Person, made by the Covenant of every man with every other man, in such manner, as if every man should say to every man, *I Authorise and give up my Right of Governing my selfe, to this Man, or to this Assembly of men, on this condition, that thou give up thine Right to him, and Authorise all his actions in like manner.* This done, the Multitude so united in one Person, is called a COMMON-WEALTH, in latine CIVITAS... And in him consisteth the Essence of the Commonwealth; which (to define it,) is *One Person, of whose acts a great multitude, by mutuall Covenants one with another, have made themselves, every one the Author, to the end he may use the strength and means of them all, as he shall think expedient, for their peace And Common Defence.* And he that carryeth this Person, is called SOVERAIGNE, and said shall have *Soveraigne Power*; and every one besides, his SUBJECT.[7]

As a treatise on what the words might mean if they are to be used in a consistent manner, and on what prudence might demand, Hobbes' case might seem attractive. But as an account of the legitimacy of political rule in terms of a one-off act by a past generation, with no possibility of questioning subsequent acts by the sovereign, the normative argument

---

[4] Thomas Hobbes, *Leviathan*, ed. Richard Tuck (Cambridge University Press, 1991), 114 [82] (square brackets refer to original page numbers) [emphasis in original]; Forsyth, 'Thomas Hobbes and the constituent power of the people', 195–6.
[5] Ibid., 200.   [6] Baker, *Inventing the French Revolution*, 225.
[7] Hobbes, *Leviathan*, 120–1 [87–8] [emphasis in original].

looks extremely weak. If what authorises the sovereign is an initial covenant, then it looks as if the authority and normative force of the sovereign's
acts derive from that covenant, or depend wholly on an argument about
utility (in which case consent seems to become marginal or redundant). If
that initial covenant is simply imposed on subsequent generations without
their consent, we seem to be ascribing supreme normative weight to the
willed acts of one generation only to discount its value for all subsequent
generations. That seems implausible, as Thomas Paine was to point out to
Edmund Burke in relation to the Act of Settlement of 1701.

Hobbes was untroubled by this issue. Indeed, in his account of acquisition by conquest, the covenant is made by each subject *to the sovereign* in
the absence of a horizontal contract. Hobbes needs to circumvent objections arising from the idea that there is a covenant *with* the sovereign,
which he denies when discussing a commonwealth by institution:
'Because the Right of bearing the Person of them all, is given to him
they make Soveraigne, by Covenant onely of one to another, and not of
him to any one of them; there can happen no breach of Covenant on the
part of the Soveraigne...'[8] In the case of a commonwealth by acquisition,
however, we seem to be missing the collective behind the sovereign. As a
result, the normative weight given through the horizontal contract of a
commonwealth by institution has no equivalent in a commonwealth by
acquisition, and the idea that the subject authorises the actions of the
sovereign seems to be merely a prudential move on his/her part. Collective
self-determination is revealed as fictive – neither collective nor self-
determining.

For Hobbes, the body politic was constituted by the free (in Hobbes'
sense) wills of its agents and its ends were unlimited, so that the manifes-
tation of the will of the whole body in the will of the sovereign retained
both a sense of the collective dimension of willing and of the will being
self-determining in the sense of free to pursue what it judged to be in its
interests. There is a major question about how strong a normative theory
this can be, but there can be no doubt that towards the end of the eighteenth century many writers found in Hobbes the components they wanted
to legitimate claims about the sovereignty of the people, and the person
who paid most attention to Hobbes, and subsequently became the touchstone for those concerned about the collective will of the people, was
Rousseau.

Rousseau took from Hobbes the importance of horizontal consent and
the need to develop from that an account of the unity of the sovereign will.

---

[8] Ibid., 122 [89–90].

While in Hobbes this was achieved through the authorisation of the sovereign as an agent, in Rousseau the sovereign remained collective and collectively expressed. Rousseau insisted that political will concerns the legislative power, and that this cannot be delegated or represented; whereas the application of political will to particular cases, and the use of force, rests with the executive power. The state is the 'minister' of the sovereign (the general will). Government is 'an intermediary body set up between the subjects and the Sovereign so that they might conform to one another, and charged with the execution of the laws and the maintenance of freedom, both civil and political. I therefore call *Government*, or supreme administration, the legitimate exercise of the executive power.'[9] On this account, the legislature forms no part of the government. In his discussion of forms of government, Rousseau talks about democracy (as a form of *government*) as uniting the legislative and executive powers, and by doing so confusing them: '[I]t is unimaginable that the people remain constantly assembled to attend to public affairs, and it is readily evident that it could not establish commissions to do so without the form of administration changing.'[10] Changed, because in entrusting activities to commissions the collectivity delegates power and creates the basis for a political élite or aristocracy. Rousseau's position, then, comes close to a form of collective self-determination. There are a number of elements to it that run against giving the collective will unconditional normative weight, however.

There is the potential disjunction between the legislative will and the executive will. At best, all we can say is that the process of collective self-determination is advanced and its normative force is increased if and when the general will is expressed through executive action. A more fundamental difficulty is that Rousseau's account involves an external agent who is to be responsible for framing the general will – namely the legislator – together with a series of conditions that have to be met for the general will to be authentically expressed, concerning the material conditions of the state, and the state of virtue of the people. For Rousseau, 'for a nascent people to be capable of appreciating sound maxims of politics and of following the fundamental rules of reasons of State, the effect would have to become the cause; the social spirit which is to be the work of the institution would have to preside over the institution itself, and men would have to be prior to laws what they ought to become by means of

---

[9] Jean-Jacques Rousseau, *Of the Social Contract*, in *Rousseau: The Social Contract and Other Later Political Writings*, ed. Victor Gourevitch (Cambridge University Press, 1997), 39–152, Bk III, ch. 1 [paras. 5–6], 83 [emphasis in original].
[10] Ibid., ch. 4 [para. 3], 91.

them'.[11] A legislator is therefore needed to create the people and to give them the institutions and confirm the *mœurs* through which they can express their wills. Rousseau makes the association a collective expression of language, customs and morals. The association precedes the state, but the state and its sovereignty sharpen people's sense of their community – as in the cases of Corsica and Poland. But the creation of the nation seems to rely on a deus ex machina. It is difficult to see this as an unequivocal endorsement of the claims of collective self-determination! Essentially, Rousseau requires a set of demanding preconditions for collective willing – basically, a combination of certain natural law, universality and particularity constraints. But, in setting up this account, the normative weight derived from the intrinsic goodness or rectitude of the general will itself is diminished. What makes the general will 'upright' either resolves into an objectivist account of the common good, or depends on a series of conditions that are partly fortuitous and partly a function of the legislator's agency – in which case, it looks more like a case of 'You get out what you put in'.

II

At the end of the eighteenth century there were several closely allied attempts to work through aspects of this position, against the background of the American and French Revolutions and the struggles for parliamentary reform in Britain. Late eighteenth-century political thinkers were not looking to develop a conception of collective self-determination; the term was absent from the discussions I am aware of. But they were consistently addressing questions about the nature of collective willing and how far it was possible to express the will of a collective through the political order. And they were aware of some of these issues and of the problems they raised for thinking about the legitimacy of state actions vis-à-vis other states and vis-à-vis their own subjects. In this sense, there was a developing problematic – an implicit framework of concepts and concerns – behind much late eighteenth-century political thought, which informed a great deal of writing and which, in turn, laid the basis for later reflection on state sovereignty and its claims.

I make no pretence to a comprehensive account; even short eighteenth centuries are long and wide. Moreover, I do not argue that their concerns contained within them a coherent account of collective self-determination. On the contrary, I want to use a few of these contributors

---

[11] Ibid., Bk II, ch. 7 [para. 9], 71.

to the debate to suggest that that account could not in fact be coherent: different dimensions of the problematic pull in different directions, and undermine the basis for a consistent and philosophically compelling account of the nature of collective self-determination. Insofar as writers at the end of the eighteenth century were working in this territory, then, they were working on a slippery conceptual terrain, and we need to see them as attempting to stabilise it through their express commitments, even though we must also recognise that every stabilisation was an incomplete one, leaving any component principle open to challenges from other parts of the conceptual framework.

Part of this conceptual structure was provided by two key strands of eighteenth-century thought. The first concerns the role of the state and commerce in international affairs. István Hont's work in particular examines the role of 'reasons of state' doctrines in relation to commercial society, and the long history of the view that the commercial interests of the state justify an aggressive foreign policy.[12] This story is not a story about *collective* self-determination so much as a continuation of a 'reasons of state' doctrine well into the eighteenth century (and beyond). There were, however, a series of ever more complex arguments that increasingly modified the reasons of state claims, not because of appeals to natural justice or the obligations to other states but largely on the grounds that 'great acts of authority' are likely to be suboptimal in terms of outcomes.[13] Commercial growth became central to the defence of the liberty of the state, but it was not a liberty that was accorded to other states (as a claim), or recognised as a constraint in which other states were involved, and it was not until late in the century that the idea of commerce as a pacific system uniting the interests of states was mooted.[14] What this material does give us is an understanding of the way that the commercial interests of states were linked to arguments for aggressive foreign policies early in the eighteenth century but became moderated in the course of the century, largely under the influence of the Scottish Enlightenment. Nevertheless, the account essentially weighs alternative courses of state action against an ever more sophisticated view of state and commercial prudence; rather than identifying an alternative moral ground for the actions of states that restrains, to some degree, the claims of self-interest. This does not give us the normative foundations we need for claims for

[12] István Hont, *Jealousy of Trade: International Competition and the Nation-State in Historical Perspective* (Cambridge, MA: Harvard University Press, 2005), introduction, chs. 2, 7.
[13] In French, 'les grands coups d'autorité': Montesquieu, *De l'esprit des lois*, Bk XXI, ch. 20.
[14] See Paine's letter to the Abbé Raynal (1782).

collective self-determination, even if it encourages the idea that self-determination on the commercial front may have generally beneficial consequences.

The second strand of argument concerns the state as a mixed polity. Any account of national willing is likely to be compromised by seeing the state as organised around a division of powers rooted in a division and conflict between orders, or by recognising the development of a legitimate form of political opposition (as in 'His Majesty's opposition', at the very beginning of the nineteenth century), in which political controversies within classes (not just between them) came to be seen as something more than the perverse effects of faction.[15] The sense that the polity in itself necessarily involves division, opposition and conflict has the effect of undermining the extent to which a collective will can be identified, and as such undermines the basis for a clear conception of collective willing. Hence, Rousseau's concerns about associations (which are essentially seen as factions that put the private or sectional interests of groups prior to the demands of the general will) are in contrast to Burke's account of party, which accords it legitimacy specifically by challenging that view (it being the view of a corrupt administration) – that 'all political connexions are in their nature factious, and as such ought to be dissipated and destroyed'.[16] There was a similar willingness to accept division, and the balancing of wills and interests, in Montesquieu and in the language of sovereignty used in *The Federalist Papers*, which reject the idea of '[a]n entire consolidation of the States into one complete national sovereignty [that] would imply an entire subordination of the parts'.[17]

Nonetheless, there was a line of argument emerging at the end of the eighteenth century that took older traditions of representing the state as principally concerned with the public or common good towards claims about the sovereignty of the people, in which the state is represented as an expression of the people's will. But there was also a powerful critique of the tendency to centralise political power, which saw the threat of despotism by this central power as necessitating countervailing powers within the state – through Montesquieu's intermediary institutions, or through the setting of interests against each other so that the will of one is checked by the will of others. In a political system in which power is divided and counterbalanced, the idea of a sovereign people, or of a collective will, is

---

[15] Archibald S. Foord, *His Majesty's Opposition, 1714–1830* (Oxford: Clarendon Press, 1964).

[16] Edmund Burke, *Thoughts on the Cause of the Present Discontents*, in *Pre-Revolutionary Writings*, ed. Ian Harris (Cambridge University Press, 1993), 116–92, 183.

[17] Alexander Hamilton, *Federalist Paper* no. 32, in *The Federalist: The Gideon Edition*, 154–5.

much harder to sustain. Moreover, we can recognise the emergence of competing languages of legitimacy, one emphasising the limits on power and the constitutionalising of rights for those whose views may not be in the majority (a line from Montesquieu through to John Stuart Mill),[18] a second claiming the will of the people as the true basis for sovereignty (the position of a line from Hobbes to Rousseau, but subject to ever more forthright criticism in the wake of the French Revolution) and a third attempting to reconcile the idea of the unity of the nation with disagreement and division but tending to be pulled in one of the other two directions, either to protecting diversity or to emphasising the sovereign will. In the work of the Abbé Sieyès, Paine, and the Marquis de Condorcet, all three elements are simultaneously present: they shared a concern with rights and their protection and with the unity of the nation, and they aspired to reconcile the competing concerns of the sovereignty of the people with the protection of the rights of citizens.

III

These three writers were closely linked at two major historical moments. They were part of a group, associated with Turgot's former circles, meeting at the time of the convening of the Estates General (when Paine spent time in Paris) to press the case *against* the model of mixed government associated with the English. Early in 1790 Sieyès and Condorcet founded the Société de 1789, and the three men's paths remained connected over subsequent years, emerging into the public eye briefly in the debate between Paine and Sieyès on republican and monarchical government following the king's flight to Varennes in June 1791.

Then, in 1792/3, the three men were appointed, as members of the National Convention, to share places on the committee charged with producing a new constitution for France. And, in the final stages of the struggle between the Girondins and the Jacobins, Sieyès and Condorcet briefly edited a journal together. Although these authors advanced different positions, they were grappling with similar questions and operating within cognate conceptual frameworks. In each case, their solutions revolved around the idea that representation could be combined in some way with the sovereignty of the people in order to produce a political order that authentically expressed the collective will of the people.

Paine, Condorcet and Sieyès were arguing in a relatively narrow intellectual space, bounded, on the one side, by advocates of constitutional

---

[18] See, for example, Aurelian Craiutu, *A Virtue for Courageous Minds: Moderation in French Political Thought, 1748–1830* (Princeton University Press, 2012).

monarchy and the English model and, on the other, by a Jacobin rhetoric for the general will. All three men saw in representation a positive mechanism (not just a second best option) for distilling ability and expertise so as to provide effective government, and their unicameralism was in line with a sense that representatives are representatives of a single sovereign people. All three retained a sense of the founding convention and the possibility of reference back to the nation as a constituent power in the event of government failing in its purposes. They differed over whether there was a role for a monarch, on the delineation of the government and its relationship to the executive and on serious matters of detail as to how to ensure that representation would effect the best possible outcomes. Nonetheless, they saw representation as compatible with a basic commitment to the sovereignty of the people, and with a sense that the people effectively will their own collective ends. They were, then, allied in seeing representative government not as an incomplete form of democracy but as something like an ideal form of government, which would allow the people to have an effective say in rule while not requiring the virtues of the democracies of the ancient world, or the associated requirements of size, etc. They were all, in an important sense, post-Rousseau thinkers – influenced by his conception of the general will, but sceptical of its feasibility in the modern commercial nation state.

A further issue that united Sieyès, Condorcet and Paine was their desire to recognise certain fundamental rights as claims prior to the constitution of government. In this move, all three departed from the Hobbes/ Rousseau view, in which natural rights are thought of as liberty rights, either transferred to the sovereign (Hobbes) or in the form of natural liberty, exchanged for civil and moral liberty (Rousseau). Paine argued that there are two types of natural rights: those that we have a perfect power to exercise (such as liberty of conscience) and those that our capacity to exercise is limited, and we therefore need support from the arm of society (such as to secure property, liberty, etc.). The remit of government is delimited by the requirement that it acts solely to remedy the inconveniences caused by these insufficiencies; thus, on Paine's view, government is a relatively simple affair, and a relatively restricted one. The people elect their representatives, the representatives legislate in areas in which the power of the people to exercise their natural rights is imperfect and, insofar as the people disapprove of the measures their representatives introduce, they may remove them at the subsequent election, or, in extremis, they may have recourse to a constitutional convention to reassess the adequacy of constitutional provision. But the people's role is essentially one of acting as the arbiter of their rights and of exercising forms of post hoc veto on those who fail adequately to respect them:

[T]he sovereign power . . . remains where nature placed it – in the people. . . This sovereignty is exercised in electing and deputing a certain number of persons to represent and act for the whole, and who, if they do not act right, may be displaced by the same power that placed them there, and others elected and deputed in their stead, and the wrong measures of former representatives corrected and brought right by this means.[19]

In his *Reconnaissance et exposition raisonnée des droits de l'homme et du citoyen*, Sieyès presented the rights of man as the prime object of every constitution. But his conception is not of a specified set of natural claims reserved to the individual so much as one of the citizens of a society engaging in a limited authorisation of those who represent them; an analogy is drawn with an attorney, in that we instruct him in his duties without having to enumerate that which does not lie in his purview. Moreover, the rights of man include not simply claims that the agent can exercise in a natural state but also claims that become possible only in a social state arising through people's reciprocal relations. Endorsing Paine's positive view of society, but not his earlier view of 'government as a necessary evil', Sieyès sees government as a positive good, and one that consolidates, enlarges and makes concrete people's rights. In part, that is why the rights of the citizens of each society may vary. Each society will have different issues and will develop in different ways, and that will have an impact on the rights they are concerned to claim and defend. Indeed, the model Sieyès uses is that of the relationship between an individual and his attorney: 'He gives the attorney *instructions*, he gives the attorney a declaration of his *duties*; he does not amuse himself by saying: as for me I wish to conserve intact such and such of my rights.'[20] So the place of rights is less as a reserve and more as the basis for a set of instructions to those who act as the citizens' representatives. That principle is still more clearly stated in a later piece, *Bases de l'ordre social*, written in the autumn of 1794 and spring of 1795:

The rights of man are hence anterior to everything. They are not lost on entering society; on the contrary the great object of the political association is to give them a stronger guarantee, by placing them under the protection of the community. . . In order to conform to usage we speak of our rights as having become *civil* through the guarantee of the city, although the law is far from being able to declare and guarantee all our rights. . . In the same way that the mutual recognition of natural rights rendered them positive; in the same way that they received a fresh guarantee by becoming civil; so I demand a third guarantee. . . [W]here is the guarantee against the powers established for the sake of protection, if the latter turn their

---

[19] Paine, *Dissertations on Government*, 369.
[20] Murray Forsyth, *Reason and Revolution: The Political Thought of the Abbé Sieyès* (Leicester University Press, 1987), 110–11 [emphasis in original].

relatively irresistible force against individual rights? It lies in the existence and exercise of political rights.[21]

Much the same perspective was present in the plan of the new French constitution of 1793. Rights are enshrined in its preamble, in which 'the object of all union of men in society' is declared to be the maintaining of natural, civil, and political rights', although in the enumeration of these rights they range from negative liberty rights to rights arising from social needs, such as to education or for 'public succour'. But, as with Sieyès, these rights are linked fundamentally to sovereignty and to the political rights of individuals:

25 The social guarantee of these rights rests on the National Sovereignty.
26 This sovereignty is one, indivisible, imprescriptible, and inalienable.
27 It resides essentially in the whole people, and every citizen has the equal right to concur in the exercise of it.[22]

In these various texts, and in the practical struggles and intellectual debates of which they were a part, we see these three men drawing on closely allied ideas and principles to identify ways in which the state can be self-determining not only in the narrow sense of ruled in its interests but by being the expression, in some way, shape or form, of the collective will of the people. As we have seen, there are other ways to do this, but they come with a price. Taking the Hobbesian road simply eradicates any real normative substance from the claim for national sovereignty to represent the will of the people; taking Rousseau's route opens a potential chasm between the legislative will and the government and requires that any state aspiring to the social contract has to be a small city state. Against those extremes, these men attempted to find a course in which representation would answer the exigent and the normative case: that it would not be just a second best deal to direct democracy but would be better than the thing itself – better by virtue of its ability to encompass the interests of all and to enlist the participation of the ablest of men, and better because, as Paine put it, in contrast to the frauds of monarchy and aristocracy it 'presents itself on the open theatre of the world in a fair and manly manner'.[23]

The striking thing about these writings is that their concerns revolved around the idea that in some way the political will can, through representation,

---

[21] Forsyth, *Reason and Revolution*, 125 [emphasis in original]; see the original text in Pasquale Pasquino, *Sieyès et l'invention de la constitution en France* (Paris: Odile Jacob, 1998), 182–4.

[22] See 'Plan of the declaration of the natural, civil, and political rights of man', in Committee of Constitution, *The New Constitution of France* (London: James Ridgway, 1793), and in Sommerlad and McLean, 'The political theory of Condorcet II', 121.

[23] Paine, *Rights of Man, Part the Second*, 235.

become an expression of the sovereign will of the people – and thereby be the expression of the collective self-determination of the people. That phrase is not used, but in different ways each of those I have discussed does seem actively to be reaching for such a principle. In doing so, however, they allow us to see how far their doctrines fall short of any such ideal, and they demonstrate the elusive character of such a principle in relation to political orders.

IV

Sieyès represents one way in which the role of the people and the implementation of the will of the nation through representatives were thought through in the period from the financial crisis of the French monarchy through to the establishment of a republic in France in 1792. Advocates of Sieyès have thought that he contributed significantly to Hobbes' position by his sense of the collective will of the nation and its continuing salience within the political system, and by his concern with the representation of that unity. For Sieyès, the 'Nation' emerges at the moment when 'millions of men heaped together without order and without design' become a nation.[24] To become itself it has to slough off and separate itself from everything alien to itself; thus the nation becomes a new source of legitimacy, from which new institutions and a new political structure can emerge. Sieyès thought in terms of recovering the rights of the nation, to restore the original body, but he had no sense of a past image of purity nor of an ethnic, racial or linguistic basis for identity.[25]

Sieyès conceived of the nation as a unified political entity, and as the product of individuals, and of individuals as self-determining beings – beings with the right to deliberate, will for themselves, to make contracts, incur obligations and so to impose laws upon themselves.[26] He shared Hobbes' individualism and his project of constructing a legitimate political order from a union of individuals. This contractual basis for the nation as a unity of individual wills was the keystone, but he combined this, like Hobbes, with a concern that this union have its own representative, distinct from the representatives that individuals and groups have within the union. The individual's will and his/her capacity to contract, exchange and act as a representative suffice to express and pursue individual interests; for the political side, a unity is necessary to express the nation's common interests. This becomes basically a Hobbesian account of engagement and collective authorisation, but one in which what is

---

[24] Forsyth, *Reason and Revolution*, 69.   [25] Ibid., 71.   [26] Ibid., 72–3.

expressed is the *constitutive* will of the people (i.e. the will that constitutes the political order). The first engagement forms the union/society/nation; it is established for purposes that they collectively will: 'A political association is the work of the unanimous will of the associates. Its public establishment is the result of the majority will of its associates.'[27] For the nation to act, it must express itself through a majority will and, when sufficiently large, through its representatives, and must express its will in an act that constitutes the government. The nation is the constituent body, and cannot itself be subject to the constitution. As a community of individuals acting by majority, it is the source of all positive institutions, and has an inalienable will.[28] The majority will of the nation expressed through a system of representative government becomes the only properly constituted will of the people: 'The people or the nation can have but one voice, that of the national legislature. . . In a country that is not a [direct] democracy – and France cannot be one – the people, I repeat, can speak or act only through its representatives.' Moreover, the representatives 'are not merely the representatives of the bailliage which has named them; they are also called on to represent the generality of the citizens, to vote for the entire realm'.[29] '[W]hen representatives try to act as delegates, the union of the whole is lost – each deputy represents the totality of the association.'[30] Crucially, there is no sense in Sieyès that the use of representatives is in any way a compromise for a more authentic collective will. On the contrary, with an emphasis on the distinction between active and passive citizens and with a clear sense of a division of labour with those in public office being those who are better equipped to handle the affairs of the nation, Sieyès regarded government by representatives much as Hobbes viewed government by the sovereign – that is, as a more authentic expression of the sovereignty of the people than any other form of government.

Sieyès drew on a view, inherited from Turgot and others, that representation involves the representation of social interests, in which 'the active exercise of the right to participate in legislation [is conferred] upon those whom greater leisure, education and enlightenment had rendered "much more capable than they of knowing the general interest and of interpreting their will in this respect"'.[31] There is no sense that the sovereign will can or must be exercised by the people (at least in a nation of any extent or cultivation); its mandate comes from its serving the public good through its ability to pursue the interests of all. This may seem

[27] Ibid., 74.   [28] Ibid., 77–8.   [29] Baker, *Inventing the French Revolution*, 249, 248.
[30] Forsyth, *Reason and Revolution*, 75.
[31] Baker, *Inventing the French Revolution*, 250, citing Sieyès, in *Joseph-Emmanuel Sieyès: Écrits politiques*, ed. Roberto Zapperi (Paris: Éditions des Archives Contemporaines, 1985).

surprising, since, in his pamphlet 'What is the Third Estate?', Sieyès' answer is 'Everything'. He sketches an association in its first form, as a collection of isolated individuals seeking unity through coming to act by the *common will*: 'A community has to have a common will. Without this *unity* of will, it would not be able to make itself a willing and acting whole.'[32] But, as it grows in size and complexity, it reaches a position at which 'it is no longer a *real* common will that acts, but a *representative* common will'. This representative common will has become the collective national sovereignty at work; and, when Sieyès says 'However a nation may will, it is enough for it to will . . . its will is always the supreme law', one recalls Paine's endorsement of Lafayette's comment 'For a nation to be free it is sufficient that she wills it'.[33]

Sieyès' final move was to argue for the importance of a monarchy that would be answerable to the constitutive power of the nation, would represent the majesty of the nation and would supervise the execution of the laws made by the parliament.[34] The monarch would choose the ministers, who would be answerable to parliament:

Make all political action, that which you call the Executive Power, center in a Council of Execution appointed by the people or by the National Assembly, and you have formed a Republic. Place, on the contrary, at the head of the departments which you call ministerial, and which ought to be better divided, responsible chiefs, independent of one another, but depending as to their ministerial existence, upon an individual of superior rank, in whom is represented the stable unity of Government, or, what is the same, of National Monarchy; let this individual be authorised to chuse and dismiss, in the name of the people, these first executive chiefs, and to exercise some other functions useful to the public interest, but his irresponsibility for which cannot be dangerous, and you have formed a Monarchy.[35]

Sieyès had supported the pro-American, popular sovereignty wing of those involved in the 1789 constitutional debates, but saw doing so as perfectly compatible with the preservation of the monarchy, as the chief magistrate and as the embodiment of the nation. The exchange with Paine in the wake of the king's flight to Varennes in June 1791 has been supposed by some to be a set-up job, to discredit monarchy, but there is no reason to doubt the sincerity of Sieyès' commitment to monarchy. What is in many ways more important is the proximity of the two men's positions on fundamentals: the sovereignty of the people; the principle of

---

[32] *Sieyès: Political Writings, Including the Debate between Sieyès and Tom Paine in 1791*, ed. Michael Sonenscher (Indianapolis: Hackett, 2003), 134 [emphasis in original].
[33] *Sieyès: Political Writings*, 137–8 [emphasis in original]; Paine, *Rights of Man*, in *Thomas Paine: Rights of Man, Common Sense and Other Political Writings*, 172.
[34] Forsyth, *Reason and Revolution*, 179.   [35] *Sieyès: Political Writings*, 169.

representation; the distinction between the constituent power of the nation and the constituted power of political institutions; the sacrosanct nature of rights; and so on. They differed because Sieyès believed (following Hobbes' account of sovereignty) that there needs to be a single point in the political system that represents the nation *qua* nation, not just as individuals with particular wills, and that point he associated with monarchy. Paine seemingly found this position impossible to understand, but that is partly because he lacked a sharp sense of the difference between the executive as the embodiment of the nation and the executive as merely the instructed agent of the legislative will – or, indeed, as an administrative committee of the legislature.

For Paine, every government had a sovereign power, and in America the sovereign remained in the people: 'The sovereignty in a republic is exercised to keep right and wrong in their proper and distinct places, and never suffer the one to usurp the place of the other. A republic, properly understood, is a sovereignty of justice, in contradistinction to a sovereignty of will.'[36] This position sits uncomfortably with more direct and active interpretations of the sovereignty of the people – hence Paine's claim in 1791 to be 'a Citizen of a country which knows no other Majesty than that of the People; no other Government than that of the Representative body; no other sovereignty than that of the Laws...'.[37] It is difficult to see much distance from Sieyès when he says 'the only system of government that can insure [sic] anything like adequate attention to every portion to an extended territory is the government that has its source in popular representation'.[38]

Condorcet too was looking for a way to sustain a sense of the people as remaining embodied and active in the willing of the state, while also recognising that the work of government itself needed to be carried out through representatives. There are a number of places in which Condorcet expressed his views, such as in his *Lettre d'un bourgeois de New-Haven...*, but his most developed position was expressed in the constitution drawn up by the constitutional committee of the National Convention, of which Sieyès and Paine were also members but which has largely been credited to Condorcet himself. The constitution was effectively rejected by the Jacobins in favour of their own empowering version. Condorcet's speech denouncing the Jacobins for this effectively ensured his proscription.

For Condorcet, the proposed constitution sought to establish itself on the basis of reason and justice, while securing each citizen in the

---

[36] Paine, *Dissertations on Government*, 375.
[37] Paine, 'To the authors of "Le Républicain"', 1315.   [38] Ibid., 1316–17.

enjoyment of his/her rights and ensuring the rule of law and the submission of the wills of individuals to the general will.[39] The proposals had three basic objectives: '[T]hat the people yielding only a provisional obedience to power established by their authority, may preserve their sovereignty entire; [...] [T]hat no power contrary to their rights may be established, even for a moment; [...] [T]hat their consent may give to the laws that power which appertains to the will of the majority.'[40] The constitution was to consist of: 'a declaration of rights adopted by the people, a statement of the conditions to which each citizen submits, by entering into the national association of rights which he acknowledges belongs to the whole, a boundary prescribed by the general will to the enterprises of social authorities, and the compact into which all these authorities enter relative to the rights of individuals; these, altogether, form a powerful shield for freedom and equality, and a sure guide for citizens when they wish for reform'.[41]

As with Sieyès and Paine, Condorcet coupled the language of rights with that of sovereignty: asserting the sovereignty of the whole, rather than of the individual assemblies, and seeing this sovereignty as most centrally exercised in the forming and ratification of the constitution – that is, as an expression of the constituent power of the people. And the appeal he was making was to the primary assemblies to act in their constitutive role to establish the constitution he had designed.

The constitution built in the possibility of remonstrance. A single citizen (with the support of fifty signatures) could ask his primary assembly to demand that any law be subject to reappraisal, or propose a new law to meet some concern. If the primary assembly agreed, it had the power to convoke all the assemblies within a territorial division. If the territorial division agreed, then all the assemblies of a more extensive division were convoked; and, if they agreed, the National Assembly was obliged to consider whether it wished to discuss the proposal. If not, then all the primary assemblies needed to be convoked to see if a majority agreed; and, if they did not, then the National Assembly would be dissolved and the law passed. Similar rules allowed a convention to be called for constitutional reform. The primary assemblies, then, had a number of functions. They should meet 'when it shall be in agitation to accept or refuse a plan of Constitution, or a change in the Constitution accepted; second, when the

[39] 'The speech of M. Condorcet', in Convention Nationale, *An Authentic Copy of the New Plan of the French Constitution as Presented to the National Convention: To which is Prefixed the Speech of M. Condorcet, on Friday, February 15, 1793, (M. Bréard, President) Delivered in the Name of the Committee of Constitution* (London: Debrett, 1793), i.
[40] 'The speech of M. Condorcet', vii.   [41] 'The speech of M. Condorcet', xiii.

convocation of a National Convention is proposed; third, when the Legislative Body calls for the opinion of all the citizens on a question that concerns the whole republic; finally, when it is in agitation, either to require the Legislative Body to take an object into consideration, or to exercise, on the acts of national representation, the censorship of the people...'.[42] What this seemed to build into the political system was a preservation of the ongoing sovereignty of the people, rather than simply equating the actions of representatives with those they represented. In this sense, it was a more developed version of Paine's view that the sovereignty remains with the people and that they can recall their representatives whenever they act contrary to their will, or rights.

Condorcet's view is that the legislative power is that of the majority and the obligation to obey this is 'in actions which must conform to a general rule, to obey not one's own reason but the collective reason of the greatest number. I say its reason and not its will, because the majority's power over the minority must not be arbitrary. It does not extend to the violation of the rights of a single individual, nor can it force submission when it clearly contradicts reason. This legislative power may be exercised directly or through representatives.'[43] 'Legislative functions are therefore limited to declaring which of the common rules that the plurality recognises as in conformity with their rights are the most in accordance with reason. Then, since the laws are (and can be) no more than consequences and applications of natural rights, the majority will have relinquished merely the forms and combinations of the principles they recognise, and will have done so only because of the impossibility of discussing these forms and analysing these combinations themselves. [...] A legislative body therefore exercises no true power; it is no more than a collective legislator for the laws subject to approval.'[44]

The second power is that which applies these laws to particular cases, or assesses that a certain action constitutes the application of the law, defined as 'the function of making a syllogism in which the law is the major premise, some general fact the minor premise and the application of the law the conclusion'.[45] This function needs to be delegated. The amount of delegation is limited: 'A nation which wants to be free and peaceful therefore needs laws and institutions which restrict the government's actions to within the smallest possible limits.'[46]

[42] *An Authentic Copy of the New Plan of the French Constitution*, 9.
[43] Sommerlad and McLean, 'The political theory of Condorcet II', 196.
[44] Ibid., 198–9.   [45] Ibid., 199.   [46] Ibid., 205.

V

With each of these writers something close to an idea of collective self-determination was partially present. We might think of Paine's insistence (borrowing from Lafayette) that '[f]or a nation to be free, it is sufficient that she wills it'; or of Sieyès' 'The community must have a common will; without *unity* of will it would not form a willing and acting totality';[47] or of Condorcet's question in writing to the Comte de Montmorency in August 1789 expressing concern at the absence of provision for constitutional revision: how can men have equal rights; how can the law be the expression of the general will, if children are forced to abide by a constitution drawn up by their grandparents? How can laws bind a nation when only a minority of its inhabitants, and after a few years not a single one of them, assisted in their formation?[48] Moreover, in each case, the author was seeking to reconcile this with claims or natural rights, with the representation of citizens rather than by direct democracy and with the establishment of a constitution.

One fundamental problem, which was not tackled in these writings but which acts as a standing obstacle to any claims for collective self-determination, concerns the issue of who counts as in or out with respect to membership. Every collective will simultaneously divides people into 'ins' and 'outs', but the grounds for making this distinction are hard to justify, save by appeal to factors that our Enlightenment writers could not accept, such as ethnicity. And any such justification, as with the more historical account given by Burke, cannot make the case by reference to collective willing but has to appeal to something primordial, as more basic than that claim. In doing so, even if the principle of self-determination might be supported, it remains unclear why this particular collective has normative significance, especially when the acts of the collective may affect those who are not themselves members of the collective. In fact, appeals to collective self-determination turn out to clash with a number of other constraints, which in various ways leave it without special normative weight or significance.

The natural law constraint. In the work of all three writers there is, as we have seen, an appeal to natural rights, which sets limits to what it is that the people can will and what the state can do. In other words, there are natural rights or natural law constraints on the wills of collectivities, which mark out a sphere of agency and activity against interference (such as liberty of conscience) and which consequently diminish the normative weight that can be claimed for

---

[47] Paine, *Rights of Man*, 172; Forsyth, *Reason and Revolution*, 73.
[48] Fiona Sommerlad and Iain McLean, eds., 'The political theory of Condorcet I', Social Studies Faculty Working Paper no. 1/1989 (University of Oxford, 1989), 321.

the collective nature of the determination and its self-willing aspect. With Rousseau, any such claims are turned into formal generality requirements for the general will: that law is to apply equally to all; that the general will cannot pronounce on individuals; and so on. In the wake of the American Revolution, and then the struggle for a bill of rights, writers in France in the late 1780s and early 1790s were clear that there needed to be some enumeration of rights that are taken to be prior to the establishment of political institutions or law. Sieyès tried to get round this problem by thinking of these rights as peculiar to each nation, but it is clear that he was uncomfortable with a complete relativism and wanted a line between those things that are subject to the majority will and those that are in some way sacrosanct. In the case of all three authors, there is a clear recognition that the power that they create to do the will of the people may also come to act in ways that turn against the very rights that government is established to preserve. One response was to deny that any authentic collective act can violate an agent's rights – Rousseau's 'The general will cannot err'. But that view was not shared by these writers. Instead, they were expressly concerned with potential divergences and with the importance of protecting the citizen from such an occurrence. This means that any sense of collective self-determination is going to be within constraints, rather than expressing an absolute sovereignty of the people – and that means that its normative appeal is going to be limited by normative principles that are independent of collective self-determination. A parallel case exists in the case of individuals: can people contract into slavery? To deny that they can seems to invoke values and principles that are independent of the value of individual self-determination, and consequently moderates the weight that can be attached to it.

The issue of membership raises a related problem. The appeal to natural rights doctrines as a general constraint implies the valuation of these rights independently of the individual's membership of any particular state. Indeed, if the protection of these rights is the end of the state, what does one say about those whose rights are not being protected outside the state? If the emphasis is placed on the collective willing underlying the nation, that confers special weight on the unities that this process creates, independent of the rights that this will is established to protect. But, by moderating the weight of natural rights claims, in favour of the collective will, one simultaneously undermines the force of claims for the collective will as that which is established to guarantee individual rights: 'Les droits de l'homme son donc antérieurs à tout . . . le grand objet de l'association politique est de leur donner une plus forte garantie. . .'[49] How

---

[49] Emmanuel-Joseph Sieyès, 'Bases de l'ordre social', in Pasquino, *Sieyès et l'invention de la constitution en France*, 182.

does one justify the separation of a people from others in a state of nature in a way that both values their natural rights and nonetheless leaves the embodied nation in a Hobbesian state of nature vis-à-vis those outside its borders?

These natural law and natural rights commitments are not extraneous to considerations of collective self-determination and cannot easily be abandoned. The point of recognising these constraints is precisely to protect the independence and agency of the individuals involved, so that their individual capacity for self-determination is protected as a condition for their collective willing. Not to value the kinds of individual rights that are demanded by these writers is simultaneously to weaken the case for the moral content of an idea of collective self-determination. Of course, issues about the authentic nature of individual preferences and interests may also lead to demands for public education, civic virtue, and so on, but this is simply one tension (starkly present with Rousseau) between the promotion of individual liberty and the preservation of a collective or common good.

The collective authorisation constraint. The principle of representation is also faced with the fundamental task of demonstrating that the relationship between those subject to political authority and those who exercise political authority on their behalf is such as to allow us to say that the one is the instrument of the purposes of the other. None of the three authors I have discussed saw delegacy as an appropriate model. It is not seen as practical; it does not allow a wide range of interests to be encompassed; and the principle of delegation sees the representative as subordinate to those who elect him/her – and that is inevitably less than the sum of all those who are members of the nation. For these reasons, representatives have to take their mandate from the higher principle of the public or collective good. The representative is the representative of the people or the nation as a whole.

One historical story Sieyès told suggests that a development of representation takes place as the society grows, but that, when representatives try to act as delegates, the union of the whole is lost. There is no sense in Sieyès, or in Paine or Condorcet, that the use of representatives in any way compromises a more authentic collective will. On the contrary, with an emphasis on the distinction between active and passive citizens and with a clear sense of a division of labour, with those in public office being those who are better equipped to handle the affairs of the nation, Sieyès regarded government by representatives much as Hobbes viewed government by the sovereign – that is, as a more authentic expression of the sovereignty of the people than any other form of government. Moreover, even if Paine and Condorcet did not go this far, they too operated with an implicit commitment to a division of political labour.

In Sieyès and Condorcet (and in Paine in the second part of *Rights of Man* and subsequently), the collective authorisation constraint is built into the process of the formation of the state itself; it is understood in terms of the constituent power and the establishment of the constitution, rather than at the point of the election of representatives to legislate. The constituent power is taken as collective authorisation. But it is hardly a powerful normative principle to think that, because people choose to form a nation and to be governed in their common concerns by a common will, they thereby will anything that the representatives they elect choose to will. Hence, in part, Condorcet's concern to retain the capacity for remonstrance, and Paine's demand (which he shared with Jefferson and Condorcet)[50] that laws be systematically subjected to a process of confirmation every generation. But in each case what we see is a concern that, without the prospect of a more fundamental type of negative or commentary, there is no sense that representatives can always be expected to act as an expression of the collective will. This concern, coupled with the idea that those elected are collectively authorised to do what they judge best serves the public good,[51] moved these writers' positions away from an idea of collective authorisation. Instead, on the one hand, we have cases for remonstrance, recall and revision by the collective against their representatives; on the other, we have a consequentialism in which the activities of representatives are measured not by the authorisation principle but by the more demanding principle of the public good – or *res publica*. If what makes their actions right is not that they express the will of the people but that they track more or less adequately the public good, then the value of what they do derives from the ends they realise, not from the fact that these ends are collectively authorised. There is little doubt that the influence of Rousseau was present for each of these men, and that they sought to find a way of treating the political system as expressing a collective will, but they did so with systems of representation that Rousseau disdained and that fundamentally compromised what could be claimed from a doctrine of the general will. The collective authorisation constraint is a major challenge to those who seek to combine representation with something like the sovereignty of the people, not because Rousseau was right about representation but because the attachment of a high normative weight to the sovereignty of the people makes it imperative to show that it is this

---

[50] Marquis de Condorcet, 'On the need for the citizens to ratify the constitution', in Sommerlad and McLean, 'The political theory of Condorcet I', 319–20.
[51] See Marquis de Condorcet, 'Advice to the electors', in Sommerlad and McLean, 'The political theory of Condorcet II', 173–6.

sovereignty that is expressed through law passed by representatives. In any moderately complex state, that is extremely difficult.

One position shared by all three thinkers involved rejecting Rousseau's ongoing legislative sovereignty of the people and his sharp distinction between the general will and government. For all three thinkers, the constituent power – that which makes the people a people and authorises the constituted powers of government – lies largely (but not entirely) dormant. Unlike with Rousseau, it is not re-enacted through the ongoing exercise of sovereignty in a general will. In the separation of constituent and constituted powers, collective authorisation is given to the representative and majoritarian process of law-making. This immediately makes the initial constituent authorisation something that operates at one remove: it authorises a process, not an outcome. He/she who says A must say B: he/she who engages to construct a political order is bound to comply with the outcomes of that order, even if they do not authentically express his/her will. This thought troubled all three thinkers; hence their concern with generational sovereignty, with 'relegislation' and with the rights that stand prior to and beyond the constituted political powers. But their anxieties simply pointed to tensions that are inherent in any attempt to link the idea of a collective will with the authorisation of law in any other system than the most direct form of democracy (and one that in each case, at least implicitly, authorises the process that generates the decision).

The rationality of willing constraint. Perhaps one of the most distressing aspects of these writers' commitments, given their experiences in the French Revolution, lies in their assumption that the will of the people is itself pure and upright – that it will be, in fact, fully reasonable. A few years later Georg Hegel would have demanded something more – some self-reflexivity: that the self must will and be aware of willing, and, being aware, must take cognisance of the willing of others. But, although all three writers believed that each must will within the constraints of the rights of others, there was less clarity on the issue of what would make the individual's will truly authentic. But, if we are to value an agent's will, and value the agent's status as a self-determining being, we need some sense of what counts as authentic self-determination. Paine and Sieyès had a very clear sense of the force and fraud that had hitherto shackled the peoples of America, Britain and France, but they assumed that it was simply a case of liberating people from those impostures for them to be able to will for themselves. But their personal experience suggests that, in some circles at least, the removal of those ties left room for equally irrational and especially vicious ambitions and desires that lacked any deeper rational content, and therefore any deeper validity, as a ground for self-willing. For all three of our writers, the Enlightenment confidence in the power of reason left them convinced of the potential rationality of the people, but in each case they came up hard against the realities of a people whose will was more often reflex or misguided than reasonable. Condorcet's constitution was itself produced at a point at which he must have seen that there was little chance of its acceptance, and that this was so not simply because France was increasingly controlled by a faction but because the faction could marshal the support of a considerable body of the (Parisian) people. Self-determination involves more than the mere fact of willing but implies that the willing is not merely reflex or natural but is one that the agent can endorse as to some extent rational.

If collective self-determination is to carry weight as a normative principle, it must involve either a powerful doctrine of the intrinsically authentic character of individual willing, which demands recognition as far as possible within a collective process, or it must make some assumptions about how those who will together will tend to converge on values and goods that justify us recognising the sovereignty of their collective will. It is difficult to see what a collective version of the former doctrine would look like, since the more persuasive individual versions of the doctrine look more individual and irrationalist (as with Friedrich Nietzsche). But the latter course vacillates between a descriptive or sociological account of the conditions for convergence and a normatively substantive claim about rational convergence that is extremely difficult to sustain.

The generalisability constraint. I have not dealt with the discussions in this period concerning relations between states;[52] it is not an easy subject to summarise. But each of these writers had a recognition that what they were arguing for was not just a particular organisation for their particular state but a more general model that would be applicable more widely for states. This is one symptom of the Enlightenment roots of these writers. But it also points to the fact that, in their hands, collective self-determination had a generalisability dimension – that it was a normative principle for states that in part legitimated their activities and in part determined rules and principles for adjudication between them. At the same time, in the French 'Edict of Fraternity' of 19 November 1792, offering aid to oppressed people wishing to recover their liberty, we can also see at work the corollary of such a position – that is, the illegitimacy of states that are not governed by their sovereign principles but are oppressed or exploited by their rulers. This not only nullifies their standing as states but, because of the values encapsulated in the demand for collective self-determination, creates the

---

[52] For which see Hont, *Jealousy of Trade*, passim.

basis for claiming that other agents have a responsibility in such conditions to help realise those values – hence the potential for outside intervention under conditions in which a political order does not meet the appropriate standards. The generalisability constraint is marked by a paradox: the stronger the claim one makes for the importance of collective self-determination, the less legitimacy states without it have, and the easier it is to justify intervention in its name. Yet, as we have seen in the discussion of these other dimensions of collective self-determination, it is not at all clear what the criterion for crossing a threshold of acceptability with respect to collective self-determination looks like in practice.

The particularity constraint. There is a further, fifth, constraint at work in these doctrines, namely a particularity constraint – in the following sense, and for the following reason: to the extent that the will that is self-determining is specific to the entity that acts, it is a particular will, among other particular wills (those of other citizens, or those of other states). It needs to be particular if the principle of *self*-determination is to be sustained, and it needs to be particular for value to attach to *self*-determination as a principle. Were self-determination simply the pursuit of what everyone rational pursues, then the value would seem to arise from the rationality of the will or the rationality of the end, not from the particular willing of this end. As such, self-determination would have no (or dramatically diminished) weight – diminished, perhaps, in the case when the end is rational but independent weight might attach to the process by which the individual reaches the end, as in late eighteenth-century arguments for the right and duty of private judgement when the weight really does attach to the personal judgement more than to the convergence of belief (except in some rather extreme sects, such as the followers of Robert Sandeman). This is part of the power of Sieyès' conception of rights as an expression of the path dependence of the particular nation, representing the issues and claims that it has historically contested. Hence also the very strong sense in all three writers that France was striking out on its own independent path, and that America could not be a blueprint so much as a model of another state insisting on its independence in the face of those who wished it subordinate.

These different constraints sometimes pull in the same direction – for example, the rationality and generalisability constraints – but in doing so they simultaneously pull against constraints relating to collective authorisation, or merging with natural law considerations that may undermine components of intentionality and the weight accorded to rationality. And the generalisability and particularity constraints are equally hard to reconcile in any stable way. We can see them pulling against each other in these ways with respect to the three authors discussed, but we can also see them more abstractly as principles that have a powerful intuitive feel, yet it remains difficult to know how to reconcile them with each other.

Although I have set out these constraints on the doctrine of collective self-determination in a relatively abstract form, we can see many of these issues at work in the debates of the 1780s and 1790s about the sovereignty of the people and how that sovereignty could be instantiated in the political order in a way that truly represented it. These discussions can be seen as attempts to track components of the principle in which we are more generally interested. Their shortcomings in articulation might be taken as evidence that I am asking the wrong questions of them – treating them as dealing with an issue in which they really had no interest. But my reading suggests, if anything, the opposite: that they were looking for a way to conceptualise the sovereignty of the people as a normative principle that would legitimate the political will and the outcomes of the political process in exactly the sort of way we mean when we talk of collective self-determination. They found it an elusive principle, sometimes because they were simply too optimistic, but more often because the principle is itself inherently subject to a range of tensions and constraints that make it impossible to grasp and hold on to firmly. That they took this route owed much to Hobbes and Rousseau; that they stuck to it owed much to the events of the day and the need to find a way to reform the French state so as to provide a stable constitutional order under dramatically suboptimal conditions. That they failed is, I believe, evidence that they were misled in thinking that there is a middle way, offered by representation, between the constitutional doctrines of a mixed polity (in which collective self-determination is not a value) and the will-based theories of Rousseau and Hobbes (in which there is no other value).

VI

These writers were working at a major transitional point in the history of political thought. They were trying to face up to the problem of how to integrate the idea of the sovereignty of the people into the state, when the state remained itself caught up in the system of states that owed much of its self-understanding to Ciceronian and Hobbesian models. The writers I have discussed saw in the people a way of providing a normative account of the legitimacy of the political regime. But, in various ways, they fell short of providing a model that was coherent and that resolved the various tensions that their commitments triggered. That they did so, I suspect, accounts for the shift in thinking over the next thirty years to a more causal and sociological account of democratic society and its varied political orders.

I have argued that some sense of collective self-determination was present in the 1790s, and especially in revolutionary France, but that the ideas of which it was composed were both immensely attractive and deeply unstable. They were attractive because they seemed to offer a way of combining the fact of state power with the legitimating principle of the sovereignty of the people. It was unstable because this project was overambitious. No version of the project could simultaneously meet and reconcile the five constraints I have raised. That no account can resolve these questions and that these accounts were, at least to some extent, attempting to raises important issues about the character of the history of political thought in this period. It undermines some of the more conceptually driven accounts of events found in the work of people such as François Furet and Keith Michael Baker. But it should also encourage us to question claims that particular ideas have been given definitive form in the work of particular thinkers. On the account I have given, no one has thought the idea of collective self-determination, because the idea is itself too unstable to warrant such a claim. There cannot really be a history of this concept, just an attempt to reconstruct different instances and their particular focuses and myopias towards its various antinomies. And it is then for a social, cultural and political history, in which this intellectual history can be located, to help explain how the flawed normative logic of such an ideal comes to exercise a powerful grip on the minds and practices of particular groups of men and women. An entirely local and particular account of the history of ideas will find it hard to recognise the tensions and contradictions I have pointed to. And, when we fail to recognise those tensions, we will not adequately understand what people thought, why they thought it and what supplementary elements needed to be appealed to in order to see sets of practical consequences and entailments flowing from this way of thinking. In other words, this intellectual history and the history of political thought must both think about the coherence of conceptual commitments, and must situate their analysis in the social, cultural and political worlds in which those commitments come to be articulated and invested with power.

11 Time to talk[1]

At the beginning of his inaugural lecture at the Collège de France, Michel Foucault voiced the wish that he might somehow be able to slip silently into the discourse that he was about to speak – as if the discourse was already there, already formed and, in a way we come to expect with Foucault, already producing the subject who would speak it. This is an attractive thought in some ways, and it is the kind of thought that has come to play a major role for many in the 'linguistic turn', and in the transformation of this turn into a method for reconceptualising what, and how and why, things happen historically.[2] In the later work of François Furet, and in that of Keith Michael Baker, and more recently in that of István Hont and Michael Sonenscher, the examination of the intellectual and conceptual apparatus that people brought to bear on their lives is taken to have a profoundly determining effect on the way in which they deal with their reality.[3] In an inversion of the classical Marxist agenda, thought becomes the agent through which change is brought about. In the closing remarks to what is one of the most important works on the discourses of political theory in the French Revolution, Baker exemplifies this view:

[T]o the extent that their acceptance of the suspensive veto implied a repudiation of Sieyès's arguments for a theory of representation based on the division of labour, the assembly was setting aside a discourse of the social, grounded on the notion of the differential distribution of reason, functions and interests in modern civil society, in favour of a discourse of the political, grounded on the theory of a unitary general will. In the most general terms, it was opting for the language of

---

[1] Jon Mee and I worked together at the National Archive during my writing of this chapter and his work on a book on 1790s radicals. Even so, I do not feel I can blame him for mistakes. He fulfilled his role of interlocutor admirably. My thanks are also due to Joe Philp for his comments.
[2] Michel Foucault, *L'ordre du discours* (Paris: Gallimard, 1971), 7.
[3] François Furet, *Interpreting the French Revolution* (Cambridge University Press, 1981); Baker, *Inventing the French Revolution*; Michael Sonenscher, *Before the Deluge: Public Debt, Inequality, and the Intellectual Origins of the French Revolution* (Princeton University Press, 2007), *Sans-Culottes: An Eighteenth-Century Emblem in the French Revolution* (Princeton University Press, 2008); Hont, *Jealousy of Trade*.

political will, rather than that of social reason; of unity, rather than of difference; of civic virtue, rather than of commerce; of absolute sovereignty, rather than of government limited by the rights of man – which is to say that, in the long run, it was opting for the Terror.[4]

It would be ambitious to challenge this way of thinking in this short chapter, but I have become more and more conscious, as I have ruminated on the 1790s and beyond, of a growing tendency to treat the march of ideas in ways that ascribe an order and coherence to people's thinking and acting that, in my view, does not match what people were saying and doing or how they experienced the world. This 'march' might vary from the kind of discursive 'determinism' that Foucault gestures to through to the more saccharine histories of the long march of particular ideas – democracy, representation, popular sovereignty, and so on; or it might be the more careful and often more persuasive attempt to understand how, in seeing the world in a certain way, certain options become more or less possible.[5] In collaboration with Joanna Innes and others, I have examined how the word 'democracy' functioned in the late eighteenth and early nineteenth centuries, and this work has led me to try to reflect more systematically on the relationships between words and ideas, and practices and commitment, in Britain at the time of the French Revolution.[6] The democracy project is not a straightforward exercise in the study of conceptual change; clearly, it does describe conceptual change at one level, but it is also an attempt to chart a history of the ways in which the word is used, rhetorically, polemically, projectively – in short, in a variety of ways in which conceptual content may be low on the register of the term's meaning – while, at the same time charting the practices and institutions in which these speech acts were embedded, and that both shaped, and were themselves in turn shaped by, these speech acts. The struggles with words that took place in the 1790s, and again following the Napoleonic Wars, and around the Great Reform Act, and later under Chartism, did indeed forge new conceptual content, but they also created new alignments between words and practices – so that, for example, elections became increasingly associated with democracy, and democracy came to be seen as something modern. But conceptual content is not always the most important component of the way in which the word was used.

In this chapter I want to try and press the methodological question a little further with respect to the 1790s and to focus on how certain political

---

[4] Baker, *Inventing the French Revolution*, 305.
[5] As in Baker's, Hont's and Sonenscher's work.
[6] Joanna Innes and Mark Philp, eds., *Re-Imagining Democracy in the Age of Revolutions: America, France, Britain and Ireland 1750–1850* (Oxford University Press, 2013).

lexicons were formed and developed, and the related issue of the tension between the tendency of certain terms implicitly to claim general – even universal – significance (or for us to ascribe that to them) and the fact that they emerge in large part as a result of more local and particular experiences. One feature of the period covered by the chapters in this volume is that there is a case for seeing it as one in which political discourse, once largely the preserve of an élite, was opened up and contested by the popular press and popular political movements – a moment in which the appeal to the abstract concept of 'the people' in Whig political discourse became taken more literally and concretised. We read that claim as involving a shift from claims to particular privileges and rights to more general claims: to equality, natural rights and equal citizenship. And it is not unusual for historians and political theorists to treat these claims as, in some ways, self-evident, as a Pandora's box that, once opened, is difficult to shut (without extensive coercion and intimidation). I do not take this view, because, as print culture expanded, its authority changed and people's relationships to it became more multidimensional.[7] Moreover, the complex case of women's rights is a good example of the weakness (the startling lack of self-evident force) of some of these conceptual links. In this chapter I want to suggest that we may, more generally, be over-reading (making too precise) the nature of people's commitments, under-reading their protean character and investing too substantive a conceptual content to the terms and phrases they used.

One of the reasons that it was '*bliss* . . . in that dawn to be alive'[8] was not because hopes and long-felt aspirations were seen as reaching fruition – but, on the contrary, because at that moment the world seemed to offer the prospect of being rethought. The sense of liberation was not in realising one or another particular expectation but in being in a position to imagine and construct (both intellectually and practically) the world anew. This sense of discovering a voice (and, in part, a hand) in the construction of possibilities was a common element in a great deal of the writing and activity of the period, and it was far from restricted to those who were advocating reform. Of course, it was one thing for privileged young men to drink to that sense of limitless possibility; it was another for those who tried to fathom and articulate what it was that they wanted in practice and to work out its implications for the political system more

---

[7] Roger Chartier, *The Cultural Origins of the French Revolution* (Durham, NC: Duke University Press, 1991), 83–91. See also Michel de Certeau, 'Reading as poaching', in *The Practice of Everyday Life*, trans. Steven F. Rendall (Berkeley: University of California Press, 1984 [1980]), 165–76.
[8] William Wordsworth, *Prelude*, Bk X, ch. 1, 692–3 [emphasis added].

widely. This process was not simply an unpacking of the discourses and political languages of the period; indeed, it was, potentially, radically transgressive of such frameworks and expectations.

This perspective needs care. For some, it will smack of too much voluntarism. But there is also a risk in thinking that what opened up was a single set of transformative possibilities, rather than multiple and potentially conflicting ones; and there is an associated risk in thinking that these possibilities stood relatively free from people's social and intellectual locations. The general interpretations of the period tend to see a unity of perspective amongst those who questioned the status quo, to think of a single public sphere whose rapid development destabilised the existing state of affairs of hierarchical order and to assume that people were talking about the same kinds of things in the same kinds of ways, sharing a common Enlightenment tradition and responding to power with a popular language that was rooted in reason and an equal right to be heard.[9] I do not deny that there is something to each of these claims; but they do need considerable nuance.

I

On 9 July 1798 George Dyson, the gifted but tempestuous young acolyte of William Godwin, set out on a journey to visit his aunt in west Wales. He wrote from Northop in Flintshire, just close to the border of north Wales with Cheshire:

The most entertaining circumstance that has attended my pilgrimage is the change of personage which has been incident to me since my departure. On quitting the English border I was in the space of 24 hours transformed into a French Spy and was regarded with a due degree of alarm and detestation. Advancing towards the West my character altered with the country and I was positively proclaimed an Irish rebel by the majority; though a few, good natured, sensible souls, observing my blackcoat with commiseration, were certain I was a refugee and whole villages were divided between contrary sentiments excited by my crimes and my misfortunes, which, heaven knows, were represented sufficiently heinous or deplorable according to the disposition of the reporter. As I proceeded into the heart of the country a new metamorphosis ensued: enquiries were made respecting the condition of the faith, the position of the saints, and nothing less than blasphemy could have saved me in Bricknock & Radnor from the reputation of a Methodist apostle.

---

[9] And one issue in the theoretical literature concerns the extent to which a single public sphere generates counter-public spheres (as in Nancy Fraser's 'Rethinking the public sphere: a contribution to the critique of actually existing democracy', *Social Text* 25/26 (1990), 56–80), as against thinking, more strongly against the grain of Jurgen Habermas's original formulation in *The Structural Transformation of the Public Sphere* (Cambridge, MA: MIT Press, 1989), of a multiplicity of competing and conflicting public spheres.

This shame, however, wore out with the rest and I was enrolled a soldier; a wild youth who in a rash frolic had sold himself to the musquet & and now sick of martial discipline was braving martial law by desertion.[10]

Dyson clearly revelled in the discovery of his multiple identities as he acted as a slate on which his interlocutors inscribed their prejudgements, and one is struck by how varied and inconsistent these were. I think we are right to be struck. We believe we would not run that particular gauntlet. We have a national (indeed, increasingly international) visual culture that trains us in a set of stereotypes and expectations, and that allows us to 'read' those we meet on a variety of registers and dimensions. In work on rational expectations, a familiar point is the validity of the claim 'If everyone believed that only prostitutes wear short skirts, then only prostitutes will wear short skirts'. The causal train is that no people who believed this to be true would wear one unless they wished to advertise their services. But that train depends on people believing the same thing and seeing things in the same way. What happens when the culture is much more diverse? Basically, it becomes much harder to say that actions, statements and symbols have a single definite meaning; and we need to think of meanings as partly projective (gesturing to, creating and fixing a meaning) and partly negotiated (something to which people feel their way), creating new understandings and initiating new possibilities.[11]

If everyone believed that only the poor and Jacobins abjured wigs and cut their hair, then only the poor and Jacobins would do this. But, when Godwin and Holcroft and others cut their hair in the 1790s, although they were making a statement to themselves and to their friends and acquaintances, they were not making the same statement to all their contemporaries. Some would simply not have registered it; others would have disdained it as a gesture; still others would have 'read' it as a part of a more general programme. It was a symbolic gesture, but the meaning of that gesture was, like Dyson's identity, contestable, open to interpretation and misinterpretation and, in important ways, not entirely under their control. They clearly sought to make a statement, but the statement that they were making could not have been wholly clear to them in advance; it could have misfired (though it was helped considerably by certain contextual factors), and it was something they could subsequently have sought to renegotiate had they needed to.

---

[10] National Archive TS 11/463.1582.

[11] See John Brewer, *The Pleasures of the Imagination: English Culture in the Eighteenth Century* (London: HarperCollins, 1997), for a sense of the languages of fashion and style in the eighteenth century. My sense is that the metropolis-centred world had become increasingly challenged and increasingly fragmented by the end of the eighteenth century, but that argument requires another work!

As in the world of visual culture, so too in the world of politics. There was a press, which sometimes achieved a national circulation, but it did so barely, and we should not overstate the extent to which it was a single world of meaning, as against a multivocal and often radically local medium. In the ensuing thirty to forty years the printing press really created something like a national print culture, albeit with powerful local inflection (not unconnected to developments in the printing process)[12] – as is suggested in the late letter of the former London Corresponding Society secretary, Thomas Hardy, to Lafayette, congratulating him on the July 1830 revolution in France:

I rejoice that it has pleased God to spare my life so long, being now in my 80th year, to witness this grand and beneficial change which has taken place in this country. And also great changes all over Europe. I ardently wish that the oppressed people of every country may be relieved from their oppressors. Political knowledge is making a great, and rapid progress. It is now diffused among all classes. The printing press is performing wonders. It was a maxim of the great *Lord Bacon* that *Knowledge is power.*[13]

In the 1790s that sense of communication was only intermittently achieved, and it was rarely experienced by ordinary men and women as a vehicle for their own voices, or as something that spoke to or for them. Yet many felt a pressure to have some kind of voice, even if only to talk. Although much has been written about the ideology of the LCS, it seems clear that the society's initial and sustaining impulse was less ideological and more a desire on the part of the members to communicate with each other. Hardy, the founding secretary, gave several accounts of the founding. One, for example, went as follows:

In the commencement of the year 1792 a small number of well-meaning men taking into consideration the many defects and abuses of our Government & considering that the great ignorance of the bulk of mankind was the greatest obstacle to obtaining redress, resolved to form themselves (under the name of the London Corresponding Society &c) into an orderly & well regulated society for the purpose of dispelling as far as in them lay, that ignorance, and instilling into the hearts of their fellow citizens, at once, a sense of their Rights as Free-men, & of

---

[12]   See David Vincent, *Literacy and Popular Culture 1750–1914* (Cambridge University Press, 1989), 2000–1: '[T]he invention of the Stanhope iron frame press ... extended rather than inhibited the possibilities of small-scale, decentralised manufacture ... it opened he field to anyone who could find as little as £30 to purchase a press and hire a room in which to install it. The consequence was the proliferation of printing establishments in the early decades of the century until every town in the country possessed the means of reproducing literature at the rate of at least 200 sheets an hour.' See also Gilmartin, *Print Politics*.

[13]   British Library, Place Papers, Add. MS 65153B, fo. 28 [emphasis in original].

their duty to themselves & their posterity, as good Citizens & hereditary guardians of the liberties transmitted to them by their forefathers.[14]

But, in many ways, the more revealing account is that contained in the letter he wrote at the time to his cousin Mr T. Newill, complaining that they had seen very little of each other and offering a solution to the problems of distance:

> If it is agreeable to you I should be very happy to establish an epistolary correspondence with you and I hope you will favour us with a visit when you come to town – As we are placed at such a distance from each other as to be deprived of a verbal conversation when we would wish we may have the privilege of conversing by letter when we please. A dish of chat about politicks Foreign and Domestick I relish very well when I have the leisure of an hour or two.
> I will give you my opinions very freely and in few words without being asked of the revolution of France that has lately and at this present moment engrossed conversation so much – It is / I think / one of the greatest events that has taken place in the history of the world. As to domestick politicks there is a good deal of talk here of societys forming in different parts of the Nation for a reform of parliament that is to have an equal representation of the people and shortening the duration of parliaments. There is one established at Sheffield for that purpose as we are informed by the newspapers and another in London of which I am a member and original projector...[15]

Hardy's emphasis was on 'chat' – on communication. He had his views; he anticipated that his cousin would have his. But the point was to deliberate. It even prompted him to correspond with his uncle, from whom he had not heard for eighteen years![16] This sense of a need to communicate and converse, by whatever means possible, infected Hardy's relationships with his distant family at exactly the time that it brought him together with his fellow craftsmen to deliberate about the state of the country and parliamentary reform. And central to their sense of deliberation was their desire to publish their resolutions and activities. Through print one could extend the conversation to others, and the establishment of the LCS was, essentially, driven by the desire to encourage others to communicate and deliberate with them.

Modern historians want to ask about doctrine. What Hardy says, and especially his reference to 'equal representation of the people and shortening the duration of parliaments', is read as evidence that the society was drawing on eighteenth-century Whig traditions in thinking about political reform, as are his references to Pitt's reform motion and the proposals

---

[14] Add. MS 27812, fo. 1.
[15] Add. MS 27811, fos.4 r–v (letter to Mr T. Newill, 15 February 1792).
[16] Add. MS 27811, fo. 12 r (letter to J. Walker, Falkirk).

made by the Duke of Richmond in 1783, in his account of the influences that led him to propose the establishment of the society.[17] The secondary literature recognises that other languages were also in play in the LCS's statements and self-conception, but the suggestion has been broadly that the core set of commitments were based around a constitutionalist language, and that this was backed by a certain tactical advantage in using the constitutionalist idiom. This was by far the most powerful and established language, with other elements being less elaborated than they would become in the tactical manoeuvrings of reform movements in the early nineteenth century. Moreover, it is seen as something that imposed costs on the society: 'Hardy's interest in the Duke's early writings did much to confine the LCS to a conservative and oddly aristocratic vision of reform.'[18]

Yet the extensive published literature of the society and its unpublished papers demonstrate a much more multivocal world, in which constitutionalist language was repeatedly accompanied by more universalist claims. Political theorists and historians of political thought want to distinguish these arguments, and rightly point to their dramatically different implications, and the very different traditions of argument into which they fitted. And they feel some discomfort in finding the claims muddled together, as if it was of little importance which was to be given priority. Nor can we claim that those in the society were ignorant of the tensions between the different traditions of thinking – as is clear from John Baxter's *New and Impartial History of England*, and, indeed, as would have been made clear in the advice they took from Paine.[19] Nonetheless, both constitutional and natural and universal rights were repeatedly claimed. In drawing up a list of resolutions 'expressive of their *Rights* and *Complaints*', they began with a preamble that drew on a powerfully universalist claim:

Man as an individual is entitled to liberty – it is his Birth-right
As a member of society the preservation of that liberty becomes his indispensable duty

---

[17] Pitt's motion for reform, 7 May 1783; Duke of Richmond's letter on a parliamentary reform addressed to Lieut. Col. Sharman, 14 November 1783.

[18] See, for example, Benjamin Weinstein, 'Popular constitutionalism and the London Corresponding Society', *Albion* 34 (2002), 37–57, 46.

[19] See John Baxter, *A New and Impartial History of England* (London: H. D. Symonds, 1796), preface, which emphasises the original purity of the constitution and its central role in protecting the people's liberties. Paine was clearly consulted by Hardy in the opening weeks of the LCS, which might account for the strongly Painite phraseology in some of the society's material. On Paine's involvement, see Add. MS 27811, fo. 6; *Selections from the Papers of the London Corresponding Society*, 9.

When he associated he gave up certain rights, in order to secure the possession of the remainder

But he voluntarily yielded up only so much as was necessary for the common good. He still preserved a right of sharing the government of his country; – without it no man can, with truth call himself *free*.[20]

In the published version of the initial resolutions of the LCS, the introductory remarks begin with the broader claim: 'Assured that Man, Individual Man may justly claim Liberty as his birthright, we naturally conclude that, as a member of Society, it becomes his indispensable duty to preserve inviolate that Liberty for the benefit of his fellow citizens, and of his and their posterity.'[21] The references to rights and liberties, and the reference in Hardy's letter to the French Revolution, suggest that the society was at least broadly acquainted with the pamphlet war that had ensued following the publication of Burke's *Reflections on the Revolution in France* (1790). Moreover, it was, at an early stage, as much influenced by Painite language as it was by constitutionalism: there is borrowing of the phrase 'fraud and force', and in November 1792 a paraphrasing of Paine's paraphrase of Lafayette: 'That a Nation like Britain should be free, it is requisite only that Britons should will it to become so.' But it followed this immediately with a reference to the 'Abuses of our *Original Constitution*'.[22]

There was also more anger and hostility to the prevailing order than is often emphasised in the secondary literature. In Hardy's letter to his uncle, J. Walker, at Falkirk in June 1792, Hardy wrote: 'There are many in England which we have corresponded with our society begun last Jan[ry] with three or four meeting in one another's houses in an evening consulting on the low and even miserable condition the people of this nation were reduced to by the avariciousness and extortion of the haughty, voluptuous and luxurious class of beings who would have us to possess no more knowledge than to believe all things were created for the use of that small group of worthless individuals.'[23] Indeed, the society seems to have been the sponsor of addresses to the French societies, which were similarly forthright in their attack on aristocracy: '[W]e have against us only the same enemy which is the enemy of justice in all Countries, a herd of Courtiers fattening on the spoils of the public.'[24]

---

[20] Add. MS 27812, fos. 1–2 [emphasis in original].
[21] 'The London Corresponding Society's addresses and resolutions', 2 April 1792.
[22] Add. MS 27812, fo. 2 v, fo. 9 v [emphasis in original]. Paine cited Lafayette's 'For a nation to be free it is sufficient that she wills it': Paine, *Rights of Man*, 172; *Address of the London Corresponding Society to the Other Societies of Great Britain United for Obtaining a Reform in Parliament* (London: LCS, 1792), 5–6. On fraud, see below, note 19.
[23] Add. MS 27811, fo. 12 r.
[24] TS 11/951, 'Address to the Friends of the Constitution known by the name of the Jacobins meeting in Paris'.

I am not suggesting that the society was initially Painite, or that the society sought to be (or to present itself as) Painite. It borrowed from and used Paine, but was aware at an early stage that some distance might be wise. As Maurice Margarot pointed out in his letter of 18 June 1792, following the initiation of the prosecution of Paine's pamphlet and the society's proposal to subscribe to his defence: '[W]e seem to make our Society a party concerned in Mr Paine's works, & while yet ignorant on what part of Mr Paine's works the prosecution may be grounded. We declare our approbation of the whole & of every sentence therein, which I cannot conceive to be the sentiments of the majority of our members and the expression in consequence of his valuable production entitled &c, &c., is liable to be twisted by malignant persons into an unwarrantable setting of our face against the laws...'[25] Margarot's point is evidence of a growing sense that the responsibilities of managing a correspondence included avoiding commitments that would alienate potential correspondents. In July 1793, writing to Norwich, the LCS correspondent emphasised: 'Union and increase being then our only resources let us diligently exert ourselves therein, with Zeal & Patience removing ignorance and Prejudice, with firmness & a consistent behaviour encouraging those who join us & and above all avoiding little bickering among ourselves, ever discountenancing selfish jealousies & private animosities, and cordially joining heart & hand in the common cause...'[26]

By reading the society's pronouncements for doctrine and tradition, I am suggesting that we tend to mischaracterise the point of its activity as the members themselves saw it: to generate discussion and communication and, through that, some kind of general or national conversation – aided by their assiduity in commemorating their activities in print and by offering a body of published material to which their diverse correspondents could refer to inform their aspirations. The commonality of the cause was more significant to most than the exact content of that cause. The aim was to communicate and to muster support, but in so doing they had to deal with a set of forces, including local differences and enthusiasms, that they subsequently had to work on to accommodate. In one of Hardy's earliest letters to John Horne Tooke, he lamented the difficulty of getting agreement on a statement of principles:

I am sorry to inform you of our defeat last night at the society. The address was not received. For one reason, it was not animated enough and another some of the sentiment were too low and contemptible to appear to the public from the

---

[25] Add. MS 27812, fo. 22; see also *Selections from the Papers of the London Corresponding Society*, 14.
[26] TS 11/953.3497.

principal city in the Nation. For example, Where it says 'Men less indebted to Education than Nature for the plain common sense they possess' some of the amendments were agreed to others were rejected the same committee were allowed another week to firmly settle upon a declaration but I have my doubts as least it for we are so full of silly importance that we will not concede to each other when we have a good thing before us.[27]

Clearly, not all thought such disagreements of 'silly importance'. In one letter to Hardy, a member of the society complained that 'the empty and incoherent language of the paper drawn up and printed for the corresponding society is what I cannot agree to, and can have no opinion but to be ashamed of having any hand in adopting it... [I]t will be a disgrace to them it is so exceedingly defective and I am afraid it will be as hurtful to the cause.'[28] This issue of what could be agreed on, and what had to be agreed to before being made public, led to further refinements in the LCS's proceedings in August 1793, but it remained a recurrent problem – not because doctrinal unity was sought so much as because they were looking for a modus vivendi among what they thought of as broadly like-minded people.[29]

II

Even when there was agreement on declarations and principles, this does not seem to have been a case of the centre proselytising to the backward provinces or London divisions. Rather, the society as a whole seemed to get better at looking for points of contact on which to build, or areas of consensus over what was 'good enough'. Political issues recurrently erupted and galvanised sectors of the population, but these tended to be dominated in the early 1790s by events that centred around Westminster and its print politics. The corresponding societies sought to make the issues that concerned them the subject of a more genuinely national conversation, with a national lexicon and a national programme. Sometimes they mooted an issue, and then dropped it because it would not float; for example, a delegate from Division 7 proposed 'the adoption of the word *Citizen* but owing to a diversity of opinions thereon in the Committee he declined pressing it any farther & withdrew his motion'.[30] Sometimes they were perceived to be too controlling; in September 1793 a motion was brought forward by Divisions 13 and 29 to the effect that

[27] Add. MS 27811, fo. 6 r; *Selections from the Papers of the London Corresponding Society*, 9.
[28] TS 11/954.
[29] See Add. MS 27812, fo. 58 v; *Selections from the Papers of the London Corresponding Society*, 78.
[30] Add. MS 27812, fo. 57 v [emphasis in original].

'circular letters be written to all the Country Societies inviting them to adopt our Title and by incorporating with us form in time a Universal Society'. The LCS had made an offer in August 1793 to the Tewkesbury Society for Political and Moral Information (and to societies in Hereford, Leeds and elsewhere) to 'willingly incorporate your society with ours under the title of the Corresponding Society in Tewksbury', but it had later to report the rejection of the offer by the Tewkesbury Society, which led them to withdraw the proposal more widely.[31] The thrust of the initiative seemed to be less one of colonising and more one of attempting to initiate a general and significant (or 'Grand') conversation – one that sought to be inclusive but relatively non-directive. But, while people could agree that it was time to talk – and to talk about fundamentals – that did not necessitate complete agreement, and it is clear that people valued their independence and that the society recognised and endorsed that.

Part of the process of organising the correspondence involved accommodating and accepting the tensions between different languages and phrasings, so that their setting alongside each other became integral to the LCS's strategy and remained recurrent throughout its history. In the controversy over the constitution for the society, which produced one version of a constitution early in 1794 and a further version shortly afterwards, we find such intermingling both within and between the versions.[32]

A Painite reading of the two constitutions is certainly possible, and would emphasise that 'all men are by nature, free, equal, and independent of each other', that they needed to give up some part of their liberty to society to enjoy its advantages, but that the majority had no right to impose upon the minority in a manner contrary to their rights. Moreover, 'all government being itself an evil' was a powerful reference to Paine's *Common Sense*. But there were more clearly constitutionalist elements, and it would also be a mistake to think that the constitutionalist tradition and Paine's writings were the only influences. The constitutions were very differently constructed; the first drew attention to abuses associated with the Corn Act, game laws, excise laws and stamp duties, the Mutiny Act and the impress service. There were also differences in language: in the

---

[31] Derek Benson, 'Ripples from the French Revolution in Tewkesbury', *Bulletin of the Tewkesbury History Society* 21 (2012), 1–7; Add. MS 27812, fos. 56 v, 57 v, 62 r, 70 v; *Selections from the Papers of the London Corresponding Society*, 82.

[32] See Add. MS 27813, fo. 36 v, which refers to the document as 'A Former report of the Constitution of the London Corresponding Society'. *Selections from the Papers of the London Corresponding Society*, 243–8, gives a copy of '*A letter &c to the Members of the London Corresponding Society (London, 6 April, 1795)* from the Friends of Liberty (formerly Division 16)'.

earlier constitution there was no discussion of subsections of the divisions; in the later version the role of 'Tythings' became prominent. But, in institutional outline, the constitutions were not dramatically different; the earlier one was steeped in detail, to the point that it became unwieldy; the later version attempted to set aside a good deal of the detail and to leave more unsaid. Both attempted in broad terms to consolidate authority in the Committee of Delegates to enable it to expedite business. In neither case was the constitution welcomed, and neither was ever implemented, with the result that the LCS lurched on with an amended 1792 constitution.

The attempt to establish a new constitution when there was already an active society exemplifies the tensions associated with allowing others to act on one's behalf. It is as if, having found a voice, members had become suspicious of even their own society's attempts to take decisions without full consultation. This testifies to the divisions' sense of the importance of their own voices and commitments. In part, they may also have been reacting against the element of self- and other-directed education in the constitution writing. The first proposal included a section on 'Order', which required that '[n]o member shall be allowed to stile himself, or any other, by any party name, whether intended to convey respect or disrespect', continuing in the next item to state:

7. All political appellations which do not in their immediate interpretation convey an idea of political sentiment or situation, are party names. The following do not fall under this objection as will appear by their explanations.

Republican, – One who wishes to promote the general welfare of his country.

Democrat, – A supporter of the rights and power of the people.

Aristocrat, – One who wishes to promote the interest of a few at the expense of the many.

Royalist, – Among the ignorant part of mankind signifies, a person attached to regal government: among artful courtiers it is a veil for their own aristocracy.

Loyalist, – A supporter of the constitution of his country.

Citizen. – The ancient appellation given to members of free states.

Subject, – Can only with propriety, be applied to a member of a State, whose government has been instituted by foreign conquest or the prevalence of a domestic faction.[33]

It is as if the constitution was in part attempting to stabilise the language in which people expressed their views and disagreements, as well as stabilising the order and the institutional structure in which they did so. It may have been more ambitious in intent than even this. Reflecting on

---

[33] *The Report of the Committee of Constitution of the London Corresponding Society* (London: T. Spence, 1794), 6.

his activities in the LCS, Francis Place acknowledged that he had been a member of the Committee to Revise the Constitution, the structure of which he described as 'assimilating its organization as much as possible to what we conceived to be the best form for governing the Nation. It was printed by the Society as "The Report of the Committee of the Constitution of the London Corresponding Society" and is, I am still of the opinion, a striking proof of the talents and judgments of the men who were selected to draw it up.'[34] Seen in the light of Place's comments, the document looks more like a general programme for structuring the government of the country and for clarifying the language and terms of engagement for the country more widely. Nonetheless, the constitution question generated very considerable controversy: the first was rejected; there was a dispute over the process of appointing a committee to revise the proposals; and when the LCS General Committee jumped the gun in adopting the revised constitution the divisions reacted badly: the proposal 'had given great dissatisfaction, it had been considered as an Act of great usurpation and Aristocracy and what was not authorized by the Constitution, it was in fact cramming a Constitution down the throats of their Constituents without asking their Opinion and exactly like the conduct of the present Minister'.[35]

The debate prompted by the constitutions did not go away but returned with a vengeance in the spring of 1795, not just over the character of the design or the concentration of responsibility[36] but, subsequently, over whether there was a need for a system of rules at all. This suggested a confidence in free discussion that tested the very idea that some sort of organisation was required. This demanded a more robust response:

IN SOME DIVISIONS IT HAS BEEN MAINTAINED

First. *'That the only means of securing social happiness is by the general diffusion of Knowledge, and this being effected, all regard to constitutional and legal rules would become unnecessary.'*

Second. *'That, as human affairs are liable to exigencies which no discernment can foresee, and which will require measures peculiar to themselves, all constitutional rules*

---

[34] Add. MS 27808, fo. 26. Oddly, the Place Papers describe the first constitution as a revision of the second, getting the order mixed up, but the published versions clearly set out the order. Francis Place was referring to the second revised constitution: Add. MS 35142, fo. 286; MS 27816, fo. 523. John Richter's examination notes by the Privy Council have him (Richter) as a member of the Committee for Reforming the Constitution from November 1793 until February 1794 – and thus before Place's membership (he joined in June 1794).

[35] *Selections from the Papers of the London Corresponding Society*, 194.

[36] See *A Letter &c. to the Members of the London Corresponding Society*, in which Division 16 announce its secession.

may prohibit or retard the adoption of such measures, and ought to be considered as fetters on Society.'

Third. *'That as it scarcely ever happens that any two cases whether civil or criminal, are precisely alike, it follows that established Laws, however numerous, cannot in their operation be perfectly equitable; and hence it is inferred, that all Law ought to be made extempore, and adapted to the particular case to which it is to apply.'*[37]

In contrast, in other divisions, a stress on the imperfections of human nature, and the limited effects of education, were seen as necessitating the adoption of constitutional and legal rules, while exigencies were thought to be likely to be responded to by passion rather than reason, as with criminal cases; therefore, some set of rules and procedures was needed for settling things on general principles without regard to the full details of particular cases.

This political lexicon was new to the society in 1794 and 1795 and drew on the work (and phrasing) of William Godwin and his *Enquiry concerning Political Justice* (1793) (while ignoring the fact that Godwin had declaimed against political associations, and was to do so still more forcibly late in 1795 following the introduction of the 'Gagging Acts'). It is likely that it derived in part from Godwin's own increased contacts with members of the LCS during the treason trials and afterwards, with him taking tea on several occasions with James Powell (the most efficient of the government's spies), alongside other members such as Richard 'Citizen' Lee and Henry Iliff.[38] Despite these ironies, it is incontestable that Godwin's *Enquiry* had an influence on some members of the LCS – so much that the General Committee felt obliged to consult the divisions on the following three propositions:

First. *Are you of opinion that this Society can be conducted without any Regulations?*

Second. *Are you of opinion that the present regulations, with such amendments as may be made in the usual way of reference by the General Committee to the Divisions, will be sufficient to answer the purposes of the Society?*

Third. *Are you of opinion that the appointing of any Committee for the special purpose of amending the present Regulations, or forming a new Constitution is necessary?*

The membership voted in favour of the second statement, but against the other two.[39]

The LCS provided a vehicle for the rehearsal and discussion of a range of principles, political languages and expectations. It focused these in

---

[37] *The Correspondence of the London Corresponding Society, Revised and Corrected* (London: LCS, 1795), 20–1 [emphasis in original].

[38] See http://godwindiary.bodleian.ox.ac.uk.

[39] *The Correspondence of the London Corresponding Society, Revised and Corrected*, 22 [emphasis in original].

large part on a set of proposals for the reform of the franchise as the necessary first step, but it was possible to support that project from a variety of positions – positions that might well be slipping and sliding partly as a function of a developing acquaintance with political writings, and that may have been informed by a whole range of local influences rather than by any comprehensive understanding or knowledge of wider political debates. There was a massive amount of literature published in this period. Historians cannot master it; and artisans and shopkeepers did not do so. What they drew on depended on what they encountered. What the LCS was trying to do was to adjudicate between a wide range of concerns so as to generate a 'correspondence' on common proposals for reform – when a range of other ambitions or expectations might simply be deferred. Crucially, there was no suggestion that an uncorrupt House of Commons was the sole, ultimate objective, since that was itself seen as instrumental to a wide range of concerns and issues that members might advance:

An Honest Parliament!
   An Annual Parliament!
   A Parliament wherein each Individual will have his own Representative!
   Soon then should we see our Liberties restored, the Press free, the Laws simplified, Judges unbiased, Juries independent, Needless Places and Pensions retrenched, Immoderate Salaries reduced, the Public better served, Taxes diminished and the Necessaries of life more within the reach of the poor, Youth better educated, Prisons less crowded, old Age better provided for, and sumptuous Feasts, at the expense of the starving poor, less frequent.[40]

At this level, there was something like a convergence on, or at least a rapport between, some of the languages the society voiced, centring on the development of knowledge and the exercise of individual powers under conditions of equality and liberty:

Equality of protection for his liberty, life and property... Equality in the exercise and enjoyments of such bodily and mental faculties as nature may have conferred upon him; [. . .] Equality of encouragement for the exercise of his talents, and consequently of the free enjoyment of the advantages thereby obtained... Freedom to publish his opinion and to exercise his religious worship without molestation... And lastly, the unrestrained exercise of his own private judgment in every action that does not trespass upon the equal rights of his fellow citizens.[41]

---

[40] *Address from the London Corresponding Society to the Inhabitants of Great Britain, on the Subject of a Parliamentary Reform* (London: LCS, 1792), 6.
[41] *Report of the Committee Appointed to Revise and Abridge a Former Report of the Constitution of the London Corresponding Society* (London: Richard Lee, 1795), 3 [emphasis in original].

The statement can be seen as expressing both their expectations of their standing in their society and their hopes for the future within society more broadly. Such broad principles linked a sense of wider ends, to be pursued through parliamentary reform, with a perception of their current situation as one in which the corruptions of government had 'deprived men of their rights and imposed upon their understandings through a combination of FRAUD OR Force, sanctioned by Custom and blind Submission'. This formulation borrowed from Paine (even if it also echoed original constitutionalist claims), and was referenced in a number of LCS and Hardy statements.[42] But it left it possible for people to subscribe to the society from a range of very different viewpoints. Place's later assessment of his colleagues in the society needs caution, given the tendency to be clearer in retrospect than one is at the time or prospect, but his view certainly confirms both the different readings of the situation that people had and the very different (and often dramatically open) views about the longer objective:

All the leading members of the London Corresponding society were republicans that is, they were all friendly to representative government. This they were taught by the writings of Thomas Paine, [. . .] A great majority of the members were also republicans but they were generally convinced that a republic could be advantageously produced in this country by slow degrees only, it was quite a common saying that 'a republic produced by our vices could not be permanent', that no change which was not the consequence of conviction of its utility could be useful. There were some however that believed a reform of Parliament would be obtained and that it was compatible with what they called the constitution, others again believed that a reform/would be obtained and that a house of Commons really chosen by the people, would in time have all the power and set aside the king and the Lords. Others expected that a reform would be obtained that would at once convert the government into a republic. Some were of the opinion that no reform would ever be obtained, that the ministers would on some occasion drive the thing to extremities and then the whole system of government would break up, that it was therefore the wisest way to ... present to the people the advantages of representative Government ... A very few were for using violence, for furthering an end to the government by any means foreign or domestic, these were always few and had no weight in the society.[43]

---

[42] 'The London Corresponding Society's addresses and resolutions', 1. See also '[T]hey have been often despoiled of their valuable rights, sometimes by fraud, and at other times by force': Add. MS 27814, fo. 18; and 'Fraud or force, sanctioned by custom, with-holds the right from (by far) the greater number of the inhabitants of this country': Add. MS 27812, fo. 2 v. The phrase seems to be Paine's, with the reference in *Rights of Man*, 121. Note the ambiguity and tensions between a view of progressive enlightenment, à la Godwin, and a view of removing shackles and blinkers previously imposed by coercion.

[43] Add. MS 27808, fo. 113.

Within this loose coalition of commitments, a range of lexicons and ideas could jostle freely, and people could experiment – as they did – with stipulative claims, original ideas and with forming and re-forming arguments. In many respects, the conflict over the society's constitution, and especially over the sense that it was being imposed upon them and that it shifted power to the centre, was a function of people's resistance to conversational control. Having formed their local divisions, people were moved by their local concerns. They may have subscribed to a broad set of commitments, but they were also jealous of their own judgement and sought their own formulations, resisting the direction of the centre. This resulted in a much richer language, the invocation of diverse lexicons, and a culture of linguistic experimentation.

Although linguistic experimentation is difficult to chart precisely it does seem clear that some terms and phrases did catch on, while some did not. 'Liberticidal' seems to have been developed in the loyalist press, used first to describe Robespierre, and then used more widely in relation to French events. Its use in a British context occurred first in Norwich, and it was brought to the LCS in correspondence, reworked by Richard Dinmore in his account of the English Jacobins, picked up by Sampson Perry but also by the loyalist John Brand; the term does not seem to have travelled further, however (although it recurred twice in 1832–4).[44] The 'hydra of despotism' was a phrase used to translate M. Leroux's speech on the execution of Louis XVI, and was used by the Birmingham Society and by J. A. O'Keefe, who credited Jacques Necker with having 'drawn back the curtain of government, and laid before their eyes the naked hydra of despotism'.[45] Arthur Young used the phrase 'domineering aristocracy' in 1780 in relation to Ireland, and Christopher Wyville used it in his 1783 *Letters Addressed to the Committee of Belfast*,[46] and the phrase was used in a number of Irish publications in the early 1790s. It was less common in Britain, though it was picked up by a member of the London Revolution

---

[44] *True Briton*, 10 June 1793; *The Correspondence of the London Corresponding Society, Revised and Corrected*, 27; Dinmore, *An Exposition of the Principles of the English Jacobins*, 32; Sampson Perry, *The Origin of Government* (London: S. Perry, 1797), 32; John Brand, *An Historical Essay on the Principles of Political Associations in a State* (London: T. N. Longman, 1796), 43.

[45] *The Correspondence of the London Corresponding Society, Revised and Corrected*, 30; *The Trial of Louis XVI, Late King of France* (London: W. Boag, 1793), 23; J. A. O'Keefe, *An Essay on the Progress of Human Understanding* (London: V. Griffiths, 1795), 42.

[46] Arthur Young, *A Tour of Ireland* (Dublin: G. Bonham, 1780), 67; Christopher Wyville, *Letters Addressed to the Committee of Belfast* (London: W. Blanchard, 1783), 12; Major John Scott, *A Letter to the Right Hon. Edmund Burke* (London: J. Stockdale, 1790), 45; John Oswald, *Review of the Constitution of Great Britain* (London: J. Oswald, 1792), 13; *The Correspondence of the London Corresponding Society, Revised and Corrected*, 36.

Society in 1790, and used by John Oswald in 1792, appearing in the LCS correspondence in a letter from Yorkshire in July 1793. An emphasis on 'the bounden duty of every [good] citizen' was infrequent, and used by loyalists and reformers alike. The idea that people should oppose, or correct and humble, 'that profligate administration, which wrings from the hand of the peasant what may corrupt the virtue of the senator, and which drains the sources of national honour' appeared in 1793 in two Dublin Association of the Friends of the Constitution, Liberty and Peace pamphlets, but it was repeated practically verbatim in an LCS letter to High Wycombe two or more years later.[47]

'Soi disant Patriots' was used in a Norwich letter, though it was probably drawn from reports of events in the French Convention in February 1793, and it then became more widely used in the 1830s. But the phrase 'soi disant' was something that seemed to come into its own in the 1790s, with only one newspaper report before 1789, and increasing use, mainly by loyalists, and often in relation to France, through the 1790s.[48] It is difficult to be entirely confident, using the existing search engines and databases, as to the origins of terms and phrases and their pattern of communication, and I am reluctant to put too much weight on the details of these two paragraphs. Nonetheless, the exercise is an important one, and as resources develop further we will be able to produce a much more sophisticated picture of the shifting sands of local popular political discourse. But what the exercise does seem to support is the idea that there may be quite local, and often serendipitous, borrowings and usages of expressions whose intellectual content may not be very deep and that we need to avoid attributing to broader languages or discourses of political thought.

III

We are accustomed to thinking in terms of shared languages, national lexicons and partisan struggles over particular terms and their meaning, and to applying a relatively consistent lexicon retrospectively to movements and ideas – democratic, republican, egalitarian, socialist, and so on. But these terminologies need to be coined and circulated, and to be rubbed smooth with use. And, even when we are scrupulous in using

[47] *The Address of the Association of the Friends of the Constitution, Liberty, and Peace* (London: James Ridgway, 1793), 7; *The Correspondence of the London Corresponding Society, Revised and Corrected*, 57.

[48] *The Correspondence of the London Corresponding Society, Revised and Corrected*, 63; *Oracle and Public Advertiser*, 16 March 1795.

terms only when they are used by the participants, we need to recognise that what they meant and what we mean by these terms is not identical, and that the establishment of a consistent reference to a term is a long process, and one that is far from linear in moving from its first utterance to acceptation and to our present. This sense of the slipperiness of language and meaning is evident in the way in which some of the reformers exploited it – as in Thomas Spence's 'The lion and the other beasts', in which 'The lion (not meaning our sovereign Lord the King) and several other beasts (not meaning the continental Kings and Powers) entered into an alliance offensive and defensive, and were to live very socially together in the forest (not meaning Europe)', and in Daniel Eaton's 'What makes a libel?'.[49] It also does much to account for the nagging repetition of definitions – even their attempted integration into the constitution of the London Corresponding Society – and the repeated puzzlement that the terms and their meaning produced in those who experienced them. As Anne Plumptre remarked in her memoirs of travelling in France, 'As aristocracy, democracy, Jacobinism, moderantism, and many terms of the like kind have no regular and settled definition, they are easily applied to any one who, for any cause whatever, is obnoxious to the person by whom he is accused; and since from being so vague and indefinite the crime is incapable of being proved, the trouble of evidence is spared, the mere accusation is sufficient for conviction.'[50] Similarly, Iolo Morganwg commented: '[W]hether my life has not been tolerantly innocent, I leave to be decided by my enemies who call me democrat, Jacobin, heretic, infidel, &c. I know not clearly what they mean by the first two epithets. As to other two, with respect to Calvinism, Trinitarianism and some other odd doctrines, I must plead guilty.'[51] (Note how much clearer religious terminology is to Morganwg, in contrast to this sense of a new, slippery and dangerous lexicon of political classification and abuse.) Examples can be multiplied.[52] Moreover, as John Barrell has shown, one of the most

---

[49] 'Examples of safe printing', in Spence, *Pig's Meat*, 3rd edn (London, 1800), vol. 3, 14–15; and 'What makes a libel?', in Eaton, *Politics for the People*, no. 5, 53.

[50] Plumptre, *A Narrative of a Three Years' Residence in France*, vol. II, 97.

[51] Iolo Morganwg, 'Letter to George Dyer, 15 February 1811', in *The Correspondence of Iolo Morganwg*, eds. Geraint H. Jenkins, Ffion Mair Jones and David Ceri Jones, vol. III (Cardiff: University of Wales, 2007), 57.

[52] See, for example, Charles Pigott, *Political Dictionary* (London: G. G. & J. Robinson, 1795); and *A Political Dictionary for the Guinea-less Pigs; or, a Glossary of Emphatical Words Made Use of by that Jewel of a Man, Deep Will* (London: J. Burks, 1795). This latter seems to have been contributed to by Joseph Burks, who was involved in the constitutional discussions at the end of 1794 and the beginning of 1795. See also *The Voice of the People, &c: Consisting of Extracts from Pigott, Gerald, &c, Printed for Citizen R. Lee, at the British Tree of Liberty* (London: Richard Lee, 1795). Or see the contrasting explanations of

sophisticated appreciations of the complexities of language, the shifting character of definitions and their exploitation for political purposes can be found in the work of William Fox. He saw quite clearly that words that were not tied down could be catastrophically inflammatory: 'A straw, or a feather, may be contended for with as much violence, and as much obstinacy, as the most important right, and the most essential interest.'[53]

But my concern here is less with the slipperiness of language, the uncertainties of meaning in the 1790s and the attempts made to contest and decontest certain terms, and more with the related but more obscured process that was going on that we may describe as an attempt to forge a general, or 'grand', political conversation from a fragmented and more local set of political, religious and other dialects ('grand' as in the ballad *The Grand Conversation on Napoleon*: wide-ranging, deep but not necessarily consensual).

Rereading the correspondence to the London Corresponding Society, I have been increasingly struck by the open character of the society's responses. Its members were concerned to welcome and sustain communication, and as such they were not strongly directive or partisan. They expressed reservations about local initiatives on occasion, such as the proposal by some 'very respectable Citizens' known to members of Division 27 to set themselves up as a division on the basis of membership consisting entirely of householders, and a quarterly subscription of two shillings and sixpence. But the reply by John Ashley and Alexander Galloway was remarkably restrained, considering that the society had had as a basic principle from the start that it was to be open to all. The strongest section was the one in which they suggested that it was a fault of this commercial country 'that property is too much respected. As an evidence of industry and oeconomy it is respectable, but it can by no means be considered as a general test of moral rectitude, and the attempt to arrogate to it more respect than it deserves, is generally proof of narrow sentiments.'[54] Moreover, while there was contention about the deism in the society, and about whether the society should be associated with an

Jacobinism in Richard Dinmore's *An Exposition of the Principles of the English Jacobins* and 'Letter to the Hereford Journal, 1799', in Marion Löffler, *Welsh Responses to the French Revolution: Press and Public Discourse, 1789–1802* (Cardiff: University of Wales Press, 2012), 103. See also the LCS understanding of loyalty: Add. MS 27812, fo. 51 v: 'Loyalty is derived from the old French word "Loyalté", and strictly signifies an attachment to the Laws; but by the fraudulent practices of Courts, exercised with too much success on vulgar ignorance, the term is often perverted to signify an attachment to Kings & their measures, even when evidently in opposition to Law & the Constitution of the Country.'

[53] William Fox, 'On Jacobinism', in *The Political Writings of William Fox*, eds. John Barrell and Timothy Whelan (Nottingham: Trent Editions, 2011), 181–94, 191.

[54] *The Correspondence of the London Corresponding Society, Revised and Corrected*, 55.

edition of Paine's *Age of Reason*, this seems to have occupied debate rather than the correspondence, and the hostile accounts of infidelism were not unchallenged.[55] That they took a conciliatory line was certainly partly tactical, but it was also indicative of the extent to which the society, and its local branches, affiliates and divisions, were feeling their way towards a common language and conversation. They were insufficiently clear themselves to lay down precise requirements; hence the several competing stories of the origins of the society and what it stood for, and hence the shifting character and language of early commitments and the evolving character of reference and discourse over the lifetime of the society.

But, at the same time, they were responding to diverse sources and influences that read situations differently and that placed their emphasis on different features of the political world, drawing on different references and allusions. This is not to say that these local organisations were uninfluenced by the national process, but it was an interactive and evolving one. In this process, there is no doubt that the legacy of Wyvill's Yorkshire Association and the Duke of Richmond's *Letter on Parliamentary Reform* served as powerful focal points – and ones that the societies tended to hark back to at moments of crisis: drawing people back to a common and (after the 1794 treason trials) widely legitimated set of principles to which people were able publicly to subscribe, at least in the first instance. Editions of the *Letter* were printed by various societies before the trials, but it remained seen as widely pertinent thereafter. In July 1795 Division 12 was suggesting that the duke's *Letter* be given to each new member of the LCS, and within a week there were similar suggestions from a range of other divisions, and further endorsements within the following weeks, with reference continuing throughout 1796 and 1797. It is wholly moot, however, whether we should take this as evidence of a commitment to constitutionalist language. The *Letter*, and other texts, seem to have functioned more as a *point d'appui* – a rallying point – that drew otherwise dispersed and potentially contending elements into correspondence, that underlined for them their common commitment against particular forces and that provided a basis for initial unity, not in the form of a common ideology or destination so much as a point from which people could move on in their chosen ways. Seen in this way, the LCS was engaged in an ongoing struggle to mobilise people, to forge a common project in what was a very diverse world and to sustain their connection by emphasising areas of agreement rather than by exploring in detail more contentious issues, such as more dubious methods of advocacy or the nature of the

---

[55] See *Selections from the Papers of the London Corresponding Society*, 306–7; Reid, *The Rise and Dissolution of the Infidel Societies*; Add. MS 27808, fos. 115–16.

ultimate destination. There were occasions on which it had to impose this common project – as when the Central Committee required a vote that was, effectively, against a more Godwinian reading of the society's character – but these occasions were rare, and there was no interest in hunting down the heresy but, rather, a concern to secure agreement that, whatever the utopian futures people might have imagined, there could be both wide-ranging discussion and a consensus on what that conversation implied for what they should expect of the existing political order.

What does this say about language as the object of study and the linguistic turn? My suggestion is that it means that we can follow the logic of arguments and the necessity of conceptual connections in only the loosest way. We have to recognise that the logic was as much in the reading as in the writing, and that the reading was always a more local experience than is assumed by the view of the unfolding of conceptual content that is often assumed by the linguistic turn. Moreover, the suggestion is that the local *habitus*, and people's practices, provided much of the framing for the readings that people undertook. (In this context, it is striking to compare the secular character of much London debate with the richly religious inflections of radical writing on the Welsh borders.)[56] This is not a determinist account, since people reacted against as well as in conformity with their local context, but in each case their reaction was shaped by that context and their practices and by the organisations and institutions they had built. Over time, of course, practices might consolidate, terminologies stabilise and principles develop roots. Later generations inherited those of the predecessors, they needed to invent less and there were models to invoke and to develop and practices to re-evaluate and innovate upon. The experiences of 1819 and the late 1830s and 1840s drew on these earlier experiences from the 1790s, partly imitating and partly developing, while drawing on the experience of those who participated in the LCS, and on their memoirs and histories. That allowed a certain amount of shorthand, and a degree of self-evidence to their activities, which the LCS and its cognate societies had to develop for themselves, or which they developed in part by drawing on the example of the Society for Constitutional Information.

This is not a general injunction about the interpretation of texts and practices, however. Methods must suit the context, and the features of this context that warrant this way of thinking about the literature of the 1790s were centrally connected to the popular character of the societies that emerged and the shared sense of an opening up of political discourse to a

---

[56] See Löffler, *Welsh Responses to the French Revolution*; and the material from *Y Geirgrawn*, 246–98.

wide audience and to sets of participants who had rarely been included in the past, or whose inclusion had been in strictly subaltern roles. The central dimension to the practices and the pragmatics of communication engaged in by the LCS was an injunction to speak and think for themselves. Of course, those who were centrally involved had a view as to what such thinking should result in, but it is striking how tolerant they were when it produced something else, and surprisingly innovative when thinking about how to encourage that process.

[I]t is by no means a difficult matter to raise general Indignation, at the idea of so small comparative number of useless, idle, & profligate *Drones*, sucking, & squandering away the honey produced by such immense numbers of hard toiling, and industrious *Bees*. If you . . . meet with Men, who have violent prejudices in favour of any *Abuses or Party* – never attack those prejudices *directly*, for that will only enflame, & confirm them the more. – pass them over for the present – & engage their attention towards something else in which they will listen with a less degree of Apprehension of being attacked in a favourite point. Once gain their good opinion, & open their eyes to one Evil: they will be more ready to hear from you on others, till at last – the favoured object by which their eyes were jaundiced, will appear in its true colours, & fall before your arguments, like all the rest.[57]

Does the fact that some people invested in this type of communication have an impact on how we understand political thinking at a more abstract level? This has to be seen as a question of the discursive pragmatics. Encouraging talking and reading and stimulating critical engagement does not inevitably develop into a commitment to radical ideas – save in the sense that this process of reflection is a worm at the root of (some features of) traditions of deference and subordination. It produced different readings and different reactions; and these resulted in different practices and demands. The implicit pragmatics of much loyalist literature tried hard to reconstitute relations of deference, but it was very difficult to do (and there was a certain irony in the project being contributed to by men and women who aspired thereby to a more active role in the polity). In a sense, a genie was out of the box, but not in ways that necessarily produced commitments to particular values or that saw certain necessary entailments. It was more a case of uncertainly flowering in the midst of the prescribed order, enabling some to find new grounds for assurance for what they thought they knew, and others to imagine and practically project new orders and vistas. It was not a moment of revolt or mere reaction, but for many it was a moment in which rethinking one's self-conception was demanded, even if the outcome of that process might be loyalist in its commitments, reformist or other. This innovative communicative

---

[57] TS 11/951.3493, 'Letter from the editors', *Sheffield Patriot* [emphasis in original].

moment opened up many possibilities but it did not prescribe a single direction. It needed to be reacted to and exploited in certain ways, and it did not touch all whom it sought to interpolate. Things, we might say, weren't necessarily so. But in that opening set of possibilities we can see the emergence of a sphere for practical political agency for many who had not previously experienced it. Men, and occasionally women, had to work out what they wanted to do with it, and with whom and to what ends, and many sought to do so through conversation and discussion, and subsequently through more systematic forms of both. But they had to work out the entailments in widely varying locations, drawing on diverse literatures and assumptions, and had to do so in a national context that was increasingly intolerant to their doing so. It was time to talk, but it became increasingly difficult to do so as the decade progressed.

Index

313

Lightning Source UK Ltd.
Milton Keynes UK
UKHW022242150519
342762UK00017B/387/P

9 781316 648490